# FAKE LAW

*Also by the Secret Barrister*

The Secret Barrister: Stories of the Law
and How It's Broken

THE SECRET BARRISTER

# FAKE LAW

## The Truth About Justice
## in an Age of Lies

PICADOR

First published 2020 by Picador
an imprint of Pan Macmillan
The Smithson, 6 Briset Street, London EC1M 5NR
Associated companies throughout the world
www.panmacmillan.com

ISBN 978-1-5290-0994-1

1 3 5 7 9 8 6 4 2

A CIP catalogue record for this book is available from the British Library.

Typeset by Palimpsest Book Production Ltd, Falkirk, Stirlingshire
Printed and bound by CPI Group (UK) Ltd, Croydon, CR0 4YY

Visit **www.picador.com** to read more about all our books
and to buy them. You will also find features, author interviews and
news of any author events, and you can sign up for e-newsletters
so that you're always first to hear about our new releases.

*To our four stars,*
*and the hope of sun tomorrow*

# Contents

# Introduction

On 20 February 2018, fifty-two years, three months and eleven days after capital punishment in Great Britain was abolished, the state ordered that a baby be put to death.[1] An unelected[2] High Court judge, sitting in the shadowy Family Division at the Royal Courts of Justice in London, rapped his gavel[3] and ruled, in accordance with government dogma, that the life of a poorly child could not be justified within the budgetary constraints of the National Health Service.[4]

Over the next two months, as the child's parents tried in vain to save their son's life, successive tiers of the silhouetted British and European judiciary would agree – on no less than eight occasions – that, notwithstanding the availability of viable medical treatment,[5] the child should die. The governmental Death Panel[6] had spoken, just as it had, barely twelve months earlier, when a similarly unwell infant was denied life-saving treatment by a legal system prioritising its fidelity to the logical conclusions of social-ised medicine ahead of basic respect for human life.[7]

In another year, in another British court, a similarly out-of-touch judge acceded to the pleas of an illegal immigrant who took the stand to contest his deportation, after he committed serious criminal offences. The reason for the decision to let this man remain? It was because – and I am not making this up – he had a pet cat.[8] A victory for the European Union's Human Rights Act,[9] putting British citizens at risk so that the nation's migrant cats might sleep sounder in their baskets.

Outside the caprice of the courtroom, hard-working taxpayers find themselves daily footing the bill for our country's voracious compensation culture, as local authorities and our National Health Service throw millions of pounds of public money at defending ridiculous claims, from cleaners pocketing nine grand for tripping over mops,[10] to the jackpot figures[11] paid to litigious employees aboard the gravy train[12] of the discrimination industry.[13] Added to our unsustainable legal-aid bill – the most expensive in the world,[14] most of which lines the pockets of illegal immigrants, criminals and their jihadist-facilitating lawyers[15] – it's no wonder the nation's finances are in their present state.

And, as for them, those foreign criminals and illegal immigrants, the law is of course on their side.[16] The statue of Lady Justice stands blindfolded atop the Old Bailey[17] for good reason: our pusillanimous justice system turns a blind eye to those who harm us, those who walk free from court despite being convicted of the most appalling crimes. The rights of the victim are subjugated to the rights of the criminal;[18] try defending your home against a burglar and you'll be arrested for a breach of their human rights before you can pick the shrapnel out of your thigh.[19] The few offenders who do go to 'prison' find something resembling a holiday camp – Butlin's with bars[20] – reclining in front of free Sky TV in four-star hospitality until they are let out early.

We shouldn't, of course, be surprised. When activist judges,[21] seeking to impose their own liberal leanings upon the downtrodden denizens of our once green and pleasant land, openly declare war on democracy,[22] defying the will of the people in service of the judiciary's secret political agenda,[23] it's a miracle that anything resembling justice is spat out of our ailing, failing legal system. Enemies of the people,[24] the lot of them.

If there's one thing you can be sure of, it is that the law, whatever it does, does not work for you.


The likelihood is that you will have heard something of the cases and themes above over recent years, whether in the press, on social media or folded into the rhetoric of an earnest politician.

The complaints are familiar and recurring. Unfurl a newspaper or click on a weblink, and the evidence is compelling. The law, as some angry blogger once said, is broken.[25]

Except, of course, that every legal detail in those stories is untrue. They are examples of what a marketing mogul with a keen eye for neologisms might term Fake Law: distortions of legal cases and judgments, spun and reformed for mass consumption. They represent a phenomenon that is far from new, but which, in an age when an errant headline can reach a million Twitter users in a single baited click, is becoming broader in scope, longer in reach and exponentially more difficult to counter.

And the above myths, and the thousands like them, are what this book aims to address. For, while most of us can equip our-selves reasonably well to critically assess news stories or commentary in many walks of life, legal stories throw up particu-lar obstacles.

Law is inherently – and often unnecessarily – complex and alienating to a non-legal audience. Finding the answer to a straightforward question – such as, *What does the law say about my right to defend myself in my home?* – is not simply a matter of going to a conveniently labelled statute online and reading what it says.

For one, we churn out new laws quicker than the government can publish them. Unfortunately, and consequently, legislation.gov.uk, the official government website responsible for publish-ing freely accessible versions of the law, has not been up to date for decades. While there have been improvements in the last few years,[26] at the time of writing, 2 per cent[27] of the statutes and statutory instruments (laws issued by ministers under powers granted by Acts of Parliament) on the website had 'outstanding effects' marked on them. In other words, one in fifty of the laws on the official government website were wrong. The website boasts 6.5 million pages.[28] That's a lot of inaccurate legislation lying in wait to trip up the casual browser.

But this is only part of the issue. Unlike civil law jurisdictions, such as France, where the bulk of the country's law is codified, we have, since Henry II's declaration at the Assize of Clarendon in 1166, been faithful to the 'common law' tradition, where the senior courts (today, the High Court, Court of Appeal and Supreme Court) have the power to 'make' law. Where a case involves an issue of interpretation or clarification of legislation passed by Parliament, our most senior judges will hand down judgments which have the effect of binding all lower courts (the doctrine of precedent). This means that, if you wish to understand what a statute means, it is not enough to simply locate an up-to-date version; once that quest is completed, you will need to know what further gloss has been coated over it by case law. And accessing case law – let alone interpreting and extracting the esoteric legal principles judicially parsed within – presents similar difficulties.

The official provider of free, up-to-date online case law is the British and Irish Legal Information Institute (BAILII), a charity subcontracted by the Ministry of Justice to publish the text of new case law on its website. BAILII performs a heroic task of uploading hundreds of new judgments each month from the various senior courts and tribunals from across the United Kingdom, but, as a charity dependent on donations (heaven forfend the Ministry of Justice fully fund this endeavour), it has its limits. A recent analysis showed that, while the leading commercial case law provider published 74,010 judgments between 2007 and 2017, BAILII was able to upload only 30,583 – well under half.[29] BAILII is also unable to offer either the search functionality of commercial legal databases used by professionals, or the helpful commentary on each case explaining the relevance and significance of the decision. Therefore, unless you know exactly what you are looking for, you will soon hit a brick wall. Ridiculously, BAILII is also restricted by copyright from publishing judgments from cases pre-1996, the very text of our laws having seemingly been procured and exploited for private gain.[30]

For a member of the public, all of this means that, unless you have access to a commercial legal database, at a subscription per year running into four figures, or the updated practitioner textbooks in every legal discipline, it is virtually impossible even to locate the applicable law.

Even if you succeed in tracking down the relevant statute and case law, comprehending its application in practice presents a separate, often insurmountable challenge. The language of the law – both its statutory drafting and judgments handed down by the courts – can appear deliberately alienating to a citizen in the third millennium. While the civil and criminal courts have formally vowed to abstain from the routine use of Latin, some participants cling onto it. Barristers in criminal proceedings will still casually slip into *res gestae, mens rea* or *novus actus interveniens*. Old-school civil practitioners still speak in terms of *ex parte, mandamus* and *certiorari*. Abstruse legalese remains scrawled throughout the legal process. The criminal law retains its fondness for old, comfy Victorian statutes to prosecute most offences of violence[31] (and some of minor public nuisance[32] – being an 'incorrigible rogue' is still a prosecutable criminal offence), and the formal courtroom exchanges between counsel and judge invariably sound lifted from another epoch. 'May it please Your Honour, my learned friend and I have considered the position and the view at the Bar is that this would fall within the *res gestae* exception' is a sentence that may trip off the tongue of a criminal lawyer, but makes little sense to anybody in the public gallery. Dragging the legal system kicking and screaming into the twentieth century is still on the to-do list in the second decade of the twenty-first.

Our education system only compounds the problem. Despite the law underpinning every facet of our existence, from prior to our birth through to and beyond our death, English and Welsh schooling has historically placed no emphasis whatsoever on legal education. How are laws made? What are our rights? How does the justice system work? What is the court hierarchy?[33] What is the difference between a solicitor and a barrister?[34] Or a judge and a magistrate?[35] Such themes, if they are explored at all, are shoehorned into unfashionable Citizenship or General Studies curricula, rather than celebrated in their own right as a key pillar of education, as important as language or maths.

Part of the blame also lies with us in the legal profession, tutting at the public's failure to understand what we do, whilst jealously guarding our knowledge. While the social-media age has brought forth a generation of writers, bloggers and tweeters doing their best to kick down the doors to the courtroom and shine a torch on the arcane activity inside, our historically well-earned reputation as aloof keepers of the keys, cloaked in black and speaking in tongues, means that many citizens feel irredeemably disconnected from the legal system and its players. The historically well-deserved reputation of the legal profession as the preserve of the privately educated, upper-middle-class Oxbridge elite – a homogeny of plummy voices and white faces – has erected barriers to access and understanding which are only now, belatedly, being taken seriously by the profession.

Putting this all together, it is little surprise that, according to research reported in 2019, the British public is 'dangerously ignorant' about the law, with more than a third of those surveyed not knowing the difference between criminal and civil courts.[36] Consequently, and inevitably, a report by Citizens Advice suggested that only two in five people have faith in the justice system.[37] And it is equally unsurprising that many people rely on secondary – and, unbeknownst to them, unreliable – sources to piece together their understanding of the law.

This disconnect, I agree, is dangerous. Because the law belongs to all of us. Society only functions if we all abide by common, agreed rules. If we don't understand our justice system, and if our comprehension is corrupted by misinformation, we can't properly engage with arguments over its functioning. We can't critically evaluate its performance, identify its flaws, propose sensible reform or even participate meaningfully in everyday conversation about the stories in the news. Our unfamiliarity also makes us vulnerable to those who would exploit the gaps in our knowledge to push ulterior agendas.

That, I hope, is where this book comes in. By examining the core principles of our legal system in action in some of the flashpoints that have occupied centre stage in the news cycle over recent years, we can see where common understanding departs from reality. We will look at how the law actually works, and why it operates in the way it does, with the aim that, when confronted with the stranger-than-fiction harrumphs of the professionally outraged, we are better equipped to scrutinise their claims.

Please don't mistake this for an apologia for the legal system. The law is not perfect. I am not proffering a full-throated defence of the justice system, its characters or how it operates. There is much wrong with the way we do justice. With criminal law alone, for instance, in which I specialise, there are enough stories of how the law is broken to fill a book. But the risk is that, by allowing our attention and energies to be diverted onto 'the law is an ass' outrages which have, on their true facts, entirely mundane explanations, we become distracted from the problems that really do exist with justice.

And so it often proves: amid the smoke and klaxons accompanying the Fake Law stories, we miss the plaintive cries of those truly betrayed or failed by the law.

This, I will suggest, is not accidental. The narratives that we are fed about how and why the law doesn't work – what is shouted from the front pages and what is muted – are deliberately configured. Sometimes, the agenda will simply be boosting circulation or garnering clicks. But sometimes it runs far deeper. Sometimes, it amounts to a calculated attempt by vested interests to undermine and chip away at our individual rights and protections, the first principles that bind us together, and, ultimately, the very foundations of our justice system.

This book is about those, real, enemies of the people. What are the truths about our justice system that they are so eager to mask? What, through coordinated dissemination of half-baked half-truths, rhetorical sleight of hand and outright lies, do they hope to gain? And what are we, the people, at risk of losing?

It is not comprehensive. It cannot cover all facets of the law. But it will drill into some of the most commonly discussed aspects of the justice system, exploring the operation and (mis) representation of the law in some of the most important areas of our lives. What does the law really say about us? Our children? Our jobs? Our society?

Similarly, not every legal myth given airtime can be debunked. However, I hope that we can cover enough ground so that, when it comes to discussing some of the bigger legal stories that elbow their way into the spotlight, we are better armed to properly understand the reality behind the headlines, to recognise the myths, the lies and the agenda, and to identify the motives of those seeking to prey on our unfamiliarity.

And if that is too ambitious, then may I at least press home, at the earliest possible stage and with as much vigour as words on a page can convey, on behalf of all legal practitioners the length and breadth of our fair nation, the following central truth of our justice system: GAVELS ARE NOT, AND HAVE NEVER BEEN, USED BY JUDGES IN ENGLISH AND WELSH COURTS.[38]

# 1. Yourself and Your Home

'Householders who act instinctively and honestly in self-defence are victims of crime and should be treated that way. We need to dispel doubts in this area once and for all.'

Chris Grayling, Justice Secretary, 8 October 2012[1]

It is 1 a.m. Lying in bed, your consciousness dancing flirtatiously on the verge of sleep as your partner rumbles soothingly beside you, a loud thud jolts you awake. You shake yourself alert, ears pricked as your brain reboots and reprocesses. Was it a dream, or something real? Was it a *thud* as much as a *smash*? Was it outside in the street, or did the sound emanate from downstairs?

As you silently contemplate the answer to each question, your mind dives into a whirlpool of possibilities. Fighting to hold onto the most mundane – the children have gone and dropped a glass of water in the kitchen – you prod the silent figure next to you. No, they heard nothing. Go back to sleep.

Curiosity unsatisfied and heart rate climbing, you grab your dressing gown from the hook on the door and step onto the landing. Flicking the switch and drenching the first floor in light, everything appears still, but, when you poke your head into each bedroom in turn, concern steadily rises as you register the child-shaped lumps under the duvets.

*BANG.*

That one was unmistakeable. You run back to your bedroom – your partner heard it that time too. They are already clambering out of bed as you head instinctively to the wardrobe in search

9

of something – anything – and alight on a small wooden coat hanger. Fear leaves no space to appreciate farce, and you seize it. Your partner follows you, mobile phone in hand, onto the landing and cautiously down the stairs.

The closer to the kitchen you move, the clearer the sound of drawers being roughly opened and shut. As your partner instinctively turns to run back upstairs to the children, they stumble. It's only a gentle clunk, but it's loud enough. The kitchen door springs open, and a man emerges. The first thing you see, and indeed the only thing you will remember when you retell this later, is that he is holding a baseball bat.

You'd always assumed that people describing such events as playing in slow motion were reciting a cliché. But every millisecond stretches in a way that confounds reality. The only thing right now that matters is your children. Your partner scrambles upwards on all fours, every step a mountain. When they eventually reach the summit, they glance back at the scene below, to the confrontation between you, wielding your flimsy coat hanger, and your better-equipped adversary. Only that's not what they see; instead, the coat hanger is on the floor and the bat has somehow been wrested from the intruder's gloved paws. You are now standing on the first stair, which affords you a slight height advantage, and you are raising the baseball bat in the air.

The crack as it crashes onto the burglar's skull is immediately followed by the thump of him collapsing to the floor. He does not move again. You don't remember the sequence of what happens next, only that you and your partner stare at each other, and then at the blood pooling around the prostrate figure on the floor, and then back at each other, and back and forth and back and forth, until someone, at some point, rushes to the children's rooms and someone calls 999.

After the police arrive and the intruder is stretchered by paramedics into the waiting ambulance, you sit in your living room, cradling an untouched cup of tea, and do your best to retell the events of the past twenty minutes, while your partner does likewise outside on the street. All you did, you both emphasise, was react instinctively in the heat of the moment. You didn't seek this confrontation; it smashed its way through your kitchen window and into the sanctity of your home. Faced with the unthinkable, one of you chose flight, one chose fight, but neither can be criticised, surely.

Surely?

The notion that you would be blamed – much less *prosecuted* – for the injury caused to the armed man who invaded your house is as offensive as it is ludicrous.

Why is it, then, that, in many cases of this type, it is the innocent householder, rather than the marauding criminal, who ends up in front of the courts?

Consider Norfolk farmer Tony Martin, convicted and imprisoned in 2000 after shooting dead a teenage burglar who broke into his home. No wonder his cause was adopted across the country, with crowds gathering outside King's Lynn magistrates' court during his first appearance, to demand his release.[2] Following his conviction for murder (later reduced to manslaughter upon appeal, due to his psychiatric condition), he was described variously as a 'folk hero'[3] and a 'hero to victims of crime'.[4] Norman Brennan, director of the Victims of Crime Trust, criticised the verdict as a 'dangerous precedent', declaring, 'This is yet another example of how the criminal justice system can make criminals out of victims.'[5]

Politicians and journalists united in support. Upon his release from prison, Mr Martin was paid £125,000 for an exclusive interview by the *Mirror*, with the Press Complaints Commission ruling that the general prohibition on paying criminals for their stories could be avoided on the grounds that he had 'a unique insight into an issue of great public concern'.[6]

William Hague, as Leader of the Opposition, purported to speak for 'millions of law-abiding British people who no longer feel the state is on their side' when he pledged that a Conservative government would 'overhaul the law' to ensure 'the state will be on the side of people who protect their homes and their families against criminals'.[7]

If a television poll was to be believed, he was sowing on fertile political ground – in the aftermath of Tony Martin's conviction, 85 per cent of voters opined that the jury had reached the wrong verdict.[8] A leaked memo by Prime Minister Tony Blair later revealed his fears that, in refusing to be drawn into the public debate, he had created a perception of being 'out of touch with gut British instincts'.[9]

This message – the law is weighted in favour of the burglar and against the Great British householder – survived and thrived throughout the next decade. It was oxygenated by the occasional tabloid flashpoint – such as the case of Munir Hussain, imprisoned along with his brother in 2008 for attacking an intruder with a cricket bat – and culminated in both Labour and the Conservatives promising changes to the law.

But even the change in the law that was duly delivered in 2012 was not enough to put the nation's minds at ease, as was demonstrated in 2018 when seventy-eight-year-old Richard Osborn-Brooks was arrested for stabbing to death a burglar in his kitchen. The 'hero pensioner'[10] feted by the *Sun* was the latest victim of laws which continue to pit 'a career criminal who sets out to deliberately burgle a house' against 'the terrified home owner who acts to protect himself and his home',[11] and come down, time and time again, against the latter.

Why is it the case, despite the best efforts of politicians, that an Englishman or woman cannot take reasonable steps to protect his or her castle? If we cannot defend ourselves and our loved ones in our own homes, how, it is reasonably asked, can we say our laws are working?

Before we return to our maligned heroes, Martin, Hussain and Osborn-Brooks, a good start would be to look at what the law actually says.

# The law of self-defence

Question: What are we allowed to do in self-defence? Answer: Quite a lot, really.

The permitted use of force in self-defence has been established in the common law of England and Wales for centuries. In fact, as an historic example of Fake Law, legal textbooks used to demonstrate how freely one could slaughter burglars by citing a nineteenth-century case in which it was claimed, 'In 1811 Mr Purcell, of co. Cork, a septuagenarian, was knighted for killing four burglars with a carving knife.' The less exciting reality was that Mr Purcell used his leftover dinner knife to kill two – not four – burglars when they attacked him with swords and a firearm, and was apparently knighted before, not because of, this incident.[12]

The law isn't quite as generous to the householder as suggested in the retelling of Mr Purcell; however, at common law, claiming that you were defending yourself can afford you a 'complete defence' to a charge of violence, up to and including murder. This means that, if successful, the accused will be acquitted of all charges; a person could be killed and yet no crime will be found to have been committed.

English and Welsh criminal law distinguishes between 'complete' and 'partial' defences. A partial defence reduces culpability – and so the level of charge – but a criminal offence has still been committed. 'Diminished responsibility' is an example of a partial defence. This arises where a person who kills another is suffering from an 'abnormality of mental functioning' arising from a medical condition, which substantially impairs the person's ability to understand the nature of his conduct, form a rational judgment or exercise self-control, and which provides an explanation for the person's actions. In such circumstances, a defendant will have a partial defence to murder, and will instead be convicted of the less serious charge of manslaughter.[13] This, as it happens, was the defence that the Court of Appeal found ought to have applied in

Tony Martin's case, after hearing expert evidence of a diagnosis of a paranoid personality disorder, and provided the reason for his conviction for murder being quashed in 2001 and substituted for manslaughter.[14]

Self-defence provides a complete defence because the law recognises that our right to physical security – indeed, our right to life – endows us with the right to defend ourselves from threatened harm. And it is not just in defence of oneself or another that a person is permitted to use force – the same principle applies to defence of property, or in the prevention of crime and the arrest or apprehension of offenders.[15] For shorthand, I shall refer simply to 'self-defence'.

The principles of the law of self-defence are relatively straightforward:

— A person acting in genuine self-defence is entitled to use such force as is reasonable in the circumstances as he believes them to be. This provides a defence to any charge of violence, up to and including the use of lethal force;

— The first question that a jury must ask is, did the defendant *believe* or may he have believed that it was *necessary* to use force to defend himself from an attack or imminent attack on himself or others or to protect property or prevent crime?

— The second question is, was the amount of force the defendant used *reasonable* in the circumstances, including the dangers as the defendant believed them to be?

— The burden is on the prosecution to *disprove* self-defence. It is not for a defendant to prove that he *was* acting in self-defence. The prosecution must prove beyond reasonable doubt (so that a jury is sure) that the defendant was *not* acting in reasonable self-defence.

The key concepts here are *necessary* and *reasonable*. It is worth briefly exploring these further.

## 'A genuine belief that force is necessary'

The question here is subjective – i.e. did the defendant genuinely believe he needed to use force in self-defence? It does not matter if the defendant was in fact mistaken, as long as he believed that at the time. So, if a six-foot man wearing a terrifying bear costume runs towards you brandishing what looks like a machete, and you genuinely believe he is about to inflict serious harm, the fact that you later realise the 'machete' is a hunny-pot and that you've KO'd Winnie the Pooh in front of a distraught crowd of Disneyland toddlers does not matter. The fact that your *belief* in the need for force was, by objective standards, unreasonable – who would mistake a hunny-pot for a machete, for Lord's sake? – does not matter at this stage. It might make the jury less likely to accept your insistence that your belief was genuine; however, the bottom line is that a mistaken, unreasonable but genuinely held belief in the need for force is enough. (An exception arises if your mistaken belief is due to your voluntary intoxication. Because, frankly, getting tanked on Stella and raining fury on Winnie the Pooh in a fountain is not something the courts can condone.)

Returning to our opening scenario, faced, in the dead of night, with an intruder standing a few feet away wielding a baseball bat, nobody could sensibly dispute that you genuinely and instinctively believed that force was necessary to protect yourself and your family.

## 'Reasonable force'

Whether force is reasonable has to be judged by the circumstances *as the defendant believed them to be*, even if, as above, he was in fact mistaken. So, if you genuinely believe that a machete attack is imminent, what is reasonable has to be assessed by reference to that belief. What is reasonable will obviously depend on the individual case, but a principle often referred to in the case law is 'proportionality'. If someone's use of force was proportionate to the threat which they honestly perceived, it would usually follow that it was reasonable.

The law also recognises that, in the heat of a frightening confrontation, it is not always easy to gauge how much force you need to deploy to protect yourself, and a wide margin of appreciation is allowed. In the famous words of Lord Morris in the case of *Palmer*,[16] which are distilled in some form to juries when they are given their directions of law by the trial judge:

> If there has been an attack so that self-defence is reasonably necessary, it will be recognised that a person defending himself cannot weigh to a nicety the exact measure of his defensive action. If the jury thought that in a moment of unexpected anguish a person attacked had only done what he honestly and instinctively thought necessary, that would be the most potent evidence that only reasonable defensive action had been taken.

Other relevant principles include there being no 'duty to retreat', although the possibility of a defendant having been able to retreat is a factor to consider when assessing whether the use of force was necessary and reasonable.[17] It is also long established that a person may strike pre-emptively – you do not need to wait to be hit. Much of this may strike a non-lawyer as intuitively commonsensical. And they'd be right.

So, in our case, the fact that you could theoretically have run up the stairs after your partner instead of confronting the burglar does not make you guilty. Disarming the burglar and striking him once to the head, doing what you honestly and instinctively thought necessary in that split second to abate the threat posed to your safety, is something which a prosecutor would struggle to prove was unreasonable or disproportionate. Even if really serious injury – up to and including death – was caused by that blow, you are not expected to be able to 'weigh to a nicety' the precise force needed to incapacitate without injuring, given the terrifying position in which you find yourself.

Putting this all together, in a nutshell, the common law defence of self-defence means that the prosecution must make a jury sure that *either* a defendant didn't really believe he *needed* to use force, or that he did, but used *unreasonable* force – for example, he killed someone with a gun in response to a slap to the face – bearing in mind the broad scope of appreciation allowed in these cases.

So, if the law allows you to use lethal force in self-defence against burglars, as long as you genuinely believe it to be necessary and act reasonably in the circumstances as you perceive them, what happened in Tony Martin's case? How did he come to be convicted?

## Tony Martin[18]

On the night of 20 August 1999, fifty-five-year-old Tony Martin was at home. He had lived alone for twenty years at the aptly named Bleak House, an isolated farm near Enneth Hungate, in Norfolk. Two convicted criminals, thirty-year-old Brendan Fearon and sixteen-year-old Fred Barras, approached the farmhouse in the dark. They broke a window to enter the breakfast room. Without warning, there followed a series of shots. Barras was shot in the back and legs, and Fearon was shot in both legs. Both managed to escape the property, although Barras collapsed and died a short distance from the house. Fearon made his way to a nearby premises and was subsequently arrested and taken to hospital.

Tony Martin told the police, and later the jury at his trial, that he had been woken by noises and had gone to the landing, where he saw a light coming from downstairs. Fearing for his safety, he retreated to his bedroom to fetch his twelve-bore Winchester pump-action shotgun. As he tentatively made his way downstairs towards the noises, a bright light was shone in his face, blinding him. Fearing for his life, he fired the gun three times, before returning to his bedroom. He waited for a while before emerging and searching the property. He could not see anybody and did not think that he had hit anyone when he fired his gun.

On that version of events, one might indeed wonder how a jury could have been satisfied that reasonable self-defence had been disproved. But it was, of course, only half the story.

The prosecution case was a little different. They said that Mr Martin had heard the burglars approaching the house and had readied himself so that, by the time they entered the breakfast room, he was already downstairs, fully dressed and with his shotgun loaded. He stepped out and shot them at least three times at short range, with the intention of killing them.

In the words of prosecuting counsel Rosamund Horwood-Smart QC, Mr Martin lay in wait and shot Barras and Fearon 'like rats in a trap'. 'This was a man,' she told the jury, 'who was prepared to be his own police force, investigating force, jury, judge and, if necessary, executioner.'[19]

Presented with the two conflicting accounts, the jury appeared to accept the prosecution's. And it is perhaps not hard to see why. Firearms experts proved that Mr Martin's claim that he had fired all the shots from the stairs was 'impossible'. A number had been fired from inside the breakfast room. The jury visited Bleak House and were able to assess the reconstruction of events for themselves. Barras' fatal wound was to his back, suggestive of a pursuit. Perhaps crucially, the jury also heard that Mr Martin had repeatedly told local Farm Watch meetings of his view that burglars should be shot. 'You know the best way to stop them – shoot the bastards.' He said that, if burglars came to his home, he would 'blow their heads off'. He also advocated putting such criminals in a field and using a machine gun on them.

These were not empty words. In 1994, Mr Martin had seen a man attempting to steal apples from his orchard and had fired at the rear of the man's vehicle as he drove away. As a result, his shotgun certificate was revoked. It follows that the firearm he used on 20 August was unlicensed.

Given this context, it is easier to see how a jury might have concluded that this was not a case of someone acting in reasonable self-defence, on any construction of the term.

And, indeed, once the full facts behind the press reports of other similar stories emerge, the sense of justified outrage starts to dissipate. The case of Munir Hussain, the 'have a go hero'[20] householder convicted and imprisoned in 2009 following an assault on a burglar, before having his sentence reduced on appeal, was variously reported as 'self-defence that went too far'.[21] Ross Clark, writing in the *Daily Express*, condemned the prosecution of Mr Hussain and his brother, Tokeer, 'all because he took action to protect his family from violent thugs who were threatening to kill them'.[22] Shadow Home Secretary Chris Grayling reacted to the case by pledging to 'change the rules' so that anyone 'acting reasonably' to stop a crime or apprehend a criminal 'could not be arrested',[23] in a baffling shuffle of horses and carts.

But, as the Court of Appeal was at pains to point out, while there was extreme provocation, which informed the decision of the Court of Appeal to suspend Munir Hussain's sentence of imprisonment, 'This is not, and should not be seen as, a case about the level of violence which a householder may lawfully and justifiably use on a burglar . . . The burglary was over. No one was in any danger. The purpose of the appellants' violence was revenge . . . It was a sustained attack with weapons. The pleas of the eyewitnesses to desist were ignored. Such violence is not lawful. No one at the trial suggested that it was.'[24]

While no doubt a terrifying ordeal for Mr Hussain, in which three men wearing balaclavas and armed with knives and cable ties forced their way into his house and threatened his wife and children, this was not a case of self-defence. It was not akin to you being confronted by a burglar on the stairs; rather, it involved rounding up a large group of men to embark upon a vigilante hunt for the burglar and, when they found him, attacking him with weapons until he suffered serious brain injury. What's more, at Mr Hussain's trial, he didn't even try to suggest that it *was* lawful self-defence; instead, he claimed that he was not part of the group administering the beating.

As with Tony Martin, the claim that Munir Hussain's conviction was an example of restrictive self-defence laws not working was baseless. In fact, the available evidence indicated that, despite what the headlines suggested, the law was being applied fairly and appropriately. In 2012, the Crown Prosecution Service conducted an 'informal trawl', which showed that between 1990 and 2005 there were only eleven prosecutions of people who had used force against intruders on private premises, and only seven of these related to domestic burglaries.[25]

As part of the same exercise, the CPS offered a series of example cases to illustrate how it was approaching charging decisions. In Derbyshire, a householder returned home to find an intruder; there followed a struggle in which the burglar hit his head on the driveway and died. In Lincolnshire, two burglars entered a house armed with a knife and threatened a woman; her husband overpowered one of the burglars and stabbed him to death. And, to return to our opening example, a householder in Lancashire disarmed a burglar carrying a baseball bat and used it to strike him on the head, fracturing his skull. In none of these cases was the householder prosecuted.

Cases where the CPS did decide to prosecute included that of a man in South Wales who approached a group of people trespassing on his land to engage in some night-time fishing. He threatened them with a shotgun and they duly ran away. As they did, the landowner fired forty shotgun pellets into one man's back. Likewise, a prosecution followed in Cheshire when the owner of a commercial premises caught a burglar, tied him up, assaulted him and then set fire to him.

Put simply, there is no evidence whatsoever to support the notion that there has been a rash of prosecutions – let alone convictions – of householders acting reasonably, as any of us might, when confronted by a burglar. The stories that trouble the bulletins – such as that of Andy and Tracey Ferrie, who in 2012 were arrested on suspicion of inflicting grievous bodily harm after firing a shotgun at intruders at their home at Welby Farm in Leicestershire – invariably conclude prosaically, with a careful investigation and review of the evidence resulting in a decision not to charge.[26] Moreover, where prosecutions are initiated, they tend to be against the surviving burglars, who can expect little sympathy from the courts. The recipients of summary justice at the barrel of Andy Ferrie's shotgun attempted to rely upon the injuries they had received as mitigation when being sentenced for the burglary, only to be told by an irate His Honour Judge Pert QC, 'Being shot is not mitigation. If you burgle a house in the country where the householder owns a legally held shotgun, that is the chance you take. You cannot come to court and ask for a lighter sentence because of it.'[27]

And on the rare occasions where householders are charged, the high standard of proof – requiring the prosecution to make the jury *sure* that the householder wasn't acting in reasonable self-defence – means that any doubt must be exercised in their favour. In 2015, in echoes of Tony Martin, an eighty-year-old farmer shot and injured a convicted burglar, whom he suspected of trying to steal diesel on his land, and was charged with inflicting grievous bodily harm. Kenneth Hugill told a jury at Hull Crown Court in 2017 that he had acted instinctively in self-defence when firing a double-barrelled shotgun at a suspicious vehicle he saw on his land at two o'clock in the morning.[28] He was acquitted in twenty-four minutes.[29]

Nevertheless, in the late 2000s, as the prosecuting authorities and the courts quietly went about applying the law of self-defence fairly and sensibly, the breathy narrative of Englishmen being unable to defend their castles became fixed in the political psyche. Something Had To Be Done.

The first legislative intervention was Labour's revolutionary move in 2008 of copying and pasting the existing common law of self-defence into a statute. That is no exaggeration – an exercise of pure political conmanship, section 76 of the Criminal Justice and Immigration Act 2008 simply restated the basic principles we considered earlier, but allowed the government to proclaim that it had Done Something. Little wonder that, during the Bill's second reading in the House of Lords, Lord Thomas of Gresford mocked 'the cheery optimism of the Minister in opening this debate', observing, 'Not only is it the fifty-fourth Bill dealing with crime and criminal justice that has come before us in the past ten and a half years, but it perpetuates muddled thinking, a lack of understanding of the fundamental legal principles that lie behind the British concept of justice, and populist but meaningless gestures towards the red tops' concerns of the day. Rhetoric and vote-catching matter more than practicality and principle.'[30]

The Conservatives, having quite rightly derided Labour's non-solution, once in government demonstrated an impressive talent for idiot one-upmanship by vowing to 'dispel doubts' where none existed. Seeking to make good on their vacuous manifesto pledge in 2010 to 'give householders greater legal protection if they have to defend themselves from intruders',[31] David Cameron and his ministers resolved to terrify citizens with ghost stories rather than honestly reassuring them that there was no monster lurking under the legal bed.

'When a burglar crosses your threshold,' Mr Cameron said, resuming his theme in 2012, 'we should worry less about their rights and more about the rights of the householder',[32] although he did not offer any actual examples of this alleged deference to 'burglars' rights' thwarting justice. He spoke of his – no doubt genuine – distress at being the victim of a burglary,[33] but not, as might perhaps have been more pertinent to the discussion at hand, of any experience of being persecuted for reasonable action he had taken against the perpetrators.

Justice Secretary Chris Grayling duly vowed to protect those who 'in the heat of the moment use force that is reasonable in the circumstances, but in the cold light of day seems disproportionate',[34] overlooking that the law already allows force that is reasonable, and that the jury's assessment of the reasonableness and proportionality of the force used is by reference to the circumstances *as the householder genuinely believed them to be.*

The change in the law that followed was about as sensible as one might expect from ministers apparently wholly unacquainted with legal reality.

On 7 October 2012, Chris Grayling announced to rapturous applause at the Conservative Party conference that he was 'strengthening the current law'.[35] His big plan? To allow the use of 'disproportionate force' against burglars. Cue the triumphant trumpet blasts of the tabloids[36] cheering what the government had briefed as the 'Batter a Burglar' law.[37]

When codifying the common law in 2008, Parliament had specified the long-standing (and rather obvious) principle that force which was 'disproportionate' was not capable of being 'reasonable'.[38] If I kick you in the shin, you gouging out my eye is disproportionate, and thus will mean your claim to be acting in reasonable self-defence will not succeed.

But, for the first time in English and Welsh criminal legal history, Mr Grayling wanted to allow the use of 'disproportionate force' between citizens. By amending the legislation, he undertook to introduce a new, undefined concept of 'grossly disproportionate' force. As David Cameron told ITV News, 'People need the certainty to know that unless they did something grossly disproportionate, as we're going to put it, then they are basically in the right.'[39]

In a 'householder case', the law of self-defence would be amended to ensure that only householders using *grossly disproportionate* force against intruders would be acting beyond the scope of reasonable self-defence. Merely *disproportionate* force, it followed, would be permitted, even celebrated. 'We're saying "you can do anything as long as it's not grossly disproportionate",' the Prime Minister beamed, while the front page of the *Sun* cheered its support: 'Homeowners who "bash a burglar" – even if they shoot or stab one in the heat of the moment – will escape prosecution.'[40] 'This,' declared Chris Grayling with something proximate to the Oxford English Dictionary definition of hubris, 'should finally lay the issue to rest once and for all.'[41]

Needless to say, it didn't. For one, Parliament didn't actually legislate what Messrs Grayling and Cameron had promised.

When the High Court was called upon to interpret the new legislative provision,[42] it confirmed that its drafting *didn't* mean that, to borrow the statesmanlike words of the Prime Minister, 'you can do anything as long as it's not grossly disproportionate'. To the contrary, the legislation on its true construction still required that the courts apply the same age-old test of 'reasonableness' when assessing the level of force. All that Grayling's Law had achieved was to state, entirely pointlessly, that 'grossly disproportionate' force could never be reasonable, and, confusingly, that 'disproportionate' force *might* in some circumstances be reasonable, but might also not be.[43]

If you are struggling to follow that last paragraph, you are far from alone. The case in question arose out of a complaint by the family of a burglar who had suffered brain damage after being apprehended by a householder. The Crown Prosecution Service had decided not to charge the householder on the basis that they understood Grayling's Law to allow all but grossly disproportionate force. The family challenged the decision not to prosecute, and claimed that Grayling's Law – allowing the gratuitous use of disproportionate force – was incompatible with the right to life guaranteed by Article 2 of the European Convention on Human Rights. The High Court found that the CPS had misinterpreted the effect of Grayling's Law; far from allowing 'disproportionate force' in all householder cases (as the ministers had told the public), all the legislation achieved was to say that 'grossly disproportionate force' was *never* reasonable, 'disproportionate force' might, in some rare cases, *be capable of being* reasonable but probably wouldn't be, but that the overall test remained whether the force was, in all the circumstances, reasonable.[44] As the High Court stated: 'The headline message is and remains clear: a householder will only be able to avail himself of the defence if the degree of force he used was reasonable in the circumstances as he believed them to be.'[45]

Tellingly, the barrister in the High Court arguing for the narrower interpretation of Grayling's Law was the QC instructed by the Justice Secretary (by this time not Chris Grayling), no doubt because *had* Mr Grayling achieved what he claimed and authorised carte blanche short of 'grossly disproportionate' force against burglars, his law *would* have been incompatible with Article 2 of the European Convention on Human Rights. Thus the judges were treated to the spectacle of a government trying to persuade a court that the correct interpretation of a law was the polar opposite of what they had repeatedly told the public it would be.

There were other divergences between what Mr Grayling promised the public and what came to pass. The *Daily Mail* was beside itself to learn, upon the legislative change taking effect, of the following features:

'Official guidance sent to judges, prosecutors and police shows:

- Homeowners cannot rely on the new defence if they find an intruder in their garden or chase them outside – the fight must take place indoors.

- Shopkeepers can only get away with disproportionate attacks on robbers if they live above their shop, and only if the two parts of the building are connected.

- Shop assistants and customers cannot get involved in the violence, unless their loved ones happen to be living in the store.

- Householders cannot use the defence if they are only trying to protect their property, rather than trying to defend themselves or their family.

The document admits: "The provision does not give householders free rein to use disproportionate force in every case they are confronted by an intruder."'[46]

The palpable disappointment at restricting who can 'get involved in the violence' is only beaten for yuck factor by the disapproval marinating the word 'admits' in the revelation that householders do not have 'free rein to use disproportionate force in every case they are confronted by an intruder'.

And this macabre dismay at the attempt to place limitations on how and when we can inflict bloody, fatal injury upon our fellow citizens should worry us.

For what this whole sorry saga shows is that the flaw in how we approach the issue of self-defence is located not in the law, nor in its application by the justice system, but in our common understanding. And, as we shall see throughout this book, that understanding – or rather lack of it – can be more influential than the law itself.

In this instance, our politicians not only wasted the best part of a decade legislating and counter-legislating to nil practical effect, but, in the process, we found ourselves passengers on a runaway political mine train, gathering furious speed as it hyped and glorified the virtue of unrestrained violence.

This is not a paean to pacifism. There will, regrettably, always be a need, in certain circumstances, for the use of force. But that has to be subject to limits. For, while the scenario that the discourse invites you to imagine, much as I did at the start of the chapter, casts you in the role of Obviously Good Householder as against Obviously Bad Intruder, human interactions are not always so clear cut. There will be the youth in your garden, eyeing up your shed. There will be the youth in your garden, retrieving his football. There will be the youth just walking in your neighbourhood. Drawing distinctions and acting reasonably and proportionately in the circumstances is self-evidently vital to minimise irreversible, mistaken consequences, up to and including the loss of life.

Furthermore, what is lost in the political arms race to permit an ever-increasing quantum of violence against our fellow citizens is that laws of self-defence are carefully calibrated not only to protect you if you perceive yourself to be in danger, but to protect you if somebody else perceives that *you* pose a threat to *them*.

Few of us intend to be burglars. But many of us have had disagreements with strangers. Many of us have felt that sense of discomfort, bordering on threat, when confronted by somebody unknown to us, and the likelihood is that most of us, whether we appreciated it at the time or not, have made somebody else feel the same way. Many of our children will, at one time or another, have wandered onto somebody's private land.

The way in which the law permits people to react matters. The limits on what can be done by others to us, and to our children, matter. We would not want someone to use violence against us, or our children, unless they genuinely believed it was necessary. We would not want somebody to be licensed by the state to use unreasonable or disproportionate force against us. We rely on the law to protect us whether we are perceived as the hero or villain.

The very real danger, therefore, is that, when we don't understand how the law works and what it in fact permits, much less the rationale behind it, we can find our misunderstanding leading us astray. We can be charmed by the half-price snake oil of the Chris Graylings of this world swearing the virtues of inflicting disproportionate force on each other, and nod along as columnists and headline writers celebrate 'bashing' burglars.

And, even if Chris Grayling lacked the competence to actually change the law in the way that he promised, others have both motive and means. Tales from the United States are cautionary.

In 2005, following lobbying by the National Rifle Association,[47] the Florida state legislature enacted an amendment to its criminal code to introduce a so-called Stand Your Ground law. The architecture of Republican governor Jeb Bush and the former president of the National Rifle Association Marion Hammer,[48] section 776.012(2) of the Florida Statutes made explicit not only that deadly force can be used where a person reasonably believes it necessary to prevent death, serious bodily harm or the commission of a forcible felony, but that, 'A person who uses or threatens to use deadly force in accordance with this subsection **does not have a duty to retreat and has the right to stand his or her ground** if the person using or threatening to use the deadly force is not engaged in a criminal activity and is in a place where he or she has a right to be.'

As we saw earlier, under English and Welsh law, there is no *duty* to retreat; however, the issue of whether a person could have retreated instead of using force is a factor to be considered in the overall assessment of the reasonableness of their conduct. Confronted with somebody in your home, for example, opportunities to retreat may be limited. Conversely, a person standing in the street and seeing an aggressive yahoo shouting threats from a hundred yards away may well, in the eyes of a jury, have a reasonable opportunity to remove themselves from the scene before it becomes a theatre of conflict. Under Stand Your Ground, you would have a legal right to remain where you are, notwithstanding that, in doing so, you may be inviting a confrontation and increasing the chances of a violent escalation. If violence is then thereby provoked, you are potentially entitled to deploy deadly force against the other person.

The obvious risks of this recalibration of self-defence were highlighted at the time of the bill's passage through the state legislature. Miami's chief of police, John F. Timoney, called the bill 'unnecessary and dangerous'. He said that children could become innocent victims and warned that gun owners might assume they have 'total immunity'. He added, 'Whether it's trick-or-treaters or kids playing in the yard of someone who doesn't want them there, or some drunk guy stumbling into the wrong house, you're encouraging people to possibly use deadly physical force where it shouldn't be used.'[49]

His fears were soon realised. Over the nine years that followed, at least twenty-six children or teenagers were killed in cases in which Stand Your Ground was cited.[50] These included a nine-year-old killed in the crossfire of a dispute in which a defendant unsuccessfully raised the Stand Your Ground defence. In another case, in West Palm Beach, an unarmed nineteen-year-old was killed after an argument about dog walking; Christopher Cote knocked on the door of his sixty-two-year-old neighbour, who answered the door armed with a shotgun, stepped outside and shot the young man dead.[51]

According to official statistics, the number of deaths in Florida caused by people acting in averred self-defence nearly tripled between 2005 and 2010, when compared to the five-year period immediately preceding the introduction of SYG, up from an average of twelve 'justified homicides' per year to thirty-five.[52] A study published by the *Journal of the American Medical Association* showed that the rate of homicides in Florida increased by 24.4 per cent between 2005 and 2014, and firearm-related homicide increased by 31.6 per cent. Not only was this over a period when the nationwide homicide rates were declining, but these trends were notably not present in comparator states which had not enacted SYG laws.[53]

Far from viewing the Florida experience as a cautionary tale, however, other – mostly Southern – states have followed suit since 2005 and brought forth their own equivalent of Stand Your Ground laws. As of 2018, a total of twenty-five states had a SYG dimension to their law of self-defence, according to the National Conference of State Legislatures.[54] While one must tread cautiously when purporting to identify causation in trends of violence, a study in the *Journal of Human Resources* in 2016 estimated that SYG laws contribute to 600 additional homicides per year.[55] Another study, published by the *European Journal of Law and Economics* in 2018, found that SYG laws had led to an increase in gun deaths in the central cities and suburbs of those states.[56]

Many of the problems, it has been suggested, lie not so much in the strict legal application of the Stand Your Ground laws, but in the way they are sold to the American people. As we have seen in England and Wales, what the law *actually* says about self-defence is, to a large extent, irrelevant. The majority of the public, without the time, expertise or inclination to pore over the statute book, will hear only the mood music of Fake Law. The US media talks about *Stand Your Ground*, not *Stand Your Ground But Only Resort To Force Where You Reasonably Believe It Is Necessary*. Back in Blighty, we have *Batter A Burglar*, not *Use Reasonable Force Against A Burglar (Carefully Treading The Line Between The Somewhat Nebulous Concepts of Disproportionality and*

*Gross Disproportionality).* To the extent that the law has an impact on individual behaviour, it is our *understanding* that matters.

If the state is understood to be encouraging citizens to be readier to resort to violence – whether by belligerently inviting confrontation or by condoning the use of disproportionate force – some receptive listeners will take the state at its word. They will shoot first and shoot often. A commentary piece by Mark Hoekstra for Reuters[57] raised the obvious question: would many of these lethal confrontations have happened at all, if there had not been a celebrated Stand Your Ground law? Would the men firing the shots have felt less emboldened had they not been subjected to a noisy soundtrack of macho, NRA-sponsored Stand Your Ground rhetoric? Is the real problem the culture that the law and its presentation fuels, rather than its strict text?

Before I return to the troubling discourse on our own shores, I would offer one final story from the United States. In September 2018, twenty-six-year-old Botham Jean was at home in his apartment in Dallas, Texas, where Stand Your Ground laws reign. Amber Guyger, a police officer who lived in the same block, walked into Mr Jean's flat in error. Not realising her mistake, and wrongly assuming him to be an intruder in her home, she drew her gun and shot him dead.[58]

While we, fortunately, are yet to share the American experience, we should not be so naive as to assume we are immune. When a prime minister tells the British public, 'When that burglar crosses your threshold . . . they give up their rights,'[59] he is not only misstating the law, but inciting a mindset where reacting to perceived threats with violence is a first, not a final, recourse.

The dominant narrative Tippexes out the nuance. Burglars, or suspected burglars, are bad. Any rights – including the right to life – are left at the point of entry. Disproportionate force is no less than they deserve. The limitations on your right to kill are causing unnecessary doubt. Trust us to dispel that for you. Just ignore the small print pointing out that this inevitably means dispelling limitations on other people's right to kill *you*.

In a paradigm where householder rights are perceived to be absolute, the right to protect life can quickly tip into a right to take life. And this matters as a tenet of basic humanity. We shouldn't take life without good reason. It matters because, without conditions on our use of force, even in situations of unimaginable terror and threat, we are marching under the flag of vigilantism. Even where we are correct in our assessment that a person poses a threat, that cannot be the end of the inquiry. Some intruders will have the shameful, unsympathetic CV of Brendan Fearon, burglar of Martin's Bleak House, but some will be children making their first stupid mistake. We see those children in the criminal courts every day of the week. And we hope that their first mistake will be their last because of their rehabilitation, not because of a Tony Martin figure inflicting their own brand of summary justice.

Our national rhetoric recently tiptoed even further towards the brink. The case of Richard Osborn-Brooks, a seventy-eight-year-old who stabbed a burglar to death using a screwdriver, occupied enraged headlines for several weeks in April 2018. He was arrested and interviewed under caution – an entirely unremarkable and expected outcome when police attend your home to find that you have killed someone in your kitchen – before the police investigation concluded that no further action should be taken against him. But, as long as fulmination sold copies and made for delectable quotables for the constituency newsletter, editors and politicians joined hands for a pious, mendacious chorus of 'Isn't the law dreadful? An Englishman's home should be his castle.' The confected rage in this case was not at Mr Osborn-Brooks' conviction, nor even his prosecution. For neither followed. No, the campaign, backed by a petition launched by the *Sun*, was for the police to be prohibited from *investigating* the death of the burglar.[60] The notion that any questions should be asked where a human life had been extinguished, that any due process should follow the discovery of a bloodied corpse at a man's home, was simply intolerable for the *Sun* and its whipped-up, misled readership.

Once again, the government could not help dipping its toe into the troubled waters. Rather than refusing to comment on an ongoing police investigation, or reminding the public of the value of due process, Justice Secretary David Gauke let it be known that his 'sympathies are with householders who have to defend themselves when intruders break in'. His spokesperson added, 'That's why we strengthened the law in 2013 to give householders greater protection from intruders.'[61]

And we can see in the middle distance, without squinting too hard, the natural confluence of these narratives. A society where we are entitled, even encouraged, to disproportionately inflict fatal violence upon each other, without the state even troubling itself to investigate; a dystopia towards which, without radical change in our understanding and discourse, we are ever faithfully stumbling.

# 2. Your Family

'It is a sad irony that while the people of the UK are busy celebrating a royal birth, its government is brushing off a commoner's right to life. It is a grim reminder that systems of socialized medicine like the NHS vest the state with power over human lives, transforming citizens into subjects.'

Ted Cruz, Senator for Texas, 25 April 2018[1]

On the evening of Friday, 23 April 2018, for the second time in little under a year, several hundred concerned citizens gathered to storm a children's hospital. As placards – *Give Him A Chance* and *I Stand With Life* – bobbed up and down in a sea of angry and anguished faces, 'Alfie's Army' charged at the line of police officers marshalling the doors to Alder Hey Children's Hospital in Liverpool, intent on breaking through the state's barriers to get to a desperately poorly twenty-three-month-old boy, Alfie Evans.[2] In an echo of the summer before, when 'Charlie's Army' had united outside Great Ormond Street Hospital in support of the distraught parents of another ill infant, the rallying cry was succinct and devastatingly powerful: *Please don't let the state kill our child.*

**Charlie Gard**'s plight had first come to public attention in early 2017.[3] Charlie suffered from a rare inherited disease called infantile onset encephalomyopathic mitochondrial DNA depletion syndrome, referred to as MDDS. He was admitted to Great Ormond Street Hospital at the age of two months, after his worried parents, Constance Yates and Chris Gard, visited their GP due to concerns over Charlie's development. Shortly afterwards, he began to suffer from seizures, and a series of tests subsequently confirmed the tragic diagnosis.

The symptoms were severe. Progressive respiratory failure meant that Charlie was dependent on a ventilator to keep him alive. He was unable to move his limbs, nor could he open his eyes enough to be able to see. He was persistently encephalopathic – there were no usual signs of normal brain activities such as responsiveness, interaction or crying. He was also deaf, and was affected by frequent seizures. The clinical consensus was that his quality of life was so poor and his condition so devastating that Charlie would derive no benefit from continued life. Accordingly, Great Ormond Street Hospital applied for a court order declaring that it was lawful for artificial ventilation to be withdrawn and substituted for palliative care – a court order, in effect, that Charlie should die.

There was, however, another option: a pioneering treatment, known as nucleoside therapy, was available in the United States. Charlie's parents traced a doctor, who said that, subject to funding, he would be prepared to treat Charlie in the US. Charlie's desperate parents appealed to the public for funds, and, with the help of social media and crowdfunding, raised £1.2 million to pay for nucleoside therapy, to take place in America.[4]

But when the case came before the High Court in March and April 2017, the judge hearing the case, Mr Justice Francis, refused to allow the pioneering treatment to take place, ruling instead that, in his judgement, Charlie should have his ventilation withdrawn.

There followed over the next few months a series of appeals through the hierarchy of the English and Welsh courts, with the Court of Appeal and the Supreme Court upholding the decision of the High Court. When those appeals failed, submissions were made to the European Court of Human Rights (ECtHR), whose judges similarly refused to step in to save Charlie's life.

Matters soon went global. The ECtHR decision attracted the attention of the American media, with the Breitbart website condemning the 'EU court' for supporting the decision of the British 'death panel'.[5] On the evening of 2 July 2017, following protests outside Buckingham Palace, the Vatican released a statement, in which Pope Francis announced that he was following Charlie's case 'with affection and sadness'. Speaking of Charlie's parents, the statement said, 'For this [the Pope] prays that their wish to accompany and treat their child until the end isn't neglected.' Within hours, US President Donald Trump tweeted, 'If we can help little #CharlieGard, as per [sic] our friends in the U.K. and the Pope, we would be delighted to do so.'[6] Within a day, the Vatican's hospital, Ospedale Pediatrico Bambino Gesù, offered to admit Charlie so as to prevent his ventilation being switched off. This offer was endorsed, and its acceptance urged, by the Italian Foreign Minister Angelino Alfano during a telephone call with UK Foreign Secretary Boris Johnson.[7] This conversation was reported on the same day that thirty-seven Members of the European Parliament published an open letter to the UK Prime Minister and Secretary of State for Health, condemning the 'outrageous outcome of Charlie's case', which it was said 'infringes Europe's most fundamental values, particularly the right to life, the right to human dignity and personal integrity'.[8]

Fox News told its American audience that Charlie had been 'sentenced to death by the British government',[9] while Breitbart warned that the courts' decisions were the inevitable corollary of 'single-payer, government-run health care'.[10] The *Austin American-Statesman* advised readers that 'European bureaucrats made the callous decision that it would not be cost effective to spend money on [Charlie], even in the face of possible treatment.'[11]

Fox News commentators excoriated the judge's 'cynical decision' to rule in favour of a 'state-run National Health Service [which is] always looking for ways to cut costs', reaching variously for parallels with Ebenezer Scrooge's entreaty to 'decrease the surplus population' and, inevitably, the Nazis, warning that the UK was teetering on the precipice of a 'full embrace of eugenics'.[12] The Speaker of the US House of Representatives, Paul Ryan, tweeted: 'I stand with #CharlieGard & his parents. Health care should be between patients & doctors – govt has no place in the life or death business.'[13]

Back at home, crowds of protestors from all over the world began to gather outside the Royal Courts of Justice on London's Strand, their chants of 'Medicine, not murder', 'Shame on you, GOSH [Great Ormond Street Hospital]' and 'Shame on you, judge' an audible, sombre percussive to the proceedings inside.

Appalled by the British refusal to grant Charlie 'the medical treatment he needs', the appropriations committee of the US House of Representatives passed an amendment on 19 July entitling Charlie to 'permanent residence' in America, only to be thwarted by the British court's refusal to allow his release.[14]

Protestors took the fight to the hospital itself, amassing at Great Ormond Street and urging the families of other patients to sign their petitions and join the campaign. The hospital responded by calling in the police.[15]

Eventually, on 24 July, after a series of further medical tests, the High Court handed down its final judgment, upholding its original declaration that palliative care should begin.[16] The decision was condemned by British politicians – with occasional UKIP leader Nigel Farage tweeting that the 'establishment closed ranks' on Charlie Gard's parents and 'took away their rights'[17] – and in America, with Texas Senator Ted Cruz among the many asking, 'WHY govt should have power to decide who lives & dies?'[18]

On 28 July 2017, Charlie passed away in a hospice. The doctors and the courts had got their wish. A child's life had ended, when, in the words of Charlie's mother, 'Had Charlie been given the treatment sooner he would have had the potential to be a normal, healthy little boy.'[19]

If the watching world had been shaken by the matter-of-fact way in which the UK establishment had ordered a child to die, it did not have to wait long for a second quake. **Alfie Evans**[20] was born on 9 May 2016, the first child of Tom Evans and Kate James. From two months of age, signs of developmental delay began to appear, and he then started to lose many of the abilities he had developed in his first months of life. At the age of six months, a series of tests showed that the delay was significant, although no specific disorder could be identified. In December 2016, Alfie was admitted to Alder Hey Children's Hospital. By February 2018, the medical consensus was that Alfie had a progressive, ultimately fatal neurodegenerative condition, most likely a mitochondrial disorder, which was both catastrophic and untreatable. There was no chance of any recovery. Alfie could not breathe or swallow unaided, and the view of the clinicians at Alder Hey Children's Hospital was that his quality of life was poor. Accordingly, in December 2017, the hospital applied to the High Court for a declaration that artificial ventilation should be withdrawn.

The sense of déjà vu does not end there. For, while Alder Hey may have felt unable to offer treatment, one medical establishment was willing and able: the Bambino Gesù in Rome, the same facility that had extended an offer to Charlie Gard. In February 2018, over several hearings at the High Court, Alfie's unrepresented parents cross-examined the medical experts and pleaded with Mr Justice Hayden to refuse Alder Hey's application and allow Alfie to travel by air to Rome for treatment.

Again, however, the High Court ruled that ventilation should be withdrawn. And again, despite arguing their case through to the Supreme Court and beyond, to the European Court of Human Rights, they were met with layers of judicial and medical resistance, notwithstanding the mounting public support in favour of keeping Alfie alive.

On 11 April 2018, after Mr Justice Hayden approved an end-of-life care plan, these supporters, like Charlie's Army before them, congregated outside the hospital, chanting Alfie's name and singing the Mariah Carey ballad, 'Hero'. They were addressed by Tom Evans, who held aloft three passports – his, Kate James' and Alfie's – as his legal representatives explained to reporters that Mr Evans had the legal right to remove his son from the hospital. Alfie, it was said, was being falsely imprisoned: 'the NHS has broken Alfie's ancient rights under habeas corpus – a 13th century legal safeguard that prevents unlawful detention.'[21]

An appeal on Facebook saw Alfie's Army grow over the days that followed, as the fresh legal challenge proceeded to court.

Protestors bearing balloons, posters, placards and teddy bears accumulated outside Alder Hey as the petition to save his life attracted close to quarter of a million signatures.[22] The family's local MEP, Steven Woolfe, a qualified barrister, told the media that 'Alder Hey is more concerned with saving face than saving a young child's life'.[23]

Mr Woolfe also evoked the 2014 case of Ashya King, a five-year-old boy with brain cancer whose parents defied NHS doctors and took him to Prague for proton-beam therapy, sparking an international manhunt. The parents were arrested, but ultimately Ashya was permitted to have the treatment in Prague, and it was a success. Speaking about Alfie, Mr Woolfe told daytime-TV show *Good Morning Britain*, 'The same applied with the Charlie Gard scenario, the same applied with Ashya King . . . We now know with Ashya King, who lived, that our professionals make mistakes.'[24]

On 15 April, the Pope once more took an interest, referring to Alfie in his Sunday prayers,[25] and, after the Court of Appeal rejected the latest appeal on 16 April, granted Tom Evans a personal audience. This was followed by Pope Francis offering his explicit support for the parents' cause, tweeting a few days later: 'I renew my appeal that the suffering of [Alfie's] parents may be heard and their desire to seek new forms of treatment may be granted.'[26]

That same day, as the European Court of Human Rights knocked back a second attempt at appealing, 200 protestors attempted to storm Alder Hey Children's Hospital, only thwarted by the lines of police officers providing state-backed muscle.

Tom Evans proceeded to initiate a private prosecution against three of Alfie's doctors, eagerly reported across the world, including by the *Daily Mail*, which asked its readers, 'Could medics face trial for conspiracy to murder?'[27] The threats, abuse and intimidation towards hospital staff that ensued were perhaps predictable.[28]

Meanwhile, in further echoes of Charlie Gard, foreign citizenship was conferred on baby Alfie – this time by the Italian Ministry of Foreign Affairs – in an effort to remove him from the jurisdiction of the murderous English and Welsh courts. The American political and media interest peaked during the final days of the legal process, in late April 2018. On 25 April, as the Court of Appeal closed the doors on the final chance of moving Alfie to Rome, a vigil was organised outside the British Embassy in Washington DC, with politicians clamouring to offer support.[29]

Nigel Farage once more provided the legal translation for US viewers, assuring Americans that, 'there is treatment available in Italy that is not available here', and nodding as the Fox News anchor suggested that Alfie was a 'hostage of the National Health Service' and that 'part of [the problem] is the NHS, they don't want to risk the fact he goes over to Italy, he gets treatment, he has some quality of life and that's a big embarrassment'.[30]

In the early hours of 28 April 2018, at twenty-three months old, Alfie died at Alder Hey. An angel had gained his wings. The state had, once more, got its way. The public mood in both cases was summarised in a post by a relative on the Charlie's Army Facebook group: 'What a sad world we live in, where judges merely look at legal arguments set out by professionals and not into the eyes of a baby they have the power to save.'[31]

Most of us will never have to confront the horror of making medical decisions concerning our terminally ill child. Even fewer of us will ever find ourselves fighting in a court of law to keep our child alive.

If pushed to imagine the unimaginable, I expect that our instinctive reaction to the plight of these parents would be not merely boundless sympathy, but solidarity. Would any of us, thrust as new parents into legal proceedings in which our child's very existence was at stake, do anything different from Connie, Chris, Tom or Kate? Even if we were not ourselves manning the protests in support of Charlie and Alfie, we may well, upon reading about the cases, have shared a link to a Facebook fundraising group, or retweeted a message in support of their Armies.

Who would not rally behind parents opposing the almighty state trying to swoop into their private lives, remove their poorly infant from their arms and extinguish all hope? Who among us would not resist to our last breath the government's attempts to harm a child, and do absolutely everything in our power to fight for their best interests?

While entirely reasonable, such questions are not as straight-forward to answer as they may appear. To do so, we first need to break down some of the premises on which they are founded, and examine more closely some of the complex issues of law, medi-cine and morality that are at play when the courts intervene in the life of a child. A theme common to the cases of both Charlie and Alfie was a deliberate muddying of the waters by a variety of special-interest groups, leading to a fundamental and wide-spread misrepresentation of what those cases were actually about. As a result, many of us were unknowingly presented with an entirely false prospectus, and our sincere and heartfelt inten-tions – like those of the parents – were appropriated and exploited in service of ulterior political agendas.

To start with, we should take a look at the term 'best inter-ests', because understanding how the law grapples with that principle – the best interests of the child – is key to understanding exactly what went on in the cases of Charlie and Alfie.


## The welfare or 'best interests' principle

First, a potted history. The jurisdiction of the courts to intervene in matters relating to the welfare of children was developed by the courts during the late eighteenth and nineteenth centuries.[32] Prior to that, the legal position was, put simply, that the father was king. He was legal guardian of his 'legitimate' children, with the mother exercising parental rights over a child born outside marriage. If a child was orphaned or otherwise parentless, the courts had powers of 'wardship' to take the child under the guardianship of the court, but had no meaningful role to play in the treatment of a child by her parents, unless and until the criminal law was breached.

Towards the end of the eighteenth century, the Court of Chancery[33] began to develop a new way of approaching cases involving children, which correlated with a growing societal awareness that children had their own rights, distinct from the wishes and whims of the father. It was recognised that not only did children need to be protected by the criminal law from abuse and injury, but that it was in the wider interests of all of us that children be educated, properly cared for and helped to become healthy and useful members of society. It followed that it would sometimes be in society's interests for the interests of the child to be promoted at the expense of the welfare or wishes of the parents, although this was heavily caveated, with the courts famously observing in one case, '[T]he father knows far better as a rule what is good for his children than a court of justice can.'[34]

Nevertheless, the slow relaxing of the paternal grip did eventually have transformative legal consequences. The mother of a legitimate child could claim custody or access from the father where the welfare of the child so required, if, for example, the father was unfit. Similar principles fell to be considered when the court was appointing or removing guardians. In 1886, the court-created notion of the welfare of the child was put on a statutory footing as a relevant consideration in custody disputes by the Guardianship of Infants Act, and gradually the balance tipped. In the twentieth century, the welfare of the child began to supplant matrimonial conduct as the deciding factor in matrimonial disputes, and the Guardianship of Infants Act 1925 not only gave mothers and fathers statutory equality in custody wrangles, but elevated the 'welfare of the child' to the 'first and paramount consideration'.

This idea, that the welfare of the child was not just *a* consideration, but *the* consideration for courts dealing with cases involving children, is what underpins our legal system today, expressed in section 1 of the Children Act 1989: when a court determines any question relating to the upbringing of a child, 'the child's welfare shall be the court's paramount consideration'.

The notion of 'welfare' is often expressed as 'best interests', which is the language used in Article 3 of the United Nations Convention on the Rights of the Child. In legal systems across the world, the absolute rights of the father have given way to the individual rights of the child.

The difficulty that can arise is that, for many children, it is hard if not impossible for them to express or enforce those rights, or to identify or take decisions in their own interests. Most of the time this is not an issue, as parents and guardians tend to agree how to raise their child, and do so, by default, with their best interests at heart. But where there is a dispute – between two parents, or between the parents and the state, or between parents and doctors – as to what is in a child's best interests, the courts can be invited to decide.

## Why might the state intervene in my child's life?

In practice, the types of case in which the courts are called upon to apply the welfare principle broadly fall into two camps – public law and private law. **Public law** cases involve the state seeking to enter uninvited into the lives of a child and her family in the name of child protection. Where the state – usually a local authority – considers a child to be suffering, or at risk of suffering, 'significant harm',[35] it can apply to the court for various orders. Two of the most common orders applied for are care orders, which transfer parental responsibility for the child to the local authority, and supervision orders, which place the child under the supervision of the local authority.

We'll put this to one side for now, as we're not immediately concerned with public law cases, and focus instead on **private law** cases involving children.

Where there is a dispute relating to the upbringing of a child between private individuals – most commonly divorced or separated parents – applications can be made to the family courts for a resolution. 'Child arrangements orders', for instance, can be applied for to regulate arrangements concerning when and with whom a child is to live, spend time or have contact. Of particular relevance for our purposes is what is known as a 'specific issue order'. Under the legislation, a party can apply for the court to resolve a specific question which arises 'in connection with any aspect of parental responsibility for a child'.[36] As the definition suggests, this allows for quite a spectrum, from questions over whether a boy should be circumcised,[37] to whether a child should be given the MMR vaccine,[38] to how children should be educated where the religions of estranged parents place them at odds over schooling. In all private law cases, the test is the same: the welfare principle. The court will hear evidence and argument from the parties, and will form its own independent view as to what order is in the child's best interests.

As for what 'best interests' entail, it depends on the scenario, but the Children Act[39] lists some factors that the court must consider:

— The wishes and feelings of the child (considered in the light of her age and understanding);

— Her physical, emotional and educational needs;

— The likely effect on her of any change in her circumstances;

— Her sex, age, background and any characteristics which the court considers relevant;

— Any harm which she has suffered or is at risk of suffering;

— How capable each of her parents or other relevant person is of meeting her needs;

— The range of powers available to the court.

To give an example of the principle in action, a high-profile case in 2012[40] saw the Court of Appeal grapple with the question of whether two young boys of Orthodox Jewish parents should be educated as the father wished – at an ultra-Orthodox Hasidic or Haredi unisex school – or as the mother desired – at a co-educational 'Modern Orthodox' school. The distinctions were stark. The Haredi community do not permit children to watch television, in the main they do not have access to the internet or social media and mixing with non-Haredi children is forbidden. The Modern Orthodox school, by contrast, was far more permissive as far as matters such as television, religious dress and socialising outside the community were concerned. As the court noted, the importance of this decision went beyond a mere choice of school; it was 'a much more fundamental way of life' for the children.

It is difficult to do justice, in a summary, to the depth of the analysis into the meaning of 'welfare' and 'best interests' that the court engaged in, and the judgment as a whole makes genuinely fascinating reading, even for those with more in their lives than law (assuming such curious creatures exist). The assessment, the court said, takes into account 'a wide range of ethical, social, moral, religious, cultural, emotional and welfare considerations', including 'everything that conduces to a child's welfare and happiness or relates to the child's development and present and future life as a human being'. The judgment ruminated on John Donne and the Aristotelian notion of the 'good life', the legal and societal imperative of respecting religious principles, and considered at length the likely impact of the two alternative schools on the children's futures. Having heard extensive evidence, the conclusion reached was that, for a number of reasons – including the educational opportunities, the emotional impact upon the children and the fact that a more liberal education would still afford the children the chance to return to their religious roots, if they so chose, when older – the mother's proposal best served the children's interests.

And so, although it is understandable why to many people the

44

notion of a court telling you how to raise your child provokes instinctive discomfort, if not outright hostility, the principle perhaps becomes easier to embrace if you view it not through the lens of the courts trampling on your parental rights, but as a societal guarantee that, wherever those who care for a child disagree, there is an independent adjudicator of last resort, whose priority above all is the best interests of that child.

It is not only warring parents, however, who can apply to the courts for specific questions to be decided. Bringing us back around to the cases in hand, the question of medical treatment of young children is also capable of being determined on a private application to the family court. Doctors have a legal and ethical duty to act in the best interests of a child or young person under eighteen years under their care.[41] Most of the time, the parents' views and the professional clinical opinions align. For the overwhelming majority of poorly children, the doctors and parents reach an accommodation on what treatment is in the best interests of the child. It is statistically exceptionally rare that clinicians and parents disagree to such an extent that a contested court hearing is required to decide the medical treatment.[42]

However, where there is a dispute, the mechanism for resolving it lies with the courts. Older children, for instance, may be competent to consent to medical treatment (the assessment of 'competence' involving a judgment on their maturity and ability to understand what is involved), but may refuse treatment that doctors believe to be in their best interests.

In 1993, in echoes of Ian McEwan's novel The Children Act, a fifteen-year-old leukaemia patient refused a life-saving blood transfusion on the grounds that it contravened a tenet of his religion as a Jehovah's Witness. The hospital applied to the High Court for permission to treat the boy in accordance with what the doctors believed to be his best interests. The court, while having regard to the boy's wishes and religious beliefs as part of the overall assessment of his best interests, nevertheless ordered that the transfusion should go ahead.[43] In a tragic footnote to this case, a few years later, when the young man was no longer a child, his leukaemia returned. As a competent adult, nobody could stop him refusing treatment, and he duly died as a martyr to his faith.

Where a child does not have capacity to consent to treatment, the decision lies with the parents, exercising their legal duties of parental responsibility. But parents, too, may not always be acting in their child's best interests. In 2014, a very young boy, 'B', suffered severe burns in an accident. The skin graft that doctors needed to carry out was likely to require a blood transfusion; without this, there was a real risk of death. The parents, both devout Jehovah's Witnesses, refused to consent to the treatment. The NHS Trust applied to the High Court for a determination. The High Court, perhaps unsurprisingly, confirmed the long-standing principle that the parents' wishes, although deserving of 'very great respect', were ultimately 'subordinate to welfare', and the best interests of the child plainly lay in receiving this life-saving treatment.[44] More recently, in 2019, Mr Justice Hayden, the judge in the case of Alfie Evans, ruled that a thirteen-month-old girl with life-threatening kidney failure should be treated with haemodialysis, as supported by Royal Manchester Children's Hospital, contrary to the wishes of the girl's parents that she be treated 'only [by] the power of prayer'.[45]

And these scenarios illustrate graphically the importance of the welfare principle. Because, as much as no good parent would envisage themselves ever acting contrary to their child's best interests, sometimes our judgment can be clouded. Whether fogged by religious dogma or stricken by grief, we can be fallible. We can, at our lowest, most hopeless ebb, conflate – entirely understandably and with the very best of motives – our own interests with those of the ones we love most. That is not a moral failing; it is to be human. But, in such circumstances, where others who love our child almost as much as we do worry that our preferred path may not be the best course for them, our society has a mechanism for ensuring, as far as we can, that the best course is followed.

This is why, in the Charlie Gard case, when Fox News' Tucker Carlson voiced the sentiments of many on his network in tweeting,

'The parents . . . should be able to decide his medical care',[46] he simply can't be right. As a catchy, retweetable homily, this is smashing. As a statement of broad unqualified principle, it is ludicrous. There *have* to be limits. Otherwise Tucker Carlson is supporting the unfettered right of parents, such as those in the case of 'B', to condemn children to death, or to subject them to pointless, painful medical procedures.

As Great Ormond Street Hospital put it in their 'position statement', lodged with the High Court and published during the maelstrom of the Charlie Gard coverage, 'A world where only parents speak and decide for children and where children have no separate identity or rights and no court to hear and protect them is far from the world in which GOSH treats its child patients.'[47]

## How can it be in a child's best interests to die?

For any parent – indeed, any person – the notion that it can ever be in the best interests of a child for their life to end runs counter to every instinct we share. But, in considering what follows, it may help to remember that the function of the law – not only in this instance but across the legal system – is to grapple dispassionately with cases that appear before the courts. That's not to say that there is no place for humanity; to the contrary, any justice system worthy of the name absolutely has to command respect for the way in which it protects and promotes what makes us human. But it also has to ensure that, when faced with the most difficult of cases, it reaches decisions that appeal to principle and reason, not just emotion.

The welfare principle – prioritising the best interests of children who are unable to stand up for themselves – operates no differently in cases involving decisions to withdraw life-sustaining treatment, where doctors and parents can't agree on the best course for the child. Awful as it is to contemplate, there are severe medical conditions causing such suffering that the view is taken that it is not in a child's best interests to undergo invasive, painful treatment in an effort to prolong a minimal quality of life.

I use the passive – *the view is taken* – because it would be a mistake to assume that the view against treatment is always held by the doctors. The courts have dealt with heartbreaking cases where loving parents of severely disabled children have found themselves arguing *against* life-saving treatment proposed by doctors, on the grounds that they fear the quality of life for their child would be so low that it is in their best interests to die. One such case in the 1980s[48] concerned the mother of an infant with Down's syndrome; the Court of Appeal ruled that a life-saving procedure should be undertaken, and this judgment, especially viewed through a twenty-first-century lens, has to be correct. But again, it gives the lie to the notion that parents should always have the final say, that there is no place for the courts in such situations.

In the cases of Charlie and Alfie, it was the doctors who were asking the court if it agreed that continuing to administer treatment was not in the child's best interests.

Where the doctors, applying their professional judgment, form the view that treatment limitation might be in a child's best interests, they apply to the High Court for a declaration. This is not because they are certain that they are right and are simply seeking a 'rubber stamp' from the court; it is because they need the court to decide what is right, and to declare, with fully evaluated reasons so that everybody involved understands, where the best interests of the child lie. As Katie Gollop QC, counsel for Great Ormond Street Hospital in the Charlie Gard case, wrote in an article with barrister Sarah Pope, 'In a strongly disputed case . . . a hospital applies to the Court because it *doesn't know* where the child's best interests lie. Of course it has a view, but even as the hospital makes its application, it knows that there is another, powerful and deeply held contrary view, that is born of parental love outside its experience. A responsible hospital knows that the parents may be right.'[49]

To further ensure that all proper considerations are put before the court, the court will also appoint a guardian to represent the interests of the child; the argument will not be left solely to the hospital and the parents. Guardians are appointed by Cafcass (Children and Family Court Advisory and Support Service), an independent body with a duty to safeguard and promote the welfare of children in the family justice system.

At the High Court, the judge will receive evidence from medical experts, parents and any other witnesses, and then hear submissions from the barristers representing the hospital, the parents and the child's guardian. There is a long stream of case law on how the 'best interests' test applies in end-of-life cases, but the key principles can perhaps be summarised as follows:[50]

i. Firstly, the question is not, *Would it be in the child's best interests for treatment to be withheld?* but instead, *Would it be in the child's best interests for invasive treatment to be continued?* If ongoing treatment would not be in the child's best interests, the courts cannot allow it to take place;

ii. There is a strong presumption in favour of life, and a 'profound respect for the sanctity of human life is embedded in our law and our moral philosophy'. However, the presumption is not irrebuttable; there will be cases where the quality of life is sufficiently small and the pain, suffering and other burdens are sufficiently great;

iii. 'Best interests' is used in its widest sense, including (but not limited to) medical, emotional, sensory and instinctive considerations. It evokes the fundamental principles that undergird our humanity;

iv. The court must consider the nature of the medical treatment in question, what it involves and its prospects of success, including the likely outcome;

v. The court is not bound to follow the clinical assessment of the doctors, but must form its own view as to the child's best interests;

vi. The views and opinions of both the doctors and the parents must be carefully considered, and may have particular value as they know the child so well. However, the court must be mindful that the views of the parents may, understandably, be coloured by emotion or sentiment;

vii. The views of the child must be considered and given appropriate weight in light of the child's age and understanding.

And this exercise, we will see, is what underpinned the decisions in Charlie Gard and Alfie Evans.

## What really happened in Charlie Gard's case?

Charlie's illness – MDDS – was caused by mutations in a gene called RRM2B. The consequence of this mitochondrial disease was that his brain, muscles and ability to breathe were all severely affected. He had congenital deafness and a severe epilepsy disorder, with his heart, liver and kidneys also affected. The disease was progressive; since birth, he had lost movement in his limbs and the ability to breathe unaided. He could not see, and his 'persistent encephalopathy' meant there were no usual signs of normal brain activity. His parents accepted that, as it stood, Charlie's quality of life was 'not worth sustaining'.[51]

By early 2017, with Charlie's life expectancy measured in months, all the treating doctors at Great Ormond Street agreed that artificial ventilation should be withdrawn, that he should be given palliative care only and that he should be allowed to die peacefully and with dignity. An expert team in Barcelona reached the same conclusion. The issue for the court was whether Charlie's best interests lay in withdrawing ventilation or in having him flown to America for 'pioneering' nucleoside therapy.

The High Court was presented with evidence over several days from the world's leading experts in mitochondrial diseases, including Dr Hirano, the neurology professor from the US offering the 'pioneering treatment'. It emerged that the term was a misnomer. Nucleoside therapy had never been used on patients with Charlie's form of MDDS; it had not even reached the experimental stage on mice. The doctor had never treated anyone with encephalopathy. There was no evidence that the treatment would have any benefit for Charlie; at best, Dr Hirano 'expressed the hope' that it might, given the modest benefit (a 4 per cent increased lifespan) it had had on patients with a different and less severe mitochondrial condition.

Great Ormond Street, nevertheless, upon Charlie's mother learning about this therapy in December 2016, took steps in January 2017 to apply for ethical permission to attempt the treatment. However, a series of further seizures that month led to irreversible brain damage and a clinical consensus that nucleoside treatment would be 'futile'.

At the time he first extended the offer, Dr Hirano had never even seen Charlie's medical notes, let alone examined him. After speaking to consultants at GOSH and reviewing the medical records, the doctor concluded, 'I agree that it is very unlikely that [Charlie] will improve with that therapy.' He agreed with the other experts that the brain damage was irreversible, and that the chances of meaningful brain recovery were 'vanishingly small'.

This caused the judge to pose the question, 'If Charlie's damaged brain function cannot be improved, as all seem to agree, then how can he be better off than he is now, which is in a condition that his parents believe should not be sustained?'

It wasn't simply a question of the likely benefit of the treatment; there was a real possibility that Charlie was in pain. The collective view of the treating doctors was that Charlie experienced 'significant' suffering, and that that outweighed the tiny theoretical chance of effective treatment. While nobody could be certain, and Charlie's parents disputed the medical opinion, the court accepted that his ongoing ventilation, suction and treatment was invasive and capable of causing pain. Nucleoside therapy – the big unknown – may also have subjected Charlie to pain. All the doctors consulted in the UK and Barcelona agreed that treatment would be futile, that it 'would be of no effect but may well cause pain, suffering and distress to Charlie'.

Charlie's guardian, having listened to the evidence over the week of the hearing, concluded that 'it is not in Charlie's best interests to travel to America to receive nucleoside therapy. This is not pioneering or life-saving treatment, but a purely experimental process with no real prospect of improving Charlie's condition or quality of life.'

The judge reached the same sad conclusion in his first judgment, on 11 April 2017.

Charlie's parents appealed to the Court of Appeal with a new legal team, arguing, among other things, that the judge had applied the wrong test in law. It was suggested that the long-standing 'best interests' test shouldn't be the only factor; instead, the courts should apply a test of 'significant harm', as they do in public law cases where local authorities are seeking to take a child into care. If the parents' choice of medical treatment does not risk 'significant harm' to the child, it should be allowed, was the thrust of the argument. The Court of Appeal, and then the Supreme Court, disagreed. The lodestar, as the Children Act makes clear, is 'best interests'. The Supreme Court pointed out that in the medical field this litmus is all the more important, as it reflects the legal and ethical duties of doctors to act in a child patient's best interests. Requiring them instead to apply a 'significant harm' threshold risked putting doctors in the untenable position where they were administering treatment which they didn't believe to be in a child's best interests. In any case, Mr Justice Francis and the Court of Appeal had found that it was likely that Charlie *would* suffer significant harm if his suffering was prolonged without any realistic prospect of improvement.[52]

The unsuccessful application for permission to appeal to the Supreme Court was followed by an attempt to appeal to the European Court of Human Rights, which upheld the domestic courts' use of the 'best interests' test, and declared the application to appeal 'inadmissible'.[53]

Throughout these appeals, GOSH continued to treat Charlie. Following the European Court decision on 27 June 2017, the parents' solicitors contacted Great Ormond Street asserting that there was new medical evidence. This prompted a flurry of excited news reporting. The 'new evidence' comprised the willingness of the Bambino Gesù hospital and Dr Hirano to accept Charlie, and new laboratory findings by Dr Hirano which had led him to the view that the likelihood of a positive effect on Charlie was 'markedly improved' compared to what was said at the hearing in April.

Accordingly, the hospital asked that the case return before Mr Justice Francis at the High Court. There followed a series of hearings between 10 and 24 July 2017, and a succession of further tests and scans.[54] It emerged on the first day that Dr Hirano had still not, at the time of giving this opinion, actually seen or examined Charlie at any stage, nor had he read the judge's findings. At the judge's invitation, Dr Hirano and a doctor from the Bambino Gesù flew to England and examined Charlie the following weekend. Dr Hirano's conclusion was that Charlie had brain damage, which was irreversible, and brain dysfunction, which was potentially reversible, although, 'I certainly don't expect that he would be normal. That's clear.' The doctor from the Bambino Gesù suggested that, at the time he offered to treat Charlie, he had not been fully aware of his condition, and stated that treatment 'will probably not have a great impact'. They remained willing, however, and stated that it was in Charlie's best interests to be treated with nucleoside bypass therapy at their respective hospitals.

A few days later, however, a full-body MRI scan confirmed 'the reality . . . that Charlie is beyond any help even from experimental treatment'. By the time Mr Justice Francis handed down his final judgment on 24 July 2017, all parties were in agreement as to where Charlie's best interests lay. The judge took the time to again praise Charlie's 'fine parents', making clear that he was satisfied they had 'nothing whatever' to do with the 'disgraceful' threats and abuse made by others towards the hospital, and observing, 'It is impossible for any of us to comprehend or even begin to imagine the agony to which Charlie's parents have been subjected in recent weeks and months as they have had to come to terms with the decision that they have now made.'[55]

And so we can see that the dominant mainstream and social-media narrative was almost completely wrong. The awful reality was that, contrary to the statement by Charlie's distraught mother, from the moment the case came before the court, Charlie never 'had the potential to be a normal, healthy little boy'. The 'pioneering treatment' was offered by a doctor who had never even visited the patient and was unaware of the severity of his condition. It was at best experimental, having never even been tested on mice, with 'vanishingly small' prospects of improving the life of a terminally ill child, who, the court concluded, was likely to suffer pain and suffering as a result.[56] By the end, what Nigel Farage conspiratorially claimed was 'the establishment closing ranks' in fact amounted to an unchallenged consensus among all medical experts involved.

But, irrespective of the medical arguments, it is clear that, at every stage, the decision revolved around the assessment of Charlie's best interests. There was never a grain of truth in the claim that financial cost of the proposed treatment was the court's primary driver; as the judge stated in the very first hearing, it was completely irrelevant. The efforts of the family raised well over a million pounds, but money was wholly unrelated to the assessment of Charlie's best interests, for the simple reason that 'best interests of the child' and funding decisions by NHS Clinical Commissioning Groups (CCGs) are entirely separate issues.

There are of course legal cases in which patients challenge recommendations made by the National Institute for Health and Care Excellence (NICE) as to which drugs and treatments are clinically and cost effective, and cases in which courts are asked to judicially review decisions by CCGs not to make available on the National Health Service certain treatments recommended by

NICE. While many such decisions turn on complex arguments of clinical effectiveness, it is not unfair to characterise these cases as based, at least in part, on financial considerations.

But – and I repeat in the vain hope that enough choruses might carry the message across the pond and through denser skulls – this had nothing at all to do with Charlie's case. The suggestion that the clinical recommendation by the hospital and the declaration by the court had any relation to the ability of the family to pay, or the willingness of the NHS to make funds available, was a monstrous lie.

Likewise, the imported fiction that Charlie was a 'prisoner of the state' or a 'prisoner of the NHS' is easily disproved. The government is represented in litigation by the relevant body or minister. In public law cases where local authorities are applying for care orders, for instance, the applicant would be the local authority. In cases involving immigration, the relevant minister would be the Home Secretary. In health cases, it would be the Secretary of State for Health. This is clear because, at the top of every published court judgment, we can see the parties involved or interested in the litigation. The only parties involved or interested in Charlie's case were the applicants, Great Ormond Street, and the respondents, Charlie's parents and Charlie (by his guardian). The fact that GOSH is an NHS establishment is immaterial; identical issues would have arisen had Charlie been a patient at a private hospital.

Confusion also abounded over the role of the judges, with the assumption raging that the politicised judicial culture in America translated to England and Wales. We will look at this in more detail in a later chapter, but the crux of the UK constitution is the separation of powers – the thick black line between government and judiciary. Judges are politically independent, appointed by the Queen upon the recommendation of an independent Judicial Appointments Commission. They are not answerable to ministers or to MPs,[57] nor do either have any influence over judicial decisions.

From whichever angle you look, the government had no role to play in this case at all.

So, when those staunch pro-death-penalty US Republicans like Paul Ryan and Ted Cruz proclaim with a straight face that 'government has no place in the life or death business', they are right, although not in the way they think. As an empirical statement of English and Welsh law, they are correct. But intended, as no doubt these comments were, as a normative judgment premised on the false yelps about English children being 'sentenced to death by the British government', they are utterly divorced from reality.

They are also irreconcilably estranged from their own legal system. The United States too, like many civilised countries in which children are recognised as having their own individual rights, has wrestled with these most difficult of cases. In 2016, a Los Angeles County Superior Court judge ruled that a toddler called Israel Stinson, who had suffered catastrophic brain injuries after an asthma attack, should have ventilation withdrawn, despite his parents' wishes.[58] Tub-thumping cries from Messrs Ryan and Cruz accusing the privatised US healthcare system of sentencing a child to death were surprisingly inaudible.

## What really happened in Alfie Evans' case?

We see markedly similar themes throughout the case of Alfie Evans. The specialist medical evidence before the High Court in February 2018 was largely unchallenged. The doctors were not able to offer a specific diagnosis, but confirmed the distressing and bleak conclusion: Alfie's progressive, ultimately fatal neuro-degenerative condition meant that his brain was entirely beyond recovery. He was deeply comatose and unaware of his surroundings. His motor responses were either of an epileptic nature or spinal reflexes. His seizures, despite various combinations of anti-epileptics, were beyond control. He could not hear and would never develop any communication, either verbally or with sign language. While the medical opinion was that it was unlikely that Alfie felt pain, it could not be ruled out, and the doctors considered that the continuation of active intensive-care treatment 'may well be causing him distress and suffering'. Alder Hey, and Alfie's guardian, were of the view that prolonging Alfie's life was not in his best interests.

At the first hearing, Alfie's parents were not legally represented, having dispensed with their experienced legal team shortly before the hearing. The judge commented on how 'extraordinarily impressive' he found Tom Evans' mastery of the issues and presentation of his case; however, in legal terms, his challenge to the hospital's case was, in the words of the judge, 'not entirely easy to state', amounting, in essence, and wholly understandably, to the pleas of 'a father unable to relinquish hope'. In the view of one of the medical experts, the conflict appeared to stem from a misunderstanding of some of Alfie's behaviour. For example, what might, entirely understandably, be perceived by his parents as Alfie reacting to their touch or voice, was very likely not purposeful, but caused by his seizures. Videos of Alfie's apparent reactions – including him appearing to yawn – were produced by Alfie's parents, and many found their way onto social media and newspaper websites.[59] The medical evidence reiterated, in spite of Mr Evans' protestations, that this 'yawn' was merely reflexive.

Mr Evans' wish was that Alfie travel by air ambulance to the Bambino Gesù hospital, or to a hospital in Germany, where he could be kept alive a little longer. All that this amounted to was 'an alternative palliative care plan', with the possibility of surgery – a tracheotomy and gastrostomy – which might allow Alfie to be ventilated at home. No further useful tests could be performed to improve Alfie's condition. Mr Evans relied upon the evidence of a Dr Hubner of the Pediatric Air Ambulance, a private German company, to the effect that Alfie could be safely transported without risk. It transpired that Dr Hubner had lied about having seen all of Alfie's files and had attended Alder Hey Hospital posing as a 'family friend' to surreptitiously – and potentially illegally – examine Alfie without the knowledge of the treating doctors. Most alarmingly, he had set out a 'travel plan' for Alfie with a recommended anticonvulsant regime that was entirely inappropriate. He further admitted in cross-examination that he had never used his service to transport a dying child.[60]

The judge accepted the conclusion of the medical evidence that treatment was 'futile'. He stated that it did not follow axiomatically that ventilation should be withdrawn, as life holds intrinsic value. He took into account the Catholic beliefs of Alfie's parents, and the position of the Roman Catholic Church as set out in an open letter by Pope Francis from November 2017. He had himself visited Alfie at the hospital; he had met the family and seen for himself the 'very happy' atmosphere surrounding Alfie. 'His life has true dignity. The far more challenging question is whether – and, if so, how – that can be maintained.'

Travelling to Italy risked exposing Alfie to infection and causing him further brain injury due to the likelihood of uncontrolled seizures during the journey. There was the prospect that Alfie could experience pain. The judge concluded that 'all of this might be worth risking if there were any prospect of treatment, [but] there is none'. He said he was satisfied that every reasonable option had been explored, and agreed with the hospital and the guardian that withdrawing ventilation was in Alfie's best interests.

The parents appealed to the Court of Appeal, and then beyond, to the Supreme Court and European Court of Human Rights, and the primary legal argument was the same as in Charlie Gard's case – that the wishes of the parents should, absent significant harm, take priority over the best interests of the child. Again, the courts affirmed the 'gold standard' of the welfare test, and again the Supreme Court emphasised that doctors 'need to know what the law requires of them'.[61] And again the European Court of Human Rights ruled the application to appeal inadmissible.

However, during this first set of appeals – more were to follow – certain facts began to emerge. It transpired that there had been *another* clandestine, potentially illegal inspection of Alfie, by Dr Jankowska, a paediatric oncologist smuggled into Alder Hey by

Mr Evans. And this particular doctor had done this before, in another high-profile case involving a boy called Isaiah Haastrup. Her involvement in both cases was hard to fathom, given that neither Alfie nor Isaiah had any form of cancer.[62]

It also emerged that a 'wholly inappropriate' legal letter had been sent to Alder Hey a few months earlier by a 'legally trained supporter' of Alfie, threatening that, if the doctors removed mechanical ventilation, this would 'constitute the offence of murder or manslaughter'.[63]

These troubling features appeared to have been instigated at the behest of 'supporters' or 'advisors' of the Evans family. Among these was an organisation called the Christian Legal Centre. On 11 April 2018, with the appeals seemingly exhausted, the case returned before Mr Justice Hayden for him to approve an end-of-life care plan for Alfie. On this occasion, Tom Evans was represented by yet another new barrister, Paul Diamond, this time instructed by the Christian Legal Centre. Mr Diamond made an application for a writ of habeas corpus – the effect of which would have released Alfie from his 'unlawful detention' at Alder Hey, and allowed him to travel. The only problem was that the application was, as the judge pointed out, 'entirely miscon-ceived'.[64] Alfie wasn't detained unlawfully; he was in the care of a hospital which was acting in what the law had determined were his best interests.

Nevertheless, this duff legal application did not shrivel and expire on the courtroom floor. It was instead circulated on social media as gospel, fuelling the ire of the crowds gathering outside Alder Hey Hospital. The following day, 12 April 2018, Tom Evans attended Alder Hey with a foreign doctor and air ambu-lance staff, armed with a copy of a letter written by a Mr Pavel Stroilov from the Christian Legal Centre. This letter, widely shared online, stated that, 'as a matter of law it is your right to come to Alder Hey Hospital with a team of medical professionals with their own life-support equipment, and move Alfie to such other place as you consider is best for him. You do not need any permission from Alder Hey Hospital or the Court to do so.'

In fact, 'as a matter of law', this advice was utterly bogus. It not only incited the distressed Tom Evans to do something wholly *un*lawful, but led to a confrontation at the hospital which culminated in the police being called, serving only to escalate the tensions as Alfie's Misinformed Army amassed at the doors. Hospital staff could not get to work due to the roads being blocked. A group of members of 'Alfie's Army' entered the Paediatric Intensive Care Unit, causing fear and upset to other patients.

Pavel Stroilov, we later learned, was a law student and case worker for the Christian Legal Centre. The morning after the riot at Alder Hey, he was summoned to appear before the judge to explain his actions. Despite a stern warning from Mr Justice Hayden, Mr Stroilov's unique interpretation of the law would not end with this letter.

Meanwhile, the misconceived litigation continued. Mr Diamond went to the Court of Appeal and argued that Alfie's best interests were 'irrelevant'; a curious interpretation of the case law. Again, he was told that his legal application had 'no foundation at all'.[65] The habeas corpus argument was taken to the Supreme Court, who repeated, yet again, the legal position that was obvious to all but Mr Evans' lawyers. The inevitable repeat application to the ECtHR met the same inevitable fate on 23 April 2018,[66] and was followed by the 200-strong attempt by Alfie's Army to storm Alder Hey Hospital.

That same day, as Alfie was due to be extubated, the Christian Legal Centre's lawyers were back at the High Court, this time arguing that the granting to Alfie of Italian citizenship by the Italian Ministry of Foreign Affairs had changed everything. It hadn't. Mr Diamond's argument was not rooted 'in any recognised law'.[67] Nevertheless, Pavel Stroilov, undeterred by the judicial fury rained upon him, now advised Tom Evans to institute a private prosecution alleging murder against the medical staff of Alder Hey,[68] a story which unsurprisingly caught alight in the press. Equally unsurprisingly, the prosecution foundered at the first hurdle, having absolutely no cogent legal basis, but the added damage was done; the hysterical shrieks of 'murderer' outside the hospital were lent a veneer of false lawful legitimacy.

At 9.45 p.m. on 23 April, Alfie's ventilation was withdrawn in accordance with the end-of-life care plan, which had been restructured by the judge to try to accommodate the parents and to ensure they could be with Alfie at the end. After he was extubated, Alfie continued to breathe unaided. This was entirely expected by the doctors, who had advised Alfie's parents that he might continue to breathe for some days once ventilation was withdrawn,[69] but was widely misreported as a significant and unforeseen improvement in Alfie's condition. The *Telegraph* was among the outlets uncritically repeating Tom Evans' untrue claim that doctors were 'gobsmacked' at Alfie's breathing.[70]

The next day, an application was made to restore Alfie's ventilation on the basis that his condition was 'significantly better' than the court had thought. It wasn't, of course, but that did not stop Pavel Stroilov submitting a witness statement 'littered with vituperation and bile'[71] attacking the hospital staff and accusing the court of reaching a decision 'on a false premise'. Mr Diamond's submissions were slapped down by the judge as 'ridiculous emotive nonsense',[72] with Pavel Stroilov described as a 'fanatical and deluded young man'.[73] Within twenty-four hours, the Court of Appeal was required to reiterate that nothing had changed, either in Alfie's condition or in the 'alternative treatment' on offer in Italy. In this, the final hearing in the case, Alfie's mother was represented by a new legal team. Her QC was instructed to put forward arguments never raised before the High Court, which were described by the Court of Appeal as 'totally without merit'.[74] The Court of Appeal was compelled to express concerns about the 'darker side' of the support offered to Alfie's parents by people 'whose interests may not in fact assist the parents' case'.[75]

Alfie passed away three days later, on 28 April 2018.

The misconceptions in the case of Alfie Evans mirror those in that of Charlie Gard. The decision had nothing to do with money, or socialised medicine, or the government, or the strained relationships between the hospital staff and those violently campaigning in what they alleged to be Alfie's interests. Alfie's welfare, as the courts confirmed on a dozen occasions, was the lodestar.

The presidential prayers for Alfie's 'recovery' were false platitudes. There was no meaningful alternative treatment plan; the claim by Nigel Farage on Fox News that 'there is treatment available in Italy that is not available here [in the UK]' was a lie. Likewise the papal suggestion that Alfie's parents were seeking 'new forms of treatment'. Ditto Ted Cruz – again – tweeting that there was 'experimental treatment' on offer. Lies, lies, lies. All that was offered in Italy was continued ventilation, with a possible tracheotomy that might allow Alfie to spend an extra few months with his parents in Munich. Fox News' imputation that Alder Hey's paediatric specialists were refusing to allow Alfie treatment that might give him 'quality of life' due to their potential 'embarrassment' is one which less forgiving doctors might have considered the appropriate subject of a defamation claim.

Much was made about the case of Ashya King, the five-year-old whose parents succeeded in treating him with proton-beam therapy in the face of contrary medical advice. But this, as with so much, was a false comparator. Ashya's parents and the treating doctors at Southampton Hospital agreed on the suitability of the parents' preferred treatment – proton-beam therapy. The sticking point was that it wasn't available in the UK on the National Health Service; NHS England would instead authorise and fund this treatment abroad for certain conditions. Ashya's precise illness, medulloblastoma, was not covered. His parents, having identified a hospital in Prague offering proton therapy, took him from England without telling Southampton Hospital staff and travelled to the Czech Republic via Spain, sparking concern for Ashya's wellbeing and a series of court orders, including ultimately a European Arrest Warrant for the parents. However – and this is key – the hospital never opposed the family's decision to obtain proton-beam therapy. The NHS could not offer it, but it would support any arrangements for Ashya to travel safely abroad if another hospital could arrange the treatment and if it could be independently funded. Ultimately, after the media circus had died down, the matter resolved with the High Court approving a treatment plan agreed between the NHS doctors and the parents, whereby Ashya would receive proton therapy in Prague, funded by private donations. And, as ever, the principle guiding the judge's decision was the best interests of Ashya. The distinction between the cases of Ashya, Charlie and Alfie was that, in the former, there was no dispute over where the child's best interests lay.[76]

For all the professed concern for the welfare of Alfie and the system's treatment of his parents, very little was said by the most vocal talking heads about an indisputably worrying facet of the story: the witches' brew of unqualified and inaccurate legal advice; the clandestine examinations of children by doctors offering dangerous and uninformed prescriptions; and the uneducated interventions of politicians and special-interest groups serving only to raise false hope and antagonise the delicate relationship between doctors and parents at the most difficult time in these young people's lives.

Regrettably, in what might most charitably be described as a gross dereliction of journalistic duty, the tabloid newspapers offering daily front-page coverage of the cases devoted little if any time to scrutinising the claims and bona fides of the groups and individuals descending on the families. Instead of exposing these legal and medical 'miracle cures' as the off-the-back-of-a-lorry wares of exploitative spivs, the media amplified the nonsensical announcements that doctors were going to be prosecuted for murder, and celebrated uncritically the bogus promises of new treatment.

And it is perhaps easy to lose sight, amid all the performative displays of public 'support' for Alfie's parents, of how uniquely vulnerable and alone those young people were. In their most desperate hour, they were targeted and exploited as pawns in the games of others. This is why there is, let me be clear, no criticism intended whatsoever of the parents of Charlie or Alfie. They could be any of us. Charlie and Alfie could be our children. The judge's description of their predicament as 'a living hell' does not even come close. To pursue every possible avenue and to turn every single stone is a fundamental condition of the parental bond; cold rationality is the expected function of the legal system, not a parent facing losing a child. To the extent that the cases of Charlie and Alfie took more circuitous and tumultuous routes than may, in hindsight, have been in the best interests of anyone involved, that is not the moral fault of Chris Gard, Connie Yates, Tom Evans or Kate James.

But the same cannot be said of the groups exploiting these parents' vulnerability – their unknowable grief – for alternative, self-serving causes. And it is important to look at exactly who was pulling those strings.


## Who was behind the agenda?

The choral chants of religious dogmatists pervaded the public campaigns in both cases, as pro-life lobbyists swooped on the stricken parents, egged on by misleading papal proclamations and Catholic heads of state, such as the President of Poland, Andrzej Duda, who tweeted, 'Alfie Evans must be saved! His brave little body has proved again that the miracle of life can be stronger than death. Perhaps all that's needed is some good will on the part of the decision makers. Alfie, we pray for you and your recovery!'[77]

The *Guardian* identified one figure in particular as instrumental – an American activist, based in Italy, called Christine Broesamle.[78] She had connections to the Italian 'Lawyers for Life' network, and together they provided advice to the parents of both Charlie and Alfie. It was she, the *Guardian* reported, who arranged for the surreptitious medical examinations of Alfie Evans and Isaiah Haastrup, and, with a 'seemingly endless pit of money and contacts', had arranged for the air ambulance to whisk Alfie to Italy. She too was credited with organising Tom Evans' personal audience with the Pope.

It was also reported that Ms Broesamle was responsible for

connecting the Evans family to the Christian Legal Centre. The CLC is an offshoot of Christian Concern, an organisation which has campaigned publicly against LGBT rights, equal marriage, stem-cell research and transgender rights.[79] It was also involved in coordinating the open letter, signed by thirty-seven MEPs, which condemned the 'outrageous outcome' in Charlie Gard's case.[80] The CLC counts among its volunteers the aforementioned Pavel Stroilov, a former researcher for ex-UKIP leader Gerard Batten and an apparent law student. It was Mr Stroilov who was responsible for drafting the more legally illiterate advice given to Tom Evans, acting in a way described by the judge as 'inconsistent with the real interests of the parents' case'.

Ms Broesamle stoked the fires back in the US as she told a Christian fundamentalist radio station that there should be 'riots' in Britain over doctors 'hell-bent' on killing children to 'cover something up'. And the messages hit home. An analysis, published by the London School of Economics, of the online campaigns by Charlie's and Alfie's respective Armies found that 'a large volume of Twitterstorm sending out negative messages about British judiciary and healthcare institutions seemed to emerge from American sources, many of whom identify with right-wing positions'.[81] During Alfie's proceedings, dozens of people gathered outside the UK Embassy in Washington DC, waving placards reading, 'Make Britain Christian Again'.[82]

Also among those organising vigils for both Charlie and Alfie was Reverend Patrick Mahoney, an executive director of the Christian Defense Coalition, known in the States for his involvement in the campaign to keep Terri Schiavo alive.[83] Back home, the domestic gallery was treated to op-eds published by Fox News in which commentators drew tenuous links between Charlie Gard's case and the unacceptably permissive British attitude to abortion.[84] The campaign to grant Charlie US citizenship was championed by Congressman Trent Franks, a long-time picketer of abortion clinics.[85]

Other major figures in the US pro-life movement hurled themselves on the bandwagon. Catherine Glenn Foster, president and

CEO of Americans United for Life, flew in to visit Charlie in hospital,[86] before holding a press conference in Washington DC in which she warned, 'This is what happens when you have laws designed to promote death over life,' sentiments uncritically repeated by Breitbart.[87]

Breitbart News Network is a self-styled 'alt-right' media outlet, formerly run by Donald Trump's one-time Chief Strategist Steve Bannon, and their interest in Charlie and Alfie feeds into a linked dimension of the Fake Law narrative: the exploitation of both cases to push political messages about American healthcare.

Charlie Gard's case in early 2017 coincided with efforts by President Trump to repeal Obamacare – characterised by US Republicans as a paving stone on the road to socialised medicine – and the opportunity to dishonestly spin the case as an example of the dangers of 'single-payer healthcare' was irresistible. Breitbart warned its readers:

> Americans may find this point of reference difficult to fathom, but it is staring them in the face with the potential for single-payer, government-run healthcare, in the new fervour for laws that allow physician-assisted suicide, and in the periodic push for acquiescence to external bodies, such as the United Nations Convention on the Rights of the Child, a treaty that allows the U.N. to decide the rights of children in any member nation.
>
> [. . .]
>
> Charlie Gard's case is one that could easily set a precedent for the power of government and the judiciary over health care, parental rights, education, and many other aspects of life. As can readily be seen throughout Europe and in the United States, such precedents and their powerful messages are difficult to rip out once embedded into the bureaucracy and the culture.[88]

Fox News, Breitbart, state media, radio shock jocks and Republican politicians clamoured to draw fallacious conclusions to leverage domestic sympathy for their campaigns. Donald

Trump's intervention – his tweeted proffering of unspecified 'help' – was the most high-profile example of this calculation in action.[89] The alleged failings of the UK health system formed a recurring theme of Trump's 4 a.m. tweets over the following year, as he railed against Democrat support for 'Universal Health-Care'.[90] Sure enough, the culture and political war still not won by the time of Alfie Evans in 2018, the Republican establishment fired the ignition once more to drive home the message that socialised medicine allows the government to kill your children.[91]

Senator Ted Cruz again expressed his horror at the consequences of 'socialised medicine',[92] echoing a high-profile US blogger, who explained, 'Free health care for your children means that they are the property of the state.'[93] Former governor of Arkansas Mick Huckabee told Fox News viewers, 'The British government has said no – we're not going to let him leave, we're going to go ahead and kill him. I just find this chilling.'[94]

The hostility to the National Health Service was not solely American. British politicians such as Nigel Farage were happy to misrepresent the cases as the unhappy products of our approach to healthcare. After being invited by Fox News presenter Lauren Ingraham onto *The Ingraham Angle* and asked why 'Britain's socialised medical system' and the 'courts in the EU and in the UK' were preventing Alfie seeking 'alternative medical treatment', Mr Farage explained: 'there is treatment available in Italy that is not available here ... Yet what happens here is our state-run medical system decides there's nothing else that can be done and, backed up by state courts, they make a decision that those parents are not fit to move their child somewhere else ... It's classic of the establishment closing ranks; the state being all powerful. And, frankly, what is happening right now is a form of state-sponsored euthanasia and I hate it.'[95]

Notwithstanding public proclamations of support for free-at-the-point-of-use healthcare, Nigel Farage was caught on video in 2012 telling party supporters that he would 'feel more comfortable' if UK healthcare was opened up to the 'marketplace'.[96] At best, his willingness to lie about the NHS' involvement in the cases of Charlie and Alfie was an exercise in self-publicity, but some may find that it sits neatly with the principles underlying a self-proclaimed libertarian movement that finds its philosophical counterparts in the red states.

The peripheral involvement of the European Court of Human Rights in the two cases also presented an open door through which to ride another tired UKIP hobby horse: anti-European Union sentiment. During the same interview on Fox News, Nigel Farage did not correct host Lauren Ingraham's claim that the decisions involved 'an EU court', a falsehood repeated by Breitbart. We will look in more detail at the European Court of Human Rights in Chapter 5, when I will unapologetically make the same point again, but, for the educational benefit of all, it cannot be stated loudly enough that the ECtHR is not 'an EU court'.

And so, as the tumult built and the lies of the various factions piled atop and alongside each other as far as the eye could see, it became apparent that it was in nobody's interests to correct anybody else; the confusion benefited all. The more scandalous the cases could be made out to be, the greater the weight they lent to the campaign, whichever of the campaigns that may be. Thus developed the silent but discernible conspiracy of global misinformation, accelerated and amplified by Twitter and Facebook, in which weeping parents were paraded as political mannequins, and hospitals were stormed and doctors were threatened with death, and judges were called Nazis, and in which, ultimately, the truth became just one among many innocent victims in two tragic cases with no winners on the ground, but a swarm of salivating vultures circling above.

The stories of Charlie Gard and Alfie Evans serve as case studies of the power of misinformation to exploit our shared humanity and manipulate our instinctive desire to help those in need. They also demonstrate our vulnerability.

By casting a fog over the facts and drilling into our deepest and most primal fears, those pushing their own agendas can persuade us that we are on the side of the angels, all the while commandeering us as unwitting components in a global social-outrage machine serving an entirely different purpose.

I can completely understand what motivated people to join Charlie's Army and Alfie's Army. For most of them, it was love. They were bound by a desire to help parents in their darkest hour, and to fight for the lives of children whom they thought needed them. What could be nobler than protecting a child from tyranny?

But *they* know this. The engineers of the outrage machine, the peddlers of Fake Law, they understand the resonance of cases like these. And they are adept at manipulating us, at harnessing the power of solidarity and twisting it into the pliable rage of the mob. So it is that we can be estranged from our first principles, convinced that the law operates so as to ignore an innocent child's best interests, rather than to enshrine them, and from there it is a wrathful hop and skip from joining a Facebook group to, as happened above, sending death threats to doctors and nurses and calling for 'murderous' judges to be hanged.[97]

The need for public legal education when cases like those of Charlie and Alfie hit the headlines cannot be starker. There was, in both of these cases, simply too great a volume of misinformation and lies for the truth to get a look-in. Calm and sober explanations by patient family law practitioners as to how and why the law operates as it does simply didn't fit the multiple agendas at play.

And one of the many tragedies of the representations in these cases was how genuine arguments of legal, moral and ethical substance were consequently drowned out. Please don't mistake my contempt for the dishonesty mongers as unqualified support for the decisions in either case, nor for the way in which the English courts balance the conflict between the best interests of the child and the views of the parents. There is a wealth of academic literature in which the decisions of the courts, and the unqualified paramountcy of the welfare principle, is criticised. Although I am personally not persuaded by them, there are strong and well-constructed arguments in favour of introducing a higher threshold in cases where the courts are determining an application which could result in life-sustaining treatment being withdrawn.[98] A 'significant harm' test has its objective attractions, even if I am not lured.

But a sensible discussion on the nuances of the legal argument was not what the special interests in these cases were seeking. They came not for principled debate, but to paint chimeras in the brightest colours on their palettes. Similarly, a genuine, unarguable scandal in Charlie Gard's case was how, due to reforms introduced in 2012 which removed legal aid from most private law family cases, Charlie's parents were refused publicly funded legal assistance or representation due to stringent means tests. They were instead reliant on solicitors and barristers working pro bono – without a fee – to fill the immoral lacuna in the law brought about by governments cynically calculating that legal aid is an easy, popular cut.

This pernicious, parsimonious approach to dealing with matters of life and death is not only offensive on principle; refusing vulnerable parents access to qualified legal representation creates the obvious risk of those parents finding themselves exploited by the Pavel Stroilovs roaming the legal wastelands, armed with their bogus advice and servicing shadowy third-party interests. At your lowest ebb, the government would rather expose you to the risk of even further harm at the grasping claws of opportunistic predators than ensure you have access to competent legal representation in matters of literal life and death. To their enormous credit, Chris Gard and Connie Yates, as part of their campaign for a 'Charlie's Law' recalibrating the 'best interests' test, are also fighting for this appalling denial of access to justice to be remedied, for means testing to be removed so that no parent has to worry about affording a lawyer when their child's life is in the balance.

But it's an injustice which those devoted activists with the placards, the megaphones, the helicopters and the prime-time TV programmes are sadly not as interested in covering.

By letting the Fake Law narratives win, and inadvertently lending our support to their cause, we become unwitting contributors to injustice, rather than its vanquishers.

# 3. Your Health

'For too long, some have exploited a rampant compensation culture and seen whiplash claims as an easy payday, driving up costs for millions of law-abiding motorists.'

Liz Truss, Secretary of State for Justice and
Lord Chancellor, 17 November 2016[1]

The compensation culture is out of control. Whatever misguided preconceptions one might previously have had about persecuted homeowners or baby-killing judges, this is one thing we all know for sure about the law. Lottery-jackpot-style payouts are showered on grasping claimants, and their avaricious lawyers, for the most trivial – and usually self-inflicted – ailments.

The ubiquity of this truism smothers us from our formative years; it underpins pop-culture references, from ambulance-chasing shyster Lionel Hutz in *The Simpsons* urging Bart to exaggerate his injuries after being hit by Mr Burns' car,[2] to 'Vinny' LaGuardia Gambini, the titular cousin in possibly the world's greatest ever legal film.[3] The compensation culture fills our headlines and moulds our expectations of lawyers, fuelled in no small part by us, the legal profession, with our billboards and TV adverts enquiring whether YOU have ever been in an ACCIDENT that WASN'T YOUR FAULT. 'Elf 'n' safety' stories gift-wrapped in red tape are recycled by pressure groups warning that 'playground games such as conkers, tag and football are being routinely banned for health and safety reasons . . . Money grabbing lawyers are sucking the lifeblood out of childhood,'[4] while columnists splutter apoplexy over bureaucrats insisting that coastal ramblers are accompanied at all times by lifeguards.[5] To borrow what the

*Daily Mail*'s Richard Littlejohn likes to remind us is his catch-phrase, You Couldn't Make It Up.

The impact is, of course, much more acute than eyebrow-raising headlines; it is felt by all taxpayers. Every time a school pupil is splashed with custard and lavished with a £6,000 pay-out,[6] or a council cleaner pockets £9,000 for falling over a mop,[7] we all end up footing the bill. The National Health Service now blows over £2.2 billion a year on paying out for clinical negligence claims – double what it spent in 2013. As the *Daily Mail* put it, '£1 in every £50 handed to the NHS is used to compensate harmed patients or settle lawyers' legal fees.'[8]

A fear expressed for some years now is that our green and pleasant land is rapidly taking on a star-spangled tinge, that we are charging towards an Americanised litigation culture in which the ridiculous US cases that have made it into our popular discourse become too close for comfort. Many of us will have heard of 'the American plonker who gulped her McDonald's coffee and took Ronald McD to the cleaners', to quote Vanessa Feltz in the *Daily Star*,[9] or the infamous case of Merv Grazinski, who, the *Daily Mail* reported, 'set his Winnebago [motor home] on cruise control, slid away from the wheel and went back to fix a cup of coffee'. When the motor home crashed, Mr Grazinski successfully sued the manufacturer for $1.75 million.[10]

A prevalent local scourge is the particularly British disease of fraudulent whiplash claims by motorists. We are, ministers have told us over the past decade, the 'whiplash capital of Europe',[11] or, according to different ministers, the 'whiplash capital of the world',[12] with fraudulent claims – including 'crash for cash' – 'being incited . . . on an industrial scale'.[13] As a consequence, roughly £90 is added onto the insurance premium of the average British driver.[14]

Occasionally the antics of rogue lawyers driving unmeritorious claims are exposed, generating further headlines as the public's suspicions about dishonest lawyers and sharp litigation practices are proved well founded.[15]

The presumption, it seems, is that these stories reveal only the tip of the iceberg. Such widespread animosity is why it is impossible for me to post a tweet or write a blog about any legal issue without my being informed, usually by an account with a username comprised largely of digits and a Twitter timeline full of retweets of racially inflammatory memes, that I and all those like me are ambulance-chasing vermin. Depending on mood, I either take the time to politely explain that, as a criminal barrister, my dealings with matters medical are usually restricted to considerations of the level and cause of injuries when prosecuting or defending allegations of violence, or, if pressed for time, I will maturely tweet them a heart emoji or a series of kisses, safe in the knowledge that nothing is assured to make them even angrier than unsolicited love.

What I rarely do, however, is tackle the 'ambulance chaser' assumption head-on. Instead, I implicitly accept the premise of the legal stereotype; my plea is simply, 'I'm not one of them.'

And this, it occurs to me, is delinquent. Because it allows to flourish unchecked the cultural meme that 'compo' is itself a problem – something unearned lavished on the undeserving. Terms such as 'windfall', 'win' and 'payout' are the building blocks of reports into personal-injury compensation awards, from the tabloids[16] through to the BBC.[17] The implication is clear: those receiving money are, by definition, 'winners'; those paying – usually the public, either directly through taxation or indirectly through raised insurance premiums – are the losers, bested in battle by a cunning foe.

The contrary argument is almost never advanced: namely that a legal system providing justice and fair financial recompense for those injured through the fault of others is an historically accepted hallmark of a fair society which benefits us all. Shifting from principle to practicality, financial compensation is usually essential for those – including us, our friends and family – whose lives are marred, even ruined, by the transformative injuries they suffer at the hands of others, and who – through no fault of their own – find themselves suddenly unable to work, unable to go about their normal daily lives and, in the most serious cases, unable even to care for themselves.

And the muting of this unpopular argument – represented in

news reports only by a perfunctory single-line quote from a personal-injury solicitor, buried at the tail end of the article – means that the direction of travel, both in public debate and in legislative reform, is forever towards clamping down on an out of control compensation culture. We rarely pause to ask how we got here. Or why the law works in the way we are told it does. Or, perhaps most critically, *whether* it works as we are told.

And, once we start tugging at those threads, other questions follow. If we are being misled, or misinformed, or even directly lied to, to what end is this being done? Whose interests are really being served? And, if it's not our interests – if it's not *your* interests – what are we – you – at risk of losing?

The law in this area is being changed, rapidly and significantly. These questions, I believe, are therefore best asked before it's too late.

## How does personal-injury law actually work?

Since early medieval times, English law has provided for a system of compensation for citizens injured by the unlawful acts of others. As the legal framework of Roman Britain was swept away following the Anglo-Saxon conquest, the invaders imported a continental concept of *weregeld* – literally 'man price' – which was a sum of money payable when one man injured another. The Law of Æthelberht, King of Kent in the seventh century, set out standard amounts for injuries – from four Saxon shillings (roughly £400 in today's money) for loss of a middle finger, to fifty Saxon shillings (£5,000) for an amputated foot. Grounded less in principle and more in the practical need to amicably resolve disputes in a society plagued by blood feuds and still centuries away from a centralised criminal justice system, *weregeld* nevertheless installed a framework in which those harmed by the wrongs of others would receive compensation.[18]

The notion of *torts* ('wrongs') causing loss and being legally actionable is what underpins contemporary personal-injury law.

Where a legal duty or obligation exists, and a person breaches that duty and as a result causes injury to you, the least they can do, the law recognises, is offer *something* to put things right. Absent the ability to undo an injury, monetary compensation – modern *weregeld* – is the best idea we have. The philosophical reasoning for compensation for injury is often geared around the question of who should bear the costs. The consequences of being injured tend to be threefold: pain and suffering; immediate financial loss, such as loss of earnings for time taken off work; and future financial loss, such as future loss of earnings or the cost of future care or treatment. Rather than abandoning the injured person to their own devices, or spreading the cost among all members of society,[19] we decree that the wrong be righted by the person at fault (or, in practical terms, often that person's insurer). Put in context, where, say, a factory owner cuts corners to save money and his employee loses a limb in some unmaintained machinery, we insist that the employer pay the costs (beyond the cost of medical treatment provided on the National Health Service), rather than have them met through general taxation.

Historically, the law was preoccupied with situations where injury was deliberately inflicted – 'trespass to the person' – but the idea of a wider concept of negligence started to be developed by the courts in the nineteenth century. Put very simply, where a person is in breach of a legal duty – not intentionally, but because they have failed to take *reasonable care* in discharging it – they will be liable for negligence.

As for when a legal duty of care arises, the general principle is derived from a case in 1932, familiar to all first-year law students, involving, as all good stories do, a dead snail and a bottle of ginger beer. In *Donoghue* v. *Stevenson*,[20] the unfortunate Mrs Donoghue poured out a refreshing ginger beer to find a decomposing *escargot* inside. She fell ill and sued the manufacturer, Stevenson. As there was no contractual relationship between a manufacturer and a consumer, her lawyers had to devise an argument that some other legal obligation existed, which Stevenson had breached. In a case that went all the way to the House of

Lords, the courts confirmed that we all owe a duty of care to those whom our actions could reasonably foreseeably affect (often referred to as 'the neighbour principle').

This has been subsequently interpreted by the courts as covering a wide range of scenarios and relationships, including manufacturers and consumers (such as Stevenson and the gastroenteritic Mrs Donoghue); motorists and other road users (we all have a duty to take reasonable care on the roads, as it is reasonably foreseeable that, if we don't, we may cause injury to others); the government and people in its care, such as prisoners; schools and pupils; and employers and employees, to list but a handful.

At the same time as the courts were developing common law duties of care, Parliament was legislating to create *statutory* duties in certain scenarios. One example arose from the need to offer explicit protection to those most vulnerable to the more brutalising side of industrialisation, in the form of health and safety legislation requiring employers to provide, as far as reasonably practicable, basics such as a safe working environment, well-maintained machinery, proper training and protective equipment.[21] Other statutory duties apply to owners and occupiers of land, obliging them to take reasonable steps to avoid harm befalling visitors, or to warn trespassers of dangers. The Highways Act 1980 places local authorities under a legal obligation to maintain public highways so that they are safe for road users.[22]

Again, a breach of any of these duties which causes injury to a person can be the subject of a claim. The exact operation of these duties varies, but, put very simply, there is in all, as with common law negligence, an underlying objective test of *reasonableness*. And the principles, again, are those with which most of us would no doubt agree. If you are an employer requiring your workers to use potentially lethal machinery, it is right that you take reasonable steps to ensure that the machinery is in good working order. If you are inviting people to your house, it is fair not to subject them to a *Home Alone*-style gauntlet of limb-threatening hazards. Taxpayers should be able to trust that the local authority has a proper system of inspection and maintenance to make public roads and pathways safe.

This, in a nutshell, is how we end up with modern personal-injury law. Essentially, the law asks three questions:

— Is there a duty of care (either common law or statutory)?

— Has there been a breach of that duty of care (i.e. has the person responsible acted objectively unreasonably?)?

— Has a reasonably foreseeable injury been caused as a result?

If the answer to all three is 'Yes', you have a viable personal-injury claim.

For clinical negligence – claims for injuries caused by medical treatment – the fault threshold is slightly different. The general test is whether the doctor has acted in a way that a responsible body of medical professionals would regard as proper.[23]

I stress that this is a simplification, and the law in practice is riddled with complexities that we don't have space to deal with. However, a headline to take away is that in almost every case of personal injury – and certainly in all cases of common law negligence – a claimant *will need to show fault on the part of the defendant*. I emphasise this because of the common misuse of the term 'accident'. A genuine accident – in which nobody was at fault – will not give rise to liability under the law of negligence (and is highly unlikely to result in a breach of any statutory duty).

This, as we shall see later, is key to understanding the manipulation of the compensation-culture narrative. Whenever you read a story in the newspaper and are encouraged to be angry about a council paying thousands of pounds to a cleaner whose feet got trapped in a Henry Hoover,[24] pause to ask yourself, *If this was just an accident and the local authority has done nothing wrong, why have they paid up?*

# Making a claim

As far as the practicalities of making a claim for personal injury are concerned, the rules of civil procedure fill textbooks the size of Yarmouth, so we shall be brief. Claims are brought in the civil courts, and proceedings must usually be started within three years of the date of the injury.[25] Before issuing proceedings, a prospective claimant is expected to comply with a 'Pre-Action Protocol', which requires steps to be taken to try to resolve the issue without formal legal proceedings. If that fails, and a claim is issued and resisted by the defendant, the court will allocate the claim to a 'track', depending on its value and complexity. For the smallest, most straightforward civil claims, up to £10,000 in value (or up to £1,000 for personal-injury cases), cases are allocated to the 'small claims track'. (Note, not the small claims *court*. There is no such thing as a 'small claims court', however much TV may suggest otherwise.) Small claims are less formal, involve a streamlined version of the Byzantine Civil Procedure Rules and, crucially, do not allow for the awarding of legal costs, even to the winner. In practice, this means that, unless you have legal insurance or particularly deep pockets, you are unlikely to be legally represented. For claims valued at between £10,000 and £25,000, the 'fast track' applies, with the highest value (over £25,000) and most complex claims allocated to the 'multi-track'. These cases usually involve lawyers on both sides.

Depending on the 'track' and the type of case, the court then sets directions to manage the case and prepare the trial. The overwhelming majority of cases settle without a contested hearing. For those that don't, the court at trial will hear evidence, including expert medical evidence, to determine whatever issues are in dispute, and make findings on liability and causation. Because we're concerned with civil, rather than criminal, proceedings, the court isn't required to find that the claimant's case is proved *beyond reasonable doubt* (the criminal standard), but *on the balance of probabilities* (the civil standard) – i.e. is it more likely than not that the claimant's case is proved? Again, because these are civil proceedings, all decisions are made by a single, legally qualified judge, rather than a jury.

An issue which often arises is *contributory negligence*. A motorist may have caused a pedestrian's injuries by being negligently distracted and failing to stop their car in time, but if the pedestrian walked out in front of the vehicle without looking, they may well be found to share some of the blame for their plight. Likewise, a council may be negligent for leaving an obvious tripping hazard on a pavement, but if it was *that* obvious, it will no doubt be said that the claimant should have spotted it. Where a court finds that a claimant was contributorily negligent, it will reflect this by reducing the damages (compensation). So, for instance, our pedestrian, staring at his phone, walking out in front of a negligently driven car, may well be found around one third to blame for his own injuries,[26] and would find his award of damages reduced accordingly. Obviously, if the fault is entirely that of the person injured, they won't receive anything.

If a claimant wins a personal-injury claim – if they can show that their injury was caused (at least in part) by the negligent actions or breach of statutory duty of the defendant – the court then looks to the issue of damages.

## What compensation am I entitled to?

The principle behind damages in tort is to restore the claimant to the position that they would have been in *had they not been harmed by the actions of the tortfeasor* (yes, it's a real word; yes, it's glorious).

Contrary to the impression that may be gleaned from reports, courts and lawyers do not simply pluck figures out of the air; assessing damages ('quantum', as you may hear it called) involves often aggressive arguments over the exact losses suffered or expected to be suffered. Readers of John Grisham may have received notions of multi-million-pound punitive or exemplary damages, far in excess of any loss actually suffered, being awarded against nefarious multinationals to mark the court's condemnation of their behaviour; this does not happen in negligence cases in England and Wales.[27] Damages in personal injury are restricted to compensation, which is calculated in two parts, as follows.

First, the court assesses **general damages**, which are designed to reflect the pain, suffering and 'loss of amenity' (effect on quality of life) caused by the injury. The Judicial College publishes guidance which operates in a similar fashion to the *weregeld* principles of Saxon England, setting out schedules of injuries and recommended brackets of compensation.[28] Where a particular case falls within a bracket depends on many factors, including the severity of the injuries, the nature, duration and prognosis of the medical treatment or surgery required, and the impact on the person's day-to-day activities.

To give some examples, at the top of the scale are the most serious, life-altering injuries, such as very severe brain damage resulting in little to no language function or awareness of environment, double incontinence and the need for full-time nursing care. The bracket for general damages is £224,800 to £322,060. At the other end of the scale, a minor back injury, where a full recovery is made within three months, would generally attract damages of up to £1,950.[29]

The court then assesses **special damages**. This is a financial calculation based on the loss incurred – such as loss of earnings, the cost of travelling to hospital for appointments, the cost of adapting your home or the cost of specialist medical or care treatment (where not provided on the NHS). The court will also look at future losses – if the medical experts say that you will be unable to work for another twelve months, that future loss of earnings will be included. These are not numbers plucked out of the air; they will be scrutinised and argued over. Claimants are expected to take reasonable steps to minimise their losses. Moreover, the damages will often be paid over a period of time.

Where you read of multi-million-pound awards for injuries,

the bulk of that will usually be special damages. Such cases often involve very young and severely injured children, such as thirteen-year-old Ben Harman, who the papers reported was 'set for millions'[30] after 'winning'[31] a 'payout'.[32] Ben's injuries, and his '£20million win',[33] arose as a result of serious negligence on the part of Kent Canterbury Hospital: a failure at birth to diagnose dangerously low blood sugar levels that caused catastrophic brain damage. He suffered from severe autism and significant cognitive impairment. He couldn't talk. He was doubly incontinent and had the mobility skills of a four-year-old, with no awareness of danger to himself or the impact of his behaviour on others. He was prone to unpredictable tantrums and lashing out physically while shrieking at the top of his voice, posing an increasing risk of injury to himself and those around him as he grew. Until the age of thirteen, he had never hugged his mother. The severity of his disability required that he remain in a residential facility until the age of twenty-five, when he would return home with a comprehensive care package and be looked after full-time by his parents.[34] The compensation he received, after lengthy and acrimonious legal proceedings against the NHS Trust that for years refused to accept liability, reflected the cost of the intensive, full-time care that he would need for the rest of his life.

At the end of the exercise, the court will apply any reduction for contributory negligence, to arrive at a total damages award.

Most people, I expect, would understand and accept the principle behind special damages. It's the more nebulous concept of non-pecuniary general damages that is perhaps more alien. It is easy to hear a large round number and feel an instinctive pang of, 'Oof. That's a lot of money.' But it is always worth breaking these figures down. Up to £12,000 for what the guidance describes as a 'modest' foot injury, such as a simple fracture or ruptured ligament, ostensibly sounds generous, but put yourself in those orthopaedic shoes, read the small print and think about what it actually reflects. That sum not only covers the agony of the injury, the corrective procedure and the immediate rehabilitation, but the practical impact on your life. The guideline figure of

£12,000 envisages a permanent limp, pain or aching, which may have a life-changing effect on aspects of your existence you take for granted. The constant, grinding ache that makes medium- and long-distance driving impossible, rendering you dependent on others to travel beyond your front door. No more jogging, yoga or five-a-side; your active gym-bunny bouncing reduced to slow, painful, limping short walks. From now on, you'll sit on the side-lines for the mums-and-dads race at school sports day. The postcard Instagram experiences you never got round to doing but always told yourself you'd try some day – skiing in Val D'Isère, ice skating at Christmas in NYC, trekking the Path of the Gods along the cliffs of the Amalfi coast as the crimson sunset illumin-ates Praiano below – torn up and tossed eternally out of reach. Not in your lifetime, my friend; instead, each climb and descent of your staircase will be a jarring, wincing souvenir of the acci-dent; every stare from a stranger in the street as you limp to the shops, a reminder that you are forever changed. For somebody in their thirties, with a good forty years of mobility left in them, this windfall would work out at around £300 a year, or the cost of two coffees a week. Would you accept that trade?

At the upper end of this miserable scale, total blindness and deafness would attract general damages of £350,000. If you have thirty-five years left to live, that's ten grand a year for the incon-venience of losing your sight and hearing. Would you consider that a 'win'?

## Is there a compensation culture?

And so it is that, when you drill down into those hysterical head-lines of jackpots,[35] windfalls and winners,[36] you will usually find a not-so-glossy tale of human misery and unearned suffering, from which compensation offers but fractional relief.

In order to successfully rebrand mundane legal reports of negligence, liability and quantum as stranger-than-fiction bonk-busters, two common devices are deployed.

Firstly, there will be a suggestion – either implied in the tone or spelled out by a fulminating backbench MP offering a blood-and-thunder quote about our something-for-nothing culture – that the claimant was either responsible for their own misfortune, or the victim of an unlucky accident, or not even really injured at all. Rarely will there be an acknowledgment of fault on the part of the organisation that has either agreed or been required to pay compensation.

And fault, as we have seen above, is critical. It underpins the entire law of negligence. While not every settlement of a personal-injury claim will include an admission of liability – some defendants may take the view that a small claim has a 'nuisance value', and that it makes commercial sense for them to offer a modest, without-liability settlement, rather than fight the claim in court – in all of the multi-thousand-pound awards and settlements that make the news, you can as good as guarantee that there will be fault. The defendant will have either admitted or have been found by a court to have acted unreasonably, in breach of a duty they had towards the injured complainant, and to have been responsible for the injuries suffered. If the individual in question was in some way to blame for their injuries – if they should have been paying more attention or had defied their training or acted contrary to basic common sense – this is contributory negligence and will be reflected in an adjustment of the compensation figure. If, as the *Daily Mirror* claimed, 'Haringey Council in London paid £9,750 to a dozy employee who walked into a lamp post and hurt their knee',[37] you can be certain that the doziness of said employee was reflected in a significant reduction to the damages to which they would otherwise have been entitled.

The second trick is to imply, by presenting gross decontextualised figures, that compensation settlements and awards are, in any given case, excessive. Or, in the less restrained words of the *Daily Express*, 'madness'.[38] You will not be given a breakdown of general and special damages. It will rarely, if ever, be explained how the figure was calculated, what the Judicial College guidance specifies for injuries of this type or what is the medical prognosis for the injured person, so that the reader can make an informed assessment of whether the damages really are as outrageous as is implied. Instead, you are provided with meaningless numbers and invited – nay, implored – to nod along and agree how ridiculous and dreadful it is that somebody would be given so much money for something so very trivial. Even though nobody has told you what the money actually represents and what the effects of the injury actually are.

Both of these rhetorical sleights of hand arise out of and rely upon an absence of information, which lies at the heart of the problem with public understanding of personal-injury law. There is, in most cases, a near-complete absence of detail as to how and why a personal-injury case has resolved. Partly this is bound up in the fact that the majority – around 96 per cent[39] – of all civil claims settle or otherwise don't go to trial, meaning there is no public record of a court's findings on liability and damages. Extracting from the parties involved the details of a settlement can be difficult, if not entirely prohibited by confidentiality clauses. Local authorities, when required by freedom of information (FOI) requests to supply information about personal-injury claims, will often compound the problem by providing only the scantest of details.

In 2015, Fylde Council responded to a FOI request by confirming that it had agreed a settlement of £341,000 with a man who 'fell off a toilet'.[40] It did not provide any detail beyond the bare fact that the man had been using a public toilet at a seaside resort when the bowl collapsed underneath him. No injuries were particularised, no explanation was offered as to how the enormous figure had been reached. This allowed commentator Ross Clark to confidently tell *Daily Express* readers that 'for too many Britons, making compensation claims has become seen as an alternative to working or doing the lottery'. While he acknowledged the possibility that 'it was a genuine freak accident involving spinal damage', he was nevertheless content to snap Occam's razor in half and conclude, absent any evidence whatsoever, that 'many [will] suspect that it is another case of a public authority giving in a little too easily to Britain's burgeoning compensation industry'.[41] Mention should also be made of Mr Clark's claim that Fylde Council had itself 'paid out' the headline sum and the assertion that 'when public services come under attack from compensation claims the inevitable result is that they start to be reduced'. The truth omitted from the piece was that, as the council had made clear, the compensation was negotiated and paid by the insurers, and the insurer in question had recognised that this case was exceptional and it had not led to any increase in premiums.[42]

But, where information is available, there is almost always an unglamorous verity belying the headline. Merv Grazinski, the million-pound-winning Winnebago driver who idiotically thought his vehicle was self-driving? He doesn't exist. The case has been conclusively debunked as a 1980s urban myth[43] – a complete fiction, notwithstanding its reporting in the *Daily Mail* as a legitimate example of 'outrageous' compensation claims.[44]

The 'American plonker' decried by Vanessa Feltz for suing McDonald's over a hot coffee that she spilt while driving, which augurs badly for our own compensation culture? The facts are a little more sober. The woman, Stella Lieback, was not driving – she was a passenger – and she opened her McDonald's coffee not knowing that it had been heated to between 82 and 88 degrees Celsius. It spilled, soaking through her trousers and causing third-degree burns. She was hospitalised for eight days, underwent skin grafts, was partially disabled for two years and scarred permanently. She didn't initially sue – she just asked McDonald's to cover her medical costs and loss of earnings for her daughter, to a total of between $10,000 and $15,000. When McDonald's only offered $500, she instructed a lawyer. At trial, it emerged that McDonald's had known that the temperature at which it served its coffee was hazardous, as there had been 700 similar complaints over the previous decade. McDonald's had done nothing to address this, and admitted that its coffee as served was not 'fit for consumption', meaning that it was in breach of statutory duty by selling a defective product. Interestingly, when a similar group claim was issued in England against McDonald's by thirty-six claimants in 2002, it failed. Under English consumer protection laws, McDonald's was held not to have sold a defective product, nor had it been negligent in how it packaged and served its (labelled) hot coffee.[45]

In response to a series of 'compensation culture' splashes in the *Daily Mail*, Bindmans Solicitors published an analysis of some of the more lurid headlines, to illustrate the level of injury that was likely to have been suffered if the quoted figures reflected general damages.[46] The school pupil splashed with custard and awarded £6,000? That child most likely sustained scarring which will remain visible at conversational distances for life. The £15,000 'given to somebody who had their elbow trapped in a Tube train'? This probably involved surgery and permanent impairment of function, such as that person never being able to stretch her elbow out fully again.

The cleaner who tripped over a mop and won £9,128 for 'a pulled groin muscle' was a figure of ridicule in the *Mail*[47] (which managed a twofer in its headline of 'Cleaning up in the small claims court', referring to a court which, as we've established, doesn't exist, and to which a claim of this value would not be allocated in any event). However, a minor soft-tissue injury which results in a full recovery within three months would attract well under £1,950, so it's obvious that there's more to this. If £9,000 represents general damages alone, there is likely to have been a fracture to the tibia or fibula, with ongoing symptoms and restriction of movement, involving time spent in plaster and a recovery period. Alternatively, the injury was somewhere in between, with the balance of special damages reflecting proven financial loss. And, it by now hopefully goes without saying, the employer would have been at fault; 'tripping over a mop' does not qualify as negligence.

This is obviously professional guesswork. But I'd suggest, with respect, that it has far more to recommend it than the immediate conclusion that there is no sensible explanation for such awards. Instead of considering that most insurers, employers and local authorities have access to highly competent lawyers, and will, in the case of settlements, be professionally advised on liability and the appropriate damages and legal costs, or, in the case of contested trials, will have been found liable by a court applying the law, editors reach instead, without any evidence, for cock-up and conspiracy.

'Taxpayers will be astounded at these payouts and the ludicrous things they're for,' stormed Jonathan Isaby of pressure group the Taxpayers' Alliance, in relation to bare figures of compensation settlements agreed by local authorities.[48] No doubt he is right. But the fault is not that of the claimants, nor (without further evidence) the defendant local authorities; it is the natural result of an informational void which is editorially exploited to *make* taxpayers astounded, assuring them of the ludicrousness of the story without offering any of the facts they need to form a view.

As for the broader question of whether there is a 'compensation culture', this is more complicated. It largely depends on one's definition. Certainly, we have a culture where it is *perceived* that compensation is awardable at the drop of a hat, whenever fault is alleged – *where there's blame, there's a claim* – and it is undeniable that certain organisations have adopted disproportionately risk-averse practices in response.

Many of these turn out, on closer inspection, to be urban myths. The Health and Safety Executive has published a handy checklist.[49] No, there is no law banning conkers in playgrounds. Trapeze artists are not required to wear hard hats. Candyfloss on a stick has not been prohibited due to a risk of impalement. The sack race has not been banned from sports day.[50] Many other 'elf 'n' safety' canards – such as Richard Littlejohn's claim[51] that coastal walkers in Stranraer were forced to be accompanied at all times by a lifeguard – crumble as untrue under the slightest scrutiny.[52] The less scandalous what-have-the-Health-and-Safety-Romans-ever-done-for-us story is that, since 1975, there has been an 81 per cent fall in workplace deaths and a 72 per cent fall in other reported workplace injuries.[53]

But it would be naive to deny the perception, and that, as a result, people's behaviours can be modified accordingly. The 'conkers' old chestnut, for example, arose due to a misunderstanding by a well-meaning head teacher who mistakenly believed that the law required children to wear goggles when playing conkers. And it would be similarly naive to ignore the symbiosis between the media and the legal profession in forging this perception. We'll return to this later, but there is no doubt that the wall-to-wall advertising of recent years by certain claims-management companies and personal-injury lawyers has added to a feeling of compensation ubiquity; if you haven't had a payout, you're missing out.

But, if the question is, *Are we more litigious?* the answer is more complex.

The figures, certainly in recent years, suggest that we are making fewer personal-injury claims. By the end of 2018, the number of new personal-injury claims issued had fallen to its lowest in almost seven years – a 20 per cent decrease over a twelve-month period.[54] Figures held by the Compensation Recovery Unit (CRU), with which all personal-injury claims must be registered, show a total of 853,615 cases registered in 2017/18, the lowest since available records from 2010. Within these, employer liability and motor liability claims were also at their lowest since 2010, with public liability (claims against government and local authorities) consistent with the pattern of the past eight years.[55]

Similarly, notwithstanding that the National Health Service paid a record £2.2 billion in compensation and legal costs in 2017/18, the number of clinical negligence claims against the NHS remained broadly flat over twelve months, at 10,673.[56] The steep increase in cost – 30 per cent in a year – was mostly attributable to a change in the way in which long-term payments are calculated. There has, according to the CRU, been a rise of 34 per cent in the number of clinical negligence claims since 2010/11. Whether this represents more trigger-happy opportunists or simply more unhappy serious clinical errors is difficult to determine; however, it is worthy of note that this rise in claims has coincided with a decade of financial austerity and well-publicised funding deficits in the National Health Service. If more people are being genuinely and seriously injured as a result of negligence by under-resourced and overwrought hospitals, it is hardly fair to dismiss those affected as opportunists.

Occasionally, context will be given from particular quarters. In 2013, the London Underground director of health, safety and environment responded to claims by a Liberal Democrat councillor that 'we are living in a compensation culture gone mad', made after (scant) details of personal-injury compensation payments made by Transport for London (TFL) were published. While nearly £5 million had been paid over three years, TFL pointed out that this represented one claim for every 2,298,850 journeys.[57]

However you approach it, though, it's an imperfect exercise. It's impossible to accurately answer the question of *How often do we claim for an injury?* as we only have raw data relating to claims made. We don't know how many unreported injuries are sustained each year; how often the national upper lip remains stiff and unquivering as we dust ourselves down and take the knocks in our stride. There are likewise no figures on how many injuries are compensated informally, before legal action is taken.

As for perhaps the key question – *Are people being routinely unjustly compensated?* – it is impossible to prove either way, but there is certainly no evidence of an epidemic. We know fraud happens – we see cases in the headlines[58] – but there are no comprehensive, reliable statistics on the incidence of fraudulent personal-injury claims; even if there were, these would mostly show those caught and *not* compensated. It is impossible to know, out of the thousands of settled claims each year, how many reflect negligent conduct by the defendant and how many are 'nuisance payments', made without liability – aside from the previously made observation that the multi-thousand-pound payments that make the news are likely to reflect at least a degree of culpability.

Nevertheless, despite what the House of Commons Justice Committee described as a 'troubl[ing] . . . absence of reliable data on fraudulent claims',[59] there is one field in particular where we have over recent years developed something of a national obsession: fraudulent whiplash claims. And this is important to look at, as, in the stampede to slay this dragon, politicians have introduced changes that strike at the heart of your right to access justice if you are genuinely injured.

## The Whiplash Capital of Europe

Whiplash refers to a soft-tissue injury to the neck, back or shoulder caused by a sudden jolting of the head or body, usually sustained in a road traffic accident. And, if our government and national press are to be believed, our country has a particular problem with 'bogus whiplash claims which push up insurance bills for honest motorists'.[60]

The difficulty with whiplash is that the symptoms largely depend on self-reporting; there is often no independent physiological evidence, so it is evidently open to abuse. However, something being open to abuse and something being routinely – as opposed to occasionally – abused are two different things. Passing around a collection plate at church is obviously *open* to abuse; it doesn't follow that there is a national crisis with kleptomaniacal worshippers helping themselves to the loose change.

Nevertheless, the rhetoric is unflinching. We are the Whiplash Capital of Europe, according to the government. Our compensation culture is 'rampant', thundered then Justice Secretary Liz Truss.[61] Prime Minister David Cameron declared in 2012, following a summit at Downing Street with 'the insurance industry, consumer and business groups', that 'Britain is now the whiplash capital of Europe, with more than 1,500 claims a day, with people claiming for whiplash injuries sustained in the most minor of incidents.'[62]

Fast-forward six years, and things were no better, with parliamentarians still anxious that 'There is no question but that the British public are being incited to submit fraudulent claims on an industrial scale.'[63] Justice Secretaries were still assuring us that our whiplash claim rate was 'higher than in any other European jurisdiction'.[64]

So ubiquitous is the mantra, there must be a solid evidential basis for it, surely? Well, not really. The House of Commons Transport Committee heard evidence from the insurance industry, the government and legal professionals in 2013, and concluded that the 'whiplash capital' claim 'cannot be conclusively proved or disproved from the information available', adding that 'It is surprising that the Government has brought forward measures to reduce the number of fraudulent or exaggerated whiplash claims without giving even an estimate of the comparative scale of the problem.'[65] An in-depth academic study by law professor Ken Oliphant traced the origins of the 'whiplash capital' claim to a report on whiplash published by the Association of British Insurers (ABI) in 2008. This was based on a 2004 European study comparing data collected from questionnaires circulated in ten European countries in 2002. Professor Oliphant found that the data was incomplete, the methodology was flawed and the 'whiplash capital' claim could only be substantiated through 'selective use of the data', alternative interpretations of which would render any of Italy, Germany or Switzerland the 'whiplash' or 'motor claims' capital of Europe. The (aged) data showed that Italy has nearly 50 per cent more whiplash claims, that in Switzerland they cost ten times as much per claim, and that bodily injury claims in general cost more in Italy, Germany, France and Spain than in the UK.[66]

The professor told the House of Commons Justice Committee, 'Such evidence as there is has been misleadingly and tendentiously presented by participants in the public debate about the alleged "compensation culture". Actually, the same evidence makes clear that, by most measures, the UK is not the whiplash capital of the world or even of Europe.'[67]

Indeed, we are not the only country repeatedly assured that its fraudulent whiplash problem renders it a world leader; an investigation by the Access to Justice Action Group found that similar claims have been made by ministers and insurance spokespersons in Ireland, Canada and Australia.[68]

Selective statistics rule the roost in the whiplash debate. The government intones that there has been a 40 per cent rise in personal-injury claims in traffic accidents between 2005 and 2018;[69] opposition MPs point out that the number of registered claims for whiplash fell by 15 per cent between 2015 and 2017.[70] But, however you slice it, the evidence to substantiate the idea that we have a quantifiable problem with fraudulent whiplash claims is simply not there. In its final report in 2018, the Justice Committee, having heard evidence from the government and the insurance industry on the rampant whiplash compensation culture, declared, '[W]e are troubled by the absence of reliable data on fraudulent claims and we find surprising the wide definition of suspected fraud that is used to collate the ABI's statistics.'[71]

Nevertheless, the premise having been implanted in the public consciousness, the government proceeded to embark upon a programme of significant legislative reform. And the consequences for victims of injury could be enormous.

## An exaggerated remedy for an exaggerated problem

Some of the responses to the compensation culture meme have been literally laughable. In 2015, Justice Secretary Chris Grayling's vaunted 'Heroism Act' was forced through Parliament despite legislators mocking Justice Minister Lord Faulks as 'the straight man in Mr Grayling's comedy routine'.[72] So exercised was Mr Grayling by the vision of Britain he'd imbibed from Richard Littlejohn columns that he introduced a new law 'to curb the Elf and Safety Culture'[73] and offer 'protection' to people who were accused of negligence while volunteering or acting 'heroically'. His worried mind brimming to its limited capacity with imagined stories of negligence claims against paramedics trying to treat patients and civic-minded gents sweeping snow from the street being sued by falling pedestrians,[74] he devised the Social Action, Responsibility and Heroism Act 2015. This legislation requires a court considering a negligence claim to 'have regard to' whether a defendant was 'acting for the benefit of society', had hitherto shown a 'generally responsible' attitude to health and safety, and whether they were 'acting heroically'. As lawyers up and down the land repeatedly pointed out to Mr Grayling, this added absolutely nothing to the existing law of negligence, which, as we've seen above, would *inevitably* involve a court considering those factors, where they arise. As the bill passed through its final stage in Parliament, it was saluted by Lord Pannick, who declared 'SARAH' (as Grayling affectionately referred to his baby) to be 'the most ridiculous piece of legislation approved by Parliament in a very long time'.[75]

Other legislative responses, however, have had more meaningful consequences.[76] Some have tackled unregulated claims-management companies encouraging healthy people to make fraudulent claims. Solicitors are now banned from paying referral fees – fees paid to third parties in exchange for having prospective personal-injury claimants referred to them. The way in which legal fees are charged in personal-injury cases has changed dramatically since 2013 ('no win, no fee' arrangements are far less lucrative for lawyers, and most claims now involve some sort of fixed-costs regime). Whiplash claims must, as of 2015, be supported by a fixed-cost medical report commissioned by an independent registered medical expert. And a court is now required to dismiss the whole of a personal-injury claim if it is satisfied that a claimant has been 'fundamentally dishonest' in relation to the claim – even if the claim would otherwise be meritorious.[77] All of these reforms have had the government's desired effect of significantly reducing the number of personal-injury claims issued since 2010.[78]

The Civil Liability Act 2018 took matters to a new level. This was celebrated as the government's solution to the alleged plague of false whiplash claims. However, although the stated intention was 'to crack down on minor, exaggerated and fraudulent soft tissue injury ("whiplash") claims stemming from road traffic accidents (RTAs)', the effects extended far beyond.

Part of the Act addressed whiplash specifically, introducing a new fixed tariff of damages to limit the compensation payable for pain, suffering and loss of amenity (general damages). This came in for significant criticism for its arbitrariness, and the fact that the deliberately low rates would, inevitably, leave injured people under-compensated. An online portal through which such claims would now have to be litigated was announced, effective from April 2020, with consternation voiced when it emerged that the portal would be funded not by the MoJ, but by the insurance industry.[79]

But whiplash, it quickly became apparent, was a smokescreen. The government's big plan was to raise the small claims limit – the maximum value of claims capable of being litigated as 'small claims' – so that a greater proportion of *all* personal-injury cases – even those entirely unrelated to traffic accidents – would fall into the small claims track. This may sound like a dry procedural reform, but the practical effects of this for claimants are vivid: legal costs can't be recovered in small claims, so many people are forced to represent themselves. It is one thing representing yourself in a very straightforward, low-value claim, where minor injury has been sustained and the stakes are relatively low, but, by raising the threshold, a host of higher-value, legally and factually complex cases suddenly fell in the small claims bracket.

The small claims limit for personal-injury cases has, since 1999, been set at £1,000, excluding special damages. This means that any claim for injury where general damages (pain, suffering and loss of amenity) were sought up to £1,000 would be dealt with by the small claims track. The aim of the Civil Liability Act was, as of April 2020, to increase this limit to £5,000 in all RTA-related claims, and to £2,000 for all other personal-injury claims. It probably does not require pointing out that a personal-injury claim against your employer for providing you with defective safety equipment has no link whatsoever to the 'Whiplash Capital of Europe' fancy; yet these claims, like all other personal-injury cases, found themselves the subject of the ostensible 'whiplash reforms'.

All of a sudden, cases involving serious injury fell into the informal small claims track. RTAs that resulted in minor brain injury, loss of part of a digit, tinnitus, fractures and significant hip/pelvic injury would be litigated as small claims. And, while the small claims track is theoretically less complicated than the fast track or multi-track, litigating any personal-injury claim is still a minefield for the unwary.

If some schmohawk texting at the wheel ploughs into your car, causing a significant pelvic injury, ruling you off work for two months, how confident would you feel in litigating that claim by yourself? Would you know how to obtain the details of the defendant and his insurer? Any idea how to achieve interim payments for ongoing medical treatment? Can you explain the respective functions of the Motor Insurance Bureau and the Compensation Recovery Unit? When it comes to litigation, where would you find the Personal Injury Pre-Action Protocol? Do you understand the significance of a Part 36 offer? Can you explain whether it applies to the small claims track? If your opponent is a legally represented insurer, are you content arguing and negotiating the finer legal points of liability, contributory negligence, causation and quantum? How conversant are you with Practice Direction 27 of the Civil Procedure Rules? Do you know how to correctly draft a witness statement? You are likely to need medical evidence to support your claim – how are you going to get around the news that three quarters of medical experts working in personal injury would not accept instructions from an unrepresented litigant?[80]

Ellie Reeves MP, a member of the Justice Committee, warned that the changes would result in 40 per cent of cases falling within the small claims track, leaving up to 500,000 people a year without legal representation.[81] In a report in May 2018, the Committee urged the government not to raise the small claims threshold, warning that 'this would represent an unacceptable barrier to justice'.[82] But the government went ahead anyway.

As for those injured at work, the Ministry of Justice didn't even bother to quantify the impact of the changes, leaving the Justice Committee 'deeply unimpressed',[83] but trade unions estimated that five times as many claims would now be dragged into the small claims track, leaving thousands of employees with the choice of battling their employers' lawyers, or simply not bothering. Research indicated that most claimants would opt for the latter, preferring to forgo the compensation to which they are entitled rather than proceeding unrepresented.[84]

The changes also threatened ruinous effects on personal-injury lawyers. Nearly half of personal-injury firms derive more than 60 per cent of their income from cases with a value of less than £5,000 – many of which would be snatched away under the reforms.[85] Many solicitors' firms, the government was warned, would find their profit margins squeezed to unsustainable levels, with 70 per cent of jobs related to personal-injury cases at high risk of being lost,[86] and 800 firms at risk of going out of business.[87]

You may instinctively have little sympathy with sob stories of hard-pressed lawyers, but bear in mind that this is not a measure targeted at shysters encouraging unmeritorious claims; those affected will be decent and honest professionals and their support staff, who work hard, for increasingly less money, to help injured people recover what they are entitled to from belligerent insurance companies. Without good personal-injury lawyers, people in desperate need of help will be at the mercy of the sharks.

What this all means is that, if you or your children are injured through the fault of a rogue driver, or your employer's negligence, or the recklessness of a local authority leaving broken glass in a children's play area, you are more likely to have to represent yourself in court proceedings, or to pay for a solicitor out of your modest compensation.

So why was it so important to push through these changes, in the face of dire warnings by experts? The sweetener for the public was that the bill would save the insurance industry £1.3 billion, meaning, the government told delighted newspapers, that the average customer would save thirty-five pounds a year on their car insurance premiums.[88] The corollary – that these savings would only be possible as a result of genuinely injured people being deterred from pursuing legitimate claims – was not shouted quite as loudly.

However, when the bill was presented, the government omitted – and, when pressed by MPs, outright refused – to include any mechanism requiring insurers to pass these savings on. Instead, the Justice Secretary was happy to hold in his hand a piece of paper signed by the leaders of twenty-six insurance companies *promising* to pass on the savings, if only the government would be so good as not to *compel* them to. The government agreed, blithely defying the Justice Committee's warning that it was being 'over-optimistic', and ignoring the fact that, despite insurers having saved £11 billion since the last round of personal-injury reforms, insurance premiums were higher than ever.[89]

When one steps back from the compensation-culture myth and asks, *Who is really benefiting here?* a familiar, repetitious response boomerangs back.

It's certainly not you, facing insurmountable hurdles seeking justice if you are injured. It is not the people you might fairly assume would benefit from a generous compensation scheme, such as victims of crime – to the contrary, since changes to the Criminal Injuries Compensation Scheme in 2012, the number of people receiving compensation for injuries caused by criminal acts has plummeted by 60 per cent.[90] Such changes are politically easy when you have successfully convinced an electorate that *compensation* is a dirty word.

If you're a driver, you may secure that bonza thirty-five-pounds-a-year discount on your insurance premium, although there is of course no meaningful legal mechanism to make sure. But that is the sum total of your promised gain. That is the best-case scenario.

So, if it's not you benefiting, then who?

Those meeting the costs of personal-injury claims are invariably the insurers. Compulsory motor insurance means that the costs of injuries, damage and legal expenses are met by the insurer for the liable party. Similarly, since 1969, all employers have been required to have insurance cover to meet potential claims by employees for injuries at work or any illness or disease resulting from their employment.[91] Many businesses have public-liability insurance to cover injuries caused to the public, and while some government departments and local authorities may self-insure, a number – such as Fylde Council, in the Case of the Collapsing Toilet Seat – take out policies with private insurers.

This is why, if you look closely, the hand of the insurance industry is detectable in each and every splash of 'compensation culture gorn mad'. Every news story will be brightened by a quotation from an insurance industry spokesperson, tutting and scratching their head at these crazy, pro-claimant times in which we sadly now exist, adding to the obfuscation and declining to offer vital context. It was they who created the 'Whiplash Capital of Europe' fallacy and dispersed it indelibly through the public consciousness, before repackaging and exporting it to be recycled abroad.

The mood music having been carefully orchestrated, our elected representatives proceeded to erect 'an unacceptable barrier to justice', blocking ordinary, poorly citizens from seeking redress at their lowest ebb. The insurance industry will stand to save £1.3 billion. For this – the enrichment of insurance CEOs and the curtailing of your access to justice – the government has calculated your price, to the thunderous applause of the media seals, at a vague, unenforceable promise of thirty-five pounds a year.

The insurers are not solely responsible for the compensation-culture myth, of course. Many hands have fed the monster. For the media, these stories are not merely staples, but catnip – a guarantee of outraged clicks and shares. And it is not just the tabloids. In 2011, when the government was seeking public support for changes to personal-injury law, insurer Aviva published a 'bizarre range of successful claims' from its archives – a medley of pratfalls over croquet hoops and bites by ferrets and fish. The *Guardian*'s 'Money Blog' dutifully reproduced the advertorial under the headline 'Compensation culture: a history of bizarre personal injury claims in Britain', uncritically listing the 'blatantly frivolous' claims decried by Aviva.[92] It failed to offer any context or explanation of how personal-injury law actually works, nor did the writer question why Aviva was required to or agreed to pay compensation if these claims were as blatantly frivolous as asserted. It made easy, copy-'n'-paste copy.

Lawyers and their third-party associates have much to answer for, too. While there has been welcome tightening, in recent years, of the rules governing claims-management companies and referral fees, for decades the legal profession has allowed its public image to be moulded by Compo4U billboards and daytime-TV adverts for claims hotlines. It has benefited lawyers to allow the something-for-nothing perception to take root, as it has helped cast the net wider and reel in the fishes. The notion that compensation automatically attaches to every accident that wasn't your fault, rather than being predicated on nuanced legal concepts of liability, causation and provable losses, is one the legal profession should have been better at refuting. Instead, we surrendered the battlefield to the minority spivs and charlatans, whether because we were happy to take home the marginal trickle-down benefits or because of complacency. The fraudsters and rogues may well be the unrepresentative minority, but we allowed them to be seen as representative. In doing so, we resourced the arsenal of those now waging war on personal-injury rights.

So it is that compensation – something to which you are legally and morally entitled if you are the victim of somebody else's unlawful behaviour – has been reimagined as the enemy of the people, instead of its ally. We are encouraged to celebrate its restriction, reduction and even removal as inherently good, a victory for Joe Public, instead of querying what it actually means for us. 'We're fighting the compensation culture!' they cry. 'Yes!' we cheer. 'Please remove our rights when we are injured!' Please remove the right to be restored to the position we were in before our lives were turned upside down by someone else's avoidable mistake.

And this is the part I can't understand. Or, at least, I can understand how we got here – I just wish we hadn't fallen so obligingly into the trap.

Make no mistake – my sentiments should not be misread as uncritically pro-claimant, nor uncritically pro-status quo. Spend half an hour with a personal-injury lawyer (should such a misfortune befall you) and you will be regaled with ways in which the law and procedure can be improved. No system is immune from abuse; there is undoubtedly fraudulent activity, by lawyers as well as claimants, and it is entirely reasonable for legislators to want to tackle it, and for insurers to resent paying for it. It is undeniable that, whether directly or indirectly, burdens are placed on the public purse by personal-injury claims, and equally undeniable that there is a legitimate public interest in accurate media reporting of cases where there is reasonable concern that an injustice has been done. There are areas of the personal-injury sector that I have not touched upon – such as the costs that lawyers are paid and the increasing, unsustainable outlay by the NHS – and over which there may well be reasoned debate (although I would add the undervalued observation that the highest legal costs are incurred in cases where defendants refuse to admit liability – if insurers or the NHS admitted blame earlier, lawyers' costs would invariably be far lower).

Personal-injury law is far from perfect. I do not offer a full-throated defence of its present operation. But I do challenge the prevailing assumption that the majority of claims are vexatious, or frivolous, or otherwise inexplicable, and that the partial accounts spun in the headlines accurately represent what the law is or how it works.

Moreover, I want us to reconnect with what we understand by compensation, and to reconfigure the perverse labelling of winners and losers. I'd like us to consider why we unquestioningly allow vested interests to manipulate our nastiest, most cynical instincts. Why, when one of our fellow citizens is injured, our reflex isn't *There but for the grace of God*, but *You lucky bastard*. Why we happily surrender ourselves to the assumption that everyone around us is on the take. Why we tut about compo windfalls, instead of pausing to ask, *Why am I being encouraged to resent a disabled child the cost of her care? Whose agenda is this serving?*

It is bizarre that, for a nation so clearly susceptible to suspicion of ulterior motive, we disengage our critical faculties and swallow blindly the propaganda of billion-pound insurance companies. We lie back and allow ourselves to be enveloped in misinformed resentment towards our suffering neighbours receiving restitution, viewing it as a sore on, rather than a credit to, a civilised society.

The key, I think, to turning us all against each other has been in convincing us that personal-injury law – like so many other aspects of the justice system – is for other people. People we will never meet, whose motives are by nature impure, and whose financial gain is the sum to our zero. It perhaps doesn't occur to us, until it's too late, that it could be us hospitalised by cheap, malfunctioning factory equipment at work, or our child injured by that driver on his mobile; that we might need the services of a personal-injury solicitor, or find ourselves limping into a courtroom preparing to duel an insurer's legal battalion armed with nothing more than Wikipedia.

Nor, when it comes to the bitterness over other people's windfalls, do we put ourselves in the shoes of the seriously injured and ask, *Would I swap lives?*

If we did, and we answered truthfully, we would see the true meaning of compensation. Not a lottery win to be coveted, but the next-best thing our society can offer to try to put things right.

# 4. Your Work

'Hallelujah! The tribunal gravy train's derailed: As workers are made to pay £1,200 fee, discrimination cases plunge by 75%.'

*Daily Mail*, 29 July 2014[1]

Twenty-eight million of us – 85 per cent of the working population – are in some form of employment. In the space of a year, Britons collectively work over a billion hours. The majority who work full-time spend on average thirty-seven hours a week in the workplace.[2] That's 85,840 hours over the course of a fifty-year working life.[3] We share more of our waking time with our employers and colleagues than we do our families and friends. Life, liberty and the pursuit of (non-work-related) happiness all play second fiddle to our jobs, and equally are dependent upon them; our ability to provide for ourselves and our loved ones – to put roofs over heads, meals on tables and shoes on tiny feet – relies on our being able to punch a clock each day and bank a wage each month. Around one third of the 15 per cent of us who are self-employed will also be responsible for the employment of others; their economic security and pastoral wellbeing will be intertwined with our own. We flourish, tumble and fall together, whirring cogs in our nation's grinding economy.

I labour these tired statistics in service of these hackneyed truisms because I find it bewildering that, given the obvious centrality of work to our existence, we are taught so little about our rights and obligations in the workplace. According to a survey in 2019, four out of five Britons are unaware of their employment rights.[4] Formal instruction in basic concepts of employment law is forsaken in lieu of a curriculum of rumour, hearsay and on-the-job testing-to-destruction, with the unsurprising result that – to mangle Donald Rumsfeld – our unknown unknowns far exceed our known knowns, and many of the latter turn out to be the former.

So it was that, as an erstwhile employment law practitioner, I would find myself wading through the same weeds when cornered by interrogators at social events. One of the advantages of practising criminal law is that, while people often have a lot of questions upon learning what I do, it is relatively rare that they are seeking advice for their own legal problems. 'I've been charged as a getaway driver in an armed robbery – can you run by me how joint enterprise works?' is a query that doesn't tend to crop up over wedding breakfasts (although I did once manage to give a business card to a young man at a friend's christening who, upon hearing my job title, excitedly told our uncomfortable corner of the room how he was 'facing a section 18 [GBH with intent] for giving this Millwall geezer a Chelsea smile' and insisted on taking my details). By contrast, with employment law, the requests for advice were relentless, and almost all geared around the same general misunderstandings.

No, you have no legal right to time off on bank holidays. No, nor time-and-a-half, double pay or time off in lieu; your statutory 5.6 weeks' holiday per year is allocated according to your contract, and bank holidays are, unless specified, just like any other day. Yes, your previous employer is generally entitled to refuse to provide you with a reference. No, calling it a 'probationary period' has absolutely no effect on somebody's statutory employment rights. Yes, you still have to pay temporary agency staff holiday pay. No, 'LIFO' – Last In, First Out – is definitely not a watertight approach to redundancy selection. Yes, asking a female interviewee when she plans to start a family is very much the sort of thing that can get you into legal hot water. No, the fact that a contract contains the words 'self-employed' does not mean that the worker whose hours you set, whose movements you control and whose exclusivity you demand *is* actually self-employed; if it walks, talks and quacks like a duck, it's probably something capable of being roasted and shredded into delicious pancakes.

The informational void is ludicrous, when you think about it. Unless you conduct your own independent research, you probably won't know what rights you have at work if, for example, you fall pregnant. How long is maternity leave?[5] Who qualifies for maternity pay?[6] How much do you get?[7] Do you have the right to time off for antenatal classes? Is that time off paid or unpaid?[8] What happens if pregnancy renders you medically unable to carry out your job? Can your employer send you home without pay?[9] What's the situation if your boss prefers the maternity cover for your role over you?[10] What can you do if you feel you're being treated less favourably by your manager because you're pregnant?

Something of which you may feel confident, however, is that, even if you don't know the specific answers to these questions, the employment protections in England and Wales are pretty strongly weighted in your favour. Or, to borrow the less temperate language of headlines in recent years, employment law and the employment tribunals that rule on disputes have created a 'compensation gravy train' and 'bonanza for parasites',[11] in which 'jackpot tribunal payouts'[12] are bestowed on opportunistic employees for the most trivial of grievances.

The *Daily Express* offered the following precis: 'A service designed to provide justice against genuinely bad bosses turned into a gigantic racket fuelled by whingeing trade unions, parasitical lawyers and money-grabbing litigants. [. . .] [T]he modern compensation culture at its worst, as a deluge of vexatious or frivolous claims punish [. . .] decent employers.'[13]

The '"discrimination" industry', to borrow from the *Daily Mail*'s Richard Littlejohn,[14] attracts particular and frequent heat. Whether it's the 'farce' of Royal Mail employees pocketing '£70k compo' for a racist note being pinned up at a sorting office (the *Sun*),[15] or a supermarket worker suing Tesco after a colleague 'broke wind in his face' (*Daily Star*),[16] or a female police officer winning £15,000 'because she could not carry a dog up a hill during a test to become a handler' (*Daily Mail*)[17] – a decision damned as 'ludicrous' by a Conservative MP[18] – popular reporting adheres to the same core message: employment law is your enemy.

And this was a drum thwacked at increasing volume during the early years of the Conservative–Liberal Democrat coalition government, as concerted efforts were made by business groups to draw attention to the scandal. The British Chambers of Commerce condemned the employment-tribunal system as 'in dire need of reform' and 'overwhelmingly weighted in favour of the employee', and warned that employers were frequently finding themselves forced into agreeing to pay settlements in unmeritorious claims.[19] Eye-watering figures were bandied about – the following passage an example from the *Daily Mail*: 'Payouts are presently unlimited. The biggest was £729,347 in a disability discrimination case. For sex discrimination the top award was £442,266, and the most successful race discrimination claimant won £374,922.'[20]

The pressure succeeded. Over the next few years, the government introduced a series of changes and, as a result, claims to employment tribunals plummeted by nearly 70 per cent.[21]

A victory for justice, surely?

Well, not if you were a pregnant woman whose employer had docked your wages by £70 for the time you lawfully took off to attend antenatal classes. Nor if you were a cleaner whose boss refused to allow you to take your statutory rest breaks during your shifts. Nor someone bullied at work, racially abused and then dismissed.

Because the way in which the dramatic fall in claims was achieved was blunt: the previously free-to-access employment-tribunal system was, in 2013, made subject to a system of application fees. By imposing disproportionately high fees on people bringing employment-tribunal claims, even for modest sums, the government priced justice beyond their reach.

To recover your docked £70 in wages for those antenatal

classes? That would now cost you £390. Obtaining a declaration from a tribunal to stop your employer preventing you from taking your rest breaks was priced at £1,200. The same fee was demanded from the newly unemployed victim of racial discrimination.

The deterrent barriers did not end there. For those who were able to afford to successfully pursue claims, and who were found by employment tribunals to have suffered loss due to their employer's unlawful behaviour, over one third were still unable to recover a single penny from their employers, who simply refused to pay.[22] People at the most vulnerable times in their lives – unemployed, penniless and with mouths to feed – were paying the government £1,200 in exchange for a form of justice that amounted to nothing more than a further two-fingered salute from their recalcitrant, lawbreaking employer.

The fee scheme culminated in a challenge before the Supreme Court in July 2017, when the court declared that the government's flagship reform 'effectively prevents access to justice' and quashed it as 'unlawful'.[23]

So, what exactly was going on? How did we end up in a position where, for nearly half a decade, our government excluded us from enforcing our employment rights, at next to no political cost? Where was the public outcry?

The answer lies in the narrative that was carefully built in the years preceding the 'reforms'. We were told that employment law was a racket – that the law operated against good employers; that jackpot compensation was gratuitously lavished on the undeserving; that tribunals were biased in favour of employees; and that there was a flood of vexatious claims by malicious employees.

And, when we look at each of these stories in turn, we can see how far they depart from the truth.

# Why do we have employment law?

Before considering the tales we are told about employment law, it is worth reminding ourselves why it exists. The principle underlying employment law, and what differentiates it from a standard contractual relationship, is the inequality of bargaining power. If I offer to supply you with a weekly delivery of home-grown organic vegetables lovingly plucked from my allotment, you have a degree of heft in that ongoing arrangement. If I suddenly change the terms – such as doubling the price once the contract is underway – or abuse your goodwill by regularly failing to deliver on time, you can either stick it out, complain, seek a renegotiation (such as a partial refund or a lower monthly cost), walk away entirely having realised the folly of sourcing vegetables from a criminal barrister, or even take legal action against me for breach of contract. None of those options, whatever happens, is going to be life-changing or irremediable. Nor indeed if I, without notice, decide to close my ill-conceived vegetable emporium and cancel our agreement completely. In any of those scenarios, you may be temporarily inconvenienced, but you can find a competitor supplier without too much hassle, and the business – me – knows that, if I don't treat you fairly, you can stand up to me or walk away without fear of adverse consequence. Being black-listed by my allotment is something your aching heart will get over.

An employment contract, by contrast, usually starts out from a position of unequal power – you need this job more than the employer needs you, as evidenced by the waiting room full of equally qualified applicants, and, certainly at entry level, you are in no position to dispute the standard terms and conditions – and it remains this way throughout the relationship. If the terms suddenly and dramatically worsen, or your working conditions become intolerable, your employer knows that you are in a bind. Finding a new job is not as quick, straightforward or guaranteed as switching a supplier, and your dependence on your income to live, pay rent/mortgage and support dependants means that your ability to walk away is hobbled. Furthermore, if you try to legally enforce your contractual rights, there is a fear that you risk damaging the relationship beyond repair – or, worse still, finding yourself persona non grata in the industry, once word spreads that you are a 'troublemaker'. If the relationship is unexpectedly brought to an end by you, it may cause the employer financial loss and inconvenience in sourcing a replacement, but it is unlikely to cause the business to fold. If you are summarily dismissed by your employer, there is a genuine risk that you could fail in the long term to secure alternative work and could lose everything.

So it is that employment law underpins working relationships by providing further minimum standards, duties and rights, additional to the formal contract between you and your employer. The content and extent of employment rights has vacillated over the twentieth and twenty-first centuries, as governments of different political hues pursued differing ideologies in striking the balance between protecting employees and ensuring that employment law does not place disproportionate regulatory burdens on employers. We'll consider specific examples in due course, but current rights include the right to be paid minimum wage, the right not to be dismissed without notice, the right to paid holiday, the right to redundancy pay, limits on working hours, the right to equal pay as persons of the opposite sex, maternity rights, the right to time off for new parents, the right to a written statement of your terms of employment, protections for whistle-blowers, protections when a business is taken over ('transfers of undertakings'), the right not to be unfairly dismissed and the right not to be discriminated against on the grounds of age, disability, gender reassignment, marital status, race, religion, sex or sexual orientation. In short, employment law is concerned with ensuring that, in the workplace, your economic rights and human dignity are not infringed or exploited as a result of that imbalance of power.

## Is employment law unfair to employers?

A full history and exposition of employment law is beyond us, but in considering this question, it is worth looking closer at the operation of two areas – unfair dismissal and discrimination – as it is on these that most media antagonism descends.

## Unfair dismissal

Unfair dismissal is a concept that has existed since 1971,[24] and today comprises the majority of employment-tribunal claims. The right not to be unfairly dismissed applies only to employees,[25] and (save for the exceptions below) only upon accruing two years' continuous service.[26]

The idea is that two years gives sufficient time for an employee to bed in, affording the employer the flexibility to easily dispense with someone's services if things aren't working out. A contrary argument would be that two years is a very long time for a person to work without security of tenure, but there we are.

In an unfair-dismissal claim, an employee has to prove that they were dismissed (as opposed to having resigned or consensually terminated the contract). It is then for the employer to show the reason for the dismissal, and that the reason is capable of being fair.[27]

Some reasons are specified as 'automatically unfair'. So serious are these, that the right not to be dismissed for these reasons applies to employees even if they don't have two years' service. They include being dismissed because of trade-union membership or participating in lawful industrial action; dismissal for reasons connected to pregnancy, adoption or other family-related leave; dismissal because of an employee's spent conviction; dismissal because an employee asserted a statutory employment right; and dismissal because of whistle-blowing.

'Potentially fair reasons' are set out in statute, and include the capability or qualifications of the employee, the conduct of the employee, redundancy, a legal restriction preventing the employee from carrying out that job (such as a lorry driver disqualified from driving), or 'some other substantial reason' to justify dismissal. Once the employer has demonstrated a potentially fair reason, a tribunal will consider whether, in all the circumstances, the employer acted *reasonably* in dismissing the employee. Critically, the tribunal isn't asking itself, *Would we have dismissed this employee in these circumstances?* Rather, it is asking, *Did dismissal fall within the 'band of reasonable responses' open to the employer?* The assessment of reasonableness includes considering whether, for example, the employee was warned about performance or conduct, and the fairness of the procedures that were followed.

We can see therefore that 'unfair' dismissal is a slight misnomer, as an employment tribunal won't in fact be concerned with 'fairness' as much as 'reasonableness'. The tribunal can easily conclude, 'Well, *we* wouldn't have dismissed you,' but find that the employer nevertheless acted reasonably.

So, to take us back to our earlier example – if you, as a cleaner denied your statutory rest breaks, raised a formal grievance with your employer, and your employer responded by sacking you on the spot, this would be an automatically unfair dismissal. If your employer sacked you because he had discovered you enjoyed a spot of live action role-playing in your spare time, this is unlikely to fall within the categories of 'potentially fair reasons', and will probably be unfair. But if your performance was continuously poor, despite being given multiple warnings and opportunities to improve, your employer would have little difficulty in showing that their decision was reasonable.

# Discrimination

The first point to note about discrimination is that it is not, of itself, unlawful. We all discriminate every day in every walk of life; to discriminate is simply to distinguish and treat differently. The problem in the employment field arises when we discriminate not on the basis of legitimate factors – such as performance or attitude – but on the basis of 'protected characteristics'.

These protected characteristics have developed piecemeal since the 1970s – starting with sex[28] and race[29] – and are largely influenced by EU law. Since 2010, the disparate legislation has been consolidated in the Equality Act, which lists protected characteristics as age, disability, gender reassignment, marriage and civil partnership, race, religion or belief, sex, pregnancy, and sexual orientation.

What sort of treatment is prohibited under discrimination law? Slightly different considerations apply, depending on the characteristic, but, speaking very broadly, discrimination encompasses the following behaviours:[30]

— **Direct discrimination** – This is where, due to a protected characteristic, a person (A) treats another (B) less favourably than A would treat others. An example would be your employer overlooking you for promotion because of your sex.[31]

— **Indirect discrimination** – Where an employer adopts a policy which applies equally to everyone but which has a disproportionate impact on a certain group of people of a protected characteristic, the employer has to show a good reason.[32] For example, a policy stating that, in order to be eligible for promotion, an employee has to be over six feet tall would obviously place women, who are on average shorter, at a particular disadvantage. Unless the employer could justify this policy, it would amount to indirect discrimination. This was the principle at play in the case involving the female police officer who couldn't carry an Alsatian seventy yards uphill and so failed a dog-handler training course. The employment tribunal found that this requirement indirectly discriminated against women, who are on average less able to complete this part of the test, and the requirement was in fact not justified, as at least half of existing dog handlers had not been forced to go through this unnecessary dog-carrying challenge.

— **Harassment** – This is where A engages in unwanted conduct related to a protected characteristic, which has the purpose or effect of violating B's dignity or creating an intimidatory, hostile, degrading, humiliating or offensive environment.[33] So, if an employee racially abuses a black colleague – say, by distributing KKK propaganda in the workplace[34] – the employer will, following long-established common law principles, be vicariously liable for that misconduct (in the same way that an employer would be liable if, say, his employee negligently injured a customer).

— **Victimisation** – This is where your employer subjects you to a detriment – for instance, demotes you – because you have made an allegation of discrimination.[35]

— **Disability discrimination** – Although covered by the above, disability discrimination operates in a slightly different way. Crucially, employers are under a duty to make 'reasonable adjustments' to avoid a disabled person being put at a substantial disadvantage. A reasonable adjustment may include, for instance, provision of equipment or accessibility aids.[36]

This is the speediest of whirlwind tours, but I hope it assists in setting out the basic framework. And the rationale behind discrimination law is, hopefully self-evidently, an effort to protect human dignity. None of the above behaviours are acceptable in a tolerant, pluralist society; none of them should we simply be expected to accept in our working environment.

There is also a business case in favour of discrimination law; it seeks to eliminate irrational economic behaviour from the market economy (such as promoting a less-competent white man over a better-qualified Asian woman).

And ultimately – as with so much of employment law – the issues in both unfair dismissal and discrimination boil down to reasonableness. If, as an employer, you have acted reasonably and fairly, the law is on your side. If you adopt fair disciplinary and grievance procedures, as recommended by ACAS (Advisory, Conciliation and Arbitration Service) and published for free on their website,[37] and treat employees fairly and with respect – as most employers do – there is not much in the theory to offend you.

The resistance to this area of law tends to be manned by commentators, newspaper editors and politicians who have had the good fortune not to have been subjected to discrimination themselves. Richard Littlejohn's regular polemics in the *Daily Mail* against the '"discrimination" industry', for example, are the product of a straight, white, able-bodied man, writing for a newspaper edited by consecutive straight, white, able-bodied men, all of whom enjoy the twin buffers of affluence and social status. Fascinatingly, when, in 2016, a sixty-one-year-old sales rep, Alan Dove, was awarded £63,000 in compensation for age discrimination after being bullied and dismissed because of his advancing years, the sixty-two-year-old Mr Littlejohn found himself a sudden convert to the discrimination cause, scolding his readers and writing, 'Mr Dove was appallingly treated and no one, apart from his ex-employers, should begrudge him a penny.'[38]

Similar doublethink is achieved by certain Members of Parliament. David Davies MP, for example, has, according to TheyWorkForYou.com, voted against or abstained from the majority of key votes seeking to promote discrimination law, including the Equality Act 2010.[39] He has also lent some choice quotes to tabloids, mocking 'ludicrous' successful sex-discrimination claims.[40] However, when it comes to religion, the Christian Mr Davies is an outspoken advocate against discrimination against Christians and a proponent of allowing Christians to wear religious iconography in the workplace.[41]

Pulling the above together, I'd suggest it's hyperbolic to claim that the law itself operates unfairly against employers; in the fields of unfair dismissal and discrimination, it simply requires them, once an employee has shown that they have been dismissed or treated less favourably, to demonstrate that there was a good and fair reason for acting in that way. The law can be complex, for sure. It can be costly to undertake training or employ an HR specialist to ensure you understand and follow the law. Other legal requirements – such as minimum wage, holiday pay and anything else that may be loosely referred to by business interests as 'red tape' – may impose financial burdens on employers. But none of that is the same as legal bias. More is needed for this claim to stand up.

## Were employees pocketing 'jackpot' compensation awards?

Remedies at employment tribunals operate with the aim of restoring the employee to the position in which they would have been had they not been treated unlawfully. While the tribunal has the power to order reinstatement of dismissed employees, in most cases it recognises the impracticability of forcing an employer to take somebody back after acrimonious tribunal proceedings some time after the event, and compensation is the most common remedy.

The calculation of compensation is complex, but it is under-pinned by the same principle we encountered in the previous chapter: it is designed to make good on your loss, not confer a lottery bonus. If you are forced out of your job, compensation encompasses, loosely speaking, a lump sum based on your length of service that equates to your statutory redundancy entitle-ment,[42] and then compensation for other losses incurred while you're seeking re-employment.[43] If you're partially to blame for your dismissal, that's reflected in your award. If your dismissal was procedurally unfair, but otherwise entirely deserved, you may well end up with no compensation at all. If you don't take steps to seek new work, you'll be penalised. As with personal injury, the sums awarded are not plucked out of the air; they represent the very real losses incurred by someone through no fault of their own.

What's more, often omitted from the debate about 'jackpot payouts' is that, while cases of discrimination can, as the *Mail* says, attract 'unlimited payouts'[44] – in exactly the same way as any type of lawsuit involving money attracts, in theory, 'unlimited payouts' – unfair dismissal does not. In cases not involving discrimination, Parliament has imposed an artificial cap on compensation recoverable for unfair dismissal, in a way that would be unthinkable in the ordinary civil courts.[45] Normally, if you unlawfully cause a loss, you are expected to make good on it. But this ceiling[46] means that those dismissed from well-paid, specialised jobs who struggle to find re-employment can be badly hit. It is a political gift to bad employers.

The only meaningful distinction when it comes to calculating compensation in employment law arises when the tribunal considers 'injury to feelings', a concept unique to discrimination cases. This can be controversial, particularly when contrasted to the sums that are generally awarded for physical injury, which we looked at in the last chapter, although the approved principle is that awards for injury to feelings should bear some broad general similarity to the range of awards for personal injury.[47] Most awards for injuries to feelings fall between £800 and £8,400.[48]

These undoubtedly sound like high figures, but context is vital. It is rare that claimants walk away from employment tribunals with thousands of pounds for injury to feelings. In its 2011 'jackpot payout' splash, the *Daily Mail* published 'average' discrimination awards, but relied on the mean rather than the median figures, ensuring that the 'average' was skewed by the outliers (unusually high awards). The median total compensation award that year for race discrimination – including losses and injury to feelings – was £5,400. Sex discrimination was £6,300. The highest median award was disability discrimination, at £8,600. Unfair dismissal was £4,600.[49]

So, the rash of 'jackpot' discrimination payouts was in fact illusory. Given that discrimination cases will often involve the loss of employment or the loss of opportunity (such as promotion), the median figures by themselves cannot sensibly be said to flash red as a warning of compensation culture gone mad. The most recent figures, published in 2018, show a similar trend: slightly higher medians in all categories (for reasons we'll come to later), but far, far below the 'averages' claimed by the *Mail*.[50] The six-figure awards distorting the mean figures are reserved for the cases where the financial loss is the greatest – usually involving individuals in specialised jobs on exceptionally high pay, and where the acts of discrimination are especially heinous. If, for instance, a BAME woman working for an investment bank on an income of £400,000 a year is dismissed because of her race, and as a result is unable to find an equivalent job for six months, her losses alone will exceed £200,000. In those circumstances, why should she be resented compensation? Why should the bank not be forced to fix what it broke?

## Are employment tribunals weighted against the employer?

Putting the law to one side, what about the employment tribunals themselves? Are they, in the words of the British Chambers of Commerce, 'overwhelmingly weighted in favour of the employee'?[51] Are they, as Conservative MP Brian Binley asserts, 'a hunting ground for some members of the legal profession', peppered by 'too many malicious and vexatious cases'?[52]

Let's take a look.

Industrial tribunals were established in 1964, and since 1968 have provided 'an easily accessible, speedy, informal and inexpensive procedure' for resolving employment disputes.[53] Rebranded as 'employment tribunals' in 1998, they were intended for use by workers, including the low paid and those who have recently lost their jobs, and for cases where often relatively minor sums are in issue (such as the non-payment of a few weeks' wages). In the words of the Supreme Court, 'they are designed to deal with issues which are often of modest financial value, or of no financial value at all, but are nonetheless of social importance'. An essential feature of the employment-tribunal system at its inception was that claimants would not be charged a fee to make a claim; the cost of the system would be borne by the taxpayer. This, you may think, is common sense: those who need to access employment tribunals are likely to be particularly financially vulnerable – in receipt of low pay, owed wages or recently unemployed – and it is self-evidently vital that they not be priced out of justice.

Rules of procedure are intended to be simpler in employment tribunals (ETs) than in the civil courts. Most claims must be presented quickly (within three months, as opposed to the six years for a contractual claim in the civil courts), and hearings are less formal than in court. Contested hearings for discrimination cases are heard by a panel, comprising a professional, legally qualified judge and two lay members – one drawn from a panel representing employers, one from a panel representing employees.[54] It is worth bearing this in mind whenever you hear an employer complain about 'bias' in ET decisions – they usually have one of their own involved in the judging. There is no legal aid available for claimants' representation, so they can either self-represent, pay privately for a lawyer or be represented by a trade-union rep or other chosen person. Employers, many of whom have legal insurance, are often legally represented.

On the way towards a full hearing, there are case-management hearings to clarify the issues and prepare for the full trial, but most claims do not reach that stage. This is largely due to the role played by the Advisory, Conciliation and Arbitration Service (ACAS), which has a statutory duty to conciliate – impartially attempt to settle cases for free – in every prospective employment-tribunal claim.

As for whether the outcomes support the claim of the British Chambers of Commerce (BCC) that ETs are 'overwhelmingly weighted in favour of the employee',[55] it's not clear that they do. For a start, the BCC itself has claimed that employers win 'the majority of cases',[56] which is an unorthodox starting point for a claim of anti-employer bias. The raw statistics don't offer immediate conclusions. In 2009/10 – the year following which the concerted campaign against employment tribunals began in earnest – 13 per cent of all claims presented were successful at a full hearing, with 6 per cent of claims unsuccessful. The remaining 81 per cent did not make it as far as a full hearing, either settling through ACAS (31 per cent), being withdrawn by the claimant (32 per cent), being struck out or dismissed at an early stage (11 per cent) or being uncontested by the employer (7 per cent).[57] So, depending on which way you cut it, tribunals were either finding in favour of employees at a ratio of two to one, or, adopting the BCC's vantage point, were only ruling in favour of employees in one in five cases. Statistics tell us everything and nothing. The success rate *may* be because ETs harbour pro-employee sympathies, but may equally be because employers dig their heels in and resist claims where they shouldn't. The bare statistics also tell us nothing about the merits of claims, whether pursued or abandoned. A claim failing at a full hearing does not mean that it is without merit, just as an employer resisting a claim is not necessarily acting vexatiously or maliciously – they may reasonably believe that they have a strong argument – and the tribunal is required to make a finely balanced decision. It is entirely possible that the system was and is working perfectly fairly: weeding out the weak claims early on, encouraging settlement where both sides have a decent case, and justly deciding the minority of cases where agreement is not possible.

However, moving away from outcomes and looking at the build of the system, and in particular the undeniable emphasis on settling claims, one can see why employers' groups become vexed. Many employers – particularly small and medium-sized enterprises – will have neither the time nor resources to invest in protracted legal proceedings, and may feel pressured to pay a 'nuisance value' to a claimant to make a claim go away, even if they believe their defence to be strong. Costs are rarely awarded in tribunals, meaning that the successful party still often ends up footing their own legal bill. This, it is suggested, is part of the reason for the high settlement rate – commercial decisions taken by employers to 'pay off' frivolous claims rather than fight them. The justification for the 'no costs' presumption is rooted part in principle, part in pragmatism. Employees will rarely have the means to pay an employer's legal costs, and the threat of paying costs could deter deserving claims. An employer can insure against legal claims; an employee cannot insure against being dismissed.

But, certainly, in this model there is *scope* for abuse by employees chancing their arm. However, is there proof that this is a widespread problem?

## Is there a flood of vexatious claims?

The Chartered Institute of Personnel and Development told the *Telegraph* in 2011 that 55 per cent of employers surveyed had 'endured a complaint on malicious grounds'.[58] And why not make a complaint, if there are no adverse consequences?

Well, the first observation is that that self-reported figure of 55 per cent does not sit easily alongside the conclusion of a government-commissioned review, four years earlier, that 'weak and vexatious claims make up only a small minority of tribunal claims'.[59] Nor with the small business survey for the Department of Business, Innovation and Skills which showed that only 6 per cent of businesses considered employment regulation a problem.[60] Nor does it chime with the experience of tribunal panel members, such as Baroness Whitaker, who told the House of Lords in 2013, 'I sat on employment tribunals for several years and I do not remember any vexatious claims. Although some were poorly argued, they would actually have done better with a lawyer.'[61]

But the second observation, often overlooked in this debate, is that, where a tribunal is satisfied that a claim is 'scandalous or vexatious or has no reasonable prospect of success',[62] it can strike out the claim early in proceedings. If a tribunal considers that a claim has 'little reasonable prospects of success' – as opposed to *no* prospects – it can order that the claimant pay a deposit, up to £1,000, in order to continue the claim.[63] And, while generally no legal costs are awarded against either party in tribunal proceedings, there is an exception where a party has acted 'vexatiously, abusively, disruptively or otherwise unreasonably', or where a party's case had no reasonable prospect of success.[64] So there are control mechanisms in place. Genuinely hopeless claims can be booted out by a tribunal at a very early stage, before an employer has incurred any real cost. Rationally, an employer faced with a truly vexatious claim should not be settling; they should be inviting the tribunal to strike the claim out at an early stage, or seeking a deposit, or, if it goes as far as a hearing, applying for costs at the end.

As for the suggestion that the high rate of claims settled or withdrawn – roughly 60 per cent every year from 2009/10 to 2017/18[65] – is evidence of a stampede of unmeritorious claims being indulged by a lopsided system, yet again we are limited in the inferences that we can sensibly draw from the statistics. Is a settlement rate of two thirds a sign of a problem, or of a system working as it should? Businesses may say that it is evidence of employers compelled by economic necessity to pay off a plague of money-grabbing claimants, out for what they can get. Employees may say that the same figures show how employers can consistently get away with paying wronged employees far less than they would receive at a tribunal, exploiting the imbalance of power and financial muscle to coerce the little man to settle for less than he's worth. The build of the system is undoubtedly imperfect, and allows for exploitation both ways. To borrow from the wisdom of Larry David, if the sign of a good compromise is that both parties are unhappy, an equally available conclusion is that the system is in fact working rather well.

The difficulty lying behind any analysis of this issue is that claims of a vexatious compensation culture are, upon inspection, almost entirely based on the subjective views of surveyed employers. And here's the thing about litigation, particularly when the issue in question is a relationship between two parties: it is rare that people admit acting unreasonably. Even if settlement is reached, it will often be preceded with a blustery throat-clear denying liability and insisting that this is a commercial decision; the employer who says, 'I treated you badly, I am at fault and your claim is entirely justified,' is uncommon. That is not a criticism; employers are humans, and we as a species are terrible at accepting genuine fault. In much the same way, you are unlikely to find a claimant who will accept, even after a finding that they were vexatious, that they were indeed acting without good reason. We deceive ourselves, our cognitive dissonance only resolved by our brains reassuring us that, in spite of what anyone else might think, we *know* we're in the right.

To invoke the product of that psychological trait as empirical evidence of an external phenomenon – as opposed to mere *perception* of the phenomenon – is a classic error in reasoning. But, from 2011 onwards, the government fell for it. It disregarded the absence of empirical evidence of widespread abuse of the tribunal system by malicious employees, and started reforming employment law based on little more than 'feels'. It swallowed and regurgitated those four unevidenced shibboleths – *the law is unfair, jackpot payouts are pandemic, tribunals are biased* and *vexatious claims are endemic* – in service of a fundamental re-engineering of the entire system.

And the results were devastating.


With the lobbying cries of employers' bodies ringing around the Ministry of Justice from 2011, a series of pro-business reforms were enacted. The MoJ enlisted the services of Oxford- and Harvard-educated venture capitalist Adrian Beecroft to recommend employment law reforms to help foster a 'flexible labour market', which he did in a report[66] described by Citizens Advice as 'a rogue's charter'.[67] Although the most radical proposal – the scrapping of unfair dismissal and introduction of a 'no fault dismissal' scheme by which employees could be fired at will, for any reason, upon payment of a fixed sum – was not enacted, a number of changes did follow.

The qualifying service for claiming unfair dismissal was doubled from twelve months to two years in 2012, celebrated by the *Telegraph* as 'powers to sack the slackers',[68] in apparent ignorance of the reality that, as we've seen, 'slackers' were already eminently sackable, as long as you went about it in a fair way. This was, more accurately, a 'power to unfairly sack people inside the first two years of their employment', which admittedly has less of a zing to it, and had the effect of removing the right to claim unfair dismissal from 3 million people.[69] A voting threshold was brought in for industrial action (a threshold which, incidentally, the vote to leave the European Union, heralded by then Justice Minister Dominic Raab as 'a remarkable direct democratic mandate', would not have satisfied).[70]

But, most significantly, in 2013, Chris Grayling's Ministry of Justice introduced secondary legislation to impose fees on workers seeking to bring employment-tribunal claims. In contravention of the founding principle of the industrial tribunal in the 1960s, and despite the absence of fees having been identified in an official review as one of the three elements that had rendered ETs a success,[71] a financial barrier was erected. 'We're gonna build a wall,' the MoJ might as well have announced to cheering business leaders, 'and prospective claimants – out of pocket and seeking money owed – are gonna pay for it.'

The stated rationale of the fees scheme was threefold: to transfer the cost burden of the tribunal system away from the taxpayer and onto those using the system; to incentivise earlier settlements; and to disincentivise the flood of weak and vexatious claims about which ministers had read so much in the *Telegraph*.

The scheme separated claims into two types – A and B. Each had a fixed 'issue fee', payable when the claim form was presented, and a fixed 'hearing fee', payable on a date in advance of the final hearing. A type-A claim – which included unpaid wages, holiday pay and other relatively straightforward claims – would cost a total of £390 (an issue fee of £160 and a hearing fee of £230). A type-B claim – the more complex claims, including unfair dismissal and discrimination – would set you back a total of £1,200 (issue fee of £250, hearing fee of £950).

Now, court fees are chargeable in civil court proceedings, but there are key differences. For a start, the fee varies according to the value of the claim. So, if you are only making a small claim, say for £200 owed to you by a customer, you only pay £50. By contrast, under the ET fee scheme, a claim for £200 owed in wages would cost you £390. While that fee would potentially be recoverable from the employer as costs upon succeeding at a hearing, it's a giant initial outlay for a modest, and non-guaranteed, reward. When you add into the mix the fact that 35 per cent of successful claimants who are awarded money by the ET in fact receive *not a single penny* – the employer simply ignores the tribunal's order and refuses to pay – forking out that £390 appears even riskier.[72]

Furthermore, claimants at employment tribunals are, by their very nature, more likely to be in financial difficulties and so unable to meet the upfront cost of fees. As part of the scheme, there was a fee remission system, which the government claimed would ensure that the least well-off would not have to pay. But this was so narrowly construed as to be meaningless. If you and your partner combined had £3,000 in 'disposable capital' *or* together had a gross monthly income of £2,195, you would not be entitled to a penny. To put that into context, it means that a couple each working forty hours a week at minimum wage would not be entitled to a penny under this supposed remission scheme. Or a nurse with thirty years' service, sexually harassed and then made 'redundant' with a 'redundancy payment' of £3,000, would be forced to spend that derisory sum on an effort to recover what she was fully entitled to. Would she? Would *you*? Recently unemployed, with a family to support, with no recourse to legal advice and up against an employer with a well-drilled employment solicitor on his insurance policy – would you gamble your last penny and take a step in the dark into intricate employment litigation?

The likely effect of the Fees Order was obvious. This was not about deterring vexatious claims; it would have the inevitable effect of deterring *all* claims, including the most meritorious, brought by the most vulnerable.

And the government was warned. Repeatedly. It was told, while the secondary legislation was making its passage through Parliament in 2013, that employment-tribunal claims were already falling. It was told that the fees proposed were wildly disproportionate to the median values of claims made, and that the reforms were 'not about vexatious claims'. It was told by MPs that fees would be 'the final nail in the coffin for people who are not represented by trade unions and who are unable to access the justice system'.[73] The government's *own research* showed that those most likely to be deterred were the low paid and those seeking modest sums for unpaid wages.[74]

Lord Monks, in the House of Lords, pointed out that the fees were 'not going to deter the well-paid executive who can see a crock of gold at the end of the case', but instead the 'low paid and vulnerable who will not find it easy to get a comparable job'.[75] Baroness Whitaker, speaking from her own experience as a tribunal panel member, said:

> There is exploitation and ill-treatment; I saw plenty of evidence of people sacked when pregnant or being sexually harassed. They were not glamorous bankers in the way that we read about them in the newspapers but, for instance, three cleaners whose lives were made a misery every day and people who were dismissed without a proper reason. The cases we found proved were brought by ordinary poor people who had lost their jobs. How could they afford to bring such cases under these regulations?[76]

The government had only that year introduced mandatory pre-claim conciliation, requiring would-be claimants to attempt conciliation through ACAS before making a claim; why not wait and see the impact this could have on settlements and the discouraging of vexatious claims?

But the Ministry of Justice, sledgehammer in hand, was not taking its eye off this nut. The Fees Order was brought into law,[77] to dramatic effect.

Claims overall fell by approximately 70 per cent. Despite the *Daily Mail*'s celebratory headline at this chapter's outset, even the MoJ, when it released its belated review into the fee scheme in 2017, admitted that 'the overall scale of the fall ... is troubling'.[78]

The greatest fall was, as predicted, in low-value type-A claims, such as unpaid wages and unpaid annual leave. The median award for unpaid-wage claims is £500, contrasted to the fee of £390. We looked earlier at the right when pregnant to paid time off to attend antenatal classes; if your boss refuses, you can make a claim for the pay that you should have received. This may, in practice, be only a few hours' pay, barely scraping into three figures. In real terms, it's money you can't afford to be without – but are you going to pay £390 to try to chase your £70 claim?

A matter to which the MoJ had had no regard was that a number of claims to employment tribunals don't involve financial awards at all; employees can make a claim where, for example, an employer refuses to provide a written statement of their terms of employment. In such cases, no money changes hands; the tribunal simply makes an order that the employer comply with the law. But such claims still fell to be charged fees as 'type A'. Who on earth would pay £390 to make such a claim? Hardly anyone, it turned out. Likewise, a worker has the right under the Working Time Regulations to make a claim if there is a dispute over the rest breaks to which they are entitled. Even if successful, compensation may not be awarded. This was a type-B claim. Pay £1,200 for a moral victory? Why bother?

In discrimination and unfair dismissal, again it was the low-value claims which were affected. As a result, the median value for discrimination claims rose. Whereas, pre-fees, 52 per cent of race-discrimination awards were for sums below £5,000, post-fees the figure fell to 19 per cent.[79] Maternity claims were particularly poorly hit; Maternity Action estimated a 40 per cent drop in the number of pregnancy-related discrimination claims.[80] As Sir Ernest Ryder, Senior President of Tribunals, said, 'If you are a pregnant woman saving for your baby – for the toys, the bedding and so on – that money falls to be taken into account. All those small capital elements might prevent you from getting remission of fees in an employment tribunal case.'[81]

The stingy remission system worked as well as had been predicted. The number who qualified was 'far lower' than even the government had anticipated.[82] In its damning review into the Fees Order in 2016, the Justice Committee concluded that the regime 'has had a significant adverse impact on access to justice for meritorious claims'.[83]

Initially, despite his promise to hold a prompt review into the impact of the Fees Order, Justice Secretary Chris Grayling refused to do so, in what his coalition partner Vince Cable described as 'an act of remarkable bad faith'.[84] Eventually, after a torrent of criticism, the post-Grayling Ministry of Justice pushed out a report confirming what everybody already knew.

By that time, judicial review proceedings had been brought by the trade union UNISON, supported by the Equality and Human Rights Commission and the Independent Workers Union of Great Britain, challenging the lawfulness of the Fees Order. The case made its way through the British court system until, in March 2017, it came before the Supreme Court. On 26 July 2017, the Supreme Court handed down judgment. It was excoriating.

For a start, the scheme had failed in all three of its stated aims. So many people were deterred from making a claim, the government recovered only a fraction of the costs it had predicted.[85] Far from promoting early settlement, the scheme coincided with a decrease in the rate of ACAS settlements, due in part to employers holding out to see if employees would give up when forced to pay the fee.[86] And, as the government itself accepted before the Supreme Court, the scheme had absolutely no impact on vexatious claims:

'The Lord Chancellor accepts that there is no basis for concluding that only stronger cases are being litigated.'[87] To the contrary, evidence given by employment judges was that 'misguided but determined litigants remain undeterred by fees'.[88]

But it was not just that the scheme was a failure on its own terms; the courts do not strike down secondary legislation simply because it's useless. The real problem – and the grounds for the judicial review – centred on what the scheme had done to the founding principles of our constitution.

The Fees Order, the Supreme Court held, 'effectively prevents access to justice, and is therefore unlawful'. The scheme had rendered it 'futile or irrational' for employees to bring low-value claims. There had been an obvious deterrent effect on the bringing of such claims, not least in light of the poor statistical likelihood of recovering your award, let alone the fee you had to pay.

The court gave examples of people who would be cut adrift by fees and the government's approach to remission. A single mother with one child, working as a secretary in a university with a gross income of £27,264, would have a net monthly income of £2,041. The Joseph Rowntree Foundation's report, 'A minimum income standard for the UK in 2013', assesses that she would need £2,273 to achieve acceptable living standards for her and her child, so she is already having to make cuts to make ends meet. Nevertheless, she would be required to pay the full £390 for a type-A claim, and £720 for a type-B claim (with a partial remission). The Ministry of Justice's argument – that they seriously advanced in a court of law – was that this woman should suspend purchasing clothing (for her and her child), personal goods and services, social and cultural participation and alcohol, for a period of two months, to save the money for a type-A claim. To save for a type-B claim, she should make those sacrifices for a period of three and a half months. Employment-tribunal claims, you may recall, have to be presented within three months.

The Supreme Court was unimpressed, remarking that 'fundamentally, the question arises whether the sacrifice of ordinary and reasonable expenditure can properly be the price of access to one's rights'.[89]

But such was the world in which the Ministry of Justice operated. Accessing rights was an optional commodity, to be added to the bucket list along with that nice pair of shoes you've been dying to buy. If you want that luxury, you should expect to scrimp and save for it.

And it was this mindset – the notion that access to justice was an individual luxury, rather than a fundamental shared right – that was met with particular astonishment by the court, for it misunderstands the entire premise of our legal system and the rule of law. Lord Reed deprecated the MoJ's 'assumption that the administration of justice is merely a public service like any other, that courts and tribunals are providers of services to the "users" who appear before them, and that the provision of those services is of value only to the users themselves . . .'

At this point, I can do no better than paste, wholesale, paragraph sixty-eight of Lord Reed's judgment:

At the heart of the concept of the rule of law is the idea that society is governed by law. Parliament exists primarily in order to make laws for society in this country. Democratic procedures exist primarily in order to ensure that the Parliament which makes those laws includes Members of Parliament who are chosen by the people of this country and are accountable to them. Courts exist in order to ensure that the laws made by Parliament, and the common law created by the courts themselves, are applied and enforced. That role includes ensuring that the executive branch of government carries out its functions in accordance with the law. In order for the courts to perform that role, people must in principle have unimpeded access to them. Without such access, laws are liable to become a dead letter, the work done by Parliament may be rendered nugatory, and the democratic election of Members of Parliament may become a meaningless charade. That is why the courts do not merely provide a public service like any other.

Lord Reed proceeded to offer the chastened government an impromptu history lesson, traversing Magna Carta, Sir Edward Coke, William Blackstone and centuries of English and Welsh jurisprudence to explain, in idiot-proof terms, the value to society of individuals being able to enforce their legal rights through access to the courts. The judgment is available for free on the Supreme Court website.[90] I would sincerely urge every reader to track it down and absorb its magnificence in full.

The Supreme Court's decision had immediate effect. The Fees Order was quashed, and the government was forced to set about reimbursing all those who had made payments under it. The real victims are the many, low paid and exploited, who were unable to afford the fees and now find themselves years out of time for bringing their meritorious claims.

And, again, we find ourselves nursing self-inflicted wounds, as contagious tabloid hysteria convinces us to welcome, and then celebrate, blow after blow after blow to our fundamental rights. We accept without question the unrepresentative six-figure discrimination award lambasted in the *Sun* as indicative of the average function of employment law. We believe the venture capitalists when they assure us that these pesky, gratuitous employment laws are sticking in the gears of our economy, and that we'll *all* be better off if we can stop employers having to pay silly money to slackers taking us for a ride. And we swallow the MoJ's premise that tribunals, and access to justice, are just for other people. Until it bites us, until we hear about our friend being abused by her co-workers for wearing a hijab, or see our ashen-faced husband come home, laid off without notice and with no idea where to turn, or learn that our teenage daughter is being paid below minimum wage and denied holiday pay by her leering, groping pub landlord, we can dismiss the true meaning of the protections we've spent decades constructing.

And lest it need repeating, I say once more: I am not denying that employers have sincere concerns. I am not for a moment saying that employment law is perfect, that there is not legitimate scope for debate as to how and where lines are drawn, and how competing rights and obligations are delicately balanced. Economists would no doubt find me easy prey in a debate over macroeconomics; I don't present the status quo as inevitable or unimpeachable. I understand wholeheartedly, for instance, the concerns that awards for injury to feelings in discrimination cases, even at the mid range, can appear out of kilter with the compensation payable for pain, suffering a loss of amenity in cases of physical or psychiatric injury (although I would add an important caveat that such judgements are best made by those who have found themselves the victim of discrimination, rather than the bastions of inherited privilege who preach from their tabloid pulpits).

I do try, however, to push back against those tired assumptions and lazy clichés which set the tone and framework of debate. *The system is biased against employers. Employees are all on the take. Tribunals hand out jackpot bonanzas. Most claims are vexatious. The reduction of employment-tribunal claims is ipso facto a Good Thing.* Because those myths hurt us. We've learned, from bitter recent experience, how they hurt us. An accessible, low-cost and relatively informal disputes-resolution procedure where employees can enforce their rights in relationships of unequal power – this, we must keep telling ourselves, is vital. Not just to us, the employees, but to other employers. It ensures that the good employers who play by the rules are not undercut by the rogues who seek to gain a competitive advantage by breaching them. Why should the business next door be allowed to boost its profit margins by paying its staff below minimum wage, withholding holiday pay and refusing to make reasonable adjustments for disabled employees? Why is it the business of government to make it harder for these cheats to be held to account? These questions – this framing – one doesn't often see.

And while I don't seek an inverted narrative, casting all employees as virtuous saints and all employers as neo-Dickensian sportswear retailers, I do find it a curious act of self-flagellation that we so rarely allow ourselves to contemplate the possibility that we, the little people, might be entitled to stick up for ourselves. Employment law, the horrified media shows us, permits David to bully Goliath with alarming regularity. That we often read such tales in *Goliath News* does not seem to shake our faith; we accept its bona fides and pledge allegiance to its cause.

But looking where the statistics do allow conclusions – that over half of tribunal awards, *legally binding court orders*, are not paid in full by employers – we can see that other headlines are available to the subeditors. There is an alternative to the jackpot-bonanza malicious-claims reiteration. They simply choose not to give it to us. And we don't think to demand it.

# 5. Our Human Rights

'We all know the stories about the Human Rights Act. The violent drug dealer who cannot be sent home because his daughter – for whom he pays no maintenance – lives here. The robber who cannot be removed because he has a girlfriend. The illegal immigrant who cannot be deported because – and I am not making this up – he had a pet cat.'

Theresa May, Home Secretary, 4 October 2011[1]

As the clock approached 3 a.m. on 7 May 2003, Fiona[2] decided to call it a night. A friend's birthday had been suitably celebrated with a meal at a Soho restaurant and some follow-up drinks at a late-night bar, and the time had come for the group to bid each other farewell, and for Fiona to retire to her boyfriend's address. Her friends hailed a black hackney cab for her, Fiona got in and the cab set off.

The driver, Fiona recalls, was talkative; he had just won a large sum of money and was eager to share his good fortune. He offered Fiona a celebratory tipple, which Fiona politely declined. The driver was insistent, though, and so Fiona, not wishing to appear rude, accepted. He pulled the car into a side street and poured Fiona a drink – something orange and strong-tasting, not unlike Malibu. The driver then got out of the front seat and climbed onto the back seat next to her. There was a cigarette, and a compliment, and an arm around the shoulder. And then everything went black.

Fiona woke up in Whittington Hospital later that morning. Disorientated and confused, she went to the toilet. She realised that her tampon had fallen out, and that her vagina was sore and covered in lubricant. She immediately suspected that she had been drugged and raped. When her boyfriend arrived at the hospital, they made a report to the police.

It later emerged that the driver had enlisted the help of an unwitting member of the public, Kevin, to help him deal with the drugged, helpless Fiona after the assault. Kevin suggested that they take Fiona to the police station, and the driver, whether because of Kevin's insistence or an arrogant confidence that Fiona would not be able to remember what he had done, agreed. Fiona was taken to Holloway police station, and from there, by ambulance, to hospital.

From her prompt complaint that morning, Fiona cooperated fully with the investigation by the Metropolitan Police, including undergoing invasive forensic scientific tests and giving a painstaking video interview. She quickly got the impression, however, that the police were not holding up their side of the bargain – that not enough was being done to trace the driver.

Fiona didn't know the half of it.

From the outset, when Fiona arrived at the police station, no record was made. The police assumed that Fiona was 'either drunk or an addict', and so not only failed to record the details of her initial attendance, but, incredibly, failed to take any details of Kevin or, more importantly, the driver or his vehicle. The notion – well established in the training that ought to have been given to these officers – that a woman presenting in such a state might be the victim of an offence, simply didn't occur to them.

The failures snowballed from there.

Kevin was never interviewed. Fiona even located him herself – but the police didn't bother, despite the fact that he would have been in a strong position to identify the driver. CCTV would have covered the route that Kevin and the driver took when Fiona was driven to Holloway police station, and might have captured the vehicle registration of the cab. It was never sought. The forensic scientific testing came back inconclusive – not uncommon in sexual offences, as offenders usually use a condom and 'date rape' drugs may not stay in the system for very long – but more could have been done; in particular, DNA testing could have been carried out on Fiona's handbag. It was not. Subsequent investigations found that there had been 'an endemic failure' to treat Fiona's complaint seriously and keep an open mind. Officers were particularly influenced by the fact that the driver had attended the police station with Fiona on the night. *Why, if he was a rapist, would he be so bold as to bring her to the police station?* the police asked themselves with a wide-eyed innocence forgivable in a PCSO on his first day, but unthinkable for a professional with any experience of the way in which manipulative, sophisticated criminals operate.

A Senior Investigating Officer should have been appointed at the outset, but only became closely involved months into the investigation. The training and policies in place for officers dealing with allegations of serious sexual offences – particularly where victims are drugged – were seriously inadequate. Those that were in place were not followed. The combined result was that, on 13 February 2004, the investigation was closed, the police having formed the view that Fiona was 'a drunk with a coke habit' and that 'the facts of this case do not support' there having been a sexual assault. Fiona's pleas and her prescient warning that this man would strike again were ignored.

But Fiona *was* raped. And the taxi driver was John Worboys. Between 2003 and 2008, he committed over a hundred rapes and sexual assaults upon female passengers in his cab. He was clinical and conniving, and his methodology was distinctive: he would drug women, usually under the pretext of offering them a drink to celebrate a supposed lottery or casino win, and then seriously sexually abuse them when they lost capacity. When the police finally searched Worboys' car in 2008, they found what was grimly described as a 'rape kit', containing small bottles of champagne, plastic cups, strips of Nytol tablets, condoms, a vibrator, gloves and a torch. He was eventually convicted of a sample of his offences in 2009 and sentenced to an indeterminate period of imprisonment.

However, despite the fact that, following Fiona's complaint in

2003, the police were made aware of numerous similar incidents over the next four years, nobody connected the dots. Fiona's case remained closed. And Worboys remained at liberty to reoffend.

One of his later victims, in July 2007, was Manisha. She too was drugged and raped, and she too suffered a catalogue of errors in the investigation. In her case, the police managed to quickly identify the cab as belonging to Worboys, but inexplicably failed to carry out a search of his home or his vehicle. Instead, they merely interviewed Worboys – before a full statement had been taken from Manisha – and simply accepted his denials at face value. When evidence later emerged that contradicted his account, he was not re-interviewed, the police deeming him to be 'a good chap' who 'would not do that sort of thing'.[3]

The systemic errors overlapped with Fiona's experience: failures to provide training to relevant officers; failures in supervision and management; failures to use intelligence resources; failures to maintain confidence with victims and take their complaints seriously; failures to allocate appropriate resources. Some operational failings were specific: the police (again) failed to obtain relevant CCTV; Manisha's case was not recorded as a suspected sexual offence and her details were not entered onto the relevant database. The investigation was abandoned after three months, only being reopened when police finally spotted the pattern in 2008.

And, of course, the deficiencies in Fiona's investigation had a direct and terrible impact upon Manisha. For, as the High Court would later find, but for the police's failings in the period up to 2007, it was probable that Worboys would have been apprehended, and that Manisha 'would not have been raped at all'.

The impact upon both women is hard to estimate. For Fiona, the worst thing that could happen had been made worse still by entirely avoidable errors by police officers failing to treat her complaint seriously, leading to severe psychiatric harm. Manisha not only suffered the indignity and trauma of an amateur investigation by incredulous police officers, but her suffering could have been avoided entirely had the Metropolitan Police done their job properly in the preceding years.

However, despite the overt and damaging negligence of the police, up until 2014 there was no legal redress for Fiona and Manisha. The law of negligence, which we considered with personal injury earlier, does not apply to police investigations. It is not possible to make a claim for damages for loss or injuries suffered due to serious failures by police in investigations.

Even where, as with Manisha, those state failures led to her being raped.[4]

In 2014, Fiona and Manisha nevertheless brought a claim to the High Court. What's more, they won. The Metropolitan Police, despite accepting that they had manifestly failed these two women, appealed all the way to the Supreme Court, and, in a landmark judgment in 2018, the Supreme Court confirmed that both women were entitled to compensation.[5]

How?

This grievous injustice was not resolved by our elected parliamentarians. No balm was offered by prospective governments in general-election manifestos. Instead, Fiona and Manisha found their salvation in 'the hated Human Rights Act'.[6]

Yes, those dreaded anti-British[7] 'Yuman Rites'.[8] This 'Europe-inspired human rights legislation',[9] which 'undermines democracy'[10] and is 'protecting the wrong people';[11] which has 'devalued Magna Carta';[12] which prevents us from deporting foreign sex offenders;[13] whose 'unelected euro judges'[14] have told us 'that we have to give votes to prisoners and stop sending the most brutal murderers to prison for the rest of their lives';[15] which ordered that an Iraqi insurgent 'caught red-handed with a bomb' be awarded £33,000 for being detained in breach of his human rights;[16] which handed victory to prisoners claiming that 'hardcore pornography is a human right';[17] which 75 per cent of us believe is a 'charter for criminals';[18] and which allowed an illegal immigrant to stay in the United Kingdom because – and Mrs May was not making this up – he had a pet cat. The very same.

Fiona and Manisha were only able to hold the state to account for its devastating misconduct due to the Human Rights Act and the European Convention on Human Rights (ECHR), which, the Supreme Court confirmed, operated so as to impose a duty on the police to conduct investigations into this kind of serious crime in a timely and efficient manner. Where there were failures as serious as these, victims were entitled to a remedy.

But for the Human Rights Act, and the European Convention on Human Rights, these women would have been left completely powerless – acknowledged as victims of the most appalling state failings, but without any legal redress against the system that had failed them.

This story about the Human Rights Act arrived too late to make it into the future Prime Minister's speech at the Conservative Party conference in 2011, in which, armed with the stranger-than-fiction tale of the illegal immigrant and his cat, she told the assembled tub-thumpers that 'the Human Rights Act needs to go'.[19]

But one wonders whether she might have found space for it. After all, she played a key role in Fiona and Manisha's case. When the Metropolitan Police applied for permission to appeal to the Supreme Court in 2015, Home Secretary Mrs May, in an 'unprecedented and highly politicised'[20] move, intervened. She not only supported the Metropolitan Police's application, but made the legal submissions which enabled the police to obtain permission to appeal. Without her intervention, the police would have had permission to appeal refused, and Worboys' victims would not have had to wait another two years for justice.

Mrs May's fractious relationship with the Human Rights Act 1998 is far from unique. Her party has been promising to scrap 'Labour's Human Rights Act'[21] since 2006, when new leader David Cameron told the BBC that the Act 'has actually hindered the fight against crime, it has stopped us responding properly in terms of terrorism, particularly in terms of deporting those who may do us harm in this country, and at the same time it hasn't really protected our human rights'.[22]

A vow to repeal the HRA and replace it with 'a modern British Bill of rights' has been renewed at regular electoral intervals ever since, although is still – nearly a decade after the Conservative Party re-entered government – to come to fruition. The anger towards the Human Rights Act nevertheless shows no signs of subsiding. Justice Minister Edward Argar suggested in 2019 that scrapping the Human Rights Act would still very much be on the government's agenda once the United Kingdom had left the European Union,[23] and Dominic Cummings, the architect of the Vote Leave campaign in the EU Referendum and subsequently senior advisor to Prime Minister Boris Johnson, has promised, 'We're leaving the EU . . . Then we'll be coming for the ECHR.'[24]

But this, as we have seen, is the same legislation that delivered justice to rape victims who would otherwise have been left high and dry by the good ol' British justice system. So what is the truth about our human-rights laws? And why might the government be so eager to take the Human Rights Act away from you?

The principal objections to the Human Rights Act and European Convention on Human Rights tend to fall within three categories: human rights are inherently 'European' or 'un-British'; anti-British judges use human rights to overrule the democratically expressed will of our national Parliament; and, in practice, human rights disproportionately favour the 'wrong' sort of person.

Let's start with some of the basics.

## What is the European Convention on Human Rights?

The first thing to emphasise is that, no matter how many times the *Sun*,[25] the *Daily Mail*,[26] Breitbart,[27] the *Daily Star*,[28] the *Independent*[29] or the former Prime Minister[30] suggest otherwise, the European Convention on Human Rights – and the European

Court of Human Rights – have *nothing whatsoever to do with the European Union.*

In fairness, it's easy to see where, for the layperson, confusion may arise. The European Convention on Human Rights is the invention of the Council of Europe. This was formed in 1949 by the Treaty of London and was focused primarily on values of human rights and democracy. The European Union, by contrast, has had an historic emphasis on trade and economics, with its roots in the 1952 European Coal and Steel Community (which, in 1957, was superseded by the European Economic Community, and then, in 1992, by the European Union). But the various institutions of the EU share preposterously similar names. There's the European Council (headed by the President of the European Council and responsible for defining the EU's policy agenda). There's also the Council of the European Union, formerly the Council of Ministers, which is a body composed of government ministers from each member state.

So, as a running total, we have the European Council, the Council of the European Union (formerly the Council of Ministers) and the Council of Europe. The first two are EU institutions. The latter is not. To add to the fun, the European Union now requires that all member states be signatories to the European Convention on Human Rights, and has also introduced its own human-rights document, the Charter of Fundamental Rights of the European Union (in respect of which the United Kingdom secured various opt-outs).

However, the distinction remains important: the European Convention on Human Rights and the European Court of Human Rights are completely independent from the EU.

The Council of Europe was forged in the aftermath of the Second World War, with the specific aim of promoting and protecting democracy and human rights. The United Nations had adopted the (lovely sounding, but unenforceable) Universal Declaration of Human Rights (UDHR) in 1948, but the nations of Europe, scarred by the horrors they had witnessed inside their own borders, wanted their own enforceable human-rights charter, and a court with the power to impose sanctions against member states who breached it.

The European Convention on Human Rights (ECHR) was the fruit of the Council's labours. Drawing inspiration from the UDHR, it provided a series of rights, freedoms and protections which applied to all citizens across the continent. The universality of these rights is central. The countries of Europe had learned, in the most explicitly violent way, the human cost of denying or infringing the rights of sectors of society deemed undesirable by government. This framework was designed to provide basic minimum standards for each and every one of us, with the express aim of ensuring that national governments could never again set off down the pathway trodden in 1930s Germany. The tyranny of the majority would always find resistance in the sanctity of human rights.

Although described by the *Sun* as 'Europe-inspired human rights legislation',[31] the ECHR had a particularly British flavour. The Council of Europe was something that Winston Churchill had been calling for as long ago as 1943, and the rapporteur of the committee that drafted the convention was Churchill's Solicitor General, David Maxwell Fyfe. He was the Deputy British Prosecutor at the Nuremberg trials and successfully cross-examined Goering and Ribbentrop. At the signature of the convention in Palazzo Barberini, in Rome, on 4 November 1950, Fyfe described his hope that 'our light will be a beacon to those at the moment in totalitarian darkness and will give them a hope of return to freedom'.[32] Furthermore, when the European Court of Human Rights was established in 1959, its first president was a British judge, Lord McNair. All of this makes the common claim that there is something 'un-British' about the ECHR a little less credible than may first appear. When we turn shortly to look at what the protected rights and freedoms actually are, their familiarity rather underscores the point.

# What is the European Court of Human Rights?

The United Kingdom became a signatory to the court (as opposed to simply the convention) in 1966. The effect of this was that UK citizens who believed that the state was infringing their convention rights could bring cases directly to the European Court of Human Rights (ECtHR) in Strasbourg, once they had exhausted the domestic court process.

Today, there are forty-seven signatories to the ECHR and the ECtHR, meaning some 820 million citizens qualify for its protections. There are correspondingly forty-seven judges, one drawn from each member state. The judges are frequently criticised by outlets such as the *Daily Express* for being 'unelected',[33] although it's perhaps worthy of note that no judges in the United Kingdom are elected (we instead have independent appointment commissions), and that judges at the ECtHR are chosen by a procedure involving each country nominating three candidates, and the Council of Europe's Parliamentary Assembly (which comprises MPs from domestic parliaments, including the UK) voting for their favourite, a process bearing the uncanny hallmarks of an election.[34]

Depending on the complexity and nature of an application, it will either be heard by a three-judge 'Committee', a seven-judge 'Chamber' or, in the most serious cases, the 'Grand Chamber' of seventeen judges. Whenever a case is brought against a state, the state's 'national judge' will always be a member of the Chamber or Grand Chamber hearing the case.

The number of cases brought has increased as membership has widened. Around 50,000 applications are lodged every year, although the court filters around 85 per cent of cases[35] (until 1998 there was a European Commission on Human Rights which performed this task), so only a relative handful make it as far as a full hearing.[36]

Where, in the court's judgement, a state has violated a convention right, the state is bound by that decision and expected to take steps to avoid future violations, including amending its domestic law. If an applicant has suffered damage, the court will award 'just satisfaction' – usually in the form of compensation.

## Is the ECtHR biased against the UK?

In 2012, outlets including the *Mail*[37] and the *Telegraph*[38] reported a study by backbench Conservative MPs purportedly showing that the United Kingdom had 'lost three out of four cases' at the ECtHR between 1966 and 2010. In 2014, the *Sun* provided an update, putting the figure at '3 out of 5 cases', a figure which qualified lawyer and future Foreign Secretary Dominic Raab MP dutifully stepped up to condemn as 'staggering'.[39]

In order to arrive at these statistics, the researchers on both occasions chose to ignore the overwhelming majority of applications which the court struck out at an early stage – decisions which were in the UK's favour – and to focus instead on the tiny percentage which made it to a final hearing – cases which, by virtue of having not been filtered out at an earlier stage, were meritorious. As human-rights barrister Adam Wagner put it, this is akin to observing the ten finalists in *The X Factor* and concluding that one in ten of all *X Factor* auditionees go on to win the competition.[40]

A parliamentary report later confirmed that the true proportion of cases which the UK lost in the ECtHR in 2010 was, in fact, 1.3 per cent. In 2012 and 2013, the proportion of cases involving the UK in which the ECtHR found a violation was 0.6 per cent. At the time that the *Sun* ran its piece, the UK in fact had more judgments in its favour than any of the other forty-six contracting states.[41] If this was 'Europe's war on British justice',[42] as the *Mail* had it, Europe was in dire need of target practice.

None of that is to say that the court doesn't get decisions wrong; inevitably, it does. All courts do. But if your hypothesis is one of institutional anti-British bias, I'd suggest the facts – that the institution in question is the brainchild of a British prime minister, runs on rules inspired by British common law and resolves 99.4 per cent of cases in favour of Britain (or, more properly, the United Kingdom) – may call for further investigation.

In fact, over the past two decades there has been 'a significant downward trend' in the number of cases in which the UK has been found by the ECtHR to be in breach – down to only two, in 2017.[43]

And one of the main reasons for this is the introduction of the Human Rights Act.

## The Human Rights Act 1998

In 1997, the new Labour government sought to swiftly make good on its manifesto pledge to 'bring rights home'.[44] For too long, UK citizens had been forced to take complaints of human-rights violations to Strasbourg, waiting an average of five years and paying an average of £30,000[45] – there surely had to be an easier way. So it was that, in 1998, the Human Rights Act (HRA) was enacted with cross-party support, and in 2000 it came into force.

In short, the HRA enabled our domestic courts to consider the types of cases that had previously been taken to Strasbourg. To do this, the Act made it unlawful for a public authority to act (or fail to act) in a way which is incompatible with a convention right.[46] Where this happens, a claim can be made before a domestic court, and the court can provide a remedy (such as a declaration or compensation).[47] In other words, rather than victims like Fiona and Manisha having to book a flight and join the queue in Strasbourg, they could bring legal proceedings straight before a court in England and Wales.

Does this mean that the European Convention and the rulings of the European Court automatically override our own national courts, or, worse, our own Parliament? Simply, no.

Courts are required, when considering any case, to interpret domestic legislation 'in a way which is compatible with the Convention rights',[48] and to 'take into account' any relevant judgments or decisions by the European Court,[49] but they do not have to follow the ECtHR blindly. As we will see, judges can and do depart from Strasbourg case law, to take account of our national laws and traditions.

What if it is not possible for one of our courts to interpret a piece of legislation 'compatibly' with the law of the European Court? Can the courts override an Act of Parliament? Again, no. In cases where an Act of Parliament is clearly in breach of the ECHR, and there is no way for the court to creatively interpret it so that it is not in breach, the senior courts (High Court and above) can issue a 'declaration of incompatibility'. This doesn't have a quashing effect – the courts can't 'strike down' Acts of Parliament – but it does create a mechanism for the courts to bring to Parliament's attention where there is a clash. The courts of course still have the long-standing power to strike down *secondary* legislation if it is unlawful, but Acts of Parliament, passed by our democratically elected legislature, remain supreme.[50]

Finally, the Human Rights Act requires that ministers certify that any proposed legislation is ECHR compliant. But, ultimately, Parliament remains sovereign. If Parliament wanted to enact non-compliant laws and suffer the consequences, no court – either domestic or the ECtHR – could stop it.

So, by 'bringing rights home', Parliament aimed to transfer as much as possible of the decision-making process in human-rights cases *away* from Europe and towards our own courts and Parliament. The right of a UK citizen to petition the ECtHR still exists, of course, once you've exhausted the domestic court process, but the purpose of the HRA was to reduce the need for this to happen. In theory, if Parliament is passing laws certified as consistent with the ECHR, and courts are interpreting existing law consistently with the ECHR and the case law of the ECtHR, it should only be the smallest minority of cases which result in successful applications to the European Court. And so it has proved: applications to the ECtHR fell from 2,047 in 2002 to

507 in 2017. Judgments fell from twenty-four in 2002 to five in 2017. Findings of violations fell from ten to two.

The duties, it must be emphasised, lie on the state: government, public authorities or private organisations contracted to carry out 'public work', such as private companies running care homes. I couldn't make a claim against you, a private citizen, under the Human Rights Act. However, if I made a claim against you under a different head of law – such as employment law or a negligence claim – the Human Rights Act would mean that the courts would have to ensure that they acted consistently with the convention rights when dealing with the claim. Likewise, the criminal courts have to ensure, when dealing with people who come before them, that the trial procedure complies with ECtHR standards.

As for your remedy if you succeed in a claim against a public authority – this depends. Compensation or damages are not automatic; the HRA says that these can only be awarded where 'necessary to afford just satisfaction'. In many cases, the mere finding and declaration of a violation will be sufficient.

So, if there is little evidence to suggest that the European Convention was an un-British conception, or that the European Court is biased against the UK, or that any court – European or British – can 'overrule' Parliament, what about the content of the human rights themselves? What exactly are the trivial, superfluous rights that the convention and the Human Rights Act suffuse throughout our law?

## What human rights do we have?

The European Convention on Human Rights consists of some fifty-one articles and fifteen protocols, but the key provisions are as follows:

— **Article 2 – The right to life.** You have the right not to be unlawfully killed by the state. The state is required to investigate suspicious deaths, and in some circumstances is required to take reasonable steps to prevent a loss of life.

— **Article 3 – The prohibition of torture and inhuman or degrading treatment or punishment.** This applies irrespective of a person's conduct, and extends to a prohibition on deporting or extraditing individuals to states where they might be subjected to such treatment.

— **Article 4 – The prohibition of slavery, servitude and forced labour.** This does not apply to lawful sentences of imprisonment, compulsory military service or work considered to be part of a person's normal 'civic obligations'.

— **Article 5 – The right to liberty and security of person.** This includes the right not to be unlawfully arrested or detained, and the right to promptly access a court to determine the lawfulness of your arrest or detention. It also includes the right to trial within a reasonable time, or release pending trial.

— **Article 6 – The right to a fair trial.** You have the right, in criminal and civil proceedings, to a public hearing before an independent and impartial tribunal. Where charged with a criminal offence, you have additional rights, including the right to a presumption of innocence, the right to access legal representation where the interests of justice so require, the right to an interpreter and the right to challenge witnesses.

— **Article 7 – No retroactive criminalisation.** A person cannot be punished for an act that was not a criminal offence at the time it was committed.

— **Article 8 – The right to respect for a private and family life, home and correspondence.** This includes the right to start a family and to not have the state poke around in your private life.

— **Article 9 – The right to freedom of thought, conscience and religion.** This includes the freedom to change belief and to manifest belief through worship, teaching or other observance.

— **Article 10 – The right to freedom of expression.** This includes the right to hold opinions and receive and impart information and ideas without state interference.

— **Article 11 – The right to freedom of association with others.** This includes the right to form trade unions.

— **Article 12 – The right to marry.** This does not extend to same-sex marriage.

— **Article 13 – The right to an effective remedy if your rights are violated.**

— **Article 14 – The prohibition of discrimination.** Discrimination relating to legal rights is prohibited where it is based on sex, race, colour, language, religion, political or other opinions, national or social origin, association with a national minority, property, birth or other status (including sexual orientation).[51]

Some of these rights are *absolute*. The right not to be tortured, for example, cannot be violated by the state under any circumstances. Others are *qualified*, meaning that they have to be balanced against the interests of, for instance, national security, public safety or the protection of rights and freedoms of others. Where the state interferes with a right, it must generally be for a pressing social need, and must be *proportionate* to the aim being pursued.

Articles 8 to 11 are examples of qualified rights. Article 10 – free speech – is not absolute; states are entitled to impose restrictions, such as criminalising hate speech or incitement to violence. Likewise, as we'll see shortly, despite popular media presentation, an individual's Article 8 right to family life has to be balanced against competing public-interest considerations. It does not provide an automatic get-out-of-jail/avoid-deportation card.

These rights may strike you as, on their face, eminently reasonable – very much the sort of thing you would want in a tolerant, pluralistic country. And tolerance and pluralism are key, because the ECtHR does not demand uniformity of laws, culture or politics among the diverse contracting states. When considering whether a state action is an unjustified interference with a convention right, the court affords states a *margin of appreciation* in recognition of the fact that different states will have different views. The idea is that each state retains sovereignty over how to govern itself and its people; there is simply an expectation that, in doing so, it respects those rights. This much is obvious from the vastly different ways in which contracting states' electoral systems, criminal justice systems and other national infrastructure have lawfully differed since 1950.

On their face, there is little to object to, I would suggest, in the thirteen rights and freedoms above. They have – unsurprisingly, given their origin – a recognisably British flavour. The controversy tends to arise in their interpretation, and especially when the courts appear to extend the ambit of the convention rights. And these fears are neither baseless nor unreasonable; the scope of the convention as we know it in 2020 is far broader than Maxwell Fyfe and his co-authors ever envisaged in 1951. Part of the reason for this is that the convention is treated by the ECtHR as a 'living instrument', to be interpreted to reflect modern conditions, values and mores. And, inevitably, there is proper debate as to what those values are, and the way in which they are divined by the courts as opposed to being explicitly and exhaustively determined by Parliament.

However, I fear that we are too often thrown off track from measured and informed debate over the nature of our protected rights by selected examples of human-rights cases presented as egregious distortions of what the law actually says. Some of the most famous stories are simply lies. The front page of the *Daily Mail* on 15 December 2017 carried the headline 'Another human rights fiasco!' above a story claiming that a 'suspected Iraqi insurgent' who was 'caught red-handed with a bomb' had 'won £33,000 – because our soldiers kept him in custody too long'. The front page carried a rented quote from Colonel Richard Kemp decrying the 'insanity' of 'courts decid[ing] the human rights of terrorist suspects are more important than the human rights of potential victims'.[52] The truth was that the Iraqi man in question, Abd Al-Waheed, was neither an insurgent nor a terrorist (as the court awarding compensation confirmed), had not been caught 'red handed with a bomb' (described by the same court as 'pure fiction') and had only been awarded £3,300 for being unlawfully detained, the balance representing compensation for inhuman treatment (breach of Article 3) after Mr Al-Waheed was beaten with rifle butts, punched in the face, and subjected to abuse and sleep and sensory deprivation by British soldiers while in custody.[53] Following a ruling by the Independent Press Standards Organisation (IPSO), the *Mail* was forced to issue a full-page correction.

The widely reported story[54] that 'hardcore pornography' had been ruled a human right was similarly false – a speculative claim had simply been launched by a prisoner, before being dismissed by the courts at an early stage.[55] Theresa May's cat story – that she was definitely not making up – was, in fact, made up. The feline in question had a cameo role in an immigration case in which the Human Rights Act played absolutely no part; instead, it involved a Bolivian student who was in a four-year relationship with a UK national and was seeking leave to remain in the UK. The existence of a cat was one strand of evidence presented to the tribunal to demonstrate the genuineness of the relationship – along with bank statements, diaries, witness statements and the like – but played no role at all in the ultimate decision to let the man stay. That decision by the Asylum and Immigration Tribunal hinged on the fact that the Home Office had misapplied its own policy when refusing the man's application to remain. The cat, although mentioned in jest by the judge, who said it 'need no longer fear having to adapt to Bolivian mice', was in the end immaterial to the tribunal's decision.[56]

Other causes célèbres rely on selective or misleading reporting to achieve the same effect. Two recent high-profile examples stand out:

1. **'We should not be told by an international court . . . that we have to . . . stop sending the most brutal murderers to prison for the rest of their lives.'[57]**

Chris Grayling, as Justice Secretary, was not alone in his rage when, in 2013, we were told that the ECtHR had banned us from passing whole-life terms of imprisonment on the most brutal murderers. But the court said no such thing. In the case of *Vinter*,[58] the applicants – all serving life sentences – claimed that it would amount to inhuman treatment contrary to Article 3 for the state to pass a whole-life sentence without any prospect of release. The ECtHR said that a whole-life sentence *was* consistent with Article 3, as long as there was 'a prospect of release and a possibility of review'. This is because, in the court's view, the justifications for detaining someone (including punishment, deterrence, public protection and rehabilitation) may – not *will*, but *may* – change over time. Even the worst among us may be capable of making 'exceptional' progress towards rehabilitation. Citing English judges in its judgment,[59] the court said that it was a matter of 'human dignity' that whole-life prisoners should have the possibility of a review of a whole-life sentence.

Now, whether you agree with the ECtHR on this or not, the UK has in fact had such review mechanisms in place for decades. Up until 2003, whole-life prisoners had their sentence automatically reviewed by the Home Secretary at the twenty-five-year point, and every five years thereafter. In exceptional circumstances, the Home Secretary could order release. Since 2003, the Secretary of State (today the Justice Secretary), although not conducting regular reviews, has had the power to direct the release of a whole-life prisoner in exceptional circumstances (usually 'compassionate' grounds).[60]

But, in 2013, the ECtHR said that the rules that governed the ministerial exercise of this power (set out in the so-called 'Lifer

Manual') were overly restrictive and lacked 'clarity'. That is why it ruled against the UK. It *never* said that we couldn't sentence murderers to whole-life imprisonment. Once the scope of the Lifer Manual had been clarified by our Court of Appeal in 2014,[61] the ECtHR confirmed, in a case in 2017, that the English and Welsh criminal justice system was in fact compliant.[62] Applying the margin of appreciation doctrine, this mechanism was a satisfactory way for the UK to comply with its Article 3 obligations. Whole-life sentences could still be passed by English and Welsh courts. The baddest and most brutal would still spend the rest of their lives in prison. All that was required was the *possibility* of review, where exceptional circumstances arose. Where that possibility arises (which is a matter for our government), there is no requirement that any prisoner *be* released. That is all, ultimately, a decision for the UK.

### 2. 'The Human Rights Act . . . guarantees everyone the right to a family life, no matter how depraved their crimes or who they have hurt.'[63]

Perhaps the most potent bane of the tabloid press is Article 8, the right to respect for a private and family life, and its interaction with immigration law. Few cases raise more hackles than foreign nationals breaching our criminal law, only for the government's attempts at deporting them to be frustrated. It is why Theresa May as Home Secretary told Parliament in 2013 that 'some judges have [. . .] chosen to ignore the will of Parliament and go on putting the law on the side of foreign criminals instead of the public'.[64] And why, that same year, she put her name to a *Mail on Sunday* piece entitled, 'It's MY job to deport foreigners who commit crime – and I'll fight any judge who stands in my way'.[65]

And make no mistake – this is a valid public concern. The expectation that a foreign national committing a serious offence should forfeit the privilege of remaining in their host country is enacted in legal systems across the world, and I expect many people would agree with the broad principle. However, it will inevitably be subject to limits. One arises from Article 3 – the prohibition on torture. We don't deport people, however undesirable, where there is a risk of the receiving state subjecting them to that sort of harm, in the same way that we don't send people to their deaths at the hands of foreign executioners. To do so would make us complicit; blood would be on our hands, even if the axe, noose or syringe were wielded by a Saudi, Iranian or American official.

Article 8 is different. It is, as we've seen, a qualified right. It is absolutely not, as the *Sun on Sunday* columnist Tony Parsons claims, 'better than a British passport'.[66] But it is something that courts have to take into account when balancing the public interest in deporting criminals with the individual's rights.

Space prevents a full analysis of the workings of immigration law, but the statistics show that a small minority of appeals by foreign nationals facing deportation – 14 per cent in the year that Mrs May was bobbing up and down in the ring and issuing smack talk to judges – actually succeed on Article 8 grounds.[67] There is a legal presumption that any foreign national sentenced to a prison sentence of twelve months or more will be liable for deportation,[68] and the courts have made clear – again, in the same year as Mrs May's open challenge – that 'it is only exceptionally that such foreign criminals will succeed in showing that their rights under Article 8(1) trump the public interest in their deportation . . . The scales are heavily weighted in favour of deportation and something very compelling (which will be "exceptional") is required to outweigh the public interest in removal.'[69]

But occasionally, in that minority which somehow find their way from the Home Office to the editor's desk, the courts will rule that, even though an individual has committed a serious criminal offence, to deport them would constitute such a grave interference with their family life – would have such far-reaching and severe consequences – that the balance tips in favour of allowing them to stay.

One of the difficulties in aiding public understanding is that most such decisions are made by immigration judges sitting in the First-tier Tribunal, whose judgments are not easily accessible by the public. It is only when cases are appealed to the Upper Tribunal (Immigration and Asylum Chamber) or beyond that judgments are routinely published. But what we can see in the reported cases is that, where Article 8 arguments succeed, the courts explain at great length how the competing interests have been balanced, and how cases meet the 'exceptional' circumstances requirement. It is never, as Mr Parsons thoughtfully told his readers, as simple as a court allowing an Article 8 argument because a 'foreign felon has knocked up some local slapper'.[70]

Often, it will not be the right of the foreign national which informs the decision as much as the right of his children, whose interests, you will recall from earlier, play a primary role in court decision-making. It is possible for people who have done dreadful things to nevertheless be caring and doting parents, without whose love and support a family unit might crumble. If a non-UK national has lived here for many years and has a British partner and young British children who know nothing of life outside this country, the parent's threatened removal poses a horrific, insoluble dilemma. Do they rip the children out of school, away from friends and family, and move them thousands of miles away to a land they have never known, where they might not even speak the language, so that the family unit remains intact? Or does the family attempt remote parenting – a permanent, long-distance relationship kept afloat by annual visits and buffering Skype chats? In some cases, imposing such a burden on the children cannot be avoided. But, in some, it can, and it must.

A hugely controversial case with which readers may be familiar is that of Mohammed Ibrahim.[71] In 2010, the Prime Minister told the country, 'We have an Iraqi asylum seeker who has killed a child and there is no way he can be sent back.'[72] Mr Ibrahim was an Iraqi national who entered the UK illegally in 2001. His asylum claim was refused, but no action was taken to effect his removal. On 24 November 2003, he was involved in a road traffic accident involving a twelve-year-old girl. Ibrahim fled the scene, leaving the child to die under the wheels of his vehicle. He was at the time disqualified from driving and uninsured. He was convicted and imprisoned, but when the Home Office attempted to deport him, Ibrahim successfully appealed on Article 8 grounds. The case understandably filled headlines for months. But much of the vital explanatory context was omitted.

Firstly, although described as the 'asylum seeker death-crash driver',[73] Ibrahim was never prosecuted for causing the girl's death. He was convicted instead of offences of disqualified driving, having no insurance and failing to stop after an accident, which carry a total maximum of six months' imprisonment (he was sentenced to four). While he shouldn't have been driving, and while his conduct in fleeing the scene was cowardly and reprehensible, the Crown Prosecution Service appeared to form the view that the evidence did not show that there was anything in the manner of Ibrahim's driving or his behaviour that led to the tragic fatality. Nevertheless, given that he had no lawful basis for being in the UK, and was in the custody of the state as a prisoner, the Home Office could easily have taken steps to remove him in 2003. But it didn't. Instead, it waited until 2009. In this interval, Ibrahim developed a family life. He had two children and became de facto father to his partner's children from a previous relationship, who 'spoke in glowing terms of [Ibrahim] as a father'.[74] The Immigration Tribunal heard evidence from his partner and the children, and ruled that this was 'a strong family unit, which has been subjected to a number of stresses over the years and has withstood them'.[75] The children were all British citizens and had spent their entire lives in the UK. The judge found that, having regard to the best interests of the children, the disruption and interference in their family lives would not be proportionally justified if Ibrahim were removed.

Now, you may reasonably disagree with this decision. As the Upper Tribunal noted when the Home Office appealed in 2010, Ibrahim's general behaviour was reprehensible, and his persistent criminality 'gives rise to deep-seated and understandable anger not only from her grieving parents but also the public more generally. His presence continues to give pain to [the girl's] family.'[76] You may say that the rights of the four blameless children should cede to the public interest in deporting a man with no legal right to enter the country, who went on to commit imprisonable offences. But it is simply wrong to suggest that this case – or any other – shows Article 8 providing an automatic right to remain. The court at every tier struggled with the difficult balance between the rights of those involved – applicant and his children – and the public interest in deportation. Evidence was called, witnesses were cross-examined and a fully reasoned judicial decision was given, and then scrutinised and upheld on appeal.

Anger might better be directed at the Home Office, which failed to take any action to remove Ibrahim in 2003, when it had ample opportunity. As the tribunal said, '[T]he reason he has become entitled [under Article 8] is the Secretary of State for the Home Department's delay in making a lawful decision in relation to his removal.'[77]

I am of course not suggesting that, in every Article 8 case, the court strikes the right balance. There will undoubtedly be cases in which the public are right to be aggrieved, and where politicians feel justifiably frustrated that undesirable characters are permitted to remain. But to adopt Parsons' Law and suggest that Article 8 is 'better than a British passport', and that the easy solution in every case is to 'kick them out', is in defiance of both reality and humanity. These are rarely simple cases. The right to a family life, although not absolute, is nevertheless important in a way we all, if we think about our own lives, immediately, instinctively understand. The Windrush scandal in 2018 was a stark, brutal demonstration of what happens when due process and human rights are subjugated to populist, kick-'em-out agendas. President Donald Trump's order, in 2017, to forcibly separate 2,000 children from their asylum-seeking parents at the southern border was eventually injuncted, over a year later, by a San Diego judge, but, as Lord Wilson of the UK Supreme Court told an American audience, Article 8 would mean 'that our courts would have stopped the abuse more quickly'.[78]

Lives are overturned by these decisions. It is only right, surely, that the courts give them careful consideration.

The statistics show that successful Article 8 appeals are a minority, but the media don't report the thousands of successful deportations of foreign offenders, nor the majority of cases in which Article 8 is unsuccessfully raised. Instead, by seizing solely on the 'exceptional' cases, those who so desire can misrepresent them as the norm.

And it is in the unreported cases that the everyday value of human rights is often most keenly felt. So we should end where we started this chapter: on the human-rights stories about which we *don't* often hear.

## What have human rights ever done for us?

If I were a modern-day Reg from *The Life of Brian*, demanding my brethren in the People's Front of Judea join my rhetorical denunciation of our invading human-rights overlords, the twenty-first-century conversation would probably echo the screenplay.

In fact, this very conceit made it into a skit in 2016,[79] with Patrick Stewart playing the lead, and while it's fair to say that it's not the sharpest pastiche, it does provide a valuable reminder of what human rights have done for *us*.

We have already looked at the successful claims brought by the victims of John Worboys, but the Human Rights Act is credited with numerous other high-profile victories for victims of injustice failed by the state.

And those four words are crucial, for they underpin not only the theory of human rights, but the motivations of those who seek their destruction. The losing party, in almost every human-rights horror story flogged in the press, is the state. Human rights provide a brake on agents of the state, and in particular politicians, doing as they damn well please. They ensure that, no matter how lowly or poor or unpopular, you cannot simply be trodden underfoot by majoritarian states without regard for what makes you human. Respecting and safeguarding rights may well be inconvenient, or expensive, or a thorn in the side of your most popular manifesto pledges, but that is the point. Behind nearly every human-rights case is an individual standing up for themselves, and a state official trying to make his own life easier. And if sympathy is, perhaps understandably, in short supply for those individuals whose cases spark howling, bile-spattered headlines, it may be in greater supply for some of the following.

The Hillsborough inquest, in which the families of the ninety-six who died in the stadium disaster of 1989 finally obtained answers regarding the circumstances of that fateful day, was only possible due to the Article 2 right to life, which requires the state to conduct a full investigation into the wider circumstances surrounding a death. This meant that the narrow verdicts of 'accidental death' recorded at the original inquests in 1991 could be reopened and a new inquest convened with a far wider remit, including the emergency response, stadium safety, the history of near misses and planning. As a consequence, the jury that heard the inquest between 2014 and 2016 were able to hear much fuller evidence and deliver a narrative verdict answering fourteen questions, in which they found widespread failings in the planning, operation, regulation and emergency response, which led to the unlawful killing of the ninety-six on 15 April 1989.[80]

Article 2 also offered justice to the families of thirty-seven soldiers who died in Iraq and Afghanistan due to substandard Snatch Land Rovers – dubbed 'mobile coffins' – provided by the Ministry of Defence. The MoD spent £750,000 of taxpayers' money challenging the suggestion that the Article 2 duty to protect life applied to the MoD in relation to soldiers fighting abroad, in an attempt to avoid liability for supplying its soldiers with inadequate equipment.[81] When, in 2013, the Supreme Court held that the duty did apply,[82] the MoD belatedly apologised and paid recompense to the bereaved families.[83]

The public inquiry into the scandal at Mid Staffordshire Hospital ('Mid Staffs'), at which 'conditions of appalling care' between 2005 and 2008 led to the deaths and maltreatment of numerous patients, was only possible due to a challenge brought under the HRA. As Health Secretary, Alan Johnson and his successor Andy Burnham were reported to have together resisted eighty-one requests[84] for a public inquiry into the reports of patients being wrongly medicated, treated by receptionists, neglected to lie in soiled bedding and forced to drink water from flower vases.[85] It was only when a claim was threatened under the Human Rights Act, citing the Article 2 and 3 duties to investigate loss of life and degrading treatment, that, in 2010, new Health Secretary Andrew Lansley agreed to a full public inquiry.

In 2012, Theresa May, usually of the view that the Human Rights Act 'added nothing'[86] to our law, nevertheless relied upon Article 3 of the ECHR when she intervened after widespread media pressure to prevent the extradition to the United States of alleged hacker Gary McKinnon. The risk posed by extradition to his health – there was cogent evidence that Mr McKinnon, who was diagnosed with Asperger's, would take his own life in a US prison – was something that the statutory extradition process at the time paid little heed towards. As Gary McKinnon himself said in an op-ed for the *Guardian*, 'Where extradition legislation failed, the Human Rights Act delivered.'[87]

The age of consent for sex between men was only equalised in 2001 following an application to the Commission of the ECtHR under Article 8 (right to a private life) and Article 14 (right to non-discrimination).[88] In 2014, even the *Sun*, four days after its latest headline calling for the abolition of 'the hated Human Rights Act', instigated legal proceedings before the Investigatory Powers Tribunal in reliance on Article 10 (right to freedom of expression), after the phone records of one of its reporters were unlawfully obtained.[89] Likewise, the *Daily Mail*, while publishing editorials headed, 'A nation imperilled by the Human Rights Act',[90] has repeatedly relied on and cited its Article 10 rights in litigation.[91]

More plentiful still are the cases that cross the desks of lawyers rather than journalists, but which transform people's lives for the better. Amnesty offers a list of examples. There's the elderly couple whom Social Services refused to allow to stay together in a residential care home, reunited after an Article 8 challenge.[92] A young man with autism and learning disabilities was kept in a unit away from his father for a year, until Article 5 (right to liberty) was invoked.[93] There's the family who were wrongly suspected by the local authority to be lying about living in a school catchment area, and who were subjected to a campaign of unlawful covert surveillance until Article 8 stepped in.[94] Local authorities in charge of polling stations which were inaccessible to disabled voters have been challenged under Article 14 (non-discrimination).[95] A mother of six, left severely disabled after a stroke, suffering from paralysis, diabetes and double incontinence, was housed by the council in what it conceded was 'totally unsuitable' accommodation, which, due to its layout, left her unable to care for her children and unable to access a toilet. Despite being ordered to move the lady to alternative accommodation, the council did nothing for twenty months. Only a successful claim under Article 8 secured action and the return of her dignity.[96]

In each instance, the reflex of the state was to resist, to fight and scrap and squeal, either to avoid taking an utterly reasonable step that could have changed the course of a person's life for the better, or to defend an unreasonable step they had already taken, which was making somebody's life worse.

Now, of course, these examples do not themselves 'settle' the debate in favour of the HRA any more than the negative stories win the argument against. However, they provide a fuller picture than the dominant narrative evokes, and also help to explain quite why human rights are so fiercely defended by what the *Mail* likes to term 'the human rights lobby'.[97]

For it is here, on the everyday level, that human-rights law has the deepest impact. Far from being a 'charter for terrorists, criminals and prisoners', the figures show that, between 1975 and

2015, only fourteen successful cases at the ECtHR involved terrorists, thirty-five involved criminals, forty-five involved prisoners and 203 involved 'other people' – law-abiding folk like you and me. When the *Daily Mail* ran a story claiming that the ECtHR had ordered the UK government to pay £4.4 million in 'taxpayer-funded payouts' to 'murderers, terrorists and tràitors', it was forced to publish a correction, explaining that the true compensation figure was £1.7 million, and that 'the money went to a range of claimants', many of whom were not criminals at all.[98]

For sure, there will still be a disproportionate percentage of unpopular people making claims against the state, for the rather obvious reason that those we are encouraged to fear most – prisoners and those in immigration detention centres – have twenty-four-hour-a-day contact *with* the state.

But this is the point of rights: they don't only apply to people we like. Rights – indeed, the law – if they mean anything, have to apply equally to all. That's not to say that they don't have to be balanced against the rights of others or against the wider public interest, but we don't ride roughshod over them, nor remove them entirely, simply because a person is deemed 'undeserving'. What a straightforward world Tony Parsons and his columnist bedfellows inhabit, where all justice requires is to draw a dividing line between goodies and baddies, and for the goodies to have untrammelled power to make miserable the lives of the baddies. Hang 'em, torture 'em, separate 'em from their children and kick 'em out. Simples. No shades of grey; no concessions to human frailty. Justice is vengeance. Nothing more, nothing less.

As Lady Hale, President of the Supreme Court, has it, '[Human rights are] premised on the inherent dignity of all human beings whatever their frailty or flaws . . . It may be that those rights have sometimes to be limited or restricted . . . but the starting point should be the same as that for everybody else.'[99]

This has to be right. We are encouraged to forget that, although our rights are individual, in the sense that they apply to each of us, they are also by definition common. It is further forgotten that the engine of law runs on a fuel of precedent; as soon as a decision is made in respect of A, the same decision will apply to B under the same circumstances. We may, in our darker thoughts, care little about whether a suspected terrorist is extradited to a state where he might be executed, or tortured, or might not receive a fair trial; but a legal system which permits this for a suspected terrorist would have to allow it for your partner, or friend, or teenage son whose computer whizz-kiddery lands him in hot water with the security services of a foreign power. Tearing down the edifice of human rights, as we are urged is in our interests, simply because it occasionally results in a benefit to people we don't like, is the politics of the kindergarten. To reinflate a health analogy I've pumped up before, we would not support the abolition of universal healthcare just because the NHS is sometimes used by murderers, terrorists and paedophiles.

And as I've said earlier, and will say again, my argument is not that human-rights cases are all correctly decided, nor that the current framework cannot be improved, nor that public confusion, anger and frustration is unreasonable. Many cases, including those the reporting of which I've criticised, are borderline; a strong argument can be made against the court's decision as to where the margins lie and how the delicate balancing exercise tips one way or another. There are valid criticisms of judicial overreach, and of how the 'living instrument' doctrine used by the ECtHR risks stepping beyond human-rights protection and over the boundary into social policy. I would not seek to stop anyone from arguing the toss.

But I would ask that we conduct that debate on facts, not distortions of the exceptional cases branded as the norm. After all, if the case against the Human Rights Act is as compelling as the government assures us, surely the argument will succeed on its merits, without the need for a smog of misinformation to confuddle the voters.

Because this smog is not incidental. It is a deliberate smoke-screen pumped by those yanking the levers of power and wishing away the resistance. *Governing would be so much easier, would it not, if it weren't for all these damn laws, telling us what we can and can't do from behind our ministerial desks.* Replacing 'European' human rights with a 'British' bill of rights may sound reasonable to the casual listener, but ask the question that no advocate for a British bill of rights has yet been willing to answer: which of these rights, which forty-seven other countries – including Russia and Azerbaijan – find themselves able to subscribe to, are ones we cannot tolerate? Are our values so different that we have no choice but to abandon the court we helped create and join Belarus, Europe's last remaining dictatorship, as the only European state not in the ECHR?

A system of human rights which pleases those who rule over us is not a system of human rights at all; it is a system of unchecked executive power. Yet it is a system we are encouraged nearly every day to embrace. *You don't need human rights. They're not for people like you.* Like Kaa whispering *Trust in me* as he wraps himself tighter and tighter around your chest, the state promises you that it has your best interests at heart. They just happen, funnily enough, to coincide with the interests of the state.

And this sleight of hand, the misconception that rights only affect other people rather than underpinning our common humanity, is a narrative that has been employed to devastating effect, as we shall now see when we consider our ability to access the justice system.

# 6. Our Access to Justice

'Since being established in 1949, legal aid has grown into a
£2billion-a-year industry far removed from its original,
noble purpose of providing Britain's poor with access to
justice. For precious little is now off limits to taxpayer-
funded assistance. Immigrants who have never set foot in
the UK appealing against visa decisions . . . prisoners
claiming their bed is too hard . . .'

*Daily Mail*, 16 November 2010[1]

Little is off limits to taxpayer-funded legal assistance. Whether
paedophile, prisoner or illegal immigrant, if you want to make a
claim, however speculative, the largesse of the English and Welsh
legal-aid budget – the most generous in the world[2] – is there for
you, filling the pockets of fat-cat lawyers with rates of up to
£1,000 an hour.[3] Not only will you get your day in court, however undeserving you may be, but your lawyers will be showered
with cash to guarantee a Rolls-Royce service.

Even after reforms in 2012, introduced by Ken Clarke as Justice Secretary and designed to reduce the legal-aid budget, the
expense of our legal system would remain unrivalled. As Mr
Clarke assured us when interviewed in 2011:

If I manage to get all my changes through the House of
Lords, we will still have *by far* the most expensive legal
system of legal aid in the world. No other Western democracy would make taxpayers' money so widely available for
so much litigation and legal advice *after* I've made the reduction . . . If anyone's running the risk of losing their house

and their home, they will get legal aid, as long as they qualify financially, in other words. All cases of domestic violence, abuse of children, we're still giving legal aid.[4]

And, as headlines to this day indicate, the age-old racket[5] of taxpayer millions being squandered on the undeserving – such as £1 million in legal aid being handed to a paedophile gang to fight deportation[6] – shows that the problem is there is too much legal aid, not too little.

So, listening to the headlines, and in particular to the soothing bonhomie of Mr Clarke, one would presume that Rachel[7] would be OK. After years of serious violent and sexual abuse at the hands of her husband, she managed to flee with their two children. Two years later, after the divorce, he initiated legal proceedings to secure contact with the children. Rachel had a wealth of evidence to prove the domestic violence: a caution for assault which he had admitted; Social Services records; findings of fact made in the divorce proceedings; counselling records from a Rape Crisis centre. Her right to legal assistance *had* to be guaranteed.

Likewise Florence. She was brought to the UK as a tiny child by her mother and abandoned in the care of a friend. Florence had no idea that she was 'undocumented', until, after years of witnessing abuse, she was made homeless and taken into care, aged sixteen, when the true picture emerged. In order to avoid her eighteenth birthday heralding detention by the immigration authorities and potential deportation to her country of birth, she needed to go through a complex legal process to 'regularise' her status.[8]

Or Rita,[9] evicted with her daughter by the local authority from her temporary accommodation after they deemed her to have made herself 'intentionally homeless'. Rita, who was in a low-paid job and receiving tax credits, wanted to challenge this decision so that she and her child might retain a roof over their heads.[10]

Jenna,[11] too, was surely entitled to legal help. She suffered life-changing 50 per cent burns to her face and body in an acid attack, which left her housebound and unable to work. She was wrongly assessed by the Department of Work and Pensions as fit to work, and needed to appeal the government's decision to strip her of her disability benefit.[12]

A legal-aid system as excessively generous as ours would not hesitate to provide legal assistance in these cases, surely? If the winds of fate cast you into these most dreadful circumstances, if you were forced to navigate the labyrinth of our legal system to secure your basic rights to safety, shelter or statehood, you would be assured by Mr Clarke's words that you would get the help you need.

In each of these cases, legal aid was refused.

No lawyer was made available by the state for any of these women. Nor for Florence, a child facing deportation to a country she had never visited. Presenting themselves at the law's equivalent of A & E, they were informed that trained medical care was not included. *No doctor or nurse for you. Feel free to pay privately, or grab a scalpel and have a go at treating yourself.*

These stories are far from unusual. They occur with a tragic frequency that gives the lie to the narrative fashioned about legal aid in the headlines. For that – a lie – is what it is. You – we – have been lied to for years. And we are still being lied to today. We are lied to about who and what legal aid is for, why we have it and how much it costs. And the consequences of the lies, and what they permit those in power to get away with, threaten to undermine the entire basis of our justice system.

## Why do we need legal aid?

The circumstances in which you might need legal assistance are often those you would rather not contemplate. A sobering rule of thumb is that, if you are seeking legal help or representation, something in your life has most likely not gone to plan. Getting divorced, becoming injured, losing your job, losing a loved one, fighting a belligerent local authority or ex-partner to ensure your child gets the support she needs, facing homelessness, having state financial support withdrawn, fleeing your homeland, being sued by somebody, being accused of a crime – the association between our lowest moments and the brilliantine grins of perma-tanned legal professionals is probably a significant contributing factor to many people's aversion to lawyers.

In any of those instances, the importance of being able to access justice – to access the courts to ensure a fair and lawful outcome – is self-evident. The consequences to you or your loved ones if things go wrong can be life altering. This is why our country has, since Magna Carta, prized the right of access to the courts, and to the timely and fair administration of justice, as the principle underpinning the edifice of our system: 'We will sell to no man, we will not deny or defer to any man either Justice or Right.'[13]

Access to justice, although necessarily including access to the courts, does not simply mean the right of access to a physical court building. To return to our medical analogy, 'access to medical treatment' amounts to more than the ability to present yourself at a hospital; it is meaningless unless it also includes trained professionals to diagnose and treat you.

Similarly, inherent in the right to access the courts is a requirement that we are able to understand the laws on which they run. And, absent a sudden campaign of free universal legal tuition, that is going to require access to professional legal advice and, where appropriate, representation at court to ensure that our case is presented and argued as well as it can be.

In many cases, legal advice will be enough in itself. It will either satisfy the individual that there is nothing they can do, or arm them with the knowledge they need to confront and resolve the issue. For others, litigation – contested legal proceedings – will be unavoidable. In which case, if it is to be done properly, so that the individual has as fair a crack of the whip as their legally represented opponents, equality of arms will require that they have a lawyer to represent them in court.

For those who can easily afford to pay for legal advice and representation, there might sensibly be no objection to them being required to shoulder at least some of the financial burden, as long as there is a mechanism for full recovery in the event that their case succeeds. But, where anyone falling under the jurisdiction of English and Welsh law does not have the means to pay, assistance should be provided and the cost shared among all of us. Justice only for those able to pay for it is not justice at all.

That is why legal aid matters. Without legal aid, without access to the knowledge and the skills by which we can enforce our rights, we are voiceless.

However, its significance does not end there. The importance of each of us being able to meaningfully access justice spreads deeper and wider than the impact upon the individual in a given case. We considered earlier the judgment of Lord Reed in the *Unison* employment-tribunal fees hearing before the Supreme Court (p. 129), and the point he makes cannot be laboured enough: the right to access the courts matters not only to the individual with a legal problem, but to every single one of us living under these laws. Making a legal claim is not merely a private activity, of interest only to the parties involved; it affects all of us.

Contested legal cases result in judgments, which become added to the sum of our common law. Some of these cases establish principles of huge general importance – Lord Reed offers the example of *Donoghue* v. *Stevenson*, which is the case involving the snail and the ginger beer that we met in Chapter 3 when considering duties of care in negligence cases. Hundreds of thousands of claims have, since 1932, been litigated, won, settled or successfully defended on the basis of that single decision; many other cases have involved the courts refining or interpreting the principles further, as the shape of the law of negligence evolves and adapts. Another example offered by Lord Reed is court decisions on the interpretation of equal-pay law, which have had life-changing impacts for millions of people beyond the handful of parties physically sitting in that courtroom. The examples in criminal law are manifold, but to offer just one: in 1991, the House of Lords (the predecessor to the Supreme Court) declared that the common law 'marital rape exemption', which had historically allowed men to rape their wives with impunity, was henceforth 'a legal fiction'. 'The time has now arrived when the law should declare that a rapist remains a rapist subject to the criminal law, irrespective of his relationship with his victim.'[14]

But the value of access to the courts extends far beyond the reported judgments of great renown; in our everyday lives, we need to know that the law is enforceable. We need to know that, if a crime is committed, the prosecuting authorities and the person accused have access to the courts for a fair trial to take place. When you go to work tomorrow, you rely on the security that, if your employer is tempted to withhold your pay, you are both aware of your right to go to a court to enforce the contract. When a landlord lets you a flat, both parties need to know that, if the accommodation is unsanitary or unsafe, there is a body of laws setting out the landlord's responsibilities, and a package of protections to prevent him simply summarily evicting you to avoid his obligations. When you buy a new washing machine, the manufacturer and supplier need to know that their responsibilities to provide a safe and operational product are as enforceable as the duty on you to pay the instalment plan. Every day in a thousand ways we interact with and rely upon the law without it even occurring to us.

This is why I say, and make no apology for repeating, that the law belongs to all of us. Even if we have no direct contact with the courts for the majority of our lives, the law is both the engine of our democracy, quietly whirring away in the background, and its foundation – the giant turtle atop which our daily existence is unknowingly, delicately balanced.

# How did legal aid come about?

Legal aid is often characterised as a pillar of the post-war welfare state, although its development was technically discrete from the true 'four pillars' – the National Health Service, universal housing, state security and universal education. Prior to 1949, if you required legal advice or representation, whether in criminal or civil matters, you would generally either have to pay privately, or hope to secure the charity of a lawyer working pro bono (for free).[15]

In 1944, the government set up the Rushcliffe Committee to consider the issue of access to justice, and, after the committee reported in 1945, its recommendations were accepted. The Legal Aid and Advice Act 1949 was the result, with the aim expressed: 'to provide legal advice for those of slender means and resources, so that no one would be financially unable to prosecute a just and reasonable claim or defend a legal right; and to allow counsel and solicitors to be remunerated for their services.'[16]

While initially targeted at divorce cases, the scope of legal aid had, by the 1960s, broadened into other areas of civil (i.e. non-criminal) law, and around that time a system of criminal legal aid also took root. Legal aid was not – and has never been – a universal entitlement. Since its inception, it has operated on a dual testing system, comprising a means test and a merits test. Depending on your means, you would be expected to contribute towards the cost of your legal aid.

Although legal aid is funded by the taxpayer, it is not nationalised. Instead, privately run solicitors' firms and (largely) self-employed barristers carry out the work, at legal-aid rates set centrally by the state. The distinction between solicitors and barristers, to put it simply, is that, if you have a legal problem, a solicitor is your first point of contact. They will advise you and, depending on the nature and complexity of the case, may instruct a barrister on your behalf. Where you have a solicitor and a barrister on the same case, they work as a team, with the solicitor handling the litigation – the legal administrative side, for want of a better term – and the barrister providing specialist advice and, if it goes to court, advocacy services. The common analogy deployed to illustrate the solicitor/barrister dynamic is the relationship between a GP and a consultant (where the consultant invariably takes all the credit for the GP's hard work).

The role of lawyers in our legal system is an active one. The adversarial system, a tradition forged in medieval times to which England and Wales still adhere today, pits two parties against each other in front of an independent tribunal. Each party is responsible for gathering the evidence that supports their case and presenting it before a court, arguing how the law as applied to the evidence operates in their favour. This is contrasted with *inquisitorial* models, as are common on the Continent, in which the state has a far greater investigative function, gathering the evidence for itself and conferring on the lawyers a (generally) more limited role.[17]

A key component of the legal-aid system since the 1970s has been Law Centres. These are easy-access local community centres providing free legal advice and assistance to those in need. Their work includes offering advice in housing, social welfare and employment law, and helping people negotiate the legally and bureaucratically discombobulating warrens of the system, whether it be filling in benefits forms, negotiating debt settlements or representing their clients at court. Each Law Centre generates its own funding – chiefly legal-aid contracts, local authority contracts and charitable donations. They are designed to complement the network of solicitors' firms undertaking legal-aid work, and are crucial in helping people who might otherwise fall through the cracks.

When legal aid was first brought in, 80 per cent of the population were eligible. There were fluctuations in the decades that followed, as different areas of law were brought within and taken outside the ambit of legal aid, but, as of 1979, some 79 per cent of the population were covered. The assumption rested that the remaining 21 per cent were of sufficient means to afford legal advice and representation, so it could properly be said that there was a general and unimpeded right of access to the courts.

The problem that has arisen since that peak in 1979 is that legal aid, like any system in which the state pays for its citizens to receive the services of highly trained professionals, is not cheap. As the ambit of legal aid increased, and as the number of cases being brought before the courts increased, so did the cost to the taxpayer. In the 1980s, the cost of the legal-aid budget became a political issue. Suddenly, successive governments were scrambling to bring the rising total down. Means-testing was tightened, rates paid to lawyers were cut or frozen, and the scope of coverage was reduced. By 1999, the percentage of the population who would qualify for civil legal aid had fallen, in twenty years, from 79 per cent to 51 per cent.

That same year, the Labour government introduced an absolute cap on overall expenditure. While a cap may sound superficially reasonable as a response to increasing costs, its fundamental flaw is that it overlooks the fact that the law is a demand-led frontline service, much like the NHS. A particular issue was that the Labour government was extremely keen on prosecuting as many people as possible in the criminal courts, only to be perplexed at the concurrent rise in criminal legal-aid costs. The cap failed, and the budget continued to increase, peaking at £2.2 billion in 2009/10. By this time, legal-aid eligibility among the general public had crashed to 29 per cent.

The only way, it seemed, that real reductions could be achieved was by doing three things: removing legal aid completely from whole areas of law, such as personal injury; radically cutting the rates of pay; and restricting even more severely the eligibility of those for whom legal aid was originally intended.

And in order to facilitate this, to persuade the population to surrender their hard-won right to access justice, a message needed to be reinforced. Legal aid, the public had to believe, was their bane, not their shield.

The Legal-Aid Lies campaign had begun.

\* \* \*

The success of the Legal-Aid Lies campaign was in its simplicity and its relentlessness. In the latter regard, the movement was assisted by a broad coalition of interests supportive of its aims, which ensured that, whenever the opportunity to inflame public sentiments arose, it was not missed. The front benches of all three major political parties when in government – Labour from 1997 to 2010, the Liberal Democrats from 2010 to 2015 and the Conservatives from 2010 to the present day – have all promulgated the fear and misinformation required to purchase public support for their budgetary ambitions. Raucous backing is traditionally roared by the self-appointed guardians of common sense and anti-political correctness who congregate on the Conservative back benches, but the issue does not divide neatly along party lines. Even when in opposition, in 2010, Labour parroted the government's claim that legal aid was at 'unsustainable levels'.[18] Similarly, antagonistic anti-legal-aid reporting was not confined to the traditional right-leaning outlets generally supportive of lower government spending; the *Mirror*, positioned since the 1930s as a left-leaning supporter of the working class, continues to regularly run headlines inciting outrage at legal-aid expenditure.[19] Add into the mix a ready supply of commentators, pressure groups and think tanks for whom legal aid is an easy cut on the road to a small state utopia, and you have a formidable machine.

As for the simplicity of the campaign, its focus was on two core messages: *Look who legal aid is for* and *Look how much legal aid costs.*

## Look who legal aid is for

When you think of somebody entitled to legal aid, what is the first image you conjure in your mind? Is it, to step back a chapter, a young person with severe disabilities, desperate to be accommodated closer to their parents? Is it Gary McKinnon, fighting life-threatening extradition to the United States? Is it a twelve-year-old victim of child trafficking and sexual exploitation, rescued from her immediate perdition and now seeking asylum? Perhaps your mind's eye brings into focus the iconic footage of the Birmingham Six outside the Royal Courts of Justice, arms aloft as they celebrate belated vindication, their wrongful convictions finally quashed and their seventeen-year prison sentences brought to an end?

Or is your default association with legal aid somebody a little less, well, *deserving*? Do you think of the *Sunday Mirror* screaming, 'Telford child sex monsters handed almost £2.5 MILLION in legal aid'?[20] Or the sullen faces below the *Sun*'s headline, 'AID FOR PAEDOS: Rochdale paedophile gang handed £1m in legal aid to fight deportation'?[21] What about the sinister character lurking behind the *Daily Express*' 'Fury as terrorist gets £250,000 to FIGHT deportation out of UK'?[22] Possibly you think of the protagonists behind the *Daily Mail*-exposed 'abuses of the [legal aid] system by prisoners and failed asylum seekers'?[23] Or the brutal murderers of toddler James Bulger, on whom countless headlines have been expended on the same theme, as per the *Daily Star*: 'Staggering cost of legal aid given to James Bulger killers REVEALED'?[24]

The frequent and uniform tendency to report legal-aid expenditure in the vein above successfully communicates a clear message: legal aid is for the sole benefit of undeserving individuals.

They are undeserving because of their status as society's fallen, and we know it is only such wrong'uns who benefit because we are never told of the millions of 'ordinary' people – people like us, and towards whose circumstances we'd no doubt be extremely sympathetic – who qualify for legal aid. We only hear of the villains. And we know that the public expenditure is for their sole benefit because we are reminded that they 'pocket' or 'receive' or are 'handed' the thousands or millions of pounds alleged to have been paid (we'll look at what is actually paid a little later). But this language is misleading to the point of rank dishonesty. Nobody eligible for legal aid 'receives' or is 'handed' a penny. If legal aid is granted, then the solicitors and barristers involved submit a bill, at the end of the case, to the Legal Aid Agency – usually calculated on strict fixed rates, well below market value – and the funds are paid directly to the solicitor and/or barrister.

It is only because the Ministry of Justice readily discloses the cost of legal aid in individual cases, in a way that would be unthinkable in the context of the Department of Health and a patient, that our understanding in this respect can be so easily warped. The vision we are encouraged to summon and berate is of gold-plated paedophiles, diving, Scrooge McDuck style, into a pool of taxpayer cash, to be frittered away as they see fit. But people eligible for legal aid no more 'pocket' the cash than a patient receiving a heart transplant 'pockets' the £44,000 it costs the NHS.[25]

However, by framing legal aid as a direct financial gain paid to the people we are told to fear and despise most, the narrative succeeds in divorcing us from the founding principles we examined above. Legal aid is *not* a private benefit, nor a public subsidy for a private transaction between a loathed stranger and the state; it is not a luxury to be conferred only on the morally pure; it is the key – the price of which is shared among us – to guaranteeing access to justice for all of us, whatever we've done and however unpopular we may have made ourselves, and to keeping the heart of our democracy beating.

Those immigration cases pursued by terrorists and paedophiles? They matter. They matter because, going back to Lord Reed, whether these men are sinners or saints, the law applies, and the state has to know that the law applies. If there is no means by which the state can effectively be challenged or held to account in the way it deals with immigration law, we quickly find ourselves in the territory of the Windrush scandal, with arbitrary deportations and unchecked injustice. If, as the UKIP MEP quoted in the *Daily Express* 'terrorist deportation' piece says, 'Terrorists have opted out of the system', and it is for politicians to choose to whom the law applies, the rule of law shatters. The same reasoning pertains to prisoners: the law does not cease to matter because of the seriousness of their crimes. The state still has duties to respect the rights of people in its charge. If, but for the grace of God, we or someone we loved found ourselves in prison, we would want to know that the law still applies. That our mistakes, however serious, do not outlaw us and leave us at the capricious mercy of the mob.

The criminal cases – they matter, too. It matters that we ensure, as best we can, that the right people are convicted, and that somebody prosecuted by the state machinery and a highly competent, legally qualified prosecutor has their own, equally competent legal representatives safeguarding their interests. Where the charges are as serious as child sexual abuse, it is all the more imperative that we provide a fair trial, so that, if convicted, we can be satisfied that justice has been done. And, if the argument has to be made personal, it's because you, sitting there, reading this book on the train, minding your own business, could be accused of a crime you didn't commit. The criminal appeal reports are stuffed with miscarriages of justice where innocent men and women lost years of their lives because the state wrongly believed they were guilty. You are not immune. And if it happened, you would want your trial to be scrupulously fair. And you would certainly, I expect, hold no truck with suggestions that you should be denied legal assistance because of the depravity of what you were *alleged* to have done, and the fear of how a bored news editor at the *Sun* might choose to fill an empty page.

What is invariably omitted from the legal-aid coverage is the practical benefit of legal advice and representation. Good and honest lawyers – and there are rogues, of course, but they should be dealt with in their own right – will advise sensibly and act as a gatekeeper to deter spurious claims and caution against the merits of running a particular defence.[26] At court, for all that *Jarndyce* v. *Jarndyce* still occupies the popular imagination of litigation lawyers, the truth is that legal proceedings are better for everyone where the parties are legally represented. There is an oft-repeated claim that legal aid saves the taxpayer six pounds for every one pound spent, and while the evidence suggests that the calculation is not quite that straightforward,[27] it is an observable fact, in every court in the land, that litigants-in-person greatly increase the time and cost of legal proceedings, in much the same way as somebody trying their hand at removing a gall bladder for the first time would take far longer, and create far more mess, than a trained professional. When you consider that many people who are involved in bringing legal-aid claims are among society's most vulnerable, including those with educational needs or learning difficulties, the barriers erected by forcing them to self-represent can be insurmountable.

Moreover, legal representation is often vital to protecting the dignity of those involved, particularly in criminal proceedings. It ensures that witnesses are questioned competently and appropriately by somebody who knows what they are doing, rather than being taken round the houses for hours on end by a self-representing defendant firing a stream of irrelevant, unfocused interrogatives. It means that victims of serious, life-changing offences don't have to be confronted in court by the perpetrator. When the *Mirror* casts a false choice, suggesting that the legal aid spent on the defences of the Telford grooming gang should have been paid instead, somehow, to the victims,[28] it does so in either wilful ignorance or dishonest defiance of the reality that, without the fair trial enabled by legal representation, the victims would have received no justice at all.

## Look how much legal aid costs

From around 2010, a new catchphrase caught on in the Ministry of Justice: *The most expensive legal-aid system in the world.* Barely a news report or Commons debate would pass without a minister or spokesperson for the MoJ solemnly reminding the public that, at an annual cost of £2.2 billion, England and Wales had either 'the most expensive' or 'the most generous'[29] system of legal aid. Whether this was in the world[30] or in Europe[31] varied dependent on the messenger, but the message was crystalline: legal aid was 'exorbitantly expensive',[32] legal firms were 'rak[ing] in millions from legal aid',[33] and urgent cuts – £350 million a year – were required at a time of national belt-tightening.[34]

As Chris Grayling, who succeeded Ken Clarke as Justice Secretary in 2012 and accelerated the cuts announced by his predecessor, told the *Daily Mail*: 'At around £2billion a year, we have one of the most expensive legal aid systems in the world. At a time of major financial challenges, felt by businesses and households across the country, the legal sector cannot be excluded from our commitment to getting the best value for money for the taxpayer.'[35]

This reasonable-sounding sentiment was expressed at a time when what Tony Blair once described as the 'gravy train' of legal aid,[36] as demonstrated by the millions of pounds paid to 'fat cat lawyers',[37] was a regular target of criticism across the media spectrum. And it persisted through the cuts brought into effect in 2012 and through successive governments, with Justice Minister Dominic Raab MP telling MPs in 2017 that 'last year, the UK spent more per capita than any other Council of Europe member'.[38]

But the premise was flawed in two key respects: the 'most expensive legal-aid system' meme was, and remains, wholly dishonest. And the individual stories relied upon as illustrations were – and, to this day, still are – jaw-droppingly misleading.

## The most expensive legal-aid system in the world

Readers of *The Secret Barrister: Stories of the Law and How It's Broken* may recall that we explored this myth in the context of criminal legal-aid reductions, but it was deployed equally in the justification to cut civil legal aid. As of 2009/10, the total legal-aid bill for England and Wales was £2.2 billion. Roughly half went on civil legal aid, half on criminal. And no doubt £2.2 billion is, out of context, a lot of money. But, put in certain contexts, the figure doesn't appear quite so terrifying. For a population of 65 million people, it works out at nine pence per day, per person, or £2.82 a month. The total spending of the entire Ministry of Justice that year – that's everything, from legal aid, to the Crown Prosecution Service, to the courts, to probation, to prisons – was £9.3 billion. Total public spending on health in 2009/10 was £116 billion. Education was £67.3 billion. The Department of Work and Pensions spent £156.15 billion. That year, £30 billion was spent on debt interest. Winter fuel payments, which the government famously refused to subject to means-testing, meaning that multi-millionaires still received their £200 supplement, cost £2.74 billion that year, some half a billion pounds more than the 'unsustainable' legal-aid bill.[39]

But it was the cost compared to other justice systems that formed the central plank of the Ministry of Justice's concerns. *The most expensive legal-aid system in the world.* This claim, it transpired, was based on a 2009 report entitled 'International comparison of publicly funded legal services and justice systems'.[40] The authors analysed the costs of eight justice systems, using data from between 2001 and 2007, and found that, indeed, England and Wales spent considerably more on criminal legal aid (€33.50 per capita) than any of the other seven countries.

The flaws in the conclusions that the MoJ subsequently drew and circulated in the media were astonishing. For a start, eight countries do not a world make. But, more importantly, the report, as the authors acknowledged, was not comparing like with like. The comparator nations – France, Netherlands, Germany, Sweden, Australia, New Zealand and Canada – all had such different legal systems that a meaningful comparison was almost impossible. The adversarial model in England and Wales means that a disproportionate portion of the cost of legal proceedings goes towards legal aid, but the corollary is that our courts' budget, say, is much smaller than that of other countries. Some, for instance, have state-employed defence lawyers, and so the cost of defence advocacy falls into a different budget. Isolating legal-aid budgets and comparing the cost between systems – some of which barely *have* legal aid, but have significant costs elsewhere in their judicial processes – was an act so fundamentally dishonest that it is staggering a responsible government thought they could get away with it. Even more staggering was the fact that this report was brandished as the justification for quick-fix swingeing legal-aid cuts when the authors themselves warned that the sources of the comparative data were 'insufficiently robust to support much in the way of inferences', and that the 'high level of legal aid spending in England and Wales appeared to have multiple causes. This makes it difficult to produce "quick fixes".'[41]

A far better comparative exercise would consider the overall cost of justice systems between nations. And, happily, this is an endeavour undertaken by the Council of Europe every two years, comparing the costs of different aspects of justice systems between the forty-one member states. The 2010 report, based on 2008 figures, showed that, at the time the *most expensive legal-aid system* was being debuted by Ken Clarke, the total annual spending on the judicial system (courts, legal aid and prosecution) in England and Wales was 0.33 per cent of GDP per capita. The average figure among the forty-one countries? 0.33 per cent. We were bang on average, level with Russia and Lithuania, spending a fraction more than Moldova but significantly less than FYR Macedonia.[42]

From 2012, legal-aid expenditure fell sharply – as we shall see, well in excess of the £350 million predicted by Ken Clarke – but, fast-forwarding to 2017, we see Dominic Raab recycling the 'we spend more on legal aid than anyone else' trope, purporting to rely on the Council of Europe figures for 2016. But, again, it is not so much sleight of hand as shoving a dove up your jumper in plain sight of the audience and yelling, 'Magic!' For, as we've seen, comparing legal-aid expenditure alone is an utterly meaningless exercise.[43] Due to the build of our system, we will *always* be spending more than other countries, in the same way that they will *always* be allocating more of their budget towards the spreadsheet marked 'courts'. The *Daily Mail* breathlessly reported in 2014 that, based on 2012 figures, 'We spend seven times more on legal aid than the French,'[44] but found no space to point out that, when you look at the total spend on the justice system, we in fact spent less than France as a proportion of our public expenditure.[45]

The vacuity of the approach is difficult to illustrate, but it is perhaps like comparing the efficiency of a four-wheel drive and a motorbike. It's a peculiar exercise in itself, but a conclusion that there's an obvious problem with the car because 'we spend twice as much on wheels for the car', or that the motorbike needs urgent reform because 'the handlebars on a bike cost exorbitantly more than those on a car' would be dismissed as the ravings of a madman.

Had Mr Raab been interested in a more honest discussion, he might instead have advised his parliamentary colleagues that, as a percentage of overall public expenditure, England and Wales' spend on the justice system (including prisons and probation)[46] in 2016 was 1.6 per cent, well below the median. In 2018, it was the same story.[47]

If raw statistics tell us anything, it is that we have never spent more than the European average on our courts, legal aid and prosecution combined, and, since the cuts started, now spend well below the median. For the government to continue to isolate the legal-aid figures as probative of excessive 'generosity' is purely and simply a deceit.


## The stories we're told

Every good legal-aid horror story starts with an impres-sive-sounding number. Take the Telford grooming gang, who the *Mirror* tells us were 'handed almost £2.5 MILLION in legal aid' for their criminal trials.[48] On a slightly more modest, but still substantial, scale, the killers of Bristol teenager Becky Watts 'received £400,000 in legal aid', reported the BBC.[49] The *Guardian* couldn't resist informing its readers that 'Lee Rigby's killers received more than £200,000 in legal aid'.[50]

Chris Grayling told the *Daily Mail* in 2014 that 'a single trial can cost more than £10 million in fees'. The same article fixated on a single solicitors' firm receiving £15 million in civil legal aid in a year, with another receiving £8.27 million in criminal legal aid.[51] Criminal barristers earn an average of £84,000 a year, the Ministry of Justice announced to the press in 2014.[52] When allied to the headline £2.2-billion-a-year spend from 2010, the desired impression is plain.

There are a lot of tricks at play in this part of the narrative. Firstly, there are often outright lies. A common ploy, where an individual has been deemed eligible for legal aid for different purposes, is to group all the payments and allocate them to the most unattractive cause. For example, the *Telegraph* reported in 2017 that 'a terrorist described as the "very model of a modern Al Qaeda terrorist" has won £250,000 in legal aid to fight deportation'.[53] But that was a lie. For those who read down to the bottom of the article, there's a sheepish disclaimer that the bulk – £210,000 – was legal aid paid in respect of his criminal trial. The deportation fight was funded by some of the 'almost £40,000' granted in respect of 'other cases, including his deportation'. Make no mistake, £40,000 is still, out of context, a large sum of money. But it is less than a sixth of the figure claimed in the opening line.

The *Sun*'s headline in 2019 – 'Rochdale paedophile gang handed £1m in legal aid to fight deportation' – was, according to the reporter, based on information obtained in a Freedom of Information request.[54] I subsequently obtained the same information from the Ministry of Justice. The total spend on legal aid for the deportation proceedings was, as of March 2019, precisely zero. The *Sun*'s story was utterly false; they had simply taken the total figure for the lengthy criminal trials of the 'gang' and pretended that they applied to immigration proceedings.

The second trick is to exploit the (in some cases, fully deserved) caricature of the wealthy, pin-striped, well-fed commercial lawyer, and conflate it with their scrawny poor relation in publicly funded law. On average, lawyers as a homogenous blob do very well, financially. If you have ever paid privately for a solicitor or a barrister – say, for commercial conveyancing or a contested divorce – you will find it hard to believe the claims of penury that you may hear from legal-aid lawyers. But the private/public distinction is absolutely critical. It's akin to the difference in income between Premier League footballers and their League Two counterparts.

Commercial solicitors and barristers, working in the City on multi-million-pound company litigation, can bill an hourly rate which usually ranges between the hundreds of pounds to the thousands. And while there may, I hear from colleagues who were practising in the 1980s, have been shades of a similar mentality at play in legal aid in bygone years, in the twenty-first century, in both criminal and civil law, things are completely different. For a start, despite the allusion that legal-aid barristers pluck a figure out of the air and whizz a six-figure invoice to the taxpayer at the end of a case, the fees are fixed by the Legal Aid Agency, at what you may consider to be surprisingly low rates. Many cases, especially in crime, now attract a fixed fee for the solicitor and/or barrister, meaning that, irrespective of how much time a case takes you to prepare, you receive the same fee. For the types of case in which hourly rates do apply, they work out as *far* more generous than fixed fees (which can result in hourly rates below minimum wage), but the hourly rate still hovers around the £50 to £70 mark in civil,[55] and the £39 mark in crime.[56] While that may appear an attractive headline figure, it is gross income, not profit. For solicitors' firms, the fee has to cover all overheads – wages, support staff, office rent, utilities, professional insurance, IT equipment, professional subscriptions, training and all the associated costs of being an employer, and then, of course, tax. For barristers, most of whom are self-employed, it is a similar story. My gross income has to pay for my chambers expenses (such as the wages of my clerks and support staff), chambers rent, travel, insurance, practising certificate (I pay several hundred pounds a year for the privilege of doing my job), legal textbooks, ongoing training, wig, gown, subscriptions, as well as tax. To give context, I take home just under 38 per cent of my gross income.

The claim by the Ministry of Justice that criminal barristers 'earn £84,000 a year on average' was false, and the UK Statistics Authority rapped the government's knuckles for 'misleading' the public by publishing figures which not only included VAT (which, of course, goes back to the Treasury), but by deliberately excluding all the low earners to skew the average.[57] The true median figure in 2014 was in fact a net income of around £27,000 a year.[58] Not small beans, but hardly in keeping with the impression Mr Grayling was eager to create.

That is not to deny that some legal-aid barristers do very well – like anyone at the top of their profession, the superstars involved in the most serious and complex criminal and civil cases will be well rewarded. But this is a fraction of the incomes of their commercial law counterparts. And, to put one flagrant untruth to bed, the *Sun*'s suggestion of any link between legal aid and lawyers charging '£1,000 an hour' is wholly dishonest.[59] At best, that will be the figure chargeable to private-paying criminal clients, such as multinational corporations accused of regulatory or white-collar offences, and will never, ever be footed by the taxpayer.

The third trick is that, where the legal-aid figures quoted for a particular case are accurate, the context is deliberately stripped out. You are not told how the figure was calculated, nor what it represents. You are not told that it includes, for instance, fees paid to medical or scientific experts involved in the case. You are not told that it includes VAT at 20 per cent, which is money that ultimately finds its way back to the Treasury. You are not told what work went into that particular case – how many lawyers, working how many hours – so that you can assess whether it's an outrageous extravagance or fair professional remuneration.

If it is a simple matter, involving minimal work, in which a very junior legal-aid lawyer is bringing home several hundred pounds an hour, there may well be justifiable cause for concern. Even if it is an extremely serious case, involving QCs and issues of life and limb, I would accept that there will be a rate at which, compared to other publicly funded professionals, it can be argued that the legal-aid scheme is operating too generously towards the lawyers.

But you are never provided with that context, only ever the bare figures, from which you are urged to agree that Something Is Wrong. It's a con.

Fourthly, in the criminal legal-aid field, a common favourite is to present a fabulously wealthy defendant and decry 'multi-millionaire criminals claiming a fortune from legal aid'.[60] Under means-testing, nobody with a joint disposable income of £37,500 or more is entitled to criminal legal aid. However, what has almost always happened in these cases is that the prosecution has successfully applied to have the defendant's assets and bank accounts restrained, so that the defendant can't dissipate the contents, and the prosecution can confiscate the assets as the 'proceeds of crime' upon a conviction. This means that the defendant can't access his assets to pay for legal representation and so he qualifies for legal aid, even though he is notionally very rich indeed. However, if the defendant is convicted, those legal-aid costs will invariably be reimbursed from his restrained assets. So, the taxpayer does not lose a penny. That minor, but rather important, detail is often omitted.

Fifthly, and finally, in a familiar move, the myth relies on the public believing that these few high-profile, high-spend cases are representative of the norm. The solicitors' firms turning over millions each year will be the biggest firms with staffs of thousands. The average criminal legal-aid solicitors' firm operates on profit margins of 5 per cent, with 50 per cent of firms assessed by an independent report in 2014 as 'at medium or high risk of financial difficulty'.[61] The cases in which hundreds of thousands, or millions are paid will be the lengthiest, most serious and most complex of their type, requiring months, if not years of work by numerous professionals.

According to the most recent figures, the average cost of a legal-aid case in England and Wales is €1,325, or £1,165.[62] That includes all legal advice, all legal representation and any other disbursements – such as expert fees – incurred in the proceedings.

Many cases – including serious and complex cases – are resolved with barely a few hundred pounds of taxpayers' money being spent. It happens every day, inside and outside courtrooms across the land. You're just not told about it.

None of this is to say, of course, that there are no problems with legal aid, and that there is never any public interest in reporting cases that might cause the public concern. It is only right that, given limited resources, there be some restraints, and that taxpayer money is not frittered on obviously vexatious civil claims, or conferred on wealthy criminals who have no need for it. Nor do I pretend that the efficiency of our system as a whole shouldn't be scrutinised – that is the very function of the media and those in power.

But the arguments that we are fed and are encouraged to adopt aren't based on evidential rigour or honest philosophy; they are myths, lies and distortions which service a defined agenda, namely the blunt reduction of legal aid, irrespective of the merits of this course, or of the dangers.

And with the twin myths – *Look who legal aid is for* and *Look how much legal aid costs* – burned into the public psyche, the government in 2012 put its grand plan into action.

The Legal Aid, Sentencing and Punishment of Offenders Act 2012 (LASPO) was the flagship legislative reform of the governmental agenda to reduce the budget of the Ministry of Justice, which, between 2010 and 2020, it achieved to a greater extent than any other government department – a cut of 40 per cent. As the title suggested, legal aid was uppermost in the MoJ's sights, and, confident that the *most expensive legal-aid system* myth had been swallowed, Justice Secretary Chris Grayling set about his 'reforms'.

To achieve the usual anodyne-sounding objective of 'deliver[ing] better overall value for money for the taxpayer',[63] LASPO reached for a buzz saw and cleaved legal aid entirely from swathes of civil law, including claims against public authorities;

most clinical negligence; consumer law; compensation for criminal injuries; education; most employment law; private family law; housing; immigration; prison law and most welfare law.

To the government, these were simply abstract categories of legal practice on a spreadsheet. But in the real lives of real people, it was removing support from children suffering catastrophic injuries due to medical negligence; rape victims seeking redress; parents like Chris Gard and Connie Yates facing losing their baby; single parents at the mercy of predatory rogue landlords; desperately sick or disabled people screwed over by the incompetent bureaucracy of the Department of Work and Pensions. People whose lives didn't need to be made any harder.

LASPO also drastically changed the means-testing to bring down the number of people who would be eligible for legal aid for the few areas of law still covered. Previously, if you received means-tested welfare benefits, you would automatically qualify for legal aid, it being recognised that you were clearly of limited means. LASPO changed that. It introduced a capital means test that took into account the equity in your home (which benefits means tests exclude), the assumption being that, if justice mattered that much to you, you should sell the roof over your head. The income means test was set so low, and the contributions that people had to pay were so high, that an independent report concluded, 'Many people living substantially below [the minimum income standard] are excluded from legal aid entirely or are awarded it but required to make contributions that bring their income even further below [that standard].'[64]

To keep a rein on access to legally aided early advice and representation for people concerned about discrimination, debt or special educational needs (SEN), the government introduced a mandatory 'telephone gateway'. Anyone with a legal problem in those areas had to ring a government helpline, where they would be assessed by a telephone operator without legal training to see whether they qualified to be referred to another (legally trained) operator, who would determine whether the individual was deserving of face-to-face legally aided advice. The referral rate for this service spoke to its true purpose: in 2016–17, not a single discrimination case was referred through the gateway for legally aided advice. One case of SEN was referred. The number of people calling the gateway for debt advice was 90 per cent lower than the government had forecast.[65] A parliamentary report in 2016 expressed 'concern that this has created barriers for people for whom telephone advice is not appropriate, including those with physical and mental health conditions and those whose first language is not English'.[66]

An 'exceptional case funding' mechanism existed to ensure that nobody fell through the cracks. We saw such a mechanism with the employment-tribunal fee scheme in Chapter 4, and how well that worked. LASPO was no better. The government promised when debating the bill in Parliament that between 5,000 and 7,000 cases would be funded per year. In 2017, the total was 954.[67] Part of the reason was that the government had made the application forms so complex that it took *lawyers* three to four hours to complete.[68] Many of the people reliant on – *desperate for* – this safety net had vulnerabilities, including mental-health and learning difficulties. The government knew this when it designed this hideously complex bureaucratic process. It gave these people no chance.

The combined consequences were vivid. The number of people accessing civil legal aid plummeted by 82 per cent in eight years. The savings were successful beyond the Treasury's wildest dreams: forget the £350 million the MoJ had promised to save, legal aid was so restricted that, by 2018, spending had fallen by 37 per cent to £1.6 billion, over double the savings expected.[69] Mr Grayling was able to bow out as Justice Secretary in 2015 believing he had accomplished his mission.

History would quickly prove him wrong.

The effect on 'private family law' cases was perhaps the loudest canary in the mine. When legal aid was removed from these proceedings – which include divorce, applications for restraining orders[70] and child contact – the government's solemn vow was that victims of domestic violence would still qualify (as long as they satisfied the stringent means test). But the conditions that the government attached, which required narrow and specific forms of evidence that many victims of serious domestic and sexual violence simply could not obtain, rendered the exemption a dead letter for many. The example of Rachel at the start of the chapter was a real case brought before the Court of Appeal, in which the charity, Rights of Women, sought a judicial review to challenge the legality of the regulations that specified these evidential conditions. The Ministry of Justice fought the challenge all the way, so desperate was it to exclude as many potential victims as possible from legal aid, but the Court of Appeal ruled in 2016 that the MoJ's scheme operated 'in a completely arbitrary manner'.[71] Eventually, in late 2017, the government announced plans to relax the criteria.[72]

But that, of course, is only half the problem. Because, even if an abused partner is legally represented, they will, in contested legal proceedings, usually give evidence in court, and be cross-examined by the other side. And if the other side is not legally represented, this can lead to the appalling – and, for a victim, terrifying – situation where an abuser is cross-examining their victim in person. In the criminal courts, there is a legal prohibition against alleged perpetrators cross-examining their alleged victims in person in cases of this type, and, if a defendant is unrepresented, the court will appoint an independent advocate for the specific purpose of cross-examining the complainant. But no such provision existed in the family courts in 2012. So, when LASPO kicked in, family judges were confronted with countless cases where women who had complained of rape and serious violence were being subjected to direct cross-examination by the men who they alleged had abused them. As Women's Aid point out, 'Allowing a perpetrator of domestic abuse who is controlling, bullying and intimidating to question their victim when in the family court regarding child arrangement orders is a clear disregard for the impact of domestic abuse, and offers perpetrators of abuse another opportunity to wield power and control.'[73]

Family judges spoke out in cases that resonated around the legal echo chamber, but struggled to make a dent in the public consciousness. As Mr Justice Hayden said, 'It is a stain on the reputation of our family justice system that a judge can still not prevent a victim being cross examined by an alleged perpetrator . . . [T]he process is inherently and profoundly unfair. I would go further, it is, in itself, abusive.'[74]

Mr Justice Bodey went even further still: 'I find it shaming that in this country, with its fine record of justice and fairness, that I should be presiding over such cases.'[75] The government promised to address the issue, but the proposed legislative reform in 2017 found itself the victim of Theresa May's snap election and was lost in the wash. It took until 2019 for the government to bother to revisit it.

Meanwhile, the number of litigants-in-person soared. In 2012–13, 42 per cent of parties in private family law cases were unrepresented. By 2016–17, this had increased by 50 per cent, to 64 per cent.[76] Only 20 per cent of hearings saw both parties represented; in more than a third, nobody was represented. The government's bold intention that parties would be encouraged to take up mediation instead of litigation flopped, with both uptake rates and success rates falling significantly, partially because there were no lawyers to signpost warring parties to mediation services. The rise in litigants-in-person was not just confined to the family courts; the Personal Support Unit, which assists litigants-in-person, helped 7,000 people in 2010–11. By 2017–18, the number was over 65,000.[77] When investigative journalist Emily Dugan tried to obtain an MoJ-commissioned report, which contained comments from judges highly concerned about litigants-in-person in the criminal courts, the MoJ tried to bury it.[78]

Away from family law, housing and welfare law was particularly badly hit. Both are highly technical and complex areas of law – alienating enough to lawyers in other fields, like me; utterly incomprehensible to many of the people who rely on them.

In housing, there was a 58 per cent fall in 'legal help' (legally aided advice, as distinct from representation at court) between 2012/13 and 2018. Almost all areas of housing law advice were removed from the scope of legal aid,[79] leaving families at the mercy of rogue landlords. Previously, if your rental property was falling into disrepair, a housing lawyer could send a letter of claim to your landlord, which would usually prompt him to take action. The cost of this was £157 plus VAT.[80] Now, unless the disrepair poses 'serious risk of harm to health and safety' – a high threshold – you would be ineligible for assistance. As homelessness increased, LASPO removed legal help for housing benefit claims and for issues such as rent and mortgage arrears, making it just that little bit more likely that those clinging onto the bottom rung of society would fall off completely.

As a consequence of the cuts, the number of legal-aid providers specialising in housing fell by a third, creating 'legal advice deserts' – huge areas of the country where there are no legal-aid providers at all. As of 2018, for example, there was not a single housing legal-aid provider in the whole of Surrey, Shropshire or Suffolk. Law Centres, crucial sources of free advice for many, saw their incomes fall by 50 per cent, forcing many to close. Between 2013 and 2019, half of all Law Centres and not-for-profit legal advice services shut their doors.[81] Low-income families seeking help are now forced to travel long distances to other counties, at their own expense. Many just can't.

Legal aid for welfare benefit law saw the greatest decline: over 99 per cent. Legal help, which provided support to people challenging benefits decisions in the tribunals – such as those who are wrongly sanctioned or assessed as ineligible for disability benefits – was slashed from 82,500 cases in 2012 to fifteen – *fifteen* – in 2014. The government readily admitted that the removal of legal aid from most welfare law would have 'a disproportionate impact on disabled people',[82] but considered it a price worth paying. The Law Centres Network, in its evidence to the Bach Commission, which was set up to examine the effect of LASPO, said its experience was that 'major social security reforms and an increasingly punitive approach from DWP have led to a sharp rise in inaccurate decisions and benefit sanctions'.[83] The removal of legal aid created a perfect storm. One of many affected was Jenna, the victim of an acid attack whom we met in the introduction to this chapter, whose disability benefits the government wrongly tried to stop. She was only able to secure the overturning of the DWP's monstrous mis-assessment of her needs thanks to the pro-bono efforts of a Law Centre, which helped her take the case to a tribunal.

In June 2018, British citizens were as outraged as their trans-atlantic counterparts to learn that, in President Trump's America, children were being forced to represent themselves in deportation proceedings.[84] But, thanks to LASPO, we had been requiring non-British national children to do the same thing. While *millions-of-pounds-to-terrorists-claiming-Article-8* head-lines sought to give an impression of unrestrained largesse in this arena, statistics show that, even before LASPO, England and Wales spent a much smaller portion of its legal-aid budget – 2 per cent – on immigration cases than most comparable countries, such as Belgium (17 per cent) and the Netherlands (13 per cent).[85] After the changes, nobody, not even children, could seek publicly funded legal help or representation – or disbursements, such as translators – in most cases of non-asylum immigration and all cases where the right to a family life under Article 8 was pleaded as the grounds to remain.

This meant that children such as Florence in the chapter's introduction were denied help. If they wished to remain in the country they'd lived in for as long as they could remember, they would have to self-represent in complex legal proceedings, poten-tially taking on Home Office lawyers in court.

It also meant that adults with genuine and worthy cases – people who had lived in Britain for decades, but who were lacking the correct documentation – were powerless to challenge arbitrary, unfair and unlawful decisions by the Home Office. Anyone caught up in the Windrush scandal would need to find the money for private legal fees, on top of the £2,389 application fee for indefinite leave to remain. Before she resigned as Home Secretary in 2018, Amber Rudd took the time to inform Parlia-ment that she still did not see good reason to reconsider the legal-aid cuts in this area.[86]

In August 2018, following a legal challenge, the government belatedly agreed to change the rules to bring unaccompanied children back within the scope of immigration legal aid.[87] The damage that was done to thousands of children[88] in the intervening years, however, is probably irremediable.

We've touched, above, on a few legal challenges that arose as a result of LASPO and its associated regulations, but there were many more. There was a successful challenge to the 'exceptional case funding' criteria in 2014. The attempt to restrict the grant of legal aid to those who had been resident in the UK for at least a year was deemed unlawful (April 2016), as were the cuts to legal aid for prisoners (April 2017).

The response of the Ministry of Justice to being told repeatedly by the courts that it was acting unlawfully was not as contrite as you might hope. Chris Grayling penned an op-ed in the *Daily Mail* blasting 'Left-wing campaigners' launching judicial reviews to thwart his department,[89] and promptly introduced restrictions on the ability of citizens to apply for judicial review. The criteria for granting legal aid in judicial review cases was tightened, choking off 50 per cent of claims between 2013 and 2017. A House of Commons report in 2018 expressed concern that, 'very clearly these changes are cutting into cases where there is a valid human rights concern and where access to justice is required'.[90]

But the government had its wish: legal aid removed, stopping millions of people from challenging the state. And a double lock achieved by preventing people challenging the decision to remove it.

And, to return to where we started this chapter, this assault on access to justice did not only affect the individuals directly involved – the vulnerable and destitute exiled from the law's protections. It affected us all. LASPO was an act of gross constitutional vandalism, scything at the legal ties that bind us. The devastation lies not merely in the individual lives ruined, nor the people cut adrift from their own courts, but in the denigration of our whole justice system. The cases never pursued; the judgments never written; the claims lost, which might have been won if only for the availability of a qualified lawyer to make the arguments; the precedents never set; the unjust laws and policies never challenged. Negligent landlords and uncaring state jobsworths and self-serving ministers were granted a free pass, as they saw their victims' shields torn from their hands. Our society is both reflected and landscaped by what takes place in our courtrooms. The damage done by LASPO is incalculable.

The government was warned. Time and time again. By MPs, peers, charities, lawyers, judges. Its own Civil Justice Council, the body set up to advise the government on civil justice matters, cautioned against the cuts. But the government didn't care. And the MoJ conceded as much in 2014. Its senior civil servants admitted before the House of Commons Public Accounts Committee that the Ministry of Justice had not conducted *any* research before bringing in the LASPO cuts. It had not considered, for instance, the knock-on costs to other areas of government spending. It did not research whether, in removing £2 million of legal aid for housing early advice, the Ministry was creating £100 million of mental-health costs for the NHS to pick up. 'The government was explicit it needed to make these changes swiftly,' MoJ permanent secretary Ursula Brennan told MPs. 'It was not possible to do research about the current regime.' When asked what evidence had been considered, the response came: 'The evidence required was that government said we wish to cut the legal aid bill.'[91]

And this, in fairness, was clear from 2010. When the Civil Justice Council's concerns that costs would be shifted to the NHS were put to Ken Clarke in an interview, he airily dismissed them as 'campaigning nonsense', falling back on the *most-expensive-legal-aid-system* chestnut.[92] As concern grew once Chris Grayling accelerated the cuts to criminal legal aid, the *Mail* reassured its readers that 'it is hugely misleading to suggest Mr Grayling's reforms are designed to target the poor and vulnerable. Rather they will reduce the income of some of the best paid lawyers in the land, stop prisoners making frivolous claims against the State and turn off the legal aid tap to the very wealthy.'[93] Leo McKinstry, in the *Express*, pooh-poohed the suggestion that the cuts undermined the rule of law, chuckling that 'this kind of alarmist talk could hardly be more absurd'.[94]

But it wasn't alarmist. It wasn't absurd. It was correct. Real and lasting damage was being done to the fabric of our justice system. The people who needed legal aid to enforce their rights were being consciously and deliberately cut adrift. And lives were ruined as a result.

I have spent most of this chapter in the past tense, as if LASPO and its effects are a shameful aberration in our history, but this is very much our present. Right now, if you are unfairly dismissed from your work, you are on your own. If, unable to navigate the employment-tribunal system without legal help, you fall back on the safety net of the state and receive benefits, and the obnoxious DWP wrongly sanctions you, you are on your own. If your house falls into disrepair and your landlord unlawfully refuses to fix it, you are on your own. If, as a consequence, you fall ill through stress and are unable to work, but are erroneously declared fit to work by an incompetent private contractor and lose your Employment Support Allowance, you're on your own. If you become the victim of a serious crime and need compensation to try to piece together your shattered life, you're on your own. If, heaven forbid, you lose your husband or wife or child in a terrible accident and there is an inquest, the state will pay for lawyers to represent its police officers or its officials. But not for bereaved families. You are on your own.[95]

Chair of the Public Accounts Committee Margaret Hodge described the MoJ's approach to LASPO as one of 'endemic failure'. She was probably too kind. It was a concerted campaign, years and governments in the making, to deceive the electorate about legal aid in order to make the lives of those in power that little bit more comfortable. That ministers such as Dominic Raab were, even post-LASPO, still peddling the *most-expensive-legal-aid-system* myth, and that even when the government, in

2019, finally published, nearly a year late, its post-implementation review into LASPO, then-Justice Secretary David Gauke still, in the first paragraph of his foreword, defended the reforms and cited the long-gone £2 billion legal-aid budget,[96] suggests that candour and sincerity in discussions about legal aid are still a bridge too far for the Ministry of Justice. Having sliced roughly a billion from legal aid,[97] the government's solution to the problems identified was to reinvest a total of £8 million, not even rice-papering over the seismic cracks.

'The thing that really distressed me,' Margaret Hodge told the MoJ in 2014, 'is how you embarked on this with so little evidence. When you were changing the rules, you had no idea the impact it would have.'[98] Now the government knows the impact, and still sticks resolutely to its guns, the only available interpretation is that it simply doesn't care.

# 7. Our Liberty

In this chapter, I want to talk about my particular area of daily practice – criminal justice. For those who have read *The Secret Barrister: Stories of the Law and How It's Broken*, the territory trodden may have a familiar feel, but the focus here is different. Rather than concentrating on how criminal justice works (or doesn't work) in practice, over the following pages we will look at the way in which we discuss criminal justice, and the stories we tell ourselves – and are told by our betters – about who it is for.

For crime, perhaps more than any other area of law, is something on which almost everybody has a strong opinion. And it is understandable why the subject of criminal justice often provokes such heightened, visceral responses. Criminal offences are the most serious and most affecting breaches of our legal code. At the highest end, they force us to confront unimaginable truths about what we are capable of doing to each other. Even at the lowest end, crimes by their very nature represent such grave wrongdoings against the rights of others or society that the state cannot stand by. It is not enough to – as we do with the civil law – signpost the wronged party in the direction of a courtroom and invite them to assume the responsibility and cost of litigation, if they feel strongly enough about seeking redress. Instead, the state swoops in to remove the dispute from the citizens and feed it through the machinery of the criminal justice system. Private citizens retain a role, as a complainant and/or witness, but their pain and suffering is municipalised; the case passes into public ownership as a transgression not just against one, but against us all. The prosecutor is not an individual, but the Crown. Contrary to popular myth, the injured party does not decide whether to 'press charges'; the decision whether to prosecute rests with Her Majesty's Constabulary and the Crown Prosecution Service.[1]

We all have a stake in criminal justice. And, even if we are fortunate enough to have evaded its direct icy grasp, we can immediately empathise with those who are rendered victims. When we read those awful stories of harm, suffering and loss writ large, we put ourselves or our loved ones in the victim's shoes. We dare to contemplate, even if for a second, that it was *our* child who was hurt, our home that was burgled, our spouse who was killed by that driver.

By contrast, it is rare that, when a story about a criminal case breaks, our thoughts – much less our sympathies – lie with the accused. That side of the criminal justice coin does not recommend itself to us as immediately. Nobody likes to imagine, much less plans, that they will be accused of a crime. Such fates befall other people – people who invite the attentions of the state. People who deserve it.

As a result, there is, I worry, a tendency in how we discuss criminal justice – and how we are *encouraged* to discuss criminal justice – to overlook or distort the principles underpinning the system, in particular when it comes to our understanding of what the system is designed to achieve, who it is for and why it affords the protections it does to those accused of criminal offences.

The neat dichotomy between 'victims' and 'criminals', good and bad, deserving and undeserving, leads to a common conception of an unbalanced system that sprinkles privilege on the wrong people.

The idea that the protections built into the criminal process have the effect of frustrating justice, rather than securing it, is not new. But, allowed to run unchecked, this idea is dangerous, for it purchases cover for those who would, for their own purposes, like to wear down those protections. Protections which – hard as it may be to imagine right now, reclining in the comfort of your own home – you or your loved ones may, one dark day, depend upon to safeguard your liberty. It is critical, then, that when we are encouraged to agree that the criminal courts are unbalanced, and to endorse reforms to the way the system works, we understand exactly what we are discussing, and what we might be agreeing to surrender.

In order to grapple with the narratives we hear about criminal justice, we will need briefly to lay some foundations about how the criminal courts operate. That will form Part I of this chapter. In Parts II and III, we will look at how our understanding of two key principles – the burden and standard of proof, and the right to a fair trial – can become warped in the blizzard of confused and misleading rhetoric that envelops criminal justice. If you have read *The Secret Barrister: Stories of the Law and How It's Broken*, and/or have a confident grasp on the theoretical underpinnings of the criminal courts, feel free to skip ahead to Part II.


# PART I

## How our criminal justice system works

'[We have] a corrupt legal system and a police force crippled by political correctness, in a generous welfare state where the rights of criminals outweigh those of victims and society as a whole.'

Richard Littlejohn, *Daily Mail*, 24 May 2016[2]


A fuller explanation of the historical development of our criminal trial process is available elsewhere, but, for our purposes, it will assist to quickly run through some of the basics.

The criminal courts of England and Wales operate on an adversarial system, in which two competing sides – prosecution and defence – present and argue their cases in front of an independent judge and/or jury, which delivers a verdict on whether the prosecution case is proved on the evidence.

Back in the sixteenth century, the fashion was for lawyer-free 'altercation' trials, in which the prosecutor was the alleged victim and the defendant represented himself, and the court was expected to pick the bones out of a Jeremy Kyle-style confrontation, with few rules to govern the process. However, the model that has evolved since the eighteenth century has imported lawyers acting for either side. As of 1985 and the creation of the independent Crown Prosecution Service, public prosecutions[3] are mainly brought by the CPS, acting on evidence gathered by the police, and represented in court either by in-house CPS lawyers or by independent barristers (like me). Crucially, because prosecutions are now brought by the state, in the name of the Crown rather than the complainant, the potential victim is not actually a formal party to proceedings. They are often vital as witnesses, and the CPS should ensure that they are kept informed and are consulted about the progress of a case, but the case itself is not 'theirs'; the adversaries are the state and the accused.

Meanwhile, defendants are represented by independent defence lawyers, either a solicitor or both a solicitor and a barrister, depending on the nature of the case.

This theoretically guarantees equality of arms between the parties. Each has a lawyer to advise, prepare and present their case, question witnesses at trial and deal with any arguments as to how the law applies. Cases should therefore be decided on their evidential merits, rather than because one side has the advantage of legal assistance while the other is flailing in the dark.

The nature of the tribunal returning a verdict on a criminal case varies according to the type of alleged offence and the court in which it is heard. Despite the indelible cultural association between courts and juries, barely 1 per cent of the 1.37 million criminal prosecutions launched each year are determined by jury trial.[4] All criminal cases begin life in the magistrates' courts, and around 95 per cent remain there. Only the most serious cases –

generally those where a sentence of over six months' imprisonment is expected upon conviction – tend to find themselves sent to the Crown Court, where the prospect of trial by jury awaits.[5]

The magistrates' courts are presided over by either a 'bench' of three non-legally qualified volunteer magistrates (assisted by a qualified 'legal advisor'), or a single, legally qualified 'District Judge'. Magistrates (or District Judges) are responsible for the whole process: they take pleas from the defendants ('guilty' or 'not guilty'); make orders to assist in preparing not-guilty pleas for trial; decide any legal applications that might arise (such as disputes over whether a piece of evidence is admissible); hear the evidence at trial; decide cases; and, if a defendant pleads or is found guilty, pass sentence. The general idea is that, for less serious criminal offences, a quicker, cheaper and more streamlined process than applies in the Crown Court is justified. (Whether you accept that premise is, of course, another matter, but there you have it.)

Of the few that are sent to the Crown Court, the majority resolve with a defendant pleading guilty (or sometimes the prosecution dropping the case), leaving only a (relative) handful of jury trials. In contrast to the magistrates' court, there is a strict division of labour in the Crown Court. A judge presides over the trial to decide all questions of law (including, if it gets that far, the sentence), while all questions of fact, including the verdict, are in the hands of the jury. The jury comprises twelve random members of the public, drawn from the electoral roll and compelled under threat of imprisonment to attend their local Crown Court and do their public duty.

Although the first incarnation of juries, in the thirteenth century, involved gathering locals with direct knowledge of the case under discussion and inviting them to conduct their own amateur investigations as part of the trial process, the emphasis in the modern era is on independence. Jurors should not know personally any of the people involved in a case. In the American system, jurors can be quizzed about their beliefs and the parties vie to secure the most favourable jury composition, but no such process occurs here. You get who you're given, and who you're given are in turn instructed by the judge that they should not undertake any of their own research or discuss the case with anybody else. The verdict should be the views of the twelve people who have all heard the same evidence, rather than based in part on a rumour that someone has read on Twitter.

The trial itself, whether in the magistrates' or Crown Court, follows the same format. The prosecution opens the case (tells the court what the allegation is), and then calls its evidence. This is usually in the form of witnesses giving oral evidence (note, from the witness box – nobody 'takes the stand' in England and Wales), but can also include documents and other 'real evidence' – such as the bloodied knife or stolen loot. The witness tells the court what they know, and is then cross-examined by the defence advocate (usually a solicitor in the mags, and often a barrister in the Crown Court[6]). The prosecution case is followed by the defence case, in which the defendant can give evidence (if he chooses) and call any witnesses of his own, who will be duly cross-examined by the prosecutor. All evidence is subject to strict and complex rules, designed to ensure it is relevant, probative, lawfully obtained and not unduly prejudicial.

When the evidence has been heard, each advocate can address the court in a closing speech, weaving together the threads of evidence that assist their case, and, after the judge has neutrally summed up the case and (in the Crown Court) directed the jury on the applicable law, the finders of fact retire to consider their verdict.

And, after they have assessed the evidence and resolved the key issues – *Which witnesses do we believe? What really happened?* – they are ultimately required to agree, either unanimously or by a majority of no fewer than ten,[7] on the answer to one question: *Are we sure, on the evidence, that the defendant is guilty?*

If yes, the verdict is guilty. If no, the verdict is not guilty.

The idea is that this edifice provides a solid and safe laboratory for examining and testing evidence, from which the jury can reach fair conclusions. The evolution of the various elements of our trial process has taken centuries, but each part has been carefully calibrated to ensure that a criminal trial is as fair as it can be.

Yet, when it comes to discussing many of these key elements, we can see crucial misunderstandings being repeated, in a vicious circle of confusion, anger and frustration. And perhaps the greatest misunderstanding arises out of the system's most important guiding principle, as encapsulated in that ultimate question posed to the jury: the burden and standard of proof.

# PART II

## The burden and standard of proof

'Presume everyone in the country is guilty of something – which they are – and lock them up. The entire population. And anyone who can, to the satisfaction of a senior judge, prove themselves to be wholly and fundamentally innocent, will be released. There'd be a bit less fannying about then, wouldn't there?'

Detective Inspector Grim, *The Thin Blue Line*, 1995[8]

'Presumed innocent until proven guilty beyond reasonable doubt' is a concept with which we all become familiar in our early years, but is nevertheless remorselessly drummed into juries and magistrates at regular intervals throughout every criminal trial in the land. The prosecution brings the case, telling the jury what the defendant is accused of (the burden of proof); it is then for the prosecution to make the jury sure – to prove guilt beyond reasonable doubt (the standard of proof). The defendant does not have to prove his innocence. 'Sure' has, in the modern era, overtaken 'beyond reasonable doubt' in the language that judges and advocates are expected to adopt, apparently because the phrase 'beyond reasonable doubt' led to too many questions from jurors confused as to what that meant.

Probably the most striking example of a confused jury in recent times arose in the first trial of economist Vicky Pryce, in 2013, convicted (at a retrial) of perverting the course of justice after taking speeding penalty points for her husband, former minister Chris Huhne. After being directed on the law and retiring to consider their verdict, the jurors sent to the judge a list of ten questions, including not only 'Can you define what is reasonable doubt?', but the rather worrisome, 'Can we speculate?'; 'Does the defendant have an obligation to present a defence?' and 'Can a juror come to a verdict based on a reason that was not presented in court and has no facts or evidence to support it?'[9] The judge's concerns that the jury were displaying 'absolutely fundamental deficits in their understanding'[10] of their role was only slightly less damning than the conclusion invited by the *Daily Express*, which asked, 'Are some people just too stupid to serve on a jury?'[11]

But, to return to the point, 'reasonable doubt' is now out; 'sure' is in. Which is fine and dandy, insofar as it means that courts now only have to deal with questions from jurors confused as to the meaning of 'sure'.

The centrality of the burden and standard of proof cannot be overstated. Its first formal articulation is commonly traced back to 1791, when the country's best renowned defence barrister, William Garrow, told a jury at the Old Bailey that 'every man is presumed to be innocent until proved guilty'. More recently, in 1935, Viscount Sankey LC, in a House of Lords decision, provided the quote that inspired a thousand unimaginative defence closing speeches (as well as a series of *Rumpole of the Bailey*), when he remarked:

> Throughout the web of the English Criminal Law one golden thread is always to be seen, that it is the duty of the prosecution to prove the prisoner's guilt . . . If, at the end of

and on the whole of the case, there is a reasonable doubt, created by the evidence given by either the prosecution or the prisoner . . . the prosecution has not made out the case and the prisoner is entitled to an acquittal. No matter what the charge or where the trial, the principle that the prosecution must prove the guilt of the prisoner is part of the common law of England and no attempt to whittle it down can be entertained.[12]

When we examine the principle a little closer, its value becomes clear. The prosecution bears the burden of proof because it is only fair that a party making an allegation against an individual explain what the allegation is and how it can be proved. This applies throughout legal codes, both in civil and criminal law: he who asserts, must prove. Switching the burden of proof onto a defendant will often require that they prove a negative, which is usually impossible. If you can bear me explaining the joke, it is why Detective Inspector Grim's rant at the beginning of this section is funny. The notion of anyone, particularly when faced with something as serious as a criminal allegation, having to prove that they *didn't* do something, offends both our inherent sense of fairness and plain common sense.

As for the standard of proof being so high – compared to the standard that applies in the civil courts, where a claimant only has to prove his case on 'the balance of probabilities', i.e. so that a court finds it is *more likely than not* (51 per cent to 49 per cent, if you like) – the rationale lies in the peculiar nature of the criminal sanction. The consequences of a criminal conviction – from the stain on your character through to the loss of liberty – are serious and life-changing. While civil cases often raise issues of enormous importance and can have their own serious ramifications – loss of money, loss of your house, loss of your job, loss of your child – a criminal conviction can encompass all of those and much more besides.

And, if it were you standing in a courtroom accused of a crime you swear you did not commit, being judged by twelve strangers who knew nothing about you other than what they had been told in a court of law, you would want those twelve to be *sure* – not just suspicious, or semi-persuaded, or of the view that it was *more likely than not* – before they came back and gave the single-word verdict that brought your life crashing down around you.

Numerous cases in the criminal courts centre on the conflicting accounts of two people. Many more involve contested identification evidence, which is always fraught. How many times have you been *pretty sure* you recognised a friend in the street, only to discover when you next spoke to them that you were completely mistaken? The risks of allowing convictions where a jury is fairly sure that a witness was pretty sure of the correctness of their evidence speak for themselves. The unsupported evidence of a single witness, like identification evidence, *can* (and often does) found a criminal conviction, but it has to be of such high quality that the court can be sure there is no room for error.

In criminal proceedings, you also have the inherent imbalance of power between the prosecutor and defendant. The state's resources far exceed the individual's. The state can call upon a police force of over 120,000 officers imbued with both the manpower and the legal authority to search, seize, arrest, detain, question and scientifically examine in the course of their investigation. A lone defendant and his solicitor cannot even begin to compete in the evidence-gathering stakes. Placing the burden of proving an assertion on the party best placed to investigate all lines of inquiry and obtain all the relevant evidence is, again, an appeal to basic standards of fairness. If the suspect *has* committed a criminal offence, the state should, with all its power and resources, be able to prove it to the highest standard.

That is why, where there is any doubt in a criminal case, we exercise it in favour of the accused. Even though it means that, inevitably, a number of factually guilty people will benefit and be found not guilty, we prefer this as the lesser of two evils. This idea informs Blackstone's formulation, that it is better that ten guilty men go free than one innocent man suffer (a formulation which is perhaps not as well known as I'd assumed, given the 'outrage' reported in the *Daily Mail* after Cliff Richard quoted it on ITV's *Loose Women* in 2018).[13]

Unfortunately, the burden and high standard for convictions often carries invidious consequences.

The elision of the interests of the complainant and the burden of the prosecutor can make the trial process particularly horrid for victims of crime. We often hear complaints from victims' groups that complainants in criminal proceedings feel as if they are 'put on trial',[14] or being forced 'to prove they're not lying'.[15] That's because, quite simply, they are. A criminal trial requires the state to prove the truth and accuracy of its allegations. If the state's allegations are based on the testimony of a witness, the state must prove that the witness is truthful and correct, and satisfy the court that there is nothing that fatally undermines the credibility of the witness' evidence. That is unavoidable.

The standard of proof can bite even harder. It means that factually guilty people can be acquitted. It means that, in many cases, victims will leave the criminal justice system with a sense of grievance, of injustice squared, when something which they *know* happened – something terrible and unlawful, for which they deserve justice – cannot be proven on the available evidence.

There is an obvious risk that lawyers pontificating about the philosophical importance of their cherished principles appear at best stuck in an academic bubble, removed from the real lives of those affected, at worst airily and callously indifferent. *We think it's far more likely than not that this man killed your child, but our first principles mean that we're going to let him go scot-free. Yes, we accept that the evidence all points towards your complaint of rape being completely true, but find ourselves a fraction short of 'sure', so no justice for you, I'm afraid. Please be sure to complete your witness expense form – we wouldn't want you to miss out on reclaiming your parking.*

And, having spent a decade sitting post-trial in witness suites with complainants bruised by the experience of cross-examination and numbed by the pain of verdicts that fly in the face of their lived, bloodied experience, I know, from those re-victimised at its hands, the collateral cruelty of the standard of proof, how it can appear an impediment to justice, rather than its guarantor. Delivered from behind the veil of secret jury deliberations, victims will never know how and why their fate was decided as it was.

Furthermore, notwithstanding that I think Blackstone is broadly correct, I would never suggest that it follows that the pain of a victim denied justice is worth only a tenth of that of a wrongly convicted defendant. As a prosecutor, I see daily how important the state imprimatur of a conviction can be to help complainants and their families move towards closure, and the devastation when a 'not guilty' drops from a foreman's lips.

But I think perhaps the best way to explain it is that, while the official mark confirming that a crime was committed, and a sentence to match the gravity of what was done, will often be of enormous importance to a victim of crime, it is not the *only* form of justice available. It may well be the one that matters most, but other – if lesser – forms do exist. The civil courts, as we have seen, operate on a lower standard of proof, and many victims of crime have secured a different form of justice in those courts. High-profile examples from Scotland have in recent years seen complaints of sexual offences, which did not result in criminal convictions, being successfully relitigated as civil claims.[16] I'm not for a moment suggesting that this is equivalent justice, but it is *something*.

By contrast, if you are wrongly convicted, there is no alternative. That is your lot. The very best you can hope for is that you are vindicated on appeal, but, once those routes are exhausted, you are left, indelibly, with the stain and consequences of conviction. And nothing you can do will ever begin to put that right.

And, while a criminal justice system which too frequently allows the guilty to go free will quickly lose public support, one which is happy to fill its prisons with the 'possibly guilty' and 'probably guilty' will disintegrate entirely. No system, short of DI Grim's, can ever promise to catch all, or even most, guilty people. But a good system can promise not to convict you unless you do something wrong. It can prioritise and honour that term of the social contract: *if you live a law-abiding life, you need not fear the coercive sanction of the state.* Rather than a watered-down memorandum of understanding stating that *if you live a law-abiding life, the coercive sanction of the state might still on any given day uproot your life and take everything, because that's the way we catch more bad guys.*

Of course, even with the standard of proof as high as it is, wrongful convictions still occur. In the past five years, 557 convictions were found by the Court of Appeal to be 'unsafe' – the test for overturning a conviction.[17] No system is perfect. But, by calibrating the burden and standard of proof to emphasise and minimise the risk of convicting the innocent, we can, at the very least, reinforce and preserve the incentive to be good.

So that is, broadly speaking, why we have the burden and standard of proof. And much of the theory may strike as instinctual; we know it, even if we don't ever articulate it. And we would certainly expect it to apply if ever we were wrongly accused of a crime. We would want the prosecution to be forced to prove to the highest possible standard that we were guilty.

But it is when we move away from the *why*, and towards the question of *how* the principle operates in practice, that we seem to trip ourselves up. In particular, there is recurring confusion about the meaning of 'not guilty' and 'guilty', and the presumption of innocence.

## The meaning of 'not guilty'

The problem with a 'not guilty' verdict is that it means quite literally just that. Not. Guilty. Those two words embrace a wide spectrum of possibilities, from a jury being certain of innocence to their being a hair's breadth away from sure of guilt. Because we don't require juries to give reasons or explanations for their verdicts, this means that, in every acquittal at the Crown Court, there is an unsatisfactory lacuna, as those involved can only speculate about what evidence the jury did and did not accept, and what conclusions were drawn.

So it is that, following an acquittal, interested parties queue up to offer their own divination. Most commonly, a defendant will suggest that he has 'proved his innocence' by virtue of his acquittal. This, it follows from what we've looked at, is simply not true. He has been found not guilty. The legal presumption of innocence remains intact, meaning you retain immunity from coercive criminal sanction. But neither of those things amounts to a positive finding of innocence. Of course, a good number of acquitted defendants will, as a matter of fact, be innocent, but their positive vindication is not exhaustively established solely by that binary, inscrutable jury verdict. And it may sound like the pettiest 'Well, actually . . .' with which to rain on an acquitted defendant's chips, but it is vital to bear in mind the distinction. Because it feeds into other myths about the meaning of an acquittal.

A good example was the media circus that surrounded footballer Ched Evans, who was convicted of rape before having his conviction quashed on appeal and then being acquitted at a subsequent retrial. A prepared statement read outside Cardiff Crown Court following Mr Evans' acquittal declared, 'My innocence has now been established.'[18] A particular and unpleasant feature of this case, since Evans was first charged in 2011, had been the abuse piled onto the complainant by Mr Evans' supporters, including teammates.[19] Her name had been circulated online, in contravention of the legal prohibition on publishing the identity of complainants in sexual allegations, and she and her family had been subjected to appalling abuse and threats, forcing her to change her name and move house five times.[20] Following the acquittal in 2016, calls for vengeance boomed once more throughout social media. The complainant had been shown to be 'a liar'.[21] Except, of course, she hadn't. Not in the least. She, like every other complainant in a criminal trial where there is an acquittal, was no more a proven liar than the defendant was a proven paragon; the verdict simply does not allow for that inference to be drawn. The issues in this trial were whether the complainant – who was so drunk that she did not even remember having sex with Evans and his teammate, Clayton Donaldson, that fact only coming to light as part of the police investigation after the complainant reported losing her handbag on a night out – had consented, and whether Evans had reasonably believed she had consented. The verdict of not guilty could well have indicated the jury being sure that, because of her condition, the complainant was too drunk to consent, but being slightly less than sure that Evans did not reasonably believe that she was consenting. In such a scenario, there would be absolutely no finding of fact adverse to the complainant at all. But, by asserting his 'demonstrated' innocence, Ched Evans was, whether intentionally or not, signalling that he had proven the untruthfulness of the girl involved.

The prevalence of the myth that an acquittal equals a false complaint is troubling. An astonishing exchange took place in October 2017 between Radio 4 *Today* presenter John Humphrys and Director of Public Prosecutions Alison Saunders, when the latter made the obvious observation that not every acquittal at a rape trial represented a false complaint. 'Really?' spluttered Humphrys, his incredulity copied the next day in a headline in the *Sun* accusing the DPP of 'sparking outrage' with her comments.[22]

An illustration of the fallacy is the trial of DJ Neil 'Doctor' Fox in 2015. Mr Fox was acquitted at Westminster Magistrates' Court of ten allegations of indecent and sexual assault brought by six women, and announced that he had been 'vindicated'. He said, 'a lot has been said and written about me . . . [that] will need to be addressed and rectified', adding what the *Telegraph* interpreted as a 'hint that he could sue the Crown Prosecution Service'.[23]

However, as Mr Fox had been tried at a magistrates' court, rather than a Crown Court, the magistrates, when announcing their verdicts, gave reasons, as they are required to do. These were published and provided a slightly different impression than one might have gleaned from Mr Fox's punchy statement.[24] The court emphasised that they did not find that any of the complainants had been untruthful – to the contrary: 'We believed each of the complainants.' The acquittals, the court explained, were due to the bench variously not being sure of the facts alleged, sure of the context in which the events occurred or sure that the conduct amounted to the criminal offences charged, with many complications arising due to the age of the complaints.

It was a peculiar 'vindication' of Mr Fox. For one, the court was satisfied that, in respect of one of the allegations, the defendant 'has lied to us'. The magistrates were sure that, while not criminal, 'his behaviour on some occasions crossed the line of acceptable behaviour'. They were sure that he had grabbed the breasts of one of his colleagues, and described this as 'completely unacceptable'. They were sure he had simulated sex with another female colleague, an act which was 'coarse and unacceptable', which led to the woman feeling 'belittled and humiliated'. Mr Fox himself accepted tickling and simulating sexual intercourse with another woman; again the court declared this 'unacceptable'. In relation to an allegation that Mr Fox had indecently assaulted a fifteen-year-old girl by placing her hand on his penis and putting his finger in her vagina, the court stated: '[W]e believe [the complainant]. We do not think she is lying or fantasising. We are aware that for a variety of reasons events a long time ago can be misremembered. In these circumstances it is an invidious task for a court to say it is sure that what is alleged did indeed happen. We have a small doubt and that must be exercised in favour of the defendant.'

As for the implication that the CPS had erred in bringing the prosecution, the court dealt with this head-on: 'Nor should this verdict be taken as a criticism of the decision to bring this prosecution. It was a strong case and one that needed to be brought to the court for determination.'

This is another common misconception about a not guilty verdict: the notion that an acquittal is evidence that a prosecution should never have been brought. We hear this a lot, but it is a product of the same logical fallacy. The test that is applied to all prospective prosecutions (the 'Full Code' test) is twofold: (i) is there a *realistic prospect* of conviction on the available evidence? (ii) is it in the public interest to prosecute? The threshold of 'realistic prospect of conviction' is deliberately lower than the test to actually convict (sure/beyond reasonable doubt), for obvious reason. If the CPS only ever charged cases where they were sure of the suspect's guilt, not only would we have a system where large numbers of meritorious prosecutions would never be brought, but the function of the jury would be usurped by a single reviewing lawyer, modelled on something akin to Judge Dredd. Hence the CPS ask themselves, having regard to all of the evidence, *Is there a realistic prospect of conviction?* This strikes the balance between pursuing cases which are weak – risking miscarriages of justice and/or dragging witnesses and defendants through the strain of criminal proceedings where it is obvious that the evidence is too thin to convict – and not charging cases which are strong, but which the prosecution is not certain of winning.

Inevitably, prosecutors make mistakes. Cases which should be weeded out at an early stage are charged. But an acquittal is not by itself proof of this. Any working criminal trial system will result in some acquittals. The obverse – a 100 per cent conviction rate – would be far more disconcerting.

What are the signs of a prosecution that shouldn't have been brought? It's difficult, as an outsider to a case, to say. At the end of the prosecution case, if the judge considers the evidence to be so weak that *no jury properly directed could safely convict*, they are required to direct the jury to return a verdict of not guilty (referred to as a 'submission of no case to answer'). Such a direction *may* be an indication that proceedings should never have been instituted, but, again, it is not of itself conclusive. Trials are dynamic processes. Frequently, the shape of the prosecution case changes, as witnesses don't turn up, or do not give as full an account in the witness box as they did in their written statement (referred to as 'failing to come up to proof'), or give unexpected answers in cross-examination, or accept propositions put by the defence which assist the defendant's case. Sometimes, a defence lawyer will do an outstanding job in cross-examination and get the sole eyewitness to agree that, actually, they didn't get as good a look at the burglar as they'd suggested in their witness statement, and, all of a sudden, a watertight prosecution case is being booted by the judge at half-time.

Without knowing the details of an individual case, and in particular the evidence heard and the decisions reached by the fact-finders, it is impossible to draw the conclusions that many would wish. In the Crown Court, the closest we might get to an answer on acquittal will be, on rare occasions, a judicial blast at the prosecution following a not guilty verdict, with attendant reasons for the judge's ire, but most acquittals conclude without remark, the underlying reasons remaining forever unknown.

## The meaning of 'guilty'

Where a defendant pleads guilty, it means that he is accepting having committed a criminal offence in the way alleged by the prosecution. Where he admits he is guilty but disputes the factual basis of his guilt (e.g. 'I accept assaulting the complainant by punching him, but I deny kicking him'), then the parties will either agree a 'basis of plea' setting out the mutually accepted position, or, if the parties can't agree, the judge will resolve the issue, usually by hearing a trial without a jury, in which the judge alone decides whether she is 'sure' that the prosecution version of events is correct.

Where a defendant is found guilty, it means that a jury of his peers were sure, on the evidence, that he committed the criminal offence charged. Because we don't require juries to give reasons or explanations for their verdicts, it is up to the judge to consider the evidence and determine on what 'basis' the jury convicted (a situation which I personally find wholly unsatisfactory, but there you have it), and to pass sentence accordingly. The judge's sentencing remarks will make clear to the public the facts that the court – jury and judge – has found.

It follows that a guilty verdict can be more nuanced than appears from a press release – and certainly different from the 'facts' alleged by the prosecution when the prosecutor opens the case at the start of the trial. As we have seen, trials are dynamic, with the shape of the prosecution case morphing as the evidence emerges. Even where a defendant is convicted, what is actually proved by the evidence can present a radically different factual complexion, resulting in a sentence far removed from what he would have received had he been convicted on the original prosecution facts.

A graphic illustration arose in 2018, when a man called John Broadhurst was tried for the murder of his partner, Natalie Connolly.[25] The prosecution opened the widely reported case to the jury as a brutal and intentional killing, born out of jealousy. One evening, when both parties were intoxicated, Broadhurst had inflicted over forty injuries on Natalie, including severe bruising to her buttocks, back and breasts, a fracture to her eye socket and haemorrhaging of her vagina, after Broadhurst inserted, and then attempted to remove, a bottle of carpet cleaner. As she lay bleeding and dying at the bottom of the stairs, Broadhurst took himself off to bed, only calling an ambulance the following morning, by which time Natalie was, in the callously flippant words used by Broadhurst to the emergency services, 'dead as a doughnut'.

On its face, a clear case of murder – in law, unlawfully causing death with the intention to either kill or cause really serious harm. Natalie had been heavily under the influence of alcohol, and had taken cocaine, amphetamines and poppers. While it may have been the level of intoxication, rather than the injuries themselves, that was the primary cause of death, the jury were told how the prosecution pathologist would give expert evidence showing that her injuries 'at the very least accelerated her death', which would be enough to establish murder.

But as the trial progressed, and evidence was given by prosecution and defence medical experts, an alternative possible narrative emerged. Broadhurst had claimed that the injuries were either inflicted at Natalie's request, during consensual sex, or were caused when she was stumbling around, heavily intoxicated. Instinctively, many people would consider this a ludicrous defence; but the evidence, once tested, started to afford it some credence. The prosecution witnesses – Natalie's own family – gave evidence that she had previously told family and friends of how she and Broadhurst enjoyed 'rough sex', and had even shown them bruising she had sustained to her body. She was jokingly referred to as 'Anna' by her friends – a reference to the character in *Fifty Shades of Grey*. The medical experts appeared to accept that the bruising was consistent with having been caused in this way. The injuries to her head and eye socket were consistent, the experts said, with having been caused accidentally as Natalie 'stumbled around in a heavily intoxicated state and collided with objects'. Broadhurst's explanation for the vaginal injury was supported by computer evidence which the defence had indicated they would apply to put before the jury, and which suggested that Natalie had 'a proclivity for such things'. The expert evidence which dealt with the cause of death was far from straightforward. While the prosecution's pathologist maintained that, in his opinion, the cause of death was a combination of the injuries and Natalie's intoxication, he also accepted that the alcohol and cocaine levels alone were sufficient to have killed her. His opinion that the injuries and intoxication worked in tandem to accelerate her death was set against the opinion of the two defence experts, who gave evidence during the prosecution case that, in their view, the levels of intoxication, rather than the injuries, were the cause of death.

All put together, at the end of the prosecution case, the Crown were left in difficulties. The ambiguity presented serious problems in making a jury *sure* that (a) Broadhurst intended to kill or cause really serious harm, and (b) his unlawful actions significantly contributed to cause of death. This did not mean that Broadhurst had not committed a serious criminal offence – he had. He ultimately pleaded guilty to gross negligence manslaughter, on the basis that he left Natalie at the bottom of the stairs without dialling 999 when he had a duty of care towards her and it was obvious that there was a risk of death. But the facts that were eventually established as provable by the evidence varied considerably from the prosecution's initial expectations. By the end of the case, 'guilty' meant something quite different from when the trial began. After the judge heard legal submissions at the close of the Crown's case, the charge of murder was withdrawn from the jury, and Broadhurst pleaded guilty instead to manslaughter.

Understandably, when confronted with the original prosecution facts and the sentence ultimately passed – three years and eight months' imprisonment – many commentators and politicians were shocked. How could anyone not be? But much of the analysis that followed betrayed a troubling misunderstanding of the evidence, and, crucially, of the burden and standard of proof.

Some of the commentary was simply false. *Grazia* ran a feature blaming the jury for not 'buying' the prosecution case, apparently oblivious to the fact that the decision was taken away from them.[26] Harriet Harman MP told BBC *Woman's Hour* that the Broadhurst case introduced 'a new defence, which was, "Yes, it was violence, but it was violence she wanted, because . . . she was the sort of woman who wanted S & M."'

This, as we have seen, is just not true. Consent provides no legal defence to the infliction of actual bodily harm, let alone death. A famous case with which all first-year law students are invited to grapple is *R* v. *Brown*,[27] in which the House of Lords, in 1993, upheld the convictions of a group of men who had inflicted eye-watering bodily harm on other men in the course of consensual sadomasochistic sexual activity involving sharp instruments, hot wax and urethras. Consent, the Lords ruled, provides no defence to deliberately injuring another person.[28]

So, when Ms Harman went on to say, 'It doesn't matter whether or not people do want S & M . . . nobody is justified in killing another person,' implying that the Broadhurst case suggested the opposite, she misrepresented both the facts of the case and the operation of the law. Had the medical evidence established that Broadhurst inflicted the injuries in the way the prosecution alleged, and that they had caused death, he would have been guilty of murder. Consent was relevant only to the extent that it offered an explanation for the injuries to contradict the prosecution allegation of a brutal assault with an intention to kill or cause really serious harm. Theoretically, had he not pleaded guilty to manslaughter, he could have been charged with and found guilty of inflicting actual bodily harm on Natalie in respect of the injuries said to have been caused 'consensually'.

The *Independent* ran an op-ed condemning the 'catastrophic . . . second-guessing by the CPS of the jury that they would not believe Broadhurst intended to kill his girlfriend'.[29] Again, this misunderstands the issues. It was not that the CPS didn't think a twenty-first-century jury would believe that a man would brutalise his partner. Juries up and down the country demonstrate every day through guilty verdicts that they are more than capable of 'believing' that violent men inflict horrific injuries upon women. It was a fact-specific case, in which the particular combination of evidence – including the independent testimony of medical experts – meant that the prosecution could not prove the elements of murder to the required standard.

But this – the central role played by the burden and standard of proof in the outcome of the case – was lost in the fog. The *Independent* inadvertently encapsulated the confusion when it suggested that the CPS 'calculated that twelve jurors would believe Broadhurst's defence'. As far as misstatements of the principle go, this mangling of the burden of proof takes some beating. For it was not the case that the CPS calculated that the jury would believe the defence; rather they concluded that, given the evidence that emerged at trial was consistent with the account Broadhurst had given from the start, the jury couldn't be *sure* that his defence – that he did not cause the life-ending injuries – was *untrue*. This is a key difference. If the burden was on Broadhurst to prove that Natalie's death happened in the way he claimed, it would likely have been a very different story. But it wasn't – it was on the prosecution to disprove that Natalie could have died in the way Broadhurst suggested. When the prosecution realised that it couldn't, it reassessed what it *could* prove. It consulted Natalie's family, who, having been made aware of the evidential position in this highly complex and unusual case, confirmed they were content for the Crown to accept a plea to manslaughter.

The accusation voiced in the *Observer* that the CPS 'did not trust' the jury and were guilty of 'accepting the historical fallacy of domestic violence as a non-serious issue',[30] suffered from the same fundamental misunderstandings. The comment piece, having outlined the original prosecution allegations, rhetorically asked, 'Exactly what would it take for a woman's violent death at the hands of her partner to be called murder?' The short response would be 'evidence capable of making a jury sure that the accused inflicted unlawful violence causing death, with intent to kill or cause really serious harm'. Applied to this case, the outcome may well have been very different if there had not been prosecution evidence to support Broadhurst's claim that consensual sexual violence was a feature of the relationship. Or if the medical evidence had discredited Broadhurst's explanation as to how all of the injuries were caused. Or if the medical evidence had demonstrated that the infliction of injuries was a significant cause of death.

But none of that was present. Instead, had the murder charge gone to the jury (and it has been reported that the judge was not willing to allow this),[31] the jury would have been left with medical evidence capable of supporting two contrasting explanations, and only Broadhurst's evidence as to what took place. The jury may well have been suspicious. It may well have thought that the original prosecution narrative of a jealous boyfriend resorting to gratuitous violence provided an attractive and credible explanation. It may well have doubted the plausibility of Broadhurst's account. But that would not have been enough.

\* \* \*

This was an awful case, and the headline – three years and eight months for the loss of a young mother's life in this most brutal and degrading manner – understandably inflamed the public's instinctive sense of fairness. Even taking into account the fact that the sentence appears in accordance with the sentencing guidelines for manslaughter, I would not challenge anyone who read the facts and concluded that, guidelines aside, this was a sentence that was difficult to comprehend for behaviour so callous, with consequences so serious.

Cases such as these also carry the weight of the historic failure of the justice system to deal with violence against women. The concern is entirely reasonable. There is no criticism of the bona fides and noble motives at play. Sounding a warning and asking *Is this OK?* is vital. Historically, there were too few such questions; a male-dominated legal system was allowed to trample over the rights of women with little public challenge. Here, Broadhurst had obviously done something criminally wrong. A young woman had been killed in the most horrifying circumstances, redolent of the type of wanton violence committed against women which has too often gone unpunished. It would be frankly negligent to read the headline and *not* ask questions.

But the taking of the headline at face value, the failure to seek answers before publicising settled conclusions, and the carelessness with which basic facts and first principles were treated in the course of the public debate that followed must be challenged. Because it all represents deeper problems with our understanding of criminal justice.

If the picture had been as straightforward as presented in the think pieces, the outrage would have been entirely justified – no, it would not have been enough. If our courts entertained the notion that a man could secure a woman's consent to her own fatal mutilation, or if prosecutors abandoned a viable murder trial because they suspected it would not survive the inherent misogyny of the jury, this should be front-page news. If our system was geared so that all a homicidal man need do is assert,

'She was asking for it,' for an indolent prosecution service to throw in the towel, I would be hoping for marches in the street.

But none of that, in this case, was true. The prosaic reality – that an evidentially complex case meant that the prosecution could not discharge its burden of proof to the high criminal standard – was not even alluded to in the commentary. The burden and standard of proof did not even occur to writers talking about juries 'believing Broadhurst's defence'. The legal elements of the offence charged were deemed similarly unworthy of remark.

Instead, there was an immediate leap to the broad conclusion that the original prosecution allegations were true, even after the prosecution had themselves disavowed them. The allegation of a sadistic murder by a controlling partner fit a familiar narrative about criminal trials. The assumption was that any outcome at odds with that narrative had to be flawed. The state had made an allegation of guilt; therefore, it must be right.

And dispelling the confusion in this case is important. Not only because it is vital to public understanding that something as central to our justice system as the burden and standard of proof be accurately represented by those with the most prominent platforms. Not only because consistency demands that we are equally critical when the law is misrepresented by those on the side of the angels, the purity of whose cause – justice for victims of domestic violence – is not in dispute.

But it matters because, when we fail to distinguish between 'accused' and 'guilty', between a state-sponsored allegation and proven guilt, we contribute to a conflation that is exploited by those with ulterior agendas. We find ourselves nodding along as 'tough on crime' politicians reframe the delicate balance of competing interests alive in the system, from 'state versus complainant versus accused' to 'criminal versus victim', or 'criminal versus law-abiding public'.

When we buy into the message that the prosecution case is always correct, and any deviation from a guilty verdict is *by itself* evidence of a malfunctioning system, we invite changes to the law and procedure to make it easier for the prosecution case to remain intact.

And this, when we look at the changes that have been advocated to criminal justice over recent years, is precisely what legislators have set out to do.


# PART III

## The right to a fair trial

'What concerns me is that the criminal justice system always seems to put the rights of the criminal ahead of the rights of the law-abiding public and the victim.'

Philip Davies MP, 20 August 2011[32]


The pattern is formulaic. A scourge will be identified – almost always something complex, socially embedded and multifactorial, for which the solution requires careful evidence-gathering, long-term thinking, multi-agency involvement and politically unappealing decisions. A politician will tell the public that, actually, the solution is simple and located in the criminal justice system, which is perennially weighted in favour of the criminal. Shaking their head solemnly, our hero will vow to rebalance the system in favour of the law-abiding public.

The way in which this is achieved varies. Let's look at three common examples: rules of evidence; the right to legal representation; and the right to jury trial.

# Rules of evidence

Over recent decades, a quick-'n'-easy answer has been to change the laws of criminal evidence. Criminal evidence is a mystery to most people outside the criminal law. It occupies year-long modules of professional legal training courses, and takes years of practice before its idiosyncrasies sink in. It is therefore ripe for political picking.

In the 1990s, Home Secretary Michael Howard defied the advice of three Royal Commissions and introduced laws to abolish the centuries-old right to silence in criminal proceedings. The right was long considered a vital corollary of the burden of proof, with its origins often ascribed to the response to the oppression of the seventeenth-century Star Chamber, in which alleged traitors and heretics were interrogated, tortured and tried in secret. Those who refused to answer questions were immediately convicted and gruesomely punished.[33]

In the modern era, the right was reflected in the ability of a suspect to decline to answer police questions or give evidence at trial, without any adverse effect. Similar to the fifth amendment of the United States constitution, it was accepted that the prosecution should be required to prove criminal offences without the assistance of the person accused. But Mr Howard, in a climate when the IRA terror attacks were at the forefront of popular consciousness, set about changing this. In 1993, he told the Conservative Party conference, 'The so-called right to silence is ruthlessly exploited by terrorists. What fools they must think we are . . . The so-called right to silence will be abolished. The innocent have nothing to hide . . .'[34]

The changes, brought in in 1994,[35] mean that, if a suspect fails to mention when interviewed by police something he later relies on in court, or if he chooses not to give evidence at his trial, the jury can be invited to draw an 'adverse inference' against him – in other words, add it to the prosecution evidence as evidence of guilt. This was cheered by the Association of

Chief Police Officers, who remarked that the change 'will help redress the balance in favour of justice for victims, witnesses and the mass of law-abiding citizens'.[36]

Instinctively, the 'nothing to hide' mantra may be superficially attractive. But it ignores that people may remain silent for a variety of reasons unrelated to innocence or guilt. Perhaps because they are protecting someone else. Or are afraid of reprisals. Or because they are confused or overwhelmed by the experience of being arrested and interviewed in a police station. Or because they want to wait and see what the evidence against them is, so that they can give the best account of themselves. They may not give evidence at trial on legal advice, because their lawyer has made an assessment that, if the suspect gives evidence, they are liable to give a poor impression. I have given this advice to clients who screamed their innocence at me during our conferences. *The case against you is weak. I know you want to tell the jury your side, but, in my judgement, you are likely to trip up, get yourself in a tangle and inadvertently help the prosecution case. It is better for you to say nothing.*

And while, without doubt, the right to silence was relied upon and exploited by some very bad and very guilty people, they are of course not the only ones who are affected by its removal. It also affects, for instance, children with learning difficulties. In 2010, a teenager with an IQ of sixty-eight and the language ability of a seven- to eight-year-old did not give evidence at his murder trial. The judge duly directed the jury that this was something that could be added to the prosecution case against him.[37] In 2005, Sam Hallam was convicted of murder. His conviction was quashed seven years later by the Court of Appeal after it transpired that he had been a victim of 'manifestly unreliable identification evidence', a 'failure by police properly to investigate his alibi' and 'non-disclosure by the prosecution of material that could have supported his case'.[38] Part of the prosecution case against him at trial, which secured his wrongful conviction, was his decision, on legal advice, to give 'no comment' during his police interview.

The New Labour government that followed Mr Howard in 1997 was similarly wedded to the pressing need to 'reclaim the criminal justice system', as the extremes of antisocial behaviour and Islamist terrorism preoccupied the Prime Minister. Tony Blair frequently complained about 'Justice weighted towards the criminal and in need of rebalancing towards the victim,'[39] and, in 2003, introduced two major changes to criminal evidence. Hearsay evidence – something said by somebody outside court, which the prosecution wishes to rely upon to prove the truth of what is said – has historically been largely inadmissible, for obvious reason. If you are accused, say, of stealing an apple, it is not fair for the prosecution to call a random member of the public to tell the court, 'Jim told me that he saw the apple being stolen.' You want Jim himself, the primary source of the evidence, to attend to be questioned. The Criminal Justice Act 2003 made it much, much easier for the prosecution to introduce hearsay evidence. The same legislation also made it easier for prosecutors to introduce evidence of a defendant's 'bad character' – previous convictions (or even just allegations) – which was largely kept out of criminal trials to ensure that juries focused on the evidence in the trial rather than the defendant's unpleasant reputation. Towards the end of his tenure, in 2006, Mr Blair was still banging the same drum.

Now, I don't pretend that these issues are straightforward; there is a wealth of academic literature debating where the lines should lie in criminal evidence. But what *was* straightforward was the narrative publicly deployed by the government: these changes should only worry you if you're a criminal. Those are the only people affected. Criminal versus victim. Never 'accused'. Guilt is presumed.

Over the last few years, we have seen similar rhetoric applied in relation to allegations of sexual offending. The Ched Evans case made headlines after his conviction was quashed and a retrial ordered, when the Court of Appeal accepted new evidence relating to the sexual history of the complainant. In most cases, sexual history evidence is completely irrelevant. In some, however, it will have a bearing. It can never be used to attack a complainant's credibility, and has to satisfy strict statutory criteria, including, critically, that the judge is satisfied that, if the evidence is not allowed, there would be a risk of a wrongful conviction. For my part, I am not convinced that, on its facts, the Court of Appeal decision in Evans was correct; however, its presentation in the media was an exercise in shameless scaremongering. The decision was fact specific and set no precedent, but many suggested otherwise. A piece in the *Daily Mail* described the decision as creating 'a rapists' charter'.[40] MPs untruthfully claimed[41] the decision allowed a return to days where a woman's sexual history would be held up in court as evidence that she was either promiscuous or unworthy of belief – myths which have been outlawed in the courts since 1999. A shocking case in Ireland, in which a complainant's underwear was reportedly paraded in court by the defence barrister as suggestive of the complainant being 'open to meeting someone', was disingenuously rolled up into the debate, despite such behaviour being plainly prohibited in the courts of England and Wales.[42]

And quickly, entirely justified concern for the treatment of complainants in sexual cases led to a widespread refusal to acknowledge the competing interests at play in criminal trials, and the strict circumstances in which this type of evidence might be allowed. For instance, a complainant stating on oath that he would never have had consensual sex because of his devout faith may be exposed as untruthful by evidence of a contradictory sexual history. A complainant may allege a violent and unusual sexual attack involving bondage and handcuffs, which the defendant maintains was consensual; if the complainant had three partners, all of whom confirmed that she would habitually instigate this exact type of BDSM, this might be relevant to the issue of consent.

Neither would be determinative of the issue of guilt, but they would both potentially be relevant to the jury's considerations. Without this evidence, there could be an incomplete picture and a risk of injustice.

Now, there may well be a case to say that the relevant law – section 41 of the Youth Justice and Criminal Evidence Act 1999 – is not being used as it should, that it is too permissive and results in complainants being asked intimate and embarrassing questions where it is unjustified. The most recent research does not support this,[43] but no issue can be taken with a request for a full review into how the law is applied in practice, and whether judges or practitioners require further training. But that was not the political response. Instead, MPs rushed to table a Private Members' Bill seeking to force judges to exclude all and any evidence of sexual history in all circumstances, *even where judges were sure that to do so would risk a wrongful conviction.*[44] There was not even a pretence at acknowledging that this would, inevitably, result in innocent people being imprisoned. The clash was criminal versus victim, and the latter had to win out.

## Right to legal representation – 'Whose side are you on?'

Without doubt the most sustained assault on the foundations of the criminal justice system is aimed at the right to legal representation. Having just spent a chapter on the subject of legal aid, we will not revisit the pantheon of myths over its cost and purpose, but the lack of public outcry at the increasing restrictions on criminal legal aid since 2012 suggests that the regular diet of tabloid stories of criminals 'racking up huge bills'[45] on legal aid has succeeded in turning Britons against the once-uncontroversial notion that anybody accused of a crime is entitled to legal advice and representation.

That legal aid is an essential prerequisite to establishing, fairly and safely, that an accused individual is guilty of the charge alleged, is ignored. Where someone pleads or is found guilty of a criminal offence, the importance of ensuring that they are dealt with lawfully and properly at their sentence hearing is seldom championed. Of course, where someone is convicted of a crime and has the means to reimburse the state for the cost of their legal aid, I have no quarrel with requiring that as part of the overall penalty for committing an offence. But where, as is often the case, those convicted don't have a penny to their name, that should be absorbed by the rest of us, and recognised as the low price to pay for a fair and civilised system, and for the insurance that, were we ever dragged into the criminal justice system, we would not be cut adrift for lack of money, forced to single-handedly fight the prosecution's qualified lawyers, with our liberty on the line.

But criminal legal aid, the propaganda has convinced us, is for criminals. Not the accused. It follows that we, the good law-abiding denizens of this green and pleasant land, have no need for it. And if *we* don't need it, we sure as mustard shouldn't be paying for it to be frittered away on criminals.

The natural consequence is that, recast as a luxury, criminal legal aid has been removed from swathes of the population. In magistrates' courts, anybody with an annual gross household income – the income of you *and* your partner – over £22,325, does not qualify for legal aid.[46] In the Crown Court, everybody used to be eligible for legal aid, in recognition of the fact that the consequences of a Crown Court conviction extend to life imprisonment. Since 2014, anyone with an annual household disposable income of £37,500 or more is excluded from criminal legal aid.[47]

If you don't qualify for legal aid, you will be forced to pay privately. Private fees for lawyers are like private fees for dentists; it is not until you pay them that you realise how artificially low the state price is. Private fees for a long or complicated criminal trial can cost tens if not hundreds of thousands of pounds. And the kicker, courtesy of Chris Grayling's changes in 2014? If you are acquitted, you cannot claim your full legal costs back. You are only entitled to claim legal costs at artificially low legal-aid rates; the shortfall is met from your savings or selling your house. One high-profile case in 2018 saw a doctor, accused of serious offences by a 'serial fantasist', facing a £94,000 legal bill after the prosecution case collapsed.[48] Conservative MP Nigel Evans, whose party introduced this Innocence Tax, was himself stung for

£130,000 when acquitted after a lengthy trial at Preston Crown Court in 2014.[49]

It is not only the financial cost of upholding equality of arms that the public are being successfully encouraged to resent; increasingly, it is the very notion of criminal defence itself.

Since the evolution of the modern adversarial process in the eighteenth century, the role of independent defence lawyers – solicitors and barristers – has been crucial. We exist to fight our clients' causes, so that, wherever an accused person denies guilt, they have the same access to legal advice and representation as the prosecution. The age-old dinner-party question of *How can you defend someone you know is guilty?* is easily answered once it is explained and understood that we cannot ever *know* a defendant is guilty unless he tells us. If he *does* tell us, we are then limited in what we can do to help. What we absolutely cannot and will not do is stand up in court and positively assert that he is innocent; to do so would be to mislead the court, which is among the gravest of professional sins. However, if the client insists he is innocent, notwithstanding that the evidence against him may be overwhelming, it is not our job to judge, but to present his case as persuasively as we can. Because we do know, from headlines throughout our country's history, that defendants facing 'overwhelming' evidence can, in fact, be completely innocent. If lawyers were to judge, and to refuse to act based on the reprehensible nature of the allegations or the strength of the prosecution evidence, we would not only be usurping the function of the jury, but betraying our reason for being.

However, this settled principle is being undermined by a corrosive conflation of lawyers with the (alleged) sins of their clients. We saw this writ large in the 2016 US Presidential election. Republicans launched a series of attack adverts against Democratic candidate Hillary Clinton and her running mate Tim Kaine, in which the horrific acts of some of their clients from their days as criminal defence lawyers were plastered across the nation's TV screens.[50] 'America deserves better', intoned the voiceover, warning voters that the pair had 'a passion for defending the wrong people'.[51]

A marginally more subtle line of attack was adopted in the London mayoral election of the same year, when Conservative candidate Zac Goldsmith accused Labour candidate, and former solicitor, Sadiq Khan of 'providing cover' to extremists, deprecating that Mr Khan 'chose to defend' an alleged terrorist.[52] The notion that criminal defence lawyers neither choose their clients nor by association endorse the crimes that they may or may not have committed was either beyond Mr Goldsmith, or within his comprehension but merrily sacrificed in the pursuit of votes.

In 2019, Harvard Law School professor Ronald S. Sullivan Jr, a respected defence lawyer, found himself the subject of angry calls to resign from his faculty after agreeing to defend alleged sex offender Harvey Weinstein. His attempts to explain the importance of representing 'unpopular defendants' were drowned out by the rage of his students, whose petitions, marches and vandalism – *Whose side are you on?* was spray-painted on the faculty building – succeeded in evoking a shameful response from the university. Rather than reminding these bright young minds of the essential function of criminal defence, Harvard administrators promised a 'climate review' to investigate Professor Sullivan's conduct.[53] In May 2019, Harvard announced that his tenure would not be renewed.[54]

Lest we tell ourselves such things would not happen in our own country, an unpleasant reminder occurred in early 2019. After thirty-one-year-old Jack Shepherd absconded on bail prior to his trial and conviction for manslaughter, following the death of a young woman called Charlotte Brown on Shepherd's speedboat, a tabloid campaign was launched to find the fugitive. The tabloid artillery turned from the cowardice of Shepherd,[55] onto (naturally) the scandal of him being entitled to legal aid,[56] before settling on his lawyers,[57] who had the temerity to continue to represent him. Shepherd's solicitor, Richard Egan, said that, although he was in contact with his client, he did not know his whereabouts, and valiantly attempted to explain the importance of Mr Shepherd retaining the right to instruct lawyers and pursue an appeal against his conviction. 'We represent,' he explained. 'We do not judge.'

His efforts at calming the seas did not succeed. After stories in the *Daily Mail* making incorrect claims about the legal-aid fees that his firm had supposedly raked in,[58] Mr Egan received a torrent of abuse, culminating in a letter, marked with a swastika, threatening to petrol-bomb his office and kill his children.[59]

## Jury trial

As for the hallmark of criminal justice – those twelve men and women good and true, injecting democracy and public participation into the criminal process in adherence to the spirit of Magna Carta – this is also not guaranteed.

The theory in support of the jury system revolves around the notion of jurors as the bulwark against state oppression, that anybody mistreated by the state has the guarantee of a decision by a completely independent body of normal citizens. We do not select juries like in the US, where the parties vie to secure their favoured jury composition. They are randomly selected from the electoral roll, and the expectation is that they will bring a diversity of experience and skills that equip them to reach the correct verdict, as well as ensuring that the public's collective notions of justice remain central to the operation of the criminal process.

Increasingly, however, special-interest groups are identifying particular types of crime where it is said that the conviction rate is insufficient, and locating the problem in the biases of the ordinary people sitting in judgment.

The two that have featured most prominently in the media are driving offences and sexual offences. In relation to the former, a piece in the *Guardian* in 2016 by Martin Porter QC called for people accused of dangerous driving not to be allowed to elect trial by jury, on the premise that 'jurors are too ready to acquit drivers who cause death or injury to pedestrians and cyclists'.[60] Observing, correctly, that the conviction rate for all offences is higher for trials in the magistrates' court (64 per cent) than the Crown Court (52.2 per cent),[61] Mr Porter proposed depriving defendants of a trial in the latter. He listed some examples of acquittals reported in the media, in cases in which he claimed 'the evidence against the driver seem[ed] very strong', and surmised that, as there were more drivers than cyclists, jurors were predisposed to sympathising with the former. There were no statistics in support of his thesis. And the fact that Mr Porter himself was a cyclist, who had very recently taken out an unsuccessful private prosecution against a driver who had been acquitted by a jury,[62] was an interest he forgot to mention in his comment piece. But his message was nevertheless clear: the trial process isn't producing enough results to my liking, so let's change the trial process.

Cases involving sexual allegations have been the subject of similar proposals, albeit there is a body of evidence in which these are grounded. The gap between the reported rate of sexual offences and the conviction rate is well known. The figure of 6 per cent is often cited, and, although it is difficult to state with precision, appears broadly correct. The Office of National Statistics reports that only one in six offences of rape are reported to the police.[63] Of those, just over half result in a charge, and 58 per cent of rapes charged end in conviction.[64] And it is not because 94 per cent of complaints are untrue. There is a problem – that much is undeniable.

What is less straightforward is how best to address it. Many difficulties arise at the early investigation stage when crucial scientific and other evidence is gathered or lost, as we saw when we considered the problems in the John Worboys investigation. An inherent difficulty with sexual allegations is that often the only evidence is the word of the complainant against the word of a suspect, particularly where the issue is consent. While this does not bar a conviction (there is no longer any requirement for 'corroboration' evidence – the evidence of a single complainant is enough, if the jury is sure of their evidence), it inevitably makes things more difficult for a prosecutor to prove the case to the criminal standard. Cases involving young people frequently occur against a backdrop where the parties have been drinking, where memory is fragmented. This is not a judgement, but it can make the job of making a jury sure of what happened that little more difficult.

Sexual cases are also unusual because the requirement that the prosecution prove a defendant *did not reasonably believe* the complainant was consenting can result in situations where a crime both has and has not been committed. A complainant may not have consented, but the defendant may have reasonably – but mistakenly – believed that she was consenting.

The stigma – and sentence – that attaches to sex offences also plays a role in the figures, as defendants are far less likely to admit guilt. Only 35 per cent of defendants charged with a sexual offence plead guilty. The next lowest category of offence for guilty pleas is violence, to which 60 per cent of defendants plead guilty. Drugs offences attract guilty-plea rates of 80 per cent.[65]

But the fear expressed by campaigners is that juries fall prey to common societal 'rape myths', such as preconceptions as to what constitutes a 'typical' victim or 'typical' rapist; that certain modes of dress or drinking mean a woman is 'asking for it'; how a 'typical' rape victim acts in the aftermath; and the meaning of consent. Notwithstanding that the conviction rates at trial for sexual offences are broadly comparable with other offences, and that juries are given strong directions by judges on the dangers of rape stereotypes and myths, the concern is that attitudes commonly expressed in surveys and the media inevitably filter into the jury pool. And there is some academic research that suggests this could be a real problem.[66]

So it is that some MPs have called for the abolition of juries in sex cases,[67] with the stated aim of increasing the conviction rate at court.

I am by no means ideologically wedded to jury trial. I would be nervous about all decisions being taken by lone professional judges, but I do often worry about the opacity of the jury system – it is illegal for a juror to disclose what happened during their deliberations – and how that makes it impossible to assess how juries operate. However, I would suggest that the first step prior to fundamental change is to investigate how juries are working in practice, not merely in a simulated environment. Whether it's requiring jurors to provide reasons for their verdicts, as happens in other countries, or allowing researchers to observe deliberations, we need to know whether juries are working as intended before we campaign to replace them.

And the research should not be confined to one category of offence. Because it follows, surely, that if jurors are allowing prejudice to blur their assessment of the evidence in one type of trial, others are at risk too. And while the emphasis in this discussion is on wrongful acquittals, it stands to reason that widespread failures to pay heed to the evidence will be resulting in wrongful convictions as well.

But the analysis rarely extends that far. It is framed solely as an issue of increasing conviction rates in one type of offence.

And this should trouble us. An inconsistency is intolerable. We cannot swear allegiance to the rule of law while running a parallel system – providing for a mode of trial which we hold up as a gold standard for 'normal' suspects, with a second, more pro-conviction tribunal for the crimes we *really* can't abide. Either juries are what we tell ourselves they are – the democratic guarantor of liberty faithfully applying the burden and standard of proof and the law to the evidence – or they are seriously flawed, pumping out the wrong verdict with alarming frequency. If the latter, we need to know, with a view to making radical changes to our trial process for all offences, not just some. And for the protection of defendants as much as complainants.

The unifying implication is that only the guilty are put on trial. 'Suspect' and 'criminal' are used interchangeably, as we are conditioned to agree that the criminal process is in every case a matter of easing the inevitable transition from the former to the latter, and the quicker, cheaper and more painlessly this production line is oiled, the better.

Inevitably, we risk losing our bearings. We are encouraged not to think critically about what changes to our trial system would mean if we were wrongly accused, because the subtext is that we wouldn't be. The police will only arrest the guilty man. But we know this is not true. We know that innocent people are arrested and charged every single day. And we know from the history books that some are convicted and spend years of their lives incarcerated for something they didn't do.

Our conviction rate – which includes guilty pleas – was at the latest count 87 per cent,[68] meaning that, out of the 1.37 million people prosecuted in the last year, over 178,000 are either acquitted by a court or have the proceedings against them abandoned. Many of those, inevitably, will be factually guilty people against whom there was just not enough evidence to meet the standard of proof. But, equally inevitably, some will be entirely innocent. It is for them – in recognition that they could be *us* – that the protections exist.

There is, I think, a strange doublethink in our culture. From the films we laud as classics, to the TV shows we binge-watch, to the books we inhale, we cannot get enough of stories of miscarriages of justice. From *Twelve Angry Men* to *The Shawshank Redemption*; from *Making a Murderer* to *The Innocent Man*; from *To Kill a Mockingbird* to Sirius Black in Harry Potter – innocent citizens victimised by a malfunctioning judicial process are the heroes we root for the most. Yet, lifting our heads away from the screen, we are prepared to accept at face value the assurance that this wouldn't happen in our lives. We are content to live in a society where, since 2014, we routinely refuse compensation for victims of miscarriages of justice, setting them an impossible standard of proving their innocence before we will even contemplate an official apology. Where defence lawyers are monstered as accessories to their clients' alleged crimes. Where what matters is increasing the number of convictions, rather than ensuring their safety.

And there is a risk, I know, that, in focusing this discussion on cases involving sexual violence against women, I might appear as just another centurion of the law's old guard, feeding the claim from the alt-right that there is an epidemic of false complaints. I promise you, I am here not with my #HimToo banner, shouting 'What about the menz?' in a reflexive panic at modernity snapping at my privileged heels as the immunity conferred by the patriarchy is finally breached.[69] As a prosecutor, I will tell you now, in terms of numbers, there are more men getting away with it than there are wrongful convictions.

I understand why many victims of crime, particularly gender-based violence, feel so strongly that the system is unfairly weighted against them; it's because, for centuries, it has been. Complaints have not been taken seriously. The police, prosecutors, lawyers and judges have treated complainants abominably. Our justice system has for most of its existence been something run solely by men and in the interests of men, and, while things have improved a lot, I don't pretend it's all better now. It's not. The raw figures alone tell us that things have to be improved.

But we don't – can't – structure criminal justice by reference solely to numbers. The vast majority of reports may well be true, but that tells us nothing about the merits of an individual, contested allegation. That is why we have to be so cautious when presented with easy fixes to up conviction rates.

And if it appears that I pay particular attention in this chapter to sexual violence, it is precisely because it bears all the characteristics – a low conviction rate, historical institutional indifference, belated global awareness – that lend themselves to every successful campaign to make it easier to convict those accused. It is when we are confronted with cases of the utmost horror that we are at our most vulnerable to the political siren call: 'Let's just make it a little bit easier to stop these criminals getting away with it.'

Note that the political prescription is not to improve investigation or detection, or the accessibility of the trial process. It is not, in the context of sexual offending, to stop the closure of Rape Crisis centres, or tackle the crisis in forensic science. Or increase the number of Independent Sexual Violence Advisers (ISVAs), who are essential in helping victims navigate the most difficult years of their lives. We could improve training for police officers, or develop a national education campaign to teach young people about respect and consent. Instead of announcing cuts to the justice budget of 40 per cent and sacking a third of the court staff,[70] we could resource the courts so that victims do not have to wait years until there is a courtroom available to hear their trial, by which time memory – the most valuable currency in criminal evidence – has corroded.

Those things, however, cost money.

What is cheap and quick for a government in a tight spot is to hack away at one or two fundamental protections. Follow the trusted recipe: conflate 'accused' and 'guilty', and surf the popular approval of 'rebalancing' the criminal justice system.

As with so much else of what we've seen in these pages, the greatest trick they are pulling is convincing you that the alleged 'criminal' will never be you.

# 8. *Equality and Due Process*

'The Prime Minister has said that it is not acceptable and therefore it will not be accepted. It might be enforceable in a court of law, this contract, but it is not enforceable in the court of public opinion and that is where the government steps in.'

Harriet Harman MP, Leader of the
House of Commons, 1 March 2009[1]

In October 2008, the global financial system teetered on the brink. The US investment bank Lehman Brothers had filed for bankruptcy only weeks before, sending shockwaves across the world economy. Stock markets from Wall Street to London to Frankfurt to Tokyo plunged, credit markets froze and asset values tumbled. Major depositors tried to withdraw their money from the world's biggest financial institutions, leading to panic that a global run on the banks could precipitate the collapse of the banking system across the world.

A number of major UK banks were particularly exposed, including the Royal Bank of Scotland. As of the evening of Friday, 10 October 2008, RBS had run out of money. Without urgent intervention, the bank would not be able to open its doors on Monday morning. Chancellor of the Exchequer Alistair Darling would later tell of his fear that the country came within hours of the 'breakdown of law and order'.[2] Over that weekend, the UK government negotiated an unprecedented £500 billion rescue plan, including £50 billion of taxpayer money, to stabilise the markets and recapitalise the stricken banking sector.

It came to be accepted that RBS was particularly exposed due to a series of catastrophic decisions made by its chief executive, Sir Fred Goodwin – dubbed 'Fred the Shred' on account of his reputation for aggressive cost-cutting. As part of the bailout package negotiated by the government, RBS agreed that Sir Fred (as then was) should step down. The compromise agreement that secured his departure included a recognition of his entitlement under his contract to a pension calculated at £650,000 per year.

And so, when, on 25 February 2009, the details of his pension – which had by that date been revised to £703,000 per annum – were made public by BBC Business Editor Robert Peston, the public reaction was one of understandable anger. As the House of Commons Treasury Committee would later observe, 'It seemed inconceivable to many that a chief executive, who had steered his bank to such catastrophic ruin, should be so handsomely rewarded for conduct which had been so damaging to his firm's shareholders, the UK economy, and the UK taxpayer.'[3]

But such were the terms of his contract. The Royal Bank of Scotland did not provide for any performance-based reduction, and the compromise agreement that ensured his departure preserved his contractual entitlement to the full figure on early retirement.[4]

As media outrage grew, so did pressure on the government to take steps to remedy this inequitable state of affairs. Appeals to Sir Fred's better nature, beseeching him to voluntarily surrender part of his pension, gave way to stern assurances to explore legal avenues to recover the money, before ministers quickly realised that none existed.[5]

Then came an appearance from Leader of the House of Commons and Deputy Leader of the Labour Party, Harriet Harman. In an interview with the BBC's Andrew Marr on 1 March 2009, Ms Harman was pressed about what action the government might take to recoup the pension, and said, 'Sir Fred Goodwin should not count on being £650,000 a year better off because it is not going to happen . . . The Prime Minister has said that it is not acceptable and therefore it will not be accepted. It might be enforceable in a court of law, this contract, but it is not enforceable in the court of public opinion and that is where the government steps in.'[6]

Ms Harman, a qualified solicitor, was not alone in pledging allegiance to the Court of Public Opinion over the inconvenient courts of law. Former Deputy Prime Minister John Prescott told BBC Radio 4's *Today* programme that, 'If he refuses to give [the pension] back, the government should take it off him and let him sue us through the courts.' The Liberal Democrat Treasury spokesman Vince Cable made a similar proposal, suggesting that the government should unilaterally limit the pension to £27,000 a year.[7] 'Nobody disputes that Sir Fred Goodwin should be deprived of his pension,' Mr Cable declared. 'The only issue is what is practical.'[8]

However, while few would sympathise with the arrogant, incompetent Goodwin forfeiting his multi-million-pound pension pot, the constitutional enormity of Ms Harman's comments flew under the radar. Here we had a minister explicitly calling for the government to intervene to overturn a legally binding contract; for the disapplication of the law in respect of an individual considered too unpopular to warrant its protection. It took a blowtorch to the settled principle that the rule of law requires that all of us – from Crown to citizens – be governed by and subject to the democratically created laws of the land, as legislated in Parliament and interpreted and applied by the independent courts.

When the Prime Minister was asked about his party's Deputy Leader apparently signing him up to a new doctrine of extralegal action, his spokesperson distanced the PM from the comments, observing that, 'Obviously we are bound by the rule of law'[9] – with all the sincerity of a teenager mumbling that 'obviously I'm sorry'. That was all that was said.

There was no hearty defence or explanation of the rule of law, no explicit official reassurance that the Court of Public Opinion had not, in fact, been established in parallel as an adjunct to our legal system. As Mr Cable said, 'the only issue is what is practical'. Principle didn't get a look-in. What pushback there was amounted to little more than partisan posturing, such as Conservative MP Boris Johnson accusing Ms Harman of 'leftie inanity'.[10]

The lack of outcry was, I'd suggest, because the implied primacy of the Court of Public Opinion was nothing new. Ms Harman correctly calculated that this base appeal to our worst instincts would play far better politically than a sober and reasoned explanation of the importance of equal treatment under the law, no doubt because she had seen how successfully her forebears and contemporaries had navigated difficult legal cases by casually tossing the rule of law under a bus. When faced by a difficult case involving a deeply unpopular or unpleasant individual, there are few points to be scored by referring the public to our first principles. Instead, there is a pretence – acquiesced by our betters and inflamed by the media – of an easy solution: we'll just make an exception for this particular person. Special treatment becomes not merely justifiable, but necessary.

## Equal treatment under the law

Throughout this book, I have alluded to the rule of law with a casual familiarity that assumes a settled definition which we all know and agree upon, and this, as any constitutional scholar will tell you, is not the case. The exact nature and scope of the rule of law is the subject of centuries of academic debate, but, as a working definition, one would be hard pressed to better that offered by Tom Bingham, former Lord Chief Justice of England and Wales, in his seminal book *The Rule of Law*: '[A]ll persons and authorities within the state, whether public or private should be bound by and entitled to the benefit of laws publicly made, taking effect (generally) in the future and publicly administered in the courts.'[11]

A key cornerstone, of this definition and almost every other, is equal treatment. The law must apply equally to all of us. The same legal rights and obligations attach, and the same fair process applies, even if the outcome is one with which we strongly disagree.

It is popularly thought that our tradition of equality before the law stretches proudly and unimpeachably back to Magna Carta of 1215. Chapters 39 and 40 sought for the first time to limit the power of the King and bring him within the constraints of the law: 'No free man shall be seized or imprisoned, or stripped of his rights or possessions, or outlawed or exiled. Nor will we proceed with force against him except by the lawful judgment of his equals or by the law of the land. To no one will we sell, to no one deny or delay right or justice.'

However, popular retelling often omits that King John repudiated Magna Carta within a matter of months, and the centuries that followed at times resembled a tired soap opera repeating the same storyline of the Crown overreaching and seeking to put itself – or its least favourite subjects – beyond the law. Notable examples include the Star Chamber, under the jurisdiction of which political enemies of James I and Charles I were tortured, tried and convicted in secret, until its abolition in 1640. Charles I found himself in direct conflict with Parliament in 1628, when he ordered the detention by 'special commandment' of five knights who had refused to pay a forced loan to finance the King's military ambitions. The resolution was the Petition of Right of 1628, by which Charles reluctantly agreed to a package of limitations on his powers, designed to ensure 'no freeman in any such manner as is before mentioned be imprisoned or detained', before embarking upon eleven years of autocratic personal rule in which Parliament was sidelined.

The Bill of Rights of 1689, providing the terms on which William of Orange agreed to become King, sets out many of the principles that we recognise today in our modern legal settlement. Divine authority was out; the Crown was subject to the law. Rights were set out in legislation, including the authority and independence of Parliament, the right to jury trial, a prohibition on cruel and unusual punishment and a prohibition on excessive fines or excessive bail. In 1701, the Act of Settlement ensured the independence of the judiciary by conferring immunity on judges for acts done in their judicial capacity – putting them beyond the reach of monarchs seeking to influence judicial decisions – and the framework for the rule of law was in place.[12]

Obviously, full equality before the law was still some way off. Discrimination on the grounds of race, sex, disability, religion, age, sexual orientation and marital status, to name but a few, pervaded the law as it did – and still does – our society. But, by incremental improvements, we have attempted to demonstrate fidelity to the notion that each of us is equally entitled to the protections of the law and to due process when the state seeks to interfere in our lives. Certainly that is the story we tell ourselves, and others, when boasting on the international stage of the famed British adherence to the rule of law.

Yet we don't have to look very hard to see that, even in the modern era, winning favour in the Court of Public Opinion can take precedence over our principles. Three particular examples out of many are worth considering further.

## Robert Thompson and Jon Venables

The abduction and murder of three-year-old James Bulger on 12 February 1993 occupies a unique space in our criminal justice history. Twenty-five years later, the grainy CCTV images of the two killers, ten-year-olds Robert Thompson and Jon Venables, leading the toddler by the hand out of Bootle's New Strand shopping centre remain ingrained on the public consciousness. However, the case was remarkable not only because of the unspeakable horror of the crime itself or the youth of the offenders – the youngest convicted murderers of the twentieth century – but for the alacrity with which politicians and press coalesced to convince the public that vengeance, rather than principle, should govern the outcome.

Within days of the offence, Prime Minister John Major gave an interview to the *Mail on Sunday*, famously stating that 'society needs to condemn a little more and understand a little less'.[13] The shadow Home Secretary, Tony Blair, was an enthusiastic opponent in the tough-on-crime arms race, opportunistically suggesting that this isolated offence was 'the ugly manifestation of a society that is becoming unworthy of that name'.[14]

Their reactions were in keeping with the media hysteria that grew as the defendants were arrested and the case headed towards trial at Preston Crown Court in November 1993. Before the trial started, the defence barristers presented the court with 243 separate newspaper articles which either expressed an editorial opinion of the defendants' guilt; expressed the view of a politician or church leader that the defendants were guilty; were inaccurate or misleading; or were sensational or highly prejudicial. Venables' QC described the coverage as 'poisoning the stream of justice', although, somewhat surprisingly, the trial judge ruled that a fair trial was still possible.[15]

However, the role of politicians was not confined to throwing platitudinous grenades from the sidelines. The case was complicated by the fact that, at that time, the Home Secretary still played a role in fixing the sentence for adults and children convicted of murder. Since 1983, a court passing a life sentence for murder (expressed as 'detention at Her Majesty's pleasure' for offenders under eighteen) was required to recommend a tariff, which was the minimum period the offender would spend in custody before becoming eligible for release on licence. However, the decision as to when, or whether, a life prisoner would be released was for the Home Secretary, taking into account the recommendations of the parole board.

This, it may strike you, is a fairly obvious breach of the separation of powers – the constitutional principle that judicial decisions in individual cases should be made by independent judges in full possession of the facts, rather than by politicians. But, until the early 2000s, this was how the system operated. The trial judge would recommend a tariff, the Lord Chief Justice would weigh in, and then the Home Secretary would either follow the recommendation or impose his own view.

This would be an objectionable state of affairs in any context, but set against an explosive media campaign and in the hands of a politician shamelessly craving popular approval, it becomes outright abusive. And so it proved. After the trial judge, following the boys' conviction, recommended a tariff of eight years, and the Lord Chief Justice proposed ten years, Michael Howard intervened to impose fifteen years, nearly double the original recommendation.

He did so, he boastfully admitted, as a direct consequence of a targeted tabloid campaign to make examples out of Venables and Thompson. After the convictions were greeted with tabloid headlines declaring the boys to be 'Freaks of Nature' (*Daily Mirror*) and asking, 'How Do You Feel Now, You Little Bastards?' (*Daily Star*), the *Sun* called for the Home Secretary to ensure the boys 'rot in jail'.

The newspaper published cut-out 'coupons' for its readers to sign and send to the Home Secretary, each coupon demanding that the boys 'stay in jail for life'. Some 21,281 coupons were duly sent. An MP, George Howarth, lent his support to a petition demanding a 'minimum sentence' of twenty-five years, and the Bulger family submitted a petition, signed by 278,300 members of the public, calling for whole-life tariffs – meaning that the boys would never be released. When announcing his decision to increase the tariffs, Mr Howard referred directly to 'the petitions and other correspondence' that he had received from the public campaigns. The Court of Public Opinion had passed sentence on the defendants.

The tariff was appealed and was ultimately, in 1997, held to be unlawful by the House of Lords. In a scathing judgment, Lord Steyn described Mr Howard's decision to take into account a newspaper campaign when fixing a sentence as 'an abdication of the rule of law'. The letters, petitions and coupons were 'worthless' as an indicator of informed public opinion, but public opinion was in any case 'irrelevant' to the exercise of what should be a dispassionate judicial function. 'Like a judge the Home Secretary ought not to be guided by a disposition to consult how popular a particular decision might be. He ought to ignore the high voltage atmosphere of a newspaper campaign. The power given to him requires, above all, a detached approach.'[16]

After similar reasoning resulted in the European Court of Human Rights handing down a damning judgment in 1999,[17] declaring that the involvement of the Home Secretary in fixing sentences amounted to a breach of the Article 6 right to a fair trial, Lord Chief Justice Woolf restored the tariff to eight years. Following a series of decisions of the ECtHR in the 1990s, the English and Welsh law governing all life sentences was belatedly reformed to remove political involvement altogether. Now, the 'minimum term' to be served by a prisoner sentenced to life is fixed by the trial judge – the independent individual who has heard all of the evidence in the case.

The media reaction to the involvement of the ECtHR was as might be expected. 'Who gave a bunch of European lawyers, from countries with much less satisfactory and mature legal systems than ours, the right to dictate how British courts and elected British politicians should deal with child murderers?' demanded the *Sun*. The *Daily Mail* seethed at 'an outside court interfering in long-standing judicial and political procedures which have been democratically established and accepted by the British people'.[18]

The point was spectacularly missed. The conflation of the judicial and the political was precisely the mischief that the House of Lords and the ECtHR were so anxious to remedy, for obvious reason. You don't have to agree with the decision of the judges as to the length of tariff in this case to appreciate the inherent danger of judicial decisions being taken not by independent judges, but by what Lord Donaldson described in Michael Howard's case as 'a politician playing to the gallery'.[19] Because, while we may, in our darker moments, be content for examples to be made out of the ghouls among us, we should never be so complacent as to assume that we will be immune from the pointing finger of the political classes.

In 2016, the *Sun* and the *Daily Mail* threw their weight against a 'politically-driven witch hunt'[20] that had resulted in a number of criminal prosecutions. The defendants had been treated 'like exhibits in a zoo'.[21] The political winds were said to be influencing what should be an impartial and apolitical process. The Prime Minister had thrown the defendants 'to the wolves to save his own skin'. The legal process had been 'geed up by the petty grievances' of campaigners.[22]

In this case, the defendants were tabloid journalists, charged (and acquitted), as part of the disastrous Operation Elveden, with paying public officials for stories, at a time when there was widespread political interest in and public concern over the activities of tabloid journalists. All of a sudden, the *Sun* decided that the notion of the public mood influencing the judicial process was perhaps not so desirable after all.

## Sir Philip Green

On 23 October 2018, the *Telegraph* revealed that a high-profile British businessman had been using non-disclosure agreements (NDAs) to cover up allegations of sexual harassment and racial bullying.

An NDA is the name given to a contractual settlement of a potential civil claim, where, in return for not taking formal legal action, the would-be claimant agrees to accept a financial sum from the prospective defendant. The agreement contains a confidentiality clause, preventing either side from revealing the substance of the allegations, and often the existence of the agreement itself. NDAs are not of themselves necessarily bad things; they can provide a useful means of privately resolving a legal dispute where neither party wishes to enter protracted, costly or public litigation. However, they are open to abuse, particularly where there is an imbalance of power. In the wrong hands, they can be a highly convenient tool for rich, powerful men to cover up their misdeeds with impunity.

So it was that, when an eight-month *Telegraph* investigation discovered that five such agreements had been entered into by a public figure, they sought to publish the details. However, the splash omitted something rather important – the man's name. This was because, the previous day, the Court of Appeal had upheld an interim injunction prohibiting publication of the identity of the parties until a full hearing, to be held at a later date. Or, as the headline had it, 'The British #MeToo Scandal Which Cannot Be Revealed'.

Over the next few days, social media heaved under the weight of speculation as to who the man might be, fuelled by the *Telegraph*'s relentless plugging of what they characterised as 'a devastating blow [for] press freedoms'.[23]

On 25 October, the speculation ceased. Lord (Peter) Hain stood up in the House of Lords and announced that he was using the cover of parliamentary privilege – which confers legal immunity upon MPs and peers for things said in Parliament – to name the man at the centre of the story as Sir Philip Green, the billionaire chairman of the Arcadia retail group. Green was already an established figure of public displeasure due to his business dealings, including a finding by MPs in 2016 that he had extracted large sums of money from department store BHS and then sold the business for one pound shortly before it went into administration, leaving a half-billion-pound hole in the employee pension scheme.[24]

Lord Hain revealed the name behind the headline because, he told the House, he felt it his 'duty under parliamentary privilege' to provide 'the full details of a story which is clearly in the public interest'.[25]

The acclaim he anticipated duly flowed. The Pool website declared him 'a babe' and 'our new favourite ally'. His parliamentary colleague Lord Adonis applauded this 'great public service'.[26] Anti-abuse campaigners on social media thanked him for 'having the guts & decency' to tread where others feared.[27] As interviewers queued up, Lord Hain declared that he had acted 'to promote justice and liberty'.[28] To the critics, he defiantly announced that he would 'neither retract nor apologise for standing up for human rights'.

One can understand the narrative that he was hoping to cultivate. *Brave politician stands up for victims of abuse silenced by billionaires buying rich-man's justice.* But closer inspection of the details reveals a far less attractive, and far more concerning, picture.

For one, despite the *Telegraph* doing its best to downplay the word 'interim' in its reporting of the Court of Appeal's injunction, that's exactly what it was. No final decision had been made. What had happened is that Arcadia and Sir Philip, upon being notified of the impending story, had initiated proceedings for breach of confidence. They argued that the details that the *Telegraph* wished to publish, which Sir Philip denied, were subject to a lawful confidentiality agreement, and that the courts should grant an injunction prohibiting publication. The *Telegraph* responded by arguing that, even if they were bound by the confidentiality agreement (to which they were not a party), it was in the public interest that the story be published, having regard to their Article 10 rights to freedom of expression.

Where such claims are brought, there is often a degree of urgency. Newspapers want to print immediately; the subject of the story wants to prevent publication. A full hearing assessing all of the evidence and arguments can take days, if not weeks, and it can be months until the courts have a slot available, so often an 'interim' injunction is sought as a first step. The court will conduct a provisional assessment of the merits of the claim, and, if it considers that the claimant is 'likely' to win at a full hearing, can issue an interim injunction, pending a full hearing.

That was where the case was up to when Lord Hain intervened. No final decision had been made. The High Court had initially refused Arcadia's application for an interim injunction, the Court of Appeal had overturned that decision,[29] but the full determination of the issues and competing interests had still to be determined. And there was a lot to consider. For one, two of the five alleged victims expressly supported an injunction – they were fearful that publication of Sir Philip's name would lead to their identification. Although there were legitimate fears of NDAs being used to conceal malign behaviour, these settlements did not seek to prevent the complainants from reporting alleged criminality to the police or appropriate regulatory bodies. The complainants had all received independent legal advice, and it was not alleged that any were subject to undue pressure in arriving at the settlements.

But that exercise – the careful, impartial judicial evaluation of the law, evidence and competing individual and public interests – was hijacked and crashed into the ground while it was still taking off. By using parliamentary privilege to frustrate the court's interim order, Lord Hain had deprived all involved of a fair hearing and an informed judgment. This mattered not just to Philip Green, but to the alleged victims too, and indeed the press. The Court of Appeal would have had the opportunity to reassess how the balance between the public interest and commercial confidentiality should be struck in the #MeToo era; the judgment may well have provided a vital precedent for the *Telegraph* in future legal battles.

But we will never know. The litigation now being pointless, it was abandoned.[30] Due process had been successfully supplanted by vainglorious politicking, the assumption that the snap opinion of a media-savvy politician was worth more than due process under the law. When questions of the details of the case were put to a pleased-looking Lord Hain on BBC *Newsnight*, his startled expression and circumlocutory answers betrayed a man who had not thought this through. Why the haste? Why not wait for the full court judgment? What about the wishes of the complainants? Answer came there none.[31]

And so often this is how easy it is to lose sight of our basic principles. A simplistic narrative of #MeToo victims being silenced by courts indulging rich men appeals so instinctively to our sense of injustice that we can be tricked into nodding through a 'solution' which damages us far more than we realise. When the man involved is as widely reviled as Philip Green, the assumption can be made that a defeat for him, however caused, must be A Good Thing.

But it is not. Mr Green may well be an unpleasant man. He

may well be a rich man who has relied upon his deep pockets and expensive retained lawyers to cover up allegations that the public should know about. Non-disclosure agreements may well be ripe for review and potentially reform. Access to the courts may well be – for reasons we have explored in this book – increasingly the preserve of the wealthy, affording privileges beyond the grasp of the average citizen.

Those things can all be true. But none are justifications for voiding due process, fast-forwarding to the ending that we believe is deserved.

## Shamima Begum

On 17 February 2015, three British schoolgirls from Bethnal Green arrived at Gatwick Airport. They took a Turkish Airlines flight to Istanbul, and from there travelled to Syria. Their aim was to join the estimated 550 women and girls who had fled the West to join the Islamic State terror group, responsible for the deaths of thousands of innocent civilians across the world.

Four years later, almost to the day, Anthony Lloyd, a journalist for *The Times*, located one of the three tabloid-branded 'ISIS brides', Shamima Begum, in the al-Hawl refugee camp in northern Syria. She was the only known survivor of the three who had left London in 2015, and the intervening years had been cruel. She had been married to a twenty-three-year-old Dutch ISIS fighter, days after arriving in Syria, aged fifteen. She had witnessed the atrocities of the group: the severed heads in bins, the videos of hostage executions and the arbitrary torture of dissenters. She had been injured in airstrikes, had lost two children at the ages of eight months and twenty-one months, and was now nine months pregnant with her third.

As the caliphate crumbled and ISIS battled to maintain control of its last remaining territories, she took the decision to flee Baghuz and attempt to return to Britain. 'I was frightened that the child I am about to give birth to would die like my other children if I stayed,' she told *The Times*. 'I'll do anything required just to be able to come home and live quietly with my child.'[32]

Contrition was not high on her agenda. Perhaps unsurprisingly for a fifteen-year-old indoctrinated into a fundamentalist death cult, she expressed no regret for her action and little sympathy for the victims of her brethren. When asked by Sky News about the ISIS-inspired terror attack in Manchester in 2017, she suggested that it was 'justified'.[33] Arrogant, entitled, remorseless and defiant – as a public-relations exercise, it left something to be desired.

Nevertheless, as a British citizen, she was entitled by law to return home. Obviously, it would not necessarily be without consequence; a criminal investigation was likely to attach, with the threat of prosecution for terrorism offences and, upon conviction, the life-changing sanctions of imprisonment. Social Services would doubtless intervene to ensure the safety of her child. The intelligence services would likely keep her under close watch indefinitely. Coming home and living quietly with her child was not, on any view, going to be as straightforward as the nineteen-year-old had perhaps convinced herself.

The reaction of elements of the press and commentariat to Begum's impending return was less than considered. Some represented a clown car of stupid. LBC radio host and *Daily Mail* columnist Andrew Pierce, for example, demanded the introduction of a new criminal law, to apply retrospectively, just for Begum's case.[34] That this would amount to a fundamental breach of the internationally accepted principle of non-retroactivity – that people are not prosecuted for crimes that didn't exist when they committed them – did not occur to him. Nor that there were already plenty of laws under which she could lawfully be prosecuted. A scramble ensued among Conservative MPs to think of creative ways in which the label 'treason' might successfully be applied, despite the fact that existing terrorism legislation adequately provided for a suite of offences carrying substantial terms of imprisonment. Dr Julian Lewis MP suggested that 'the Home Secretary consider upgrading the law on treason', as if this were something that a politician had the power to do unilaterally, on a whim, and apply to past behaviour.[35] Defence Secretary Gavin Williamson sprang up to share his views on this British citizen being granted legal aid in proceedings that would determine the course of the rest of her life: 'Quite frankly, the British people don't like it and neither do I.'[36]

But it was on the issue of citizenship that the biggest backlash was trained. The first clue that this might be on the political chopping board came in an editorial in the *Sun*, demanding 'Strip her of her citizenship',[37] echoing a call in Richard Littlejohn's column for the *Mail*.[38] Home Secretary Sajid Javid, whose future leadership bid had for some months been the subject of media speculation, announced in *The Times* on 15 February that, 'If you have supported terrorist organisations abroad I will not hesitate to prevent your return.'[39]

While the Home Secretary has the power under the British Nationality Act 1981 to remove citizenship if deemed 'conducive to the public good', international law prohibits this where its effect would be to render an individual stateless. This, you may think, is obvious. Until the colonisation of the moon, everybody has to have at least one country on earth where they can lawfully exist. As a British citizen, therefore, it was difficult to see how Shamima Begum could be subjected to this process.

Mr Javid attempted to get around the inconvenient legal principles by suggesting that, due to her parents' Bangladeshi heritage, Shamima Begum qualified for Bangladeshi citizenship. She had never visited Bangladesh and did not hold a Bangladeshi passport, and her by-now newborn son was a British citizen, but the Home Secretary was undeterred. He revoked her British citizenship, preventing her from returning to the UK.[40]

Putting aside the moral argument over the responsibilities of a state to deal with its own problematic citizens – not least those arguably groomed as children into terrorist cults – the lawfulness of this act was questionable.[41] Bangladesh, for its part, had publicly denied that Ms Begum was entitled to citizenship.[42] There was also the matter of Mr Javid having published only a few months earlier the UK's Counter-Terrorism Strategy for 2018, in which he included 'illustrative examples' of how ISIS returnees would be dealt with. One such case study involved a young British woman joining ISIS and seeking to return with a newborn. For that case study, the Home Office suggested that the correct course would be applying to a judge for a Temporary Exclusion Order (TEO) to manage the woman's return to the UK, followed by a police investigation and (potentially) a criminal prosecution upon her homecoming. If there was no evidence of criminality, there would be a special de-radicalisation programme to assist her reintegration into society. In any case, the local authority and external organisations would be involved to safeguard the welfare of the child. Revocation of citizenship was not even mentioned as an option.[43] The only perceptible difference between the 'illustrative example' and Shamima Begum was that the case study did not have the misfortune to be returning at a time when the Home Secretary was greasing the red tops in anticipation of a run at the party leadership.[44]

Nevertheless, it was wildly popular. The *Sun* trilled, 'Well done, The Saj', praising his 'swift and bold action'.[45] The *Daily Express* front page cheered, 'Sense at last!'[46] While the Home Secretary's crass populism was criticised by *The Times*, the *Guardian* and the *Daily Mail*,[47] a Sky News poll suggested that eight in ten Britons supported Javid's move. Only one in six thought it was wrong. A similar number supported the government having the power to render UK citizens stateless if they join terrorist groups. The poll did not ask the respondents what they would do with, say, Thomas Mair, the terrorist murderer of MP Jo Cox, nor did it ask to which random, unwilling country he ought to be deported.

The lawfulness was, for some, not even a concern. Former England cricket captain and broadcaster Michael Vaughan told his million Twitter followers that, 'Sometimes laws & Rules have to be broken.'[48] Allison Pearson in the *Telegraph* agreed: 'this fanatically stupid young woman . . . must not under any circumstances be allowed to return to Britain.'[49] Alt-right social-media agitators cheered Mr Javid for 'supporting and defending LOYAL British nationals' against 'the "religion of peace"'.[50] For these people, the fact that Mr Javid's actions, even if lawful, created two tiers of British citizens, rendering those of non-British parentage at a risk of losing their citizenship where those with British parents were not, was simply not a concern.

None of the case studies in this chapter are designed to be sympathetic. Greedy bankers, sadistic murderers, alleged sexual harassers and terror supporters – even making allowances for youth or naivety, I do not expect many reading to declare an affinity with the people presented.

But each shows how easily we can be led into assenting or turning a blind eye to 'special treatment' for those whom we are assured 'don't deserve' the rights and due process afforded to the rest of us. While in each instance there were vocal elements in the press and political classes speaking out in defence of the rule of law, that the dominant narrative was advocated with such confidence says, I fear, something troubling about our susceptibility to instinctively approve of actions that substitute the Court of Public Opinion for the rule of law.

Again, we seem vulnerable to the implicit, false reassurance that it is something that only affects other people. It isn't. If equality before the law can be disregarded for *them*, it can be disregarded for you. The rule of law is like a game of giant Jenga. You can pluck isolated cases out of the system once, maybe twice, with the structure remaining upright. But its foundations are weakened with every block removed. And you don't want to be the one standing underneath it when it tumbles.

# 9. Democracy

'Do unelected judges (about which the public know almost nothing) have the right to supersede the wishes of the elected members of Parliament, and through them the Government?'

Iain Duncan Smith MP, 7 December 2016[1]

On 23 June 2016, over 17.4 million voters in the referendum on the United Kingdom's membership of the European Union expressed their desire to leave the EU, pipping the 16.1 million remain vote by 51.89 per cent to 48.11 per cent. More people voted 'leave' than had ever voted for any other national political decision, with the vote for 'remain' a close second, causing Prime Minister Theresa May to describe the referendum as 'the biggest democratic exercise in our country's history'.[2]

Just over four months later, on 3 November 2016, three unelected judges attempted to overturn the democratically expressed will of the British people. In a High Court judgment which 'stepped into new territory',[3] the 'shocking judicial activism'[4] of the judges precipitated a 'constitutional crisis',[5] 'telling Government and Parliament how to go about their business',[6] and raising a question as to 'which body is supreme, the [judiciary] or Parliament'.[7]

Ruling on judicial review proceedings brought against the Secretary of State for Exiting the European Union by Gina Miller, an investment manager and philanthropist, the High Court judges held that the process for giving notification to leave the European Union under Article 50 of the Lisbon Treaty legally required an Act of Parliament, and that the notice to withdraw could not be given by the government using its prerogative powers. Or, as the *Daily Express* summarised the case: 'Three judges yesterday blocked Brexit.'[8]

The front page of the *Daily Mail* the following day made a statement that echoed around the world.[9] 'ENEMIES OF THE PEOPLE' was emblazoned above photographs of the three judges involved: Lord Chief Justice Thomas, Master of the Rolls Sir Terence Etherton and Lord Justice Sales. The text that followed spoke of the 'out of touch judges' who had 'declared war on democracy' in an effort to 'block Brexit'. A profile of each of the aforementioned enemies was provided on the *Mail*'s companion website, MailOnline: 'One founded a EUROPEAN law group, another charged the taxpayer millions for advice and the third is an openly gay ex-Olympic fencer.'[10]

The *Telegraph*, although attracting less attention than the *Mail*, opted for a similar front page: 'Judges vs the people',[11] relying on the same outraged Members of Parliament – Iain Duncan Smith, Dominic Raab and Douglas Carswell – for the quotes, and making similar claims about the special interests of the three judges, minus the sexuality of the Master of the Rolls. The fury was trailed across the airwaves and social media by UKIP politicians, including Suzanne Evans and Nigel Farage, the former calling for the public to have the power to 'sack' the judges[12] and the latter warning the judges of 'the public anger they will provoke'.[13] The *Daily Express* editorial declared this 'a crisis as grave as anything since the dark days when Churchill vowed we would fight them on the beaches', urging its readers, 'Rise up people of Britain and fight, fight, fight.'[14]

Government ministers joined the fray. Sajid Javid told BBC's *Question Time* that the judicial decision had 'opened an important moral issue', adding, 'This is an attempt to frustrate the will of the British people and it is unacceptable.'[15] When Prime Minister Theresa May was asked whether she was concerned about the impact of the *Mail*'s headlines on the constitutional principle of judicial independence, she chided, 'It is important that we have a free press.' The Health Secretary Jeremy Hunt similarly stated that he would 'defend to the hilt the right of newspapers within the law to write what they like'.[16] When lawyers called for Liz Truss, the Lord Chancellor with a statutory duty to defend the independence of the judiciary, to say something, Ms Truss declined, remaining silent for thirty-six hours before releasing a short statement confirming that the government would appeal the decision to the Supreme Court, acknowledging the existence of the principle of judicial independence, and urging that, 'Legal process must be followed.'[17] She would later echo the Prime Minister in emphasising that she was 'a very strong believer in the free press', and would 'draw the line at saying what is acceptable for the press to print'.[18]

As the country geared up for the Supreme Court hearing in December 2016, the *Mail* was one of several papers offering further insight into the Justices of the Supreme Court, or the '11 unaccountable individuals [who] will consider a case that could thwart the will of the majority on Brexit'.[19] Each judge was given a 'Europhile' star rating based on their 'formal links to the EU', 'publicly expressed views which appear to be sympathetic to EU' and 'links with individuals who've been critical of the Leave campaign'. Nigel Farage and the unofficial Leave.EU campaign announced that they would lead a '100,000-strong march on the Supreme Court' to 'remind . . . the court that they cannot ignore the democratic vote of the people in the referendum'.[20]

Once the hearing was underway, Iain Duncan Smith offered commentary supporting the *Mail*'s coverage, explaining that the issue to be decided was that in this chapter's opening quote: 'Do unelected judges (about which the public know almost nothing) have the right to supersede the wishes of the elected members of Parliament, and through them the Government?'[21]

On 24 January 2017, the Supreme Court upheld the decision of the High Court, ruling by a majority of eight to three that legislation would be required to give notification under Article 50. As rage swirled on social media and Nigel Farage accused the 'establishment' of trying to 'frustrate' Brexit, Iain Duncan Smith was on hand to inform the Victoria Derbyshire programme that the decision had created 'real constitutional issues about who is supreme'.[22]

As future Foreign Secretary Dominic Raab soberly warned: '[A]n unholy alliance of diehard Remain campaigners, a fund manager [and] an unelected judiciary' had 'thwart[ed] the wishes of the British public'.[23]

Merely listing the errors strewn throughout reporting and commentary on the *Miller* case could by itself comfortably fill a 300-page hardback, and this final chapter is possibly not the best place to start. If pressed to highlight some of the more egregious misapprehensions, one might begin with some of the quotes above.

To start with, on no possible interpretation of the judgments did either the High Court or the Supreme Court 'block Brexit'.[24] They simply delineated how, as a matter of law, Brexit could be achieved – a route which, after the howling had subsided, the government duly followed and accomplished within two months.[25]

The details escaped many who should know better. Dominic Raab claimed that the High Court had delivered 'a vague and undemocratic verdict'.[26] Every law student knows, even if it has apparently escaped qualified lawyer Mr Raab, that a verdict is a determination of guilt in a criminal trial; a wholly distinct concept to a legal judgment. And, far from being vague, the High Court judgment spelled out, over 115 paragraphs, the minutiae of the legal argument it had heard, the statute and case law it had considered and the reasoning for the ruling. The Supreme Court went further, offering 283 paragraphs spread over 97 pages, with helpful press summaries for those without time to read the full judgment. (The charge of 'undemocratic' we will consider later.)

Similarly, the courts were not, as Iain Duncan Smith claimed, 'straying into political territory'. As the High Court judgment clearly stated, all sides to the litigation, including the government, agreed that the case raised 'a justiciable question which it is for the courts to decide', and one which was 'a pure question of law'.[27] The question was whether the government, exercising its powers under the royal prerogative (the residual executive powers vested in the Queen which she mostly exercises on the advice of and through her ministers), was legally able to give notification to leave the EU under Article 50. The royal prerogative, put simply, consists of a rump of powers that have not been formally removed from the Queen and clearly defined by Parliament. These powers range from the granting of honours, to declaring war, to the conduct of foreign affairs, which includes the signing of or withdrawal from international treaties. Critically, the prerogative cannot be used to displace or overrule Parliament, or to alter the law of the land, as confirmed in the *Case of Proclamations* in 1610.[28] The government argued that giving notification to leave the EU treaties was an act of foreign affairs that fell within its prerogative powers. The court ruled that it was not: the effect of withdrawing from the EU went beyond leaving a treaty that existed solely on the international plane; it would directly affect and remove rights that UK citizens had acquired during the UK's membership of the EU – rights which, as a result of the European Communities Act 1972, now formed part of the body of UK law. The royal prerogative cannot be used to amend or repeal domestic law; hence an Act of Parliament would be required.

Lest it needed spelling out for the likes of IDS, the High Court emphasised: 'Nothing we say has any bearing on the question of the merits or demerits of a withdrawal by the United Kingdom from the European Union; nor does it have any bearing on government policy, because government policy is not law. The policy to be applied by the executive government and the merits or demerits of withdrawal are matters of political judgment to be resolved through the political process.'[29]

As regards the referendum, the judges were at pains to emphasise that they were considering only 'a pure legal point about the effect *in law* of the referendum', adding, 'This court does not question the importance of the referendum as a political event, the significance of which will have to be assessed and taken into account elsewhere.'[30]

Thus, the species of complaint exemplified by John Redwood MP – 'I cannot believe the judges failed to read the leaflet [sent out to voters, in which the government promised to implement the result of the referendum]' – was vacuous beyond measure. The point, as he would have known had he taken the time to read the judgment, was that it didn't matter what voters had been *told*; what mattered were the legal powers of the Crown, and these could not be changed by the government printing a flyer.

But the confusion penetrated far deeper than errors of fact or law; the reporting and companion commentary betrayed a fundamental misunderstanding of how our constitution actually works. Concepts that are merrily tossed around in political discourse as if commonly and widely understood – such as parliamentary sovereignty, the separation of powers, and judicial independence: the cornerstones of our democracy – were on this occasion so poorly discussed that it suggested widespread unfamiliarity, among the political class as much as the public, with the very basics of how our country works.

On the last of those three concepts, judicial independence, there was an even graver problem. The reaction to this entire episode, by ministers, parliamentarians, media and the public, spoke to a sprawling global phenomenon in which the independence of the judiciary is under direct attack. This of itself is not new; over the preceding pages we have tasted the political and media staple diet of accusations against lily-livered liberal judges prioritising the rights of illegal immigrants, money-grabbing compo claimants and career criminals over the law-abiding British public. But the 'Enemies of the People' headline and associated commentary, not just criticising the outcome of a court decision but personally attacking the individual judges involved, felt like a significant, emblematic moment; a sudden, choking realisation of how careless we have been in our treatment of our constitutional principles, and how close we might be creeping to doing irreparable damage to the framework of our democracy.

# What do we mean by 'parliamentary sovereignty'?

Before looking further at the threats posed to judicial independence, it may assist to skirt over some of our constitutional essentials. A common misconception is that the United Kingdom does not have a constitution. It does. What it lacks is a *codified* constitution: a single document setting out the rubrics and parameters of how our country is run. Instead, the rules are scattered throughout various Acts of Parliament, the common law and 'constitutional conventions' – unwritten but respected norms, such as the convention that the House of Lords does not oppose legislation from the House of Commons that formed part of the governing party's election manifesto (the 'Salisbury Convention').[31]

The beating heart of our constitution is parliamentary sovereignty, a favoured and pithy expression of which is, *What the Queen in Parliament enacts is law*.[32]

Originally, sovereignty was vested in the Crown, and subject to few limitations. Monarchs could largely make law as they pleased. Over the centuries, as the rule of law evolved, the monarch's powers were trammelled and handed over to Parliament – comprising the elected House of Commons and the appointed House of Lords. As we saw briefly in the last chapter, there were several key milestones at the end of the seventeenth century, including the Bill of Rights 1689, which made clear that the monarch could not unilaterally change the law of the land; Parliament was sovereign. Nowadays, what few powers the monarch retains – the royal prerogative – are mostly used by or on the advice of government ministers and must be exercised consistently with the law.

The birthing of a new law involves a bill being presented before Parliament (usually it is the government introducing a bill in the House of Commons, although legislation can start life in the House of Lords), and then successfully passing through the various stages in both Houses, at which the proposed law is debated, considered, amended and ultimately voted on.[33] Upon completing its passage through Parliament, a bill must receive royal assent from the monarch before it becomes an Act. Although theoretically allowing for a royal veto, the constitutional convention is that the monarch always grants royal assent.

Parliament can make or unmake any law it chooses. This is what we mean by parliamentary sovereignty. There is at law school a fun (using that term in the sense that lawyers do) paradox posed as to whether Parliament can make a law binding future Parliaments ('Of course it can, it's sovereign' / 'Of course it can't, future Parliaments can simply overrule legislation that they disagree with'). But what is indisputable is that the executive (the government) and the judiciary (the courts) do not have the power to overrule Parliament.

Unlike many other legal jurisdictions, we do not have an overarching constitutional court, with the power to strike down legislation that contravenes our constitution. Our Supreme Court judges have far less power, in this regard, than their equivalents in the United States. Our courts can quash *secondary* legislation – regulations made by government ministers exercising powers granted to them by Acts of Parliament (primary legislation) – if ministers have acted unlawfully in making the regulations, but judges have no such power over Acts of Parliament. The closest they get is when the courts make 'declarations of incompatibility' under the Human Rights Act, where domestic legislation is irreconcilable with the European Convention of Human Rights; but this has no legal effect. It is simply the courts exercising the powers – given to them by Parliament – to send up a flare when there is a clash between statutes and ECHR principles.[34]

This is a deliberately rudimentary sketch of parliamentary sovereignty, but it is enough to expose the intellectual hollowness of the claims by Iain Duncan Smith and co that the *Miller* case created 'real constitutional issues about who is supreme'.[35] It was, to the contrary, a straightforward example of our constitution upholding the settled principle that the government can't use the royal prerogative to overrule or displace law made by Parliament. The government wanted to do something, the court was required to determine whether the government could do so lawfully, and the court ruled that the government could not, and that an Act of Parliament was required to achieve the desired effect.

The tortured phrasing of IDS' further question – 'Do unelected judges . . . have the right to supersede the wishes of the elected members of Parliament, and through them the Government?' – betrays the depths of his muddle. Judges do not have the right to supersede the wishes of MPs as expressed in legislation, but they certainly have the right to frustrate the wishes of the government where the government tries to act unlawfully. To elide, as IDS so glibly does, the supremacy of Parliament with his apparent belief in the supremacy of *government*, is to ignore another fundament of our constitution – the separation of powers.

## The separation of powers

From the above, we can see how the three branches of our constitution – legislature, executive and judiciary – interact. Parliament makes the law as it sees fit. Ministers govern in accordance with the law, and are held to account both by Parliament and by the courts. Independent courts apply and interpret the legislation – creating an ancillary body of common law – and adjudicate disputes. If the government steps outside its legal powers, its actions can be challenged in the courts by those affected.

This model is a theoretical guarantor of democracy. In order for it to work, however, it is vital that the three branches remain, as far as possible, independent of each other. This is the nub of the separation of powers. As Montesquieu put it in *The Spirit of the Laws*:

> Nor is there liberty if the power of judging is not separate from legislative power and from executive power. If it were joined to legislative power, the power over the life and liberty of the citizen would be arbitrary, for the judge would be the legislator. If it were joined to executive power, the judge would have the force of an oppressor.

All would be lost if the same man or the same body of principal men, either of nobles or of the people, exercised these powers: that of making the laws, that of executing public resolutions, and that of judging the crimes or the disputes of individuals.[36]

Historically, our purity has been muddied. Judges originated as advisors of the King – his favourite knights, clergy, aldermen and lords. From the twelfth century, they began to tour the country, applying a measure of consistency in judicial decisions that formed the basis of the common law. While notionally independent, they served at the King's pleasure, and could easily be dispensed with if they returned unpopular judgments. In 1607, in the famous *Case of Prohibitions*, James I inserted himself as a judge in a property dispute. When Chief Justice Sir Edward Coke overturned the decision, he was dismissed. The late seventeenth century saw a rash of politically motivated hirings and firings, with Charles II sacking eleven judges in the last eleven years of his reign, and his brother, James II, removing twelve judges in three years when they would not make rulings in his favour.[37]

It was against this backdrop of abusive executive power that the Act of Settlement in 1701 was passed, giving judges immunity from civil or criminal prosecution for acts done in office and placing the power of dismissal in the hands of Parliament, setting the foundations for meaningful judicial independence.

There was still a long way to go, however. Until the creation of the Supreme Court by the Constitutional Reform Act 2005, the highest court in the land was the Appellate Committee of the House of Lords, meaning that the most senior judges were both part of the legislature and key figures in the judiciary. We have even had government ministers sitting as judges, such as Lord Cave serving as both Home Secretary and an appellate judge at the end of the First World War. We saw in the last chapter how, as recently as thirty years ago, politicians played a central role in sentencing murderers.

The office of Lord Chancellor was a long-standing constitutional quirk, triple-hatting the office-holder as a senior judge, Speaker of the House of Lords and the judiciary's representative in Cabinet, until the role was redefined as part of the constitutional shake-up that saw the House of Lords' judicial functions transferred to the brand new Supreme Court.

As of 2020, we do much better, although remain far from perfect. For a start, our government is still drawn from the legislature; government ministers are either MPs or peers. The Lord Chancellor's function has been merged with that of Secretary of State for Justice, meaning that the same individual has in recent years found themselves responsible under their oath as Lord Chancellor for ensuring that the courts are properly funded,[38] while expected as Justice Secretary to make the political case for the 51 per cent cuts to the Ministry of Justice's budget.

However, when it comes to judicial independence, it is fair to say that we have come a long way. Judges are appointed by an independent appointments commission by reference to specific criteria and qualifications, in place of the old-style tap on the shoulder from the Lord Chancellor. All ministers have a statutory duty to 'uphold the continued independence of the judiciary',[39] with the Lord Chancellor's oath including a promise to 'defend' said independence. Senior judges can only be removed by Parliament, and this has happened just once since 1701.

The implicit understanding flowing throughout the constitution is that ministers and parliamentarians will respect the rule of law and the independence of the judiciary, and not seek to influence the judicial process. Judges, for their part, are not permitted to speak publicly about their decisions; a judgment is published and that stands as the full record of and justification for the judge's determination. They can and do talk to the media about the generalities of the law and their role, and the Lord Chief Justice has a statutory duty[40] to reflect the collective views of the judiciary to Parliament and the government, but there is no public engagement in individual cases. Thus it is expected that the legislature and executive be mindful that, when they comment on court judgments, the judge in question cannot answer back.

Inevitably, there is tension between the three branches; this is not only expected but inherently good. An absence of tension would be an indicator that something is seriously wrong. If the government was always able to have its legislation passed and ministers were never criticised by Parliament, it would be a sign that Parliament was not doing its job. Likewise, if the courts were always ruling in favour of government, constantly decreeing that every executive action was lawful, to the grateful applause of the front bench, one would fear that the judges were not acting independently. Governing *should* be difficult.

But there is an obvious limit if judicial independence is to be preserved. Ministers should not lash out at the judges for unfavourable decisions. If a judge is wrong, the proper course is to appeal the decision to a higher court. Similarly, if Parliament does not like the way the courts have interpreted a particular piece of legislation, it is always open to Parliament to redraft the law, clarifying its intentions.

Of course, judges are, to some extent, political animals. The judicial oath, taken by every judge, swears to 'do right to all manner of people, after the laws and usages of this realm, without fear or favour, affection or ill will', but it would be naive to suppose that judges do not bring their own idiosyncrasies, values and unconscious biases to bear on their decisions, much as they may try to avoid doing so. And it is undeniable that judicial review, and in particular claims under the Human Rights Act, increasingly requires judges to make policy-related decisions.

However, our national preference, which I am inclined to think is right, has been to try to suppress those instincts, rather than, as in the US, unleashing and inflaming them. We don't screen judicial applicants by their party politics, nor do we require them to run for election funded by special-interest groups and corporate juggernauts. Instead, we rely on the correctives in the system – the appeals mechanism for when judges are wrong, the ability to ask a judge to recuse themselves from a case where the parties fear a risk of real or apparent bias, and the Judicial Conduct Investigations Office to deal with judicial misbehaviour – to maximise the quality and independence of judicial decision-making.

It follows that, while it is both legitimate and necessary to scrutinise and criticise judicial decisions, Parliament and the executive have to tread extremely carefully. Judges are unlikely to be troubled by virulent academic criticism of a judgment, or by a more senior court scathingly overturning them on appeal. But there is a fine line. Overreach risks breaching the separation of powers and giving the appearance – or, worse, the effect – of influencing the independent judicial process. For that reason, the accepted convention is that ministers and parliamentarians should resist publicly assailing judges for decisions with which they disagree.

None of this, I would suggest, is contentious or difficult to understand. Unless, it appears, you are one of the people with the greatest influence on our democratic process.

## Under attack from the government

Examples of ministers roundly ignoring their statutory duty to uphold the independence of the judiciary are strewn throughout the preceding chapters, as well as in the opening paragraphs of this chapter, looking at *Miller*, but a few more are worthy of mention.

'It's MY job to deport foreigners who commit serious crime – and I'll fight any judge who stands in my way.' Thus spake Home Secretary Theresa May in a *Daily Mail* comment piece in February 2013,[41] in which she gave examples of immigration judges 'subverting democracy' by making decisions with which she disagreed.

This was a recurring theme for Mrs May as Home Secretary. In a parliamentary debate that same year, she stated that, 'Some judges have [. . .] chosen to ignore the will of Parliament and go on putting the law on the side of foreign criminals instead of the public.'[42] And, in fairness to her, she was simply riffing on a theme composed and turned up to eleven by the preceding Labour government. Tony Blair in 2003 announced that he wanted to restrict the right of asylum seekers to appeal the government's decisions, railing against 'judicial interference'.[43] In 2004, Mr Blair's Home Secretary David Blunkett attempted to legislate so as to remove the right of appeal in asylum cases, even where a decision was plainly unlawful.[44]

Mr Blunkett found himself frequently at odds with judges during his tenure, for what he perceived as their failure to 'live in the same real world as the rest of us'[45] and their tendency to uphold 'airy-fairy civil liberties'.[46] He accused criminal judges who passed insufficiently severe sentences of having 'lost their marbles', with fellow ministers anonymously briefing that particular judges were 'muddled and confused old codgers'.[47] In his autobiography, Mr Blunkett would later express astonishment that the Lord Chief Justice had, in 2003, declined an invitation to a private dinner so that they could 'run through issues informally and quietly',[48] describing the judge's reluctance to attend candlelit dinners with litigants appearing in cases before him as 'very strange'. This episode, perhaps more than any other, shines as a beacon of constitutional ignorance. Upon leaving the Home Office, Mr Blunkett continued his hate/hate affair with the judiciary through a column in the *Sun*, which included headlines such as, 'Our justice system is a sick joke', 'Give that judge a brain transplant', 'Bewigged menaces who make the law look like an ass', and, in respect of a judge who ruled that one of Mr Blunkett's policies was unlawful, 'Free-booting judge'.[49]

Rewinding a decade earlier, one could hear identical complaints on the radio from Home Secretary Michael Howard, personally attacking a judge who had ruled against him in a terrorism case.[50]

The Boris Johnson government charted a deliberately provocative course against the judiciary in September 2019, after the Supreme Court unanimously ruled that the Prime Minister had acted unlawfully in advising the Queen to prorogue Parliament.[51] With 31 October 2019 looming – the date by which Mr Johnson had repeatedly guaranteed that the UK would leave the European Union, with or without an exit deal – the government, in August 2019, announced a five-week prorogation (suspension) of Parliament. The official reason offered by the government in the media was to allow for the preparation of a Queen's Speech.[52] Critics suggested a less proper motive – namely, that the government was trying to avoid parliamentary scrutiny, during a time of acute national importance, by suspending Parliament for five of the remaining eight weeks before Brexit day.

The power to prorogue Parliament is one of the prerogative powers exercised by the Queen on the advice of her ministers. Legal challenges were brought, one in England and Wales by Gina Miller and one in Scotland by SNP MP Joanne Cherry, each seeking a declaration that the government's advice was unlawful. The first question for the courts was one of 'justiciability' – i.e. was the power of prorogation something that the courts could rule on? The second question, if the courts *were* able to so rule, was whether the government had exercised the power lawfully.

At the High Court of England and Wales, the judges ruled that the question was not justiciable. The decision to prorogue Parliament was purely political, not legal, and there was no role for the courts. The Inner House of the Court of Session in Scotland, by contrast, ruled that, while having a political dimension, this very much was a legal issue that they could rule upon, and found that the Prime Minister had acted unlawfully and with improper purpose. Both courts granted permission for the losing parties to appeal to the Supreme Court.

The Supreme Court's unanimous judgment, delivered by Lady Hale, was damning for the government. The court considered a wealth of constitutional case law and, drawing upon centuries-old principles of parliamentary sovereignty, ruled that the question was justiciable. The logic was straightforward: prorogation, unlike a parliamentary recess (during which the House would not sit, but other parliamentary business would still take place, committees would meet and written parliamentary questions could be asked of ministers), has the effect of suspending all legislating and all parliamentary scrutiny of government. Parliamentary sovereignty and parliamentary accountability, the foundational principles of our constitution, could be undermined if the government was able to prorogue Parliament without any legal limit. No laws could be passed and no scrutiny of the government could take place. There must, therefore, in order to maintain parliamentary sovereignty, be *some* legal limit on the power to prorogue. Therefore, it was by definition a legal question that the courts could rule upon.

How does the court assess whether a particular prorogation is lawful? A decision to prorogue Parliament will be unlawful if prorogation has the effect of frustrating or preventing, *without reasonable justification*, the ability of Parliament to carry out its constitutional functions. In this case, several factors were material. Prorogation to prepare a Queen's Speech usually didn't last more than ten days; five weeks was unprecedented. Critically, although ministers had been happy to reassure the country that the prorogation had everything to do with the Queen's Speech and nothing to do with Brexit,[53] not a single government official, least of all the Prime Minister, was prepared to sign an affidavit swearing the truth of this on oath.[54] The Supreme Court found it 'impossible to conclude, on the evidence which has been put before us, that there was any reason – let alone a good reason – to advise Her Majesty to prorogue Parliament for five weeks'. Accordingly, the prorogation was unlawful, and Parliament could be recalled.

Cue hysteria. As with the *Miller* decision, three years earlier, the ruling was quickly, falsely, reframed as the judges taking sides on Brexit. Following the Scottish court decision, minister Kwasi Kwarteng had rushed to tell the BBC that 'many people . . . are saying that the judges are biased',[55] but the response to the Supreme Court was even more furious. Leader of the House of Commons Jacob Rees-Mogg, not chastened by having been found to have given the Queen unlawful advice, denounced the judges as having effected 'a constitutional coup'.[56] The Attorney General warned the Commons that in future 'there may very well need to be parliamentary scrutiny of judicial appointments'.[57] Having previously asserted that prorogation had 'nothing to do with Brexit', Boris Johnson immediately dropped the pretence and responded to the Supreme Court's ruling with a nod and wink, saying, 'there are a lot of people who want to frustrate Brexit',[58] comments echoed by a *Telegraph* column absurdly claiming that, 'The Supreme Court has sided with usurping Remainers over the people.'[59] Nameless Cabinet Ministers and MPs told Buzzfeed News that the judgment heralded a move to 'an American-style Supreme Court', and that the solution was, in a laughable non-sequitur, to 'scrap the Human Rights Act'.[60]

In truth, while a judgment of enormous significance, which confirmed parliamentary accountability and an extended type of parliamentary sovereignty as enforceable constitutional principles, the decision, many constitutional experts argued, simply involved the application of centuries-old principles of common law to a novel situation.[61] And it was only novel because no Prime Minister had attempted to do this before. There was nothing new in the courts ruling that a prerogative power was justiciable; it was simply that this particular power had not been previously abused in this way. And this is how the common law works: it evolves to cater for new circumstances. There were claims that the Supreme Court had 'created a new law', and it had, but only in the way that any Supreme Court decision 'creates' common law. It had interpreted the scope of the existing law by reference to identified constitutional principles, and concluded that the Prime Minister had, by suspending Parliament without offering to the court 'a reason, let alone a good reason', broken that law. The refrain that we had suddenly developed a 'US-style Supreme Court' was bonkers; the Supreme Court was not striking down legislation, putting itself above Parliament; to the contrary, it was upholding parliamentary sovereignty over executive overreach.

The ministerial threats to the Supreme Court and orchestrated mischaracterisation of the judgment was all because the Supreme Court had ruled that, in a parliamentary democracy, the government cannot suspend Parliament without a good reason. That was literally it. The Prime Minister could have offered the court a reason, on oath, for his decision, and the court would have afforded him 'wide latitude'. It was because he refused to provide any reason for suspending Parliament that the court ruled he had acted unlawfully. And his government's response, rather than apologising for having given the Queen unlawful advice, was to attack the judges who pointed this out.

## Under attack from Parliament

Similar themes emerge from the back benches. *Miller* may have seen MPs accusing the Supreme Court justices who were to hear the case of having 'strong associations with EU institutions' and calling for 'gruelling hearings' to 'pore over every aspect of their legal opinions and personal lives',[62] echoed in 2019 by MPs calling for the Supreme Court to be 'abolished' for having the temerity to do its job,[63] but this is nothing new.

Constituency MPs making hay over 'soft judges' passing insufficiently punitive sentences on local yahoos is a common theme. One frequent flyer is Philip Davies MP, whose regular calls for longer prison sentences have been interspersed with an appeal to introduce the electric chair in Britain[64] and a suggestion that the criminal justice system is failing to tackle criminality by three-year-olds.[65] In 2014, Mr Davies demanded 'consequences' for any 'soft' judge who sentenced a defendant who later reoffended,[66] which led to the Recorder of Bradford (the most senior Crown Court judge of that city) inviting Mr Davies to watch a day of Crown Court sentencing. Mr Davies did so – the first time, he admitted, he had ever actually been in a Crown Court, notwithstanding years of vocal criticism of judges – and afterwards was forced to concede that all the sentences passed were 'perfectly fair and reasonable'.[67]

In 2012, Mr Davies stood up in the House of Commons and told MPs that one particular named Crown Court judge was, in his view, 'lily-livered', asking, 'How can we make sure that idiots like this are no longer in the judiciary?'[68] And the use of the protections of the House of Commons to intervene in the judicial process is increasing in frequency. In the previous chapter, we considered the case of Lord Hain relying on parliamentary privilege to thwart the effect of a court-ordered interim injunction preventing the naming of Sir Philip Green, but this was not the first time a parliamentarian had taken it upon themselves to frustrate and overturn independent judicial decisions with which they disagreed.

In September 2009, an interim 'superinjunction' (a court injunction the existence of which cannot be reported) was granted after the *Guardian* attempted to publish a report commissioned by Trafigura into a toxic dumping incident in the Ivory Coast which had led to widespread health problems. The details were revealed by Paul Farrelly MP in the House of Commons a few weeks later. Again, as with Philip Green, one may well have sympathy with the underlying cause, feel that the public interest militates in favour of shedding light on these practices, and believe that the courts too readily grant interim (or even final) injunctions; but that is not the point. Like Peter Hain, Paul Farrelly had obliterated ongoing legal proceedings in advance of the full hearing, depriving all parties of due process and sticking a parliamentary finger up to the independent judiciary.

In 2011, Liberal Democrat MP John Hemming used parliamentary privilege to reveal that footballer Ryan Giggs was the subject of a 'superinjunction'. That same year, Mr Hemming and Lord Stoneham told their respective Houses of the details of an injunction concerning Fred Goodwin. Mr Hemming topped off a bumper year by revealing in the Commons the names of the parties involved in private family-court proceedings in Doncaster, having been contacted by the woman involved, in clear defiance of a family-court injunction.[69] It later transpired that the woman whom Mr Hemming had sought to defend had made false allegations of sexual abuse against the father of her daughter, a grim reminder of why MPs should be loath to stick their oars into ongoing court proceedings.[70]

# Attacks from the fourth estate

The media does not operate under the same constitutional restraints as ministers and parliamentarians, and for good reason. A free press is a cornerstone of a democratic society. Journalists and broadcasters must be free to report and comment on legal proceedings and outcomes, as long as it is done lawfully and without the risk of prejudice to ongoing cases. A crucial component of this responsibility is to hold the justice system to account – to criticise outcomes which they consider to be wrong, and to draw attention to cases where the law and justice appear at odds.

However, there is a special responsibility, I would suggest, where reporting on individual cases, to ensure that criticism is fair, properly targeted and based on an accurate representation of the facts and issues. Given the reach and influence of the media, editors ought to be aware of the need to ensure that legitimate comment does not tip into a campaign of improper pressure; that judges do not feel persuaded, or intimidated, into deciding cases with one eye trained on the press gallery.

There are certain examples of media behaviour which I hope we can all agree would be inappropriate. Singling out individual judges by name and running incendiary campaigns seeking to persuade them to make more of a certain type of decision, such as imposing longer prison sentences or refusing more immigration appeals. Reporting intrusive and irrelevant material about a judge's personal or family life in service of ad hominem attacks. Launching accusations of judicial bias or corruption without a solid evidential base for doing so. Misrepresenting the outcome of a case, or the reasons given by a judge for a decision, in order to take potshots at the decision maker.

The *Daily Mail*'s 'Enemies of the People' story, and the follow-ups as the litigation proceeded to the Supreme Court, managed a tick against each of those boxes. The front-page headline, placing the judges' photographs above a term used throughout history by authoritarian regimes to mark and exterminate political

275

opponents, was reportedly the brainchild of editor Paul Dacre and political editor James Slack. You may recall this name from Chapter 6 – Mr Slack was the author of almost every legal-aid story in the *Daily Mail* between 2008 and 2017. In an example of the familiar revolving door between journalism and politics, he accepted a position in 2017 as Prime Minister Theresa May's official spokesperson,[71] a role which he retained after Boris Johnson entered Downing Street in 2019.

Not a shred of what was printed could sensibly be said to found a legitimate concern of bias; but that mattered not. The message was clear: we, the press, expect you, the judges, to do as we say. After the Supreme Court ruled against prorogation in 2019, Quentin Letts, in the *Sun*, demanded that the spouses of the judges be interrogated for their voting history, and insinuated 'corruption' against Lady Hale on the basis that she had agreed, upon her impending retirement, to take an unpaid position at an Oxford college.[72]

In another sphere, we see emboldened newspapers brazenly attempting to influence criminal proceedings. The *Sun* has particular form, from its campaign to increase the sentence of Jon Venables and Robert Thompson, to the petition, considered in Chapter 1, by which it sought to dissuade the Crown Prosecution Service from charging Richard Osborn-Brooks, the pensioner who killed a burglar in 2017.

Criminal sentencing is an area where the misreporting of facts and context is notably prevalent. Often a line from a judge's sentencing remarks will be quoted, out of context, as the reason behind an apparently unusual sentence; the full remarks are rarely reported. The context is almost never given. Readers are rarely told, for example, that most offences are now subject to sentencing guidelines, published by the independent Sentencing Council, and judges are legally bound to follow them. Parliament sets the maximum sentences for criminal offences, which again tie the hands of sentencing judges.

The *Sun* has run several 'name and shame' campaigns in which judges deemed to have passed insufficiently robust sentences are held up for the vilification of the readership.[73] In 2006, the *Sun* called for one judge to be 'sacked' after he sentenced a man called Craig Sweeney to life imprisonment with a minimum term of five years and 108 days, for a serious abduction and sexual assault of a three-year-old girl. The Attorney General later confirmed that the judge had correctly applied the law and sentencing guidelines, but in the interim the judge was branded 'deranged' and 'downright wicked' by the *Express*, egged on by the Home Secretary John Reid and junior minister Vera Baird rushing to tell the media that the judge was 'lenient' and 'wrong'.[74]

In all of these cases, little heed was paid to the notion that judicial independence was a principle worthy of respect. To the contrary, the media was anxious that the views of the judges, reached after consideration of the evidence, be replaced by the gag reflex of the news editor.

## 'The will of the people'

As modern technology and social media help to amplify and mobilise special-interest groups, we can see a fourth threat to judicial independence: the power of the mob.

The invocation at regular intervals of the 'will of the people' ever since the High Court decision in *Miller* has served to cement a false notion that judges should decide cases based on what is popular, rather than the legal and factual merits. Dominic Raab – I emphasise again, a qualified lawyer – criticised the High Court decision as 'undemocratic'. He would have done well to read paragraph 22 of the judgment, in which the High Court quoted the jurist A. V. Dicey: 'The judges know nothing about any will of the people except in so far as that will is expressed by an Act of Parliament, and would never suffer the validity of a statute to be questioned on the ground of its having been passed or being kept alive in opposition to the wishes of the electors.'

To believe that judges should aim to reach decisions that accord with the approval of a sector, or even a majority, of the public, is to utterly mistake the function of the judiciary. Yet the disease is spreading – the corrosive belief that judges ought to be, and can be, got at. Nigel Farage's ultimately empty threat to lead a march of 100,000 protestors on the Supreme Court was on the premise that the judges ought to be reminded 'that they cannot ignore the democratic vote of the people in the referendum'.[75]

The far right are becoming especially adept at identifying legal cases which they can adopt and exploit. We saw this with the tragic cases of Charlie Gard and Alfie Evans, as international right-wing activists descended on the UK to commandeer the cases for their own cause. The sad case of Marine A, a psychologically damaged soldier convicted of murder after shooting an Afghan detainee at point-blank range, was similarly hijacked when the conviction was appealed to the Court of Appeal. Leave.EU, the campaign group purportedly established to campaign to exit the EU during the referendum, and which, at the time of the *Miller* judgment, could be heard claiming that 'unelected judges' have 'declared war on British democracy',[76] has post-referendum turned its attention to 'the Muslim issue', tweeting about 'Londonistan' and Shariah courts[77] with a persistence that has led an All-Party Parliamentary Group to suggest that Leave.EU 'is a front organisation for a far-right group'.[78] It adopted the cause of Marine A, peppering Twitter with tweets such as, 'It seems our judges prefer paedophiles to patriots! Where did our system go wrong?'[79]

Leave.EU also lent its support[80] when Stephen Yaxley-Lennon, the founder of the English Defence League who goes by the name Tommy Robinson, was imprisoned for contempt of court in 2018, after he was found to have breached reporting restrictions imposed by a court in a child grooming trial. Social media was awash with antagonistic misinformation about this case, falsely framing it as an effort by the establishment to suppress legitimate journalism and cover up Muslim grooming gangs,[81] and the sympathy from the far right spread throughout Europe and beyond, culminating in President Donald Trump sending a diplomat to attempt to intervene in our domestic appeals process.[82] The hysteria became so heightened that, even after the Court of Appeal quashed the contempt finding due to procedural errors, some-body still took the time to send a suspect package to the judge who had passed the jail sentence.[83]

The aim with all of this, it appears, is to achieve desired out-comes in the judicial process by brute force. The merits are immaterial; if enough angry marchers can be mobilised, and enough pressure exerted on the judiciary, they will buckle to our will. That, after all, we are told by our politicians and by the media, is what judges are supposed to do.

Judges are tough critters. I appear in front of them every day, and they do not need wrapping in cotton wool. They are robust enough to deal with the rough-and-tumble of strong media criti-cism and the occasional politician stepping out of bounds. The reaction of Sir Terence Etherton to the 'Enemies of the People' story is a case in point. Author J. K. Rowling tweeted, in response to the MailOnline report, 'If the worst they can say about you is you're an OPENLY GAY EX-OLYMPIC FENCER TOP JUDGE, you've basically won life.'[84] Sir Terence and his husband had this tweet put on a mug.[85] Judges can cope with – and expect – criti-cism. Nobody can take decisions of such importance without being accountable.

However, judges are also human. And the cumulative effects of years of chipping away at the foundations is starting to show. In the immediate aftermath of the 'Enemies of the People' head-line, the Lord Chief Justice sought advice from the police for his protection – the first time in his career that he had needed to do so. Angry litigants have subsequently confronted judges in open court, calling them 'enemies of the people'.[86] Tens of thousands of pounds have been spent installing security equipment and panic alarms at the homes of certain judges. Over half of all judges surveyed reported that they had feared for their personal safety whilst in court. Threats of hostage-taking, assault and death have become common.[87] Some have been physically assaulted in court.[88]

Not all of this can be attributed to media and political comment; judges are dealing with the most combustible elements of society and making decisions that can overturn people's lives. There is a heightened risk inherent in the job.

But it would be the height of naivety to pretend that printed and tweeted words do not have consequences. Ad hominem attacks on the judiciary by those who know better set the tone for those who may not.

It is not merely a British phenomenon. The polarisation in US politics has placed the judiciary squarely in the political arena. Not only has the Supreme Court divided along party lines since 2010, with every judicial appointment reflecting the political leanings of the governing party,[89] but the unrestrained attacks by President Trump on 'so-called' judges[90] and 'Obama judges'[91] who rule against his unlawful executive conduct make headlines around the globe. While we Brits may laugh at the pantomime of Trump tweeting 'See you in court!'[92] at judges, let us not forget that we indulge Home Secretaries threatening to 'fight' judges for their liberal treatment of 'foreign criminals'. Trump's rhetoric is ours.

If we lose judicial independence, we lose the rule of law. The day a judge makes a binding decision affecting the rights and liberties of one of us, not on the legal and factual merits, but with a nervous glance to the press and public galleries, or with a beady eye on political favour or punishment, is the day that the decay in our democracy turns terminal.

Casting a glance across the world, we see the logical consequences taken to their grisly extremes. Every would-be authoritarian regime has the judiciary in its sights. From the Polish Law and Justice party attempting to remove a third of its senior judges,[93] to Turkish President Erdoğan dismissing a quarter of all judges following the failed military coup in 2016,[94] to Hungary's Viktor Orban's 'climate of fear' leading to the removal of unfavoured judges and the installation of party loyalists.[95]

Let us never be so naive as to suppose that we are immune.

# Epilogue: Our Future

William Roper: So now you'd give the Devil benefit of law!
Sir Thomas More: Yes. What would you do? Cut a great
road through the law to get after the Devil?
William Roper: I'd cut down every law in England to do that!
Sir Thomas More: Oh? And when the last law was down,
and the Devil turned round on you – where would you
hide, Roper, the laws all being flat? This country's planted
thick with laws from coast to coast – man's laws, not
God's – and if you cut them down – and you're just the
man to do it – do you really think you could stand upright
in the winds that would blow then? Yes I'd give the Devil
benefit of law, for my own safety's sake.

Robert Bolt, A Man for All Seasons, 1960

The preceding chapters offer merely snapshots of how the
stories we are told about justice corrupt and warp our understanding. Limitations of time and space necessitate selectivity;
those in touch with the law in other fields could no doubt offer
several compendia of the damaging impact that misinformation has had on their corner of the justice system. Even in the
subjects covered, far more has been omitted than could ever
practically be included.

It is easy to feel hopeless. There is so much inaccuracy and
misunderstanding, and so great an imbalance in power and reach
between those in the pulpits and the fact-checkers on the
sidelines.

I certainly feel it, at times. And there is a temptation, having
trotted around on my hobby horse and sent my flares soaring

into the night sky, to silently dismount, stride away into the darkness and leave the difficult business of solutions to others. However, it seems only right that I offer something by way of suggestions as to what might realistically be done. No spoiler warning is needed for the revelation that there is no quick and easy panacea, but I can perhaps tentatively proffer some starting points.

Before doing so, however, I want to say one final thing about the media. This book has stridently and unapologetically criticised and berated news outlets, editors and commentators across the political spectrum for the way that stories about justice are treated. Bad law reporting is rife and it is pervasive. It is also, as I have attempted to show, capable of being exceptionally dangerous. But it is not universal.

There are some brilliant journalists covering the justice system: local reporters, new media, bloggers, correspondents, industry specialists and mainstream commentators who understand the subject area and the principles, and who report and criticise the system scrupulously fairly. As I have been at pains to reiterate in each chapter, law and justice absolutely should be the subject of fierce and frequent debate. It is essential to a healthy democracy that we never become complacent about how our laws work; we should constantly seek improvement and re-evaluation; the decisions taken inside and outside our dusty courtrooms must be held up to the brightest sunlight and the professionals held to account. While I stand resolutely by the facts I have offered throughout this book, the opinions I have expressed are not inarguable; this is a polemic, not a gospel. I have aimed to offer perspectives which tend to counter the dominant narratives, but you may quite reasonably disagree with the arguments, or the interpretation of the first principles, on which they are built. Often our justice system fails its ideals. There is plenty of space – and I would call for even more – to argue over what we understand by justice, and what we expect our legal system to achieve. As I said at the very beginning, the justice system is owned by us, the people. We all have a stake in it, and all have a right to our view as to how it should function. There is often a gap, if not a chasm, between the opinions of the legal profession and the public we serve, and we should never be so arrogant as to claim the debating turf as our own. It is shared.

My complaint therefore – I hope it is clear – is not that the media amplifies views with which I might disagree; for the foregoing reasons, it is vital that they do. Rather it is that the debate is not fought on Queensberry rules. Misreporting basic facts, distorting context, establishing false premises and ignoring first principles all serve to exploit the knowledge gaps of the audience and afford an unfair advantage in the battle of ideas. If the positions that are contended for are meritorious, they will stand up on their facts. If they are weak, or advanced in service of an agenda that is counter to the readers' interests, they should not evade critical evaluation by virtue of editorial disguise or rhetorical dishonesty. I want an improved debate, not to shut it down.

I emphasise this with acute awareness of the perilous waters that journalists across the world are presently treading. Investigative journalism is needed now more than ever, and is under threat not only in the predicted autocracies, but in established allied democracies. Close to home, battles that we complacently assumed had been won are being refought on new fronts. 'Enemies of the People' was invoked in the United Kingdom against the judiciary, but has been deployed subsequently by President Trump against the American media engaged in legitimate reporting of the activities of his political circle. His frequent diatribes and hoarse squeals of 'Fake News' and 'Enemies of the People' have culminated in journalists being assaulted at his rallies[1] and bombs being sent to news outlets,[2] and similar rhetoric can frequently be found in the abuse of UK journalists by those at the political extremes, both right and left.[3] Common to each instance is a desire to avoid scrutiny, evade accountability and ultimately cow the free press into silence.

So, while I strongly encourage elements in the media to improve, I make clear that I criticise as an avid supporter of a free press. The solutions to the problems I identify do not exist in any form of state regulation – from principle as much as practicality, having regard to the spread of the social-media jungle. I would obviously encourage higher standards in self-regulation, but that is ultimately out of the public's hands.

Instead, the changes I would suggest are aimed elsewhere in our system.

There is a reason that newspapers don't run front-page stories about alien abductions: both the media and its audience are equipped to immediately recognise them as fictional. However sensationally juicy such tales might appear, editors and reporters understand the absurdity, and know that their readers simply won't buy it. There is a commonly recognised floor of public education and understanding. This creates a filter, ensuring (for the most part) that stories which insult the intelligence of both writer and reader don't make it into copy, or at least not past the subs.

There is no equivalent floor of general understanding of the law, or at least it is set so low as to be underground. This means that, faced with a press release from the Ministry of Justice about legal-aid expenditure or a Twitterstorm encircling a criminal sentencing decision, few people on the supply chain between news reporter, subs' desk, senior editor and reader have the tools to critically evaluate what they are dealing with. While some mainstream outlets still have specialist legal correspondents, the role has disappeared from many newspapers, with law reporting bundled into home affairs or politics. The accuracy of these stories therefore depends on the knowledge, understanding and motivations of the news desk and back benches. If either of the first two is lacking, the result is often superficial or misguided treatment of a complex story. If the latter is corrupted, it is possible for important stories to be wilfully distorted in accordance with editorial agenda. While I don't suggest that all of the examples contained in this book are born of malevolence – Hanlon's Razor, requiring that we should not attribute to malice something that can equally be attributed to incompetence, is a lodestar here – there is little doubt that many represent at best a reckless disregard for legal accuracy, and some can only be understood as intentional misrepresentations. The legal correspondent for the *Daily Telegraph*, the highly respected Joshua Rozenberg QC, resigned in 2007 after news editors amended one of his reports on a human-rights case to add a false claim that a court's decision 'could open the way for civilian victims of military actions [in Iraq] to sue the Ministry of Defence for millions of pounds'. As Joshua Rozenberg explained to *Newsnight* in 2015, he had told editors that, 'It would make a better story, but it just isn't true.' The *Telegraph* nevertheless printed the falsehood, and Mr Rozenberg resigned.[4]

A similar tale reverberates around Westminster and Whitehall. Despite the prevalence of solicitors and barristers in both Houses of Parliament, those on the ground report a culture of widespread ignorance of the law among those responsible for making it. Isabel Hardman, political journalist and author of *Why We Get the Wrong Politicians*, identifies a number of problems with the culture of Parliament, which means that 'MPs often don't understand the domestic legislation they are voting on.'[5] The public pronouncements of those quoted in this book arguably stand testament to that claim.

Consequently, sensationalist nonsense about the law can be sprayed across the nation with impunity, with the more cynical among the political and media classes free to adopt the rigour of the *Sunday Sport* safe in the knowledge that the information gap will insulate them from any pushback.

The remedy lies in public legal education. Our rights can only be removed and false narratives pumped throughout our culture as long as we lack the tools to identify what is happening.

There is – belatedly, but thankfully – a genuine impetus now in train, in part due to the sterling efforts of then Solicitor General Robert Buckland MP. Having established an All-Party Parliamentary Group on Pro Bono and Public Legal Education in 2017, Mr Buckland, in late 2018, published a vision statement and briefing paper offering a ten-year vision for public legal education (PLE).[6] Bringing together a number of organisations, including Young Citizens, the Law Society, the Bar Council, the National Justice

Museum, Youth Access, CILEX, the Magistrates' Association, the Institute of Paralegals, Citizens Advice, Law for Life, the Bingham Centre for the Rule of Law, the Legal Education Foundation, the Law Centres Network and the Association of Law Teachers, the paper sets out a strategy for improving public understanding of legal issues and the public's access to legal information and advice, stretching from school through to adulthood.

The problems in schools need urgent attention. While the national curriculum requires that schools teach Citizenship Education, which should in theory educate children about the rule of law and the justice system, a House of Lords Select Committee Report in 2018 concluded that, 'The Government has allowed citizenship education [and by extension PLE] in England to degrade to a parlous state.'[7] Citizenship is rarely taught by specialists (the number of trainee Citizenship teachers fell from 240 in 2010 to just 54 in 2016), and Ofsted is no longer required to inspect it as a subject. Government funding for the Citizenship Foundation, which provides training for non-specialists, has fallen to 'virtually 0 per cent'.[8]

Reimagining legal education as a priority subject, as central to preparing a child for life as language and mathematics, is needed. Further, it should not be taught solely in silos; law, justice and rights should be as infused throughout the curriculum as they are everyday life, from primary school through to secondary and beyond. An understanding of the principles of our justice system should be as essential to journalistic qualifications as shorthand. While I would stop short of demanding that inductions for new MPs include mandatory law classes, it is not too much to expect each and every representative to make sure that they fully understand the principles and practices underpinning the laws they make.

If our system is working, each of us should, upon stepping into the big wide world, have a sufficient understanding of our rights and of the justice system to at least be able to identify a potential legal problem, and to know where to turn for further information. A task force in 2007 estimated that around one million civil justice problems go unresolved every year because people do not understand their rights or know how to navigate the legal system. While the human suffering of legal exclusion is difficult to quantify, the economic cost of unresolved legal problems is estimated at £13 billion over a three-and-a-half-year period.[9]

The legal system must do more, too. I have already taken aim in the opening pages at the systemic lack of transparency, and I'll repeat the obvious, simple fixes: ensure that all primary and secondary legislation is up to date and freely available online; properly fund BAILII so that it can publish and host all judgments from the High Court, Court of Appeal and Supreme Court, with the significance of judgments explained in the same way as in the paid-for law reports; publish judges' sentencing remarks from Crown Courts wherever possible, especially in cases likely to attract media attention. More ambitious proposals would include improving public and media access to the transcripts of proceedings such as criminal trials. Presently, members of the press and public can request a transcript of the audio recording of Crown Court proceedings, but these cost between £100 and £120 per audio hour. This means that a transcript of the evidence in a week-long Crown Court trial will cost around £3,000. New automated transcribing technology is capable of cutting this cost by 90 per cent.[10] The UK is behind the US, Canada and Australia in deploying technology to improve public access to the law.

One of the main reasons for the disconnect between the courts and the public is the demise of local court reporters and local public-interest journalism. A survey in 2016 suggested that fewer than half of local newspapers have a dedicated court reporter, with 40 per cent of those not attending court more than once a week.[11] The Cairncross Review into a sustainable future for high-quality journalism identified in its 2019 report that law reporting has been ill served by commercial press models in recent years, and proposed amendment of charity laws so as to permit forms of public subsidy for public-interest local journalism.[12]

Each advance in public legal education should, if our democracy is functioning, automatically lead to another. School leavers who understand the justice system become journalists who understand the justice system, who write for a public who understand the justice system, who vote for politicians who understand – and, most importantly, respect – the justice system. The justice system itself, open, transparent and accessible, should be something on which we all feel qualified to offer informed opinion.

But it cannot all be left to fate. There is need for oversight – a politically independent guardian of the rule of law, judicial independence and the efficient administration of justice, able and willing to speak out publicly in favour of our principles and, if required, in rebuttal to government, Parliament or the media. Where a Fake Law story looks like gaining nationwide traction, a rapid refutation should be fired out. If a court decision is causing opprobrium, the watchdog should be the first port of call for journalists and broadcasters. As judges cannot personally respond to criticism, the watchdog should be unleashed all over television, radio, newspapers and social media to explain – not justify, but explain, by reference to cold facts and first principles – the way in which the decision was reached. Where public rancour is incited by dishonest foreign politicians in sensitive cases involving the life and death of British citizens, it should not be left to tweeters, bloggers and the representative bodies of legal professionals to try to drip oil onto the troubled oceans; the watchdog should already be pulling into Sky News on their supertanker. Where fiscal squeezing is resulting in damage to legal aid and the operation of the courts, the watchdog should be howling at the Treasury, reminding the public that access to justice and properly funded courts are not a political football, but the immutable foundations of our democracy.

As for who this watchdog should be, an obvious candidate emerges at the appendix of the body politic: the Lord Chancellor. This, after all, though recent history may cause us to forget, is the individual with the constitutional responsibility to uphold the rule of law and defend the independence of the judiciary.

Since the role was fused with that of Secretary of State for Justice in 2007, the inherent tension between the political loyalty and economic thrift expected of the Justice Secretary and the fearless independence of a Lord Chancellor charged with ensuring the courts are properly funded has usually seen the Justice Secretary's violent Mr Hyde triumph over the Lord Chancellor's meek Dr Jekyll. The post has bounced between candidates of varying competence and integrity, some of whom, we have seen in these pages, have been in material breach of their constitutional duties. The union has failed. Secession is required. Recast the Lord Chancellor as a non-partisan defender of the legal system, with no interest in seeking higher political office: a watchdog that barks, instead of a lapdog that wags. A retired judge, perhaps, or legal academic, who views the role as a career pinnacle, rather than a political stepping stone; someone prepared to fight without fear or favour in defence of the rule of law, and who is prepared, if the need should ever arise, to bring a government to its knees in defence of the principles that bind us.

For it is in those shared principles that we find not just the kernels of our democracy, but our humanity. In a polarised global polity, I worry that we forget that. That when we allow ourselves to be misled as to how and why our system is built as it is, we become persuadable that it is in our interests not only to condone the corrosion of our rights, but of the bonds that tie us together, that make us human.

And I worry how regularly we see this reflected in our national conversation. How quickly we revert to othering, to demanding the removal of rights for those of whom we disapprove, having been convinced by wicked whispers in our ear that the same rights do not apply to us. How swiftly we call for harsher treatment of our neighbours who transgress, in satisfied self-assurance that neither we, nor anybody we hold dear, will ever fall short.

A YouGov survey in June 2018 examined the most fertile ground for a new political party and found that the issue on which most Britons felt unrepresented was justice. This was towards the end of a decade in which legal-aid cuts had left victims of domestic violence at the mercy of their abusers in the family courts; employment-tribunal fees had prevented exploited workers from claiming unpaid wages from exploitative employers; homeless families were denied legal help to get off the streets; disabled people were unable to challenge wrongful punitive government sanctions; children were forced to represent themselves in deportation proceedings; average prison sentences reached record lengths;[13] we imprisoned more people per capita than any other country in Western Europe;[14] £1 billion cuts to prisons coincided with soaring rates of overcrowding, violence, self-harm and death,[15] giving the lie to the laughable tabloid claim that the prison estate is 'Butlins with bars';[16] and politicians routinely and boastfully ignored the rule of law where it proved politically inconvenient.

Why did the Great British public feel unrepresented? Did they feel that no party took access to justice seriously? Did they worry that the legal system had been rendered off limits to the most vulnerable? Were they irate that the government had unlawfully removed their right to seek justice against abusive employers bullying, harassing, discriminating and refusing to pay their wages? Were they outraged that those stepping through the prison gates – the innocent, the guilty and the low-paid prison staff – were dying inside in record numbers due to staffing cuts and Chris Grayling's 'spartan prison'[17] regime? Did they feel shame that Britain was forcing parentless children who had grown up in our country to defend themselves in court against the threat of deportation?

No. The complaint – about which people felt more strongly than the National Health Service, education or the economy – was that the justice system was 'not harsh enough'.[18]

The message – *surrender your rights* – is not merely working, but viral, replicating throughout our culture. Time and time again, we are encouraged to punch ourselves in the face, our instinctive reaction being not to refuse, or even to ask why, but to sock ourselves in the eye, screaming, 'Harder?' When it comes to justice, our national dialogue is a soliloquy – each of us playing Roper, refusing sympathy for the devil and demanding the laws are cut down to catch him. The role of Sir Thomas More is left uncast; neither politicians, nor media, nor public are prepared to so much as audition.

One day, I hope we might all be persuaded to read for the part.

# Acknowledgements

It takes more than a lone criminal hack to bring together a book spanning the breadth of the justice system. So it is that, for a second time, I find myself embarking upon an exercise in trying to convey my deepest and most sincere gratitude to people who have no idea who I am, and who, for no reason other than boundless generosity, have taken time to steer me on the correct course as I navigate areas of law outside my own daily practice area. In the ordinary run of things, I would offer each and every one a thank-you drink, meal or bear-hug of their choosing, but in the circumstances all I have to give are some inelegantly expressed words of appreciation, and a promise that, should our paths ever cross in daily life, I will surreptitiously drop a chocolate bar in their bag.

And so, in alphabetical order, I would like to thank, as heartily as words on a page can convey, the following, all titans in their respective fields, whose expertise far outweighs my own, and all of whom would have been fully entitled to refuse to enter into unsolicited correspondence with an anonymous person on the internet. That they did not, and instead spent hours answering questions and reading drafts, speaks to their kindness and charity, which one day, if circumstances ever permit, I hope to meaningfully repay.

Huge thanks are therefore due to Mary Aspinall-Miles, Gordon Exall, Carl Gardner, Katie Gollop QC, Steve Hynes, Sean Jones QC, Shoaib Khan, David Mason QC, Michael Mynolas QC, Giles Peaker, Adam Wagner and Harriet Wistrich.

If I, at any point over the previous 300 pages, have sounded in any way informed or knowledgeable, it is because I have greedily drawn on their wisdom. Any objectionable opinions or errors of fact, interpretation or judgement, other than those attributed to the targets of my ranty ire, are mine.

As for the idea and inspiration, I am once again indebted to the brilliance of my agent Chris Wellbelove and editor Kris Doyle, whose expert guidance and endless patience are integral to any success that I may have stumbled upon. This is an infinitely better book than would have emerged from the sprawling ideas I initially thrust in front of them eighteen months ago, and the credit is theirs. I am also eternally thankful to Chloe May and Penelope Price for their eyes for detail and powers of expression that ensured a much more refined manuscript exited the copy-editing process. That the editorial, publicity and marketing team have once more accommodated, without a whisper of complaint, the whims and caprice of an anonymous author juggling a legal practice is an indulgence for which I am truly grateful.

I would also like to thank all those in the justice system, Parliament, media, social media and beyond, who supported the first book and worked tirelessly to amplify its message about broken criminal justice. You gave me this platform to draw attention to the issues facing the wider justice system. I hope I can repay your faith.

Finally, and most importantly, I must address my debt to the person who may sometimes feel as if they rank finally and least importantly in the hierarchy of my attention. For the months of weekend solitude during the writing process, to be added to four years of evening solitude as Twitter and blogging consume the pockets of free time we would otherwise share; for accepting without demur the inconvenience of a second secret existence atop the already inestimable demands of your own work, as well as the misfortune of being partnered to a criminal barrister; for shouldering the weight of our joint personal burdens, and never once complaining – as you rightly should have – that you were carrying for both of us; for getting me – us – through the hardest days and forgiving me without request for my being too distracted to support you in the way I should have; for bringing light and hope when we needed it most; for inspiring and consoling me during the empty times and keeping me earthed when my ego ran wild.

For all of this, and a thousand things more, I owe you a quantum I will probably never be able to repay, although I will never stop trying. You know this, I hope, but because it can't be said enough: I love you, I'm immeasurably thankful for you, and I'm sorry. And I will – I absolutely promise – unglue myself from Twitter at 6 p.m. sharp every evening. Just as soon as people stop being wrong about law on the internet.

# Appendix

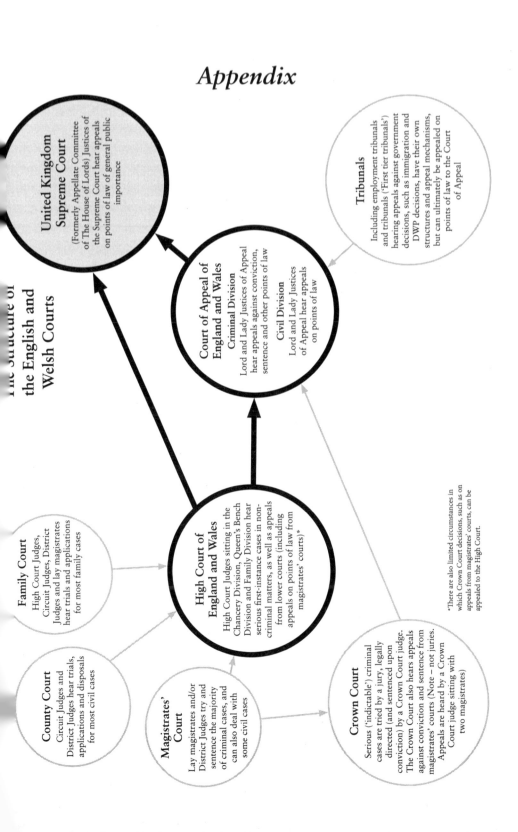

The Structure of the English and Welsh Courts

**United Kingdom Supreme Court**

(Formerly Appellate Committee of The House of Lords) Justices of the Supreme Court hear appeals on points of law of general public importance

**Court of Appeal of England and Wales**

Criminal Division
Lord and Lady Justices of Appeal hear appeals against conviction, sentence and other points of law

Civil Division
Lord and Lady Justices of Appeal hear appeals on points of law

**Tribunals**

Including employment tribunals and tribunals ('First tier tribunals') hearing appeals against government decisions, such as immigration and DWP decisions, have their own structures and appeal mechanisms, but can ultimately be appealed on points of law to the Court of Appeal

**High Court of England and Wales**

High Court Judges sitting in the Chancery Division, Queen's Bench Division and Family Division hear serious first-instance cases in non-criminal matters, as well as appeals from lower courts (including appeals on points of law from magistrates' courts)*

**Family Court**

High Court Judges, Circuit Judges, District Judges and lay magistrates hear trials and applications for most family cases

**County Court**

Circuit Judges and District Judges hear trials, applications and disposals for most civil cases

**Magistrates' Court**

Lay magistrates and/or District Judges try and sentence the majority of criminal cases, and can also deal with some civil cases

**Crown Court**

Serious ('indictable') criminal cases are tried by a jury, legally directed (and sentenced upon conviction) by a Crown Court judge. The Crown Court also hears appeals against conviction and sentence from magistrates' courts (Note – not juries. Appeals are heard by a Crown Court judge sitting with two magistrates)

*There are also limited circumstances in which Crown Court decisions, such as on appeals from magistrates' courts, can be appealed to the High Court.

# *Notes*

## Introduction

1. Nigel Farage, quoted in 'Alfie Evans: World's reaction to sick toddler's case', BBC News, 25 April 2018, https://www.bbc.co.uk/news/uk-england-merseyside-43892684
2. H. Sachs, 'Alfie Evans, the State and Us', American Thinker, 29 April 2018, https://www.americanthinker.com/articles/2018/04/alfie_evans_the_state_and_us.html
3. 'UK judge rejects bid to take sick toddler Alfie Evans abroad – Parents cucked twice, first by brain dead baby then by judge', https://kiwifarms.net/threads/uk-judge-rejects-bid-to-take-sick-toddler-alfie-evans-abroad.42288/page-5
4. Senator Ted Cruz, press release, 25 April 2018, https://www.cruz.senate.gov/?p=press_release&id=3760
5. Nigel Farage, quoted in 'Alfie Evans: World's reaction to sick toddler's case', BBC News, 25 April 2018.
6. L. Deacon, '"Death Panel": European court says terminal baby must die despite parents funding extra care', Breitbart, 29 June 2017, https://www.breitbart.com/london/2017/06/29/eu-court-terminal-baby-must-die-despite-parents-funding-extra-care/
7. D. Loucks, 'Commentary: Socialized medicine seeks Charlie Gard's death', *Austin American-Statesman*, 10 July 2017, https://archive.md/MCOmz
8. 'Theresa May speech in full', 4 October 2011, http://www.politics.co.uk/comment-analysis/2011/10/04/theresa-may-speech-in-full
9. 'EU human rights court order Italy to pay Amanda Knox £15,600 in damages for violating her rights during Meredith Kercher murder investigation', @DailyMailUK,

Twitter, 24 January 2019, https://twitter.com/DailyMailUK/
status/1088397934494994434

10. S. Johnson, 'Cleaning up in the small claims court: Council
    worker awarded £9,000 compensation for tripping over a mop',
    *Daily Mail*, 27 July 2012, https://www.dailymail.co.uk/news/
    article-2179757/Council-cleaner-given-9-000-compensation-
    tripping-MOP.html

11. D. Martin, 'Jackpot tribunal payouts face axe: Plan to limit
    discrimination at work claims', *Daily Mail*, 11 May 2011, https://
    www.dailymail.co.uk/news/article-1385731/Jackpot-tribunal-
    payouts-face-axe-Plan-limit-discrimination-work-claims.html

12. 'Comment: Employment tribunals are legalised extortion', This is
    Money, 6 January 2011, https://www.thisismoney.co.uk/money/
    article-1710536/Comment-Employment-tribunals-are-legalised-
    extortion.html.

13. R. Littlejohn, 'Unsuitable work for a woman', *Daily Mail*,
    20 February 2014, https://www.dailymail.co.uk/debate/
    article-2564235/RICHARD-LITTLEJOHN-Help-My-ID-stolen-
    Call-Fraudbusters.html

14. Interview with Ken Clarke, International Bar Association,
    November 2011, https://www.ibanet.org/Article/NewDetail.
    aspx?ArticleUid=F4A4D433-36F9-4D3B-A3CA-ED94A30EF09A

15. On 30 November 2019, Telegraph columnist Allison Pearson
    tweeted, in reference to the barrister who had represented the
    London Bridge terrorist Usman Khan: 'On the other hand,
    we have a criminal justice system – including human rights
    QCs – who facilitate violent jihadists to get away with murder'.
    This tweet was subsequently deleted. Original slugline here:
    https://twitter.com/allisonpearson/status/1200700221904-
    375808

16. Theresa May MP, House of Commons, 22 October
    2013, Hansard, column 162, https://hansard.parliament.
    uk/Commons/2013-10-22/debates/13102262000002/
    ImmigrationBill?highlight=Care%20COL:%20162

17. L. Perrins, 'The feminists who are turning British justice against
    men', *Daily Mail*, 7 September 2016, https://www.dailymail.
    co.uk/debate/article-3777053/The-feminists-turning-British-
    justice-against-men-writes-LAURA-PERRINS.html

18. Philip Davies MP, quoted in D. Barrett, 'Judges weaken rules on
    paedophiles', *Telegraph*, 20 August 2011, https://www.telegraph.

co.uk/news/uknews/law-and-order/8713203/Judges-weaken-rules-
on-paedophiles.html

19. R. Prince, 'David Cameron: when a burglar invades your home
    they give up their rights', *Telegraph*, 9 October 2012, https://
    www.telegraph.co.uk/news/politics/conservative/9595589/
    David-Cameron-when-a-burglar-invades-your-home-they-give-up-
    their-rights.html

20. M. Robinson, 'Brazen prisoners FILM a cell raid on smuggled
    mobile phone and taunt the inmate led away by officers in
    riot gear at jail they dub "Butlins with bars"', *Daily Mail*, 23
    October 2017 http://www.dailymail.co.uk/news/article-5008749/
    Brazen-prisoners-FILM-cell-raid-officers-riot-gear.html

21. Douglas Carswell MP, quoted in J. Slack, 'Enemies of the
    people: Fury over "out of touch" judges who have "declared
    war on democracy" by defying 17.4m Brexit voters and who
    could trigger constitutional crisis', *Daily Mail*, 3 November
    2016, https://www.dailymail.co.uk/news/article-3903436/
    Enemies-people-Fury-touch-judges-defied-17-4m-Brexit-voters-
    trigger-constitutional-crisis.html

22. J. Slack, 'Enemies of the people: Fury over "out of touch" judges
    who have "declared war on democracy" by defying 17.4m Brexit
    voters and who could trigger constitutional crisis', *Daily Mail*, 3
    November 2016.

23. G. Adams, 'The judges and the people: Next week, 11
    unaccountable individuals will consider a case that could thwart
    the will of the majority on Brexit. The Mail makes no apology
    for revealing their views – and many have links to Europe',
    *Daily Mail*, 3 December 2016. https://www.dailymail.co.uk/
    news/article-3995754/The-judges-people-week-11-unaccountable-
    individuals-consider-case-help-thwart-majority-Brexit-Mail-
    makes-no-apology-revealing-views-links-Europe.html

24. J. Slack, 'Enemies of the people: Fury over "out of touch" judges
    who have "declared war on democracy" by defying 17.4m Brexit
    voters and who could trigger constitutional crisis', *Daily Mail*, 3
    November 2016.

25. It was me. In my first book, *The Secret Barrister: Stories of the
    Law and How It's Broken* (Picador, 2018). If you haven't read
    it yet, I suggest that you do so. Then this self-referential jokette
    will make more sense. Although it will probably be no funnier.

26. The National Archives aimed to have all legislation updated

by the end of 2020: http://www.legislation.gov.uk/help#faqs (accessed 20 July 2019).

27. Ibid.

28. The Stationery Office website, 'The National Archives (Legislation)', http://www.tsonline.co.uk/our-expertise/case-studies/national-archives-wwwlegislationgovuk (accessed 26 August 2018).

29. D. Hoadley, 'Open access to case law – how do we get there?', Infolaw Newsletter, November 2018, http://www.infolaw.co.uk/newsletter/2018/11/open-access-case-law-get/

30. BAILII, 'Frequently Asked Questions: What case law can I find on BAILII?', https://www.bailii.org/bailii/faq.html#whatcase The problem, it seems, is that historically the courts have often not bothered to publish their own judgments, meaning that the only written records are kept by private transcription companies, who will only permit distribution of their intellectual property for a fee beyond the reach of a charity. Yes, I know.

31. Offences Against the Person Act 1861.

32. The Vagrancy Act 1824 was brought into force under William IV to address the social ills caused by the large number of homeless soldiers following the end of the Napoleonic Wars, but its scope was broadened throughout the nineteenth century to criminalise a smorgasbord of perceived immorality.

33. See Appendix for the answer.

34. A common, if simplistic, analogy is that of a doctor and a consultant/surgeon. The solicitor (doctor) is your first port of call, diagnoses the problem and, if called for, instructs a barrister (consultant) to offer specialist advice or carry out 'surgery' in court. It's not a brilliant metaphor, but captures the essence.

35. Judges are experienced, legally qualified experts who sit in courts throughout the court hierarchy. Magistrates are unpaid, non-legally qualified volunteers who sit in the magistrates' courts. These are on the bottom rung of the legal ladder, but magistrates still have the power to send people to prison (in criminal proceedings) and remove their children (in family proceedings).

36. 'Third of Britons don't know difference between civil and criminal courts', *The Times*, 8 November 2019, https://www.thetimes.co.uk/article/third-of-britons-dont-know-difference-between-civil-and-criminal-courts-nvv7rqv6h

37. Citizens Advice, 'Responsive justice: How citizens experience the

justice system', November 2015, p.2, https://www.citizensadvice. org.uk/Global/CitizensAdvice/Crime%20and%20Justice%20 Publications/Responsivejustice.pdf

38. The only known gavel in an English and Welsh courtroom is at Inner London Crown Court, where the clerk bangs a gavel to announce the entrance of the judge into court. Otherwise, they are the exclusive preserve of auctioneers and picture editors.

## 1. Yourself and Your Home

1. 'Conservative conference: Force against burglars to be allowed', BBC News, 9 October 2012, https://www.bbc.co.uk/news/ uk-politics-19879314

2. S. Morris, 'The killer who won a nation's sympathy', *Guardian*, 30 October 2001, https://www.theguardian.com/uk/2001/oct/30/ tonymartin.ukcrime2

3. Ibid.

4. R. Alleyne, 'Killer who was a hero to victims of crime', *Telegraph*, 31 October 2001, https://www.telegraph.co.uk/news/ uknews/1361023/Killer-who-was-a-hero-to-victims-of-crime.html

5. Ibid.

6. I. Burrell, 'Payment to Tony Martin was justified, says PCC', *Independent*, 3 October 2003, https://www.independent. co.uk/news/media/payment-to-tony-martin-was-justified-says-pcc-89575.html

7. P. Waugh, 'Hague calls for overhaul in laws of self-defence', *Independent*, 26 April 2000, https://www.independent. co.uk/news/uk/crime/hague-calls-for-overhaul-in-laws-of-self-defence-266716.html

8. S. Morris, 'The killer who won a nation's sympathy', *Guardian*, 30 October 2001.

9. P. Wintour, 'What the memo tells us about Tony Blair's style of leadership', *Guardian*, 18 July 2000, https://www.theguardian. com/politics/2000/jul/18/labour.politicalnews

10. M. Sullivan, 'DON'T CHARGE HIM: Join The Sun to demand an end to murder probe into hero OAP Richard Osborn-Brooks, accused of stabbing serial burglar', the *Sun*, 5 April 2018, https://www.thesun.co.uk/news/5984919/ petition-richard-osborn-brooks-murder-burglar/

11. P. Waugh, 'Hague calls for overhaul in laws of self-defence', *Independent*, 26 April 2000.
12. Cited in J. R. Spencer, 'Using force on burglars', *Archbold Review*, issue 2 (March 2016), p. 6.
13. Section 2 of the Homicide Act 1957.
14. *R v. Martin (Anthony Edward)* [2001] EWCA Crim 2245; [2002] Cr App R 27.
15. Section 3 of the Criminal Law Act 1967.
16. *Palmer v. R* [1971] AC 814.
17. *R v. McInnes* [1971] 55 Cr App R 551.
18. Facts taken from the Court of Appeal judgment, *R v. Martin (Anthony Edward)* [2001] EWCA Crim 2245; [2002] Cr App R 27.
19. R. Alleyne, 'Killer who was a hero to victims of crime', *Telegraph*, 31 October 2001.
20. '"Have a go hero" businessman Munir Hussain freed by Court of Appeal', *The Times*, 20 January 2010, https://www.thetimes.co.uk/article/have-a-go-hero-businessman-munir-hussain-freed-by-court-of-appeal-kr8p9v6057g
21. Ibid.
22. R. Clark, 'Munir Hussain: He's free but what an outrage that he was prosecuted', *Daily Express*, 22 January 2010, https://www.express.co.uk/comment/expresscomment/153368/Munir-Hussain-He-s-free-but-what-an-outrage-that-he-was-prosecuted
23. '"Have a go hero" businessman Munir Hussain freed by Court of Appeal', *The Times*, 20 January 2010.
24. *R v. Hussain & Hussain* [2010] EWCA Crim 94; [2010] 2 Cr App R (S) 60, per Lord Judge C. J. at [34].
25. 'Homeowners and self-defence – DPP issues further details of cases', Crown Prosecution Service press release, 13 January 2005, cited in S. Lipscombe, 'Householders and the criminal law of self defence', House of Commons Library, 10 January 2013.
26. 'Welby farm shooting: Couple will not face charges', BBC News, 5 September 2012, https://www.bbc.co.uk/news/uk-england-leicestershire-19496531
27. D. Batty, 'Burglars should accept risk of being shot, says judge', *Guardian*, 26 September 2012, https://www.theguardian.com/world/2012/sep/26/burglars-accept-risk-shot-judge
28. 'Yorkshire farmer, 83, claims shooting was "self-defence"', BBC News, 10 March 2017, https://www.bbc.co.uk/news/uk-england-humber-39229170

29. 'Farmer, 83, cleared over shooting man on his land', BBC News, 10 March 2017, https://www.bbc.co.uk/news/uk-england-humber-39233017

30. Lord Thomas of Gresford, House of Lords, 22 January 2008, Hansard, column 135, https://publications.parliament.uk/pa/ld200708/ldhansrd/text/80122-0003.htm

31. Conservative manifesto 2010, 'Invitation to Join the Government of Britain', p.56: 'We will give householders greater legal protection if they have to defend themselves against intruders in their homes.' http://conservativehome.blogs.com/files/conservative-manifesto-2010.pdf

32. J. Slack and J. Chapman, '"They loaded up my Skoda and drove off": David Cameron reveals he has been burgled twice as he tells homeowners they can use disproportionate force against intruders', *Daily Mail*, 8 October 2012, https://www.dailymail.co.uk/news/article-2214830/They-loaded-Skoda-drove-David-Cameron-reveals-burgled-twice-tells-homeowners-use-disproportionate-force-intruders.html

33. R. Prince, 'David Cameron: when a burglar invades your home they give up their rights', *Telegraph*, 9 October 2012, https://www.telegraph.co.uk/news/politics/conservative/9595589/David-Cameron-when-a-burglar-invades-your-home-they-give-up-their-rights.html

34. 'Chris Grayling: How I'm fulfilling my promise on new rights for householders', *Sunday Telegraph*, 24 November 2012, https://www.telegraph.co.uk/news/politics/9700895/Chris-Grayling-How-Im-fulfilling-my-promise-on-new-rights-for-householders.html

35. O. Bowcott, 'Chris Grayling's self-defence plans greeted with dismay by lawyers', *Guardian*, 9 October 2012, https://www.theguardian.com/politics/2012/oct/09/chris-grayling-self-defence-lawyers

36. G. Wilson, 'It's official: You can batter a burglar', the *Sun*, 8 October 2012, https://www.thesun.co.uk/archives/politics/975563/its-official-you-can-batter-a-burglar/

37. R. Prince, 'David Cameron: when a burglar invades your home they give up their rights', *Telegraph*, 9 October 2012.

38. Section 76(6) of the Criminal Justice and Immigration Act 2008.

39. R. Prince, 'David Cameron: when a burglar invades your home they give up their rights', *Telegraph*, 9 October 2012.

40. G. Wilson, 'It's official: You can batter a burglar', the *Sun*, 8 October 2012.
41. Ibid.
42. Section 76(5A) of the Criminal Justice and Immigration Act 2008.
43. *R (on the application of Collins) v. Secretary of State for Justice* [2016] EWHC 33 (Admin).
44. As the use of 'reasonable force in self-defence' had been previously (and consistently) found to be compatible with the Article 2 right to life, the Court's finding that section 76(5A) did not change the fundamental test of 'reasonableness' meant that the new subsection did not create any compatibility problems.
45. Per Sir Brian Leveson P., ibid at [62].
46. M. Beckford, 'You can't bash a burglar after all: Government's tough rhetoric branded a farce as it's revealed homeowners are barred from fighting raiders in garden or chasing them outside', *Daily Mail*, 27 April 2013, https://www.dailymail.co.uk/news/article-2315808/You-bash-burglar-Governments-tough-rhetoric-branded-farce-revealed-homeowners-barred-fighting-raiders-garden-chasing-outside.html
47. H. Goodman, 'NRA's Behind-the-Scenes Campaign Encouraged "Stand Your Ground" Adoption', Florida Center for Investigative Reporting, 23 March 2012, https://fcir.org/2012/03/23/nras-behind-the-scenes-campaign-encouraged-stand-your-ground-adoption-across-the-country/
48. A. O'Neill, 'NRA's Marion Hammer stands her ground', CNN, 15 April 2012, https://edition.cnn.com/2012/04/15/us/marion-hammer-profile/index.html
49. A. Goodnough, 'Florida Expands Right to Use Deadly Force in Self-Defense', *New York Times*, 27 April 2005, https://www.nytimes.com/2005/04/27/us/florida-expands-right-to-use-deadly-force-in-selfdefense.html
50. N. Flatow, 'At Least 26 Children Or Teens Died In Florida Stand Your Ground Cases', Think Progress, 5 February 2014, https://thinkprogress.org/at-least-26-children-or-teens-died-in-florida-stand-your-ground-cases-726443948a64/
51. S. Taylor Martin, 'Florida "stand your ground" law yields some shocking outcomes depending on how law is applied', *Tampa Bay Times*, 17 February 2013, https://www.tampabay.com/news/

publicsafety/crime/florida-stand-your-ground-law-yields-some-shocking-outcomes-depending-on/1233133

52. 'Deaths Nearly Triple Since "Stand Your Ground" Enacted', CBS Miami, 20 March 2012, https://miami.cbslocal.com/2012/03/20/deaths-nearly-triple-since-stand-your-ground-enacted/

53. D. K. Humphreys, A. Gasparrini and D. J. Wiebe, 'Evaluating the Impact of Florida's "Stand Your Ground" Self-defence Law on Homicide and Suicide by Firearm', *Journal of the American Medical Association*, January 2017, https://jamanetwork.com/journals/jamainternalmedicine/fullarticle/2582988

54. E. Elkin and D. Andone, 'What you need to know about "stand your ground" laws', CNN, 29 July 2018, https://edition.cnn.com/2018/07/29/us/stand-your-ground-law-explainer-trnd/index.html

55. C. McClellan and E. Tekin, 'Stand Your Ground Laws, Homicides, and Injuries', *Journal of Human Resources*, Summer 2017, vol. 52, no. 3, pp. 621–53.

56. A. Munasib, G. Kostandini and J. L. Jordan, 'Impact of the Stand Your Ground law on gun deaths: evidence of a rural urban dichotomy', *European Journal of Law and Economics*, June 2018, vol. 45, no. 3, pp. 527–54.

57. M. Hoekstra, 'The deadly consequences of "Stand Your Ground" laws', Reuters, 13 February 2014, http://blogs.reuters.com/great-debate/2014/02/13/the-deadly-consequences-of-stand-your-ground-laws/?utm_source=hootsuite&utm_campaign=hootsuite

58. 'Dallas police officer shoots neighbour dead after entering wrong apartment', *Guardian*, 7 September 2018, https://www.theguardian.com/us-news/2018/sep/07/dallas-police-officer-shoots-neighbor-wrong-apartment

59. R. Prince, 'David Cameron: when a burglar invades your home they give up their rights', *Telegraph*, 9 October 2012.

60. M. Sullivan, 'DON'T CHARGE HIM: Join The Sun to demand an end to murder probe into hero OAP Richard Osborn-Brooks, accused of stabbing serial burglar', the *Sun*, 5 April 2018.

61. S. Swinford, V. Ward and H. Dixon, 'Justice Secretary pledges to protect homeowners after "career-criminal" burglar allegedly killed by pensioner', *Telegraph*, 5 April 2018, https://www.telegraph.co.uk/politics/2018/04/05/justice-secretary-pledges-protect-homeowners-career-criminal/

## 2. Your Family

1. Senator Ted Cruz, press release, 25 April 2018, https://www.cruz. senate.gov/?p=press_release&id=3760

2. 'Alfie Evans: Protesters try to storm Alder Hey hospital', BBC News, 23 April 2018, https://www.bbc.com/news/ uk-england-merseyside-43867132

3. Facts taken from the judgment of Francis J. in *Great Ormond Street Hospital* v. *Yates & others* [2017] EWHC 972 (Fam).

4. 'Charlie Gard's parents to use £1.3m fund for charity', BBC News, 15 August 2017, https://www.bbc.co.uk/news/ uk-england-london-40940881

5. L. Deacon, '"Death Panel": European court says terminal baby must die despite parents funding extra care', Breitbart, 29 June 2017, https://www.breitbart.com/london/2017/06/29/eu-court- terminal-baby-must-die-despite-parents-funding-extra-care/

6. P. Greenfield, 'Charlie Gard: Pope shows solidarity with parents of critically ill 10-month-old', *Guardian*, 3 July 2017, https://www.theguardian.com/world/2017/jul/02/ pope-shows-solidarity-with-charlie-gards-parents

7. D. Hughes, 'Charlie Gard: Boris Johnson says terminally ill baby can't be moved to Vatican', *Independent*, 5 July 2017, https://www.independent.co.uk/news/uk/home-news/ charlie-gard-boris-johnson-italy-foreign-minister-vatican-pope- francis-paediatric-hospital-care-a7825261.html

8. 'European parliamentarians condemn "outrageous" Charlie Gard ruling in open letter to Theresa May and Jeremy Hunt', Christian Concern, 5 July 2017, https://www.christianconcern. com/press-release/european-parliamentarians-condemn- outrageous-charlie-gard-ruling-in-open-letter-to-the

9. T. Starnes, 'Charlie Gard: What kind of a nation would kill a baby in his mother's arms?', Fox News, 9 July 2017, https:// www.foxnews.com/opinion/charlie-gard-what-kind-of-a-nation- would-kill-a-baby-in-his-mothers-arms

10. S. Berry, 'Charlie Gard: How government and the courts usurp parental rights', Breitbart, 6 July 2017, https://www.breitbart.com/politics/2017/07/06/ charlie-gard-government-courts-usurp-parental-rights/

11. D. Loucks, 'Commentary: Socialized medicine seeks Charlie

Gard's death', *Austin American-Statesman*, 10 July 2017, https://archive.md/MCOmz

12. C. Thomas, 'Charlie Gard – the state is not God', Fox News, 13 July 2017, https://www.foxnews.com/opinion/charlie-gard-the-state-is-not-god

13. @SpeakerRyan, Twitter, 13 July 2017, https://twitter.com/SpeakerRyan/status/885603958756179968

14. R. Lydall and K. Proctor, 'Charlie Gard and parents given "US citizenship", but court ruling blocks baby from being taken from hospital', *Evening Standard*, 19 July 2017, https://www.standard.co.uk/news/uk/charlie-gard-and-parents-all-given-us-citizenship-but-baby-still-cant-be-removed-from-hospital-a3591456.html

15. M. MacLeod, 'Statement from Chairman of Great Ormond Street Hospital', 22 July 2017, https://www.gosh.nhs.uk/news/latest-press-releases/statement-chairman-great-ormond-street-hospital-22-july-2017

16. *Great Ormond Street Hospital* v. *Yates & others* [2017] EWHC 1909 (Fam), https://www.bailii.org/ew/cases/EWHC/Fam/2017/1909.html

17. @Nigel_Farage, Twitter, 24 July 2017, https://twitter.com/Nigel_Farage/status/889601759374708736

18. @tedcruz, Twitter, 24 July 2017, https://twitter.com/tedcruz/status/889621865161011208

19. 'Charlie Gard: Mother's full statement – "we are so sorry that we couldn't save you"', *Telegraph*, 24 July 2017, https://www.telegraph.co.uk/news/2017/07/24/charlie-gard-mothers-full-statement-sorry-couldnt-save/

20. Facts taken from judgment of Hayden J. in *Alder Hey Children's NHS Foundation Trust* v. *Evans & others* [2018] EWHC 308 (Fam), https://www.judiciary.uk/wp-content/uploads/2018/02/alder-hey-v-evans.pdf

21. T. Davidson, 'RECAP as Alder Hey Children's Hospital urges protestors to stay away as Alfie Evans' parents await fresh legal challenge', *Mirror*, 13 April 2018, https://www.mirror.co.uk/news/uk-news/live-alfie-evans-dads-emotionally-12353771

22. S. Paterson and M. Robinson, 'Alfie Evans' mother is "kicked out of hospital for complaining over visitor restrictions" as his father claims he has been threatened with jail if he tries to take brain-damaged son to Italy for treatment', *Daily Mail*, 13 April 2018, https://www.dailymail.co.uk/news/article-5611775/Alfie-Evans-

supporters-issue-fresh-call-arms-new-protest-outside-hospital.html

23. Ibid.

24. R. Hill, 'MEP Steven Woolfe makes passionate plea for Alfie's Law as he insists that doctors "make mistakes" and refers to Ashya King case', *Irish Mirror*, 27 April 2018, https://www.irishmirror.ie/tv/mep-steven-woolfe-makes-passionate-12435772

25. L. Traynor, 'Pope Francis calls for a solution in Alfie Evans case as family prepare for latest legal battle', *Liverpool Echo*, 15 April 2018, https://www.liverpoolecho.co.uk/news/liverpool-news/pope-francis-calls-solution-alfie-14533970

26. @Pontifex, Twitter, 23 April 2018, https://twitter.com/Pontifex/status/988496588283826177

27. T. Stickings, 'Could medics face trial for conspiracy to murder? Alfie Evans' father plans private prosecution against three Alder Hey doctors over son's care', *Daily Mail*, 25 April 2018, https://www.dailymail.co.uk/news/article-5657273/Could-Alfie-Evans-medics-face-trial-conspiracy-murder.html

28. 'Alfie Evans: Alder Hey Hospital defends staff against abuse', BBC News, 25 April 2018, https://www.bbc.co.uk/news/uk-england-merseyside-43900571

29. 'Alfie Evans: World's reaction to sick toddler's case', BBC News, 25 April 2018, https://www.bbc.co.uk/news/uk-england-merseyside-43892684

30. 'Nigel Farage talks Alfie Evans and Britain's medical system', Fox News, 26 April 2018, https://www.youtube.com/watch?v=rGwSNfZVKeA

31. https://m.facebook.com/groups/265101867249571/permalink/353390198420737/

32. For this historical summary, I am grateful to the Law Commission Working Paper No. 96, Family Law Review of Child Law: Custody (1986), at §6.1 onwards. http://www.lawcom.gov.uk/app/uploads/2016/08/No.096-Family-Law-Review-of-Child-Law-Custody.pdf

33. The Court of Chancery was a court of equity which operated parallel to the traditional courts of law, up until the Supreme Court of Judicature Acts of 1873 and 1875 fused the Chancery and common law courts into the High Court of Justice. Courts of equity, to crassly distil one of the most complex areas of our legal system into a snappy footnote, arose formally around the sixteenth century out of the Lord Chancellor's function as

'Keeper of the King's Conscience'. They applied somewhat vague 'equitable' principles of fairness to mitigate the harshness of the common law developed in the King's courts; a sort-of parallel justice system that led to the creation of land law and the laws of trusts, among other subjects feared and loathed by law students. In short, if there was a gap in the common law that would lead to injustice, the court of equity was your backstop. The law relating to children fell within that backstop.

34. *Re Agar Ellis* [1883] 24 Ch D 317, per Bowen L. J.
35. Section 31 of the Children Act 1989.
36. Section 8 of the Children Act 1989.
37. *Re J (Specific Issue Orders: Child's Religious Upbringing and Circumcision)* [2000] 1 FLR 571.
38. *Re B (A Child: Immunisation)* [2018] EWFC 56, at [20].
39. Section 1(3).
40. *Re G (Children)* [2012] EWCA Civ 1233 (Fam).
41. General Medical Council Ethical Guidance for Doctors, https://www.gmc-uk.org/ethical-guidance/ethical-guidance-for-doctors/0-18-years/guidance-for-all-doctors
42. For a discussion as to the difficulties in quantifying the precise number, see '10 cases like Charlie's? Actually we're not sure . . .', Transparency Project, 1 August 2017, http://www.transparencyproject.org.uk/10-cases-like-charlies-actually-were-not-sure/
43. *Re E (A Minor) (Wardship: Medical Treatment)* [1993] 1 FLR 386.
44. *An NHS Trust* v. *Child B and Mr & Mrs B* [2014] EWHC 3486 (Fam).
45. B. Farmer, 'A sick toddler's parents believe her fate should be left in the hands of God – but a judge has ruled otherwise', *Manchester Evening News*, 28 February 2019, https://www.manchestereveningnews.co.uk/news/greater-manchester-news/sick-toddlers-parents-believe-fate-15898226
46. @TuckerCarlson, Twitter, 10 July 2017, https://twitter.com/TuckerCarlson/status/884569449281531904
47. GOSH's Position Statement, Hearing on 13 July 2017, Katie Gollop QC, at §8, https://www.gosh.nhs.uk/file/23611/download?token=aTPZchww
48. *Re B (A Minor) (Wardship: Medical Treatment)* [1981] 1 WLR 1421.
49. K. Gollop QC and S. Pope, 'Charlie Gard, Alfie Evans

and R (A Child): Why A Medical Treatment Significant Harm Test Would Hinder Not Help', Transparency Project, 22 May 2018, http://www.transparencyproject.org.uk/ charlie-gard-alfie-evans-and-r-a-child-why-a-medical-treatment-significant-harm-test-would-hinder-not-help/

50. Per Baroness Hale in *Aintree University Hospital NHS Trust* v. *James* [2013] UKSC 67 and per MacDonald J. in *King's College NHS Foundation Trust* v. *Thomas, Haastrup and Haastrup* [2018] EWHC 127 (Fam).

51. First judgment, [2017] EWHC 972 (Fam) para 14.

52. Court of Appeal judgment of 23 May 2017 is at *Yates and Gard* v. *Great Ormond Street Hospital* [2017] EWCA Civ 410. Supreme Court, Permission to appeal hearing (Charlie Gard), 8 June 2017, Judgment summary, https://www.supremecourt.uk/news/ permission-to-appeal-hearing-in-the-matter-of-charlie-gard.html

53. *Gard & others* v. *United Kingdom* (application no. 39793/17), https://hudoc.echr.coe.int/eng-press#{'ite mid':['003-5768362-7332860']}

54. See the helpful commentary on the events of these dates in B. Rich, 'Update on Charlie Gard case – The last stage of the litigation: facts and sources', Transparency Project, 1 August 2017, http://www.transparencyproject.org.uk/update-on-charlie-gard-case-the-last-stage-of-the-litigation-facts-and-sources/

55. *Great Ormond Street Hospital* v. *Yates and Gard* [2017] EWHC 1909 (Fam).

56. The position statement by Charlie's guardian is worth reading, not least where they observe that, 'If novel therapies are to be offered, it appears to the Guardian to be imperative that those offering to provide them are fully aware of the clinical condition and medical history of the particular patient . . . so that offers are made on an informed basis and without setting up false hope and expectations.' Position Statement of the Guardian for Hearing, 24 July 2017, https://www.serjeantsinn.com/ wp-content/uploads/2017/08/Gard-Guardian-PS.pdf

57. Parliament technically has the power to petition the Queen to remove a judge, derived from the Act of Settlement 1701 and reflected in section 11(3) of the Supreme Court Act 1981, but this has never been exercised in England and Wales (just once in Scotland, in 1830, when a corrupt judge pinched money from litigants).

58. C. Buck, 'Brain dead toddler taken off life support in Los Angeles', *Sacramento Bee*, 25 August 2016, https://www.sacbee.com/news/local/article97861097.html

59. K. O'Neill and T. Belger, 'Alfie Evans judge questions medical evidence after watching emotional video of desperately ill baby "yawning"', *Mirror*, 8 February 2018, https://www.mirror.co.uk/news/uk-news/alfie-evans-judge-questions-medical-11994598

60. *Re E (A Child)* [2018] EWCA Civ 550, at [23] to [25], and [133] to [146].

61. Supreme Court, Permission to appeal determination (Alfie Evans), 20 March 2018, Reasons for determination, https://www.supremecourt.uk/cases/docs/alfie-evans-reasons-200318.pdf

62. *Re E (A Child)* [2018] EWCA Civ 550, at [36] and [133] to [146].

63. *Evans and James v. Alder Hey Children's NHS Foundation Trust* [2018] EWCA Civ 805, at [27].

64. *Alder Hey Children's NHS Foundation Trust v. Evans & others* [2018] EWHC 818 (Fam), at [7].

65. *Evans and James v. Alder Hey Children's NHS Foundation Trust* [2018] EWCA Civ 805, at [67].

66. *Evans v. United Kingdom* 18770/18 [2018] ECHR 357 (23 April 2018).

67. *Alder Hey Children's NHS Foundation Trust v. Evans & others* [2018] EWHC 953 (Fam), at [8].

68. See *Alder Hey Children's NHS Foundation Trust v. Evans & others* [2018] EWHC 953 (Fam) at [14].

69. [2018] EWCA Civ 984.

70. 'Alfie Evans' father reveals son has been breathing unassisted after life support stops', *Telegraph*, 24 April 2018, https://www.telegraph.co.uk/news/2018/04/24/alfie-evans-father-reveals-son-has-breathing-unassisted-life/

71. 'Judge attacks advisers to parents of Alfie Evans', *The Times*, 25 April 2018, https://www.thetimes.co.uk/article/judge-attacks-advisers-to-parents-of-alfie-evans-sft9rq39w

72. M. Scott, 'The Tragic Case of Alfie Evans', Quillette, 28 April 2018, https://quillette.com/2018/04/28/tragic-case-alfie-evans/

73. @JoshHalliday, Twitter, 24 April 2018, https://twitter.com/JoshHalliday/status/988817200940273670

74. *Evans & others v. Alder Hey Children's NHS Foundation Trust* [2018] EWCA 984 (Civ), at [33].

75. Ibid, at [39] and [40].

76. *Portsmouth City Council* v. *King & others* [2014] EWHC 2964 (Fam).

77. @AndrzejDuda, Twitter, 25 April 2018, https://twitter.com/AndrzejDuda/status/989054152155258880

78. J. Halliday, '"Call from God": American pro-lifer's role in Alfie Evans battle', *Guardian*, 28 April 2018, https://amp.theguardian.com/uk-news/2018/apr/28/call-from-god-american-pro-lifers-role-in-alfie-evans-battle?CMP=share_btn_tw&__twitter_impression=true

79. G. Peaker, 'On the Naughty Step – the questionable ethics of the Christian Legal Centre', Nearly Legal, 28 April 2018, https://nearlylegal.co.uk/2018/04/on-the-naughty-step-the-questionable-ethics-of-the-christian-legal-centre/

80. Christian Concern, press release, 5 July 2017, https://www.christianconcern.com/press-release/european-parliamentarians-condemn-outrageous-charlie-gard-ruling-in-open-letter-to-the

81. Dr Ranjana Das, 'The Charlie Gard twitterstorm: a violent and negative impact (new research)', LSE, 4 August 2017, http://blogs.lse.ac.uk/polis/2017/08/04/the-charlie-gard-twitterstorm-a-violent-and-negative-impact-new-research/

82. R. Bishop, 'Alfie Evans' supporters take to the streets in protests worldwide over parents' wishes being rejected by courts', *Mirror*, 26 April 2018, https://www.mirror.co.uk/news/uk-news/people-across-london-northern-ireland-12433984

83. 'Law Center: Husband seeks autopsy on Terri Schiavo', CNN, 29 March 2005, https://edition.cnn.com/2005/LAW/03/28/schiavo/

84. C. Thomas, 'Charlie Gard – the state is not God', Fox News, 13 July 2017, https://www.foxnews.com/opinion/charlie-gard-the-state-is-not-god

85. L. LaMaster, 'AZ Rep Trent Franks Stands Up for Charlie Gard and His Parents', Prescott News, 12 July 2017, https://www.prescottenews.com/index.php/news/current-news/item/30349-az-rep-trent-franks-stands-up-for-the-charlie-gard-and-his-parents; C. Tognotti, 'Who is Rep. Trent Franks? His 20-Week Abortion Ban Is Coming Up For A Vote', Bustle, 29 September 2017, https://www.bustle.com/p/who-is-rep-trent-franks-his-20-week-abortion-ban-is-coming-up-for-a-vote-2481919

86. 'Charlie's Army: The people fighting for Charlie Gard', *The Week*, 26 July 2017, https://www.theweek.co.uk/85153/

charlies-army-the-people-fighting-for-charlie-gard

87. S. Berry, 'US Pro-Life Leaders: We Are All Charlie Gard', Breitbart, 6 July 2017, https://www.breitbart.com/politics/2017/07/06/u-s-pro-life-leaders-charlie-gard/

88. S. Berry, 'Charlie Gard: How Governments And The Courts Usurp Parental Rights', Breitbart, 6 July 2017, https://www.breitbart.com/politics/2017/07/06/charlie-gard-government-courts-usurp-parental-rights/

89. C. K. Chumley, 'Charlie Gard makes Trump case for speedy Obamacare repeal', *Washington Times*, 3 July 2017, https://www.washingtontimes.com/news/2017/jul/3/charlie-gard-makes-trump-case-speedy-obamacare-rep/

90. @realDonaldTrump, Twitter, 5 February 2018, https://twitter.com/realDonaldTrump/status/960486144818450432

91. B. Jacobs, 'US Conservatives use case of terminally ill child Alfie Evans to criticise NHS', 26 April 2018, https://www.theguardian.com/us-news/2018/apr/25/alfie-evans-american-conservatives-criticize-nhs-ted-cruz

92. Senator Ted Cruz, press release, 25 April 2018.

93. 'Alfie Evans: World's reaction to sick toddler's case,' BBC News, 25 April 2018.

94. Ibid.

95. 'Nigel Farage talks Alfie Evans and Britain's medical system', Fox News, 26 April 2018.

96. K. Gander, 'Nigel Farage caught on video suggesting NHS should be run privately', *Independent*, 13 November 2014, https://www.independent.co.uk/news/uk/politics/nigel-farage-caught-on-video-suggesting-the-nhs-should-be-run-privately-9857389.html

97. See tweets cited in M. Scott, 'The Tragic Case of Alfie Evans', Quillette, 28 April 2018.

98. See, for example, S. Phillimore, 'What are the nature of and limits to parents' rights?', Child Protection Resource, 27 July 2017, http://childprotectionresource.online/what-are-the-nature-of-and-limits-to-parents-rights/

## 3. Your Health

1. S. Swinford and L. Hughes, 'Car insurance premiums to fall by £40 a year under plans to end "rampant compensation culture"',

*Telegraph*, 17 November 2016, https://www.telegraph.co.uk/news/2016/11/17/car-insurance-premiums-fall-by-40-a-year-under-plans-to-end-ramp/

2. 'Bart Gets Hit by a Car', Season 2, Episode 10, *The Simpsons*, first aired 10 January 1991. This episode was itself a pastiche of *Meet Whiplash Willie*, a 1966 comedy starring Jack Lemmon and Walther Matthau in which rogue lawyer 'Whiplash Willie' tries to convince his brother-in-law to fake paralysis following a road traffic accident to secure compensation.

3. *My Cousin Vinny* (1992), obviously. Obviously.

4. Christopher McGovern, Chairman of the Campaign for Real Education, quoted in R. Sabey, 'CLASSROOM COMPO: £2.9 million bill for school accident victims – for slipping in rounders and falling off see-saw', the *Sun*, 17 September 2016, https://www.thesun.co.uk/news/1803661/2-9-million-pound-bill-for-school-accident-victims-for-slipping-in-rounders-and-falling-off-see-saw/

5. R. Littlejohn, *Daily Mail*, 11 November 2009, https://www.dailymail.co.uk/debate/article-1226483/RICHARD-LITTLEJOHN-Only-Gordon-Brown-turn-tribute-gross-insult.html

6. 'Pupil awarded £6,000 for custard splash as playground "compensation culture" costs taxpayers £2million', *Daily Mail*, 4 July 2011, https://www.dailymail.co.uk/news/article-2011131/Pupil-awarded-6-000-custard-splash-playground-compensation-culture-costs-taxpayers-2million.html

7. S. Johnson, 'Cleaning up in the small claims court: Council worker awarded £9,000 compensation for tripping over a mop', *Daily Mail*, 27 July 2012, https://www.dailymail.co.uk/news/article-2179757/Council-cleaner-given-9-000-compensation-tripping-MOP.html

8. S. Adams, 'NHS blows £2.2billion a year paying for its medical mistakes, new figures reveal', *Daily Mail*, 4 November 2018, https://www.dailymail.co.uk/news/article-6350635/NHS-blows-2-2billion-year-paying-medical-mistakes-new-figures-reveal.html

9. Cited in Better Regulation Taskforce, 'Better Routes to Redress', May 2004.

10. 'Five of America's most notorious and extraordinary lawsuits', *Daily Mail*, 28 February 2014, https://www.dailymail.co.uk/news/article-2569996/Serviette-smile-McDonalds-sued-1-5-million-employee-called-Angel-gives-one-NAPKIN.html

11. Secretary of State for Transport Justine Greening, 'Britain is the

whiplash capital of Europe – and I'm going to stop it', *Mail on Sunday*, 4 February 2013, https://www.dailymail.co.uk/news/article-2096597/Justine-Greening-Britain-whiplash-capital-Europe-Im-going-stop-it.html; and, more recently, the comments of Chris Philp MP, Civil Liability Bill [Lords] Debate, House of Commons Second Reading, 4 September 2018, Hansard, volume 646, column 108, https://hansard.parliament.uk/commons/2018-09-04/debates/C5C185BA-C520-4561-B4A9-069335D3E41F/CivilLiabilityBill(Lords)

12. See Ministry of Justice, 'Reducing the number and costs of whiplash claims: A consultation on arrangements concerning whiplash injuries in England and Wales', Consultation Paper CP17/2012, Cm 8425, December 2012, at p. 3; and see Rory Stewart MP, Civil Liability Bill [Lords] Debate, House of Commons Third Reading, 23 October 2018, Hansard, volume 648, column 226, https://hansard.parliament.uk/commons/2018-10-23/debates/08FEE407-6D41-4294-9098-DA400C53EB83/CivilLiabilityBill(Lords)#contribution-F4EC132D-14B5-4C68-A669-090F6C503188

13. See Chris Philp MP, Civil Liability Bill [Lords] Debate, House of Commons Third Reading, 23 October 2018, Hansard, volume 648, column 160.

14. R. Massey, 'Europe's whiplash capital: Compensation culture makes British twice as likely to claim, adding £90 to premiums', *Daily Mail*, 20 April 2013, https://www.dailymail.co.uk/news/article-2311979/Europes-whiplash-capital-Compensation-culture-makes-British-twice-likely-claim-adding-90-premiums.html

15. N. Hilborne, 'Solicitor struck off after trying to influence medical expert', Legal Futures, 14 December 2018, https://www.legalfutures.co.uk/latest-news/solicitor-struck-off-after-trying-to-influence-medical-expert

16. K. Pickles, 'Feeling flush! Council worker hit by toilet lid gets £12,000 payout – while cleaner whose feet got trapped in a Henry Hoover also wins £12,000', *Daily Mail*, 19 July 2015, https://www.dailymail.co.uk/news/article-3167391/Crazy-compensation-payouts-Council-pays-12-000-worker-hit-toilet-lid-12-000-cleaner-feet-trapped-Henry-Hoover.html

17. 'Brain-injured teen from Sussex to get payout from NHS', BBC News, 20 June 2018, https://www.bbc.co.uk/news/uk-england-sussex-44541006

18. C. Sergeant, 'The Anglo-Saxon origins of UK compensation law', InfoLaw, 25 June 2014, https://www.infolaw.co.uk/partners/the-anglo-saxon-origins-of-uk-compensation-law/

19. As happens, for example, in New Zealand, where there is a system of state-funded social provision for those who suffer loss through injuries, irrespective of fault. There is an interesting academic debate as to whether we should adopt a similar scheme in England and Wales, and do away with our fault-based model.

20. [1932] UKHL 100.

21. The 'Six Pack' of health and safety legislation comprises the Management (Health, Safety and Welfare) Regulations 1992 (now 1999); the Provision and Use of Work Equipment Regulations 1992 (now 1998); the Manual Handling Operations Regulations 1992; the Workplace (Health, Safety and Welfare) Regulations 1992; the Personal Protective Equipment at Work Regulations 1992 and the Health and Safety (Display Screen Equipment) Regulations 1992. These have been joined by others, including the Control of Substances Hazardous to Health Regulations 2002 ('COSHH') and the Work at Height Regulations 2005.

22. There are certain absolute duties imposed under some legislation, such as the Animals Act 1971 and the Consumer Protection Act 1987 for injuries caused by animals and defective products respectively, but these 'strict liability' offences, not requiring proof of a lack of reasonable care, are rare. In the employment field, there was until 2013 an automatic right to compensation if an employer breached certain statutory duties and injury was caused, but Parliament changed the law to remove this right and inject a requirement of fault (section 69 of the Enterprise and Regulatory Reform Act 2013).

23. This is a boiled-down summary of the key principles in the landmark case of *Bolam* v. *Friern Hospital Management Committee* [1957] 1 WLR 582.

24. K. Pickles, 'Feeling flush! Council worker hit by toilet lid gets £12,000 payout – while cleaner whose feet got trapped in a Henry Hoover also wins £12,000', *Daily Mail*, 19 July 2015.

25. The Limitation Act 1980 provides the framework for calculating 'limitation'. There are many nuances – children, for example, have until their twenty-first birthday (three years after attaining majority) to issue a claim – and circumstances in which the period might be extended, but the general rule is that an injured

person has three years from the date on which the cause of action accrued (i.e. the date of the injury) *or* three years from the date that person had knowledge of a significant injury. The latter would apply in cases where, say, an employee was exposed to asbestos a decade ago but only becomes aware of the resultant disease years after the fact.

26. See, for example, *Lunt* v. *Khelifa* [2002] EWCA Civ 801, cited in D. Boyle, *An Introduction to Personal Injury Law*, Law Brief Publishing, 2017, p. 49.

27. Exemplary damages can only be claimed in cases falling within three categories: (i) oppressive, arbitrary or unconstitutional action by servants of the government; (ii) wrongful conduct by the defendant which has been calculated by him to make a profit for himself which may well exceed the compensation payable to the complainant; (iii) where a statute authorises such an award. *Rookes* v. *Barnard* [1964] AC 1129.

28. Technically, the Court of Appeal has the power to revise the recommended awards – see *Simmons* v. *Castle* [2013] 1 WLR 1239.

29. The Judicial College Guidelines, 14th Edition.

30. P. Cheston, 'Autistic boy set for millions after NHS blunder', *Evening Standard*, 12 June 2015, https://www.standard.co.uk/news/health/autistic-boy-set-for-millions-after-nhs-blunder-10315290.html

31. Ibid.

32. 'Boy made autistic by NHS blunder given millions in damages after parents sue hospital', *Mirror*, 12 June 2015, https://www.mirror.co.uk/news/uk-news/boy-made-autistic-nhs-blunder-5872815

33. P. Owen, 'We waited 13 years for NHS to admit blame for our son's brain damage', *Mirror*, 15 August 2015, https://www.mirror.co.uk/news/uk-news/we-waited-13-years-nhs-6260398

34. Facts taken from *Harman* v. *East Kent Hospitals NHS Foundation Trust* [2015] EWHC 1662 (QB).

35. 'Refugees hit jackpot with £5.2m payouts', *Sunday Express*, 18 January 2012, https://www.express.co.uk/news/uk/296341/Refugees-hit-jackpot-with-5-2m-payouts

36. E. Riley, 'Schoolgirl, 12, who has modelled for Boden and Tesco despite suffering severe cerebral palsy since birth wins £15m NHS compensation payout', *Daily Mail*, 17 July 2018, https://www.dailymail.co.uk/news/article-5962347/Schoolgirl-cerebral-

palsy-wins-15-million-compensation-NHS.html

37. N. Small, 'Council worker wins more than £12,000 in compensation after he was hit with . . . a LOO lid', *Mirror*, 19 July 2015, https://www.mirror.co.uk/news/uk-news/council-worker-wins-more-12000-6095620

38. R. Clark, '£341,000 compensation pay out for broken loo is madness, says ROSS CLARK', *Daily Express*, 5 May 2015, https://www.express.co.uk/comment/expresscomment/574840/Broken-loo-payout-just-tip-iceberg-Britain-s-compensation-culture-madness-says-ROSS-CLARK

39. Andrew Ritchie QC, 'Summary of the Personal Injury and Clinical Negligence Claims Market in England and Wales, July 2015', http://www.9goughsquare.co.uk/uploadedFiles/CN&PIMarketReview2015AR.pdf

40. 'Down the pan: Council pays man £341k after falling off toilet', *Telegraph*, 3 May 2015, https://www.telegraph.co.uk/news/politics/council-spending/11580198/Down-the-pan-Council-pays-man-341k-after-falling-off-toilet.html

41. R. Clarke, '£341,000 compensation pay out for broken loo is madness, says ROSS CLARK', *Daily Express*, 5 May 2015.

42. 'Down the pan: Council pays man £341k after falling off toilet', *Telegraph*, 3 May 2015.

43. M. Levin, 'Legal Urban Legends Hold Sway', *Los Angeles Times*, 14 August 2005, http://articles.latimes.com/2005/aug/14/business/fi-tortmyths14, as cited by Lord Dyson M.R., 'Compensation Culture: Fact or Fantasy?', Holdsworth Club Lecture, 15 March 2013, https://www.judiciary.uk/wp-content/uploads/JCO/Documents/Speeches/mr-speech-compensation-culture.pdf

44. 'Five of America's most notorious and extraordinary lawsuits', *Daily Mail*, 28 February 2014.

45. See Lord Dyson M.R., 'Compensation Culture: Fact or Fantasy?', Holdsworth Club Lecture, 15 March 2013.

46. Y. Ekici, '"Compensation Culture" – behind the Daily Mail headlines', 11 February 2015, https://www.bindmans.com/insight/blog/compensation-culture-behind-the-daily-mail-headlines

47. S. Johnson, 'Cleaning up in the small claims court: Council worker awarded £9,000 compensation for tripping over a mop', *Daily Mail*, 27 July 2012.

48. N. Small, 'Council worker wins more than £12,000 in

compensation after he was hit with . . . a LOO lid', *Mirror*, 19 July 2015.

49. 'Top 10 worst health and safety myths', Health and Safety Executive, http://www.hse.gov.uk/myth/top10myths.htm (accessed 6 January 2019).

50. H. Frankel, 'Handle with care', *Times Education Supplement*, 7 August 2009, https://www.tes.com/news/handle-care-9

51. R. Littlejohn, *Daily Mail*, 11 November 2009.

52. R. Strange, '"Elf and safety" stories should carry a warning', *Independent*, 15 March 2010, https://www.independent. co.uk/news/media/press/elf-and-safety-stories-should-carry-a- warning-1921337.html

53. Ibid.

54. J. Hyde, 'MoJ reveals 20% annual fall in personal injury claims', *Law Society Gazette*, 6 December 2018, https://www.lawgazette. co.uk/news/moj-reveals-20-annual-fall-in-personal-injury- claims/5068594.article

55. Department for Work and Pensions, 'Compensation Recovery Unit performance data', 23 April 2018, https://www.gov.uk/government/publications/ compensation-recovery-unit-performance-data/ compensation-recovery-unit-performance-data

56. 'Legal claims against NHS continue to rise', Practice Business, 16 July 2018, https://practicebusiness.co.uk/ legal-claims-against-nhs-continue-to-rise/

57. 'EXCLUSIVE: Police officer gets £10,000 for falling off a chair', *Evening Standard*, 12 April 2013, https://www.standard.co.uk/ news/uk/exclusive-police-officer-gets-10000-payout-for-falling- off-a-chair-8569997.html

58. See, for example, the members of the 'highly-organised' gang in Sheffield who were imprisoned for fraudulently orchestrating a series of 'crash for cash' traffic collisions: 'Sheffield bus crash-for-cash gang "highly-organised"', BBC News, 26 September 2013, https://www.bbc.co.uk/news/ uk-england-south-yorkshire-24283580

59. House of Commons Justice Committee, 7th Report – 'Small claims limit for personal injury', 17 May 2018, at §30, https://publications.parliament.uk/pa/cm201719/cmselect/ cmjust/659/65902.htm

60. T. Evans, 'COMPENSATION CRACKDOWN: Bogus whiplash

claims add £1billion to car insurance bills every year', the *Sun*, 17 November 2016, https://www.thesun.co.uk/living/2199963/bogus-whiplash-claims-add-1billion-to-car-insurance-bills-every-year/

61. S. Swinford and L. Hughes, 'Car insurance premiums to fall by £40 a year under plans to end "rampant compensation culture"', *Telegraph*, 17 November 2016.

62. 'Statement on outcomes following Downing Street Insurance Summit', Prime Minister's Office, 10 Downing Street, 14 February 2012, https://www.gov.uk/government/news/statement-on-outcomes-following-downing-street-insurance-summit

63. See Chris Philp MP, Civil Liability Bill [Lords] Debate, House of Commons Third Reading, 23 October 2018, Hansard, volume 648, column 160.

64. See David Gauke MP, Civil Liability Bill [Lords] Debate, House of Commons Second Reading, 4 September 2018, Hansard, volume 646, column 108, https://hansard.parliament.uk/commons/2018-09-04/debates/C5C185BA-C520-4561-B4A9-069335D3E41F/CivilLiabilityBill(Lords)

65. House of Commons Transport Committee, 'Cost of Motor Insurance: Whiplash', 4th Report of Session 2013–14, HC 117, 31 July 2013, volume 1, paragraph 28, cited in K. Oliphant, '"The Whiplash Capital of the World": Genealogy of a Compensation Myth', in E. Quill and R. Friel (eds.), *Damages and Compensation Culture: Comparative Perspectives*, Hart Publishing, 2016, https://research-information.bristol.ac.uk/files/80271070/AAM_Whiplash_Capital.pdf

66. See summary in 'Fake News and the Compensation Culture – An Access to Justice Investigation', Access to Justice Action Group, 12 January 2018, https://accesstojusticeactiongroup.co.uk/fake-news-and-compensation-culture/

67. Ibid.

68. Ibid.

69. David Gauke MP, Civil Liability Bill [Lords] Debate, House of Commons Second Reading, 4 September 2018, Hansard, volume 646, column 77, https://hansard.parliament.uk/commons/2018-09-04/debates/C5C185BA-C520-4561-B4A9-069335D3E41F/CivilLiabilityBill(Lords)

70. Jo Stevens MP, Civil Liability Bill [Lords] Debate, House

of Commons Third Reading, 23 October 2018, Hansard, volume 648, column 158, https://hansard.parliament.uk/commons/2018-10-23/debates/08FEE407-6D41-4294-9098-DA400C53EB83/CivilLiabilityBill(Lords)#contribution-F4EC132D-14B5-4C68-A669-090F6C503188

71. House of Commons Justice Committee, 7th Report – 'Small claims limit for personal injury', 17 May 2018, at §30.

72. J. Hyde, '"Ridiculous" heroism bill clears Lords hurdle', *Law Society Gazette*, 7 January 2015, https://www.lawgazette.co.uk/law/ridiculous-heroism-bill-clears-lords-hurdle/5045846.article

73. Chris Grayling MP, 'Our Bill to curb the Elf and Safety Culture', 2 June 2014, ConservativeHome, https://www.conservativehome.com/platform/2014/06/chris-grayling-mp-our-bill-to-curb-the-elf-and-safety-culture.html

74. Ibid.

75. Lord Pannick, Social Action, Responsibility and Heroism Bill, House of Lords Third Reading, 6 January 2015, Hansard, column 262, https://publications.parliament.uk/pa/ld201415/ldhansrd/text/150106-0001.htm#15010644000364

76. See 'Annex: Background to the current reforms', in House of Commons Justice Committee, 7th Report – 'Small claims limit for personal injury', 17 May 2018, at §30.

77. Section 57 of the Criminal Justice and Courts Act 2015 requires a court to dismiss the whole of a personal-injury claim in such circumstances, unless the claimant would suffer 'substantial injustice' if the claim were dismissed.

78. Department for Work and Pensions, 'Compensation Recovery Unit performance data', 23 April 2018.

79. J. Hyde, 'MoJ chief denies whiplash portal is in hock to insurers', *Law Society Gazette*, 11 February 2019, https://www.lawgazette.co.uk/news/moj-chief-denies-whiplash-portal-is-in-hock-to-insurers/5069235.article

80. House of Commons Justice Committee, 7th Report – 'Small claims limit for personal injury', 17 May 2018, at §59.

81. Ellie Reeves MP, 'The Civil Liability Bill – An Assault on Our Access to Justice', 25 July 2018, http://www.elliereeves.com/news/the-civil-liability-bill-an-assault-on-our-access-to-justice

82. House of Commons Justice Committee, 7th Report – 'Small claims limit for personal injury', 17 May 2018, at §65-66.

83. Ibid, at §81.

84. Unison survey found that 63 per cent of members surveyed said they 'would not have proceeded or been at all confident to bring their claim without legal representation', cited by Ellie Reeves MP, 'The Civil Liability Bill – An Assault on Our Access to Justice', 25 July 2018.

85. House of Commons Justice Committee, 7th Report – 'Small claims limit for personal injury', 17 May 2018, at §137-9.

86. Ibid.

87. S. McGee, 'Lawyers give dire warning as study reveals reforms will wipe out PI solicitors', *Insurance Times*, 1 March 2018, https://www.insurancetimes.co.uk/lawyers-give-dire-warning-as-study-reveals-reforms-will-wipe-out-pi-solicitors/1426462.article

88. C. Canocchi, 'Government unveils whiplash claims crackdown which it says will cut insurance premiums by £35 a year', This is Money, 20 March 2018, https://www.thisismoney.co.uk/money/cars/article-5523253/Government-unveils-plans-cut-whiplash-claims.html

89. Civil Liability Bill [Lords] Debate, House of Commons Third Reading, 23 October 2018, Hansard, volume 648, column 160.

90. O. Bowcott, 'Charities condemn Tory cuts to criminal injuries compensation scheme', *Guardian*, 23 April 2019, https://www.theguardian.com/law/2019/apr/23/charities-condemn-tory-cuts-to-criminal-injuries-compensation-scheme

91. Employers' Liability (Compulsory Insurance) Act 1969.

92. J. Insley, 'Compensation culture: a history of bizarre personal injury claims in Britain', *Guardian*, 14 July 2011, https://www.theguardian.com/money/blog/2011/jul/14/compensation-culture-personal-insurance-claims

## 4. Your Work

1. S. Doughty, 'Hallelujah! The tribunal gravy train's derailed: As workers are made to pay £1,200 fee, discrimination cases plunge by 75%', *Daily Mail*, 29 July 2014, https://www.dailymail.co.uk/news/article-2709011/As-workers-pay-1-200-fee-discrimination-cases-plunge-75.html

2. The Office for National Statistics records that, in January 2019, there were 32.53 million people in work, 15 per cent of whom were self-employed. In the year to November 2018, the total number of hours worked exceeded 1 billion. See

Office for National Statistics, 'UK labour market: January 2019', https://www.ons.gov.uk/employmentandlabourmarket/peopleinwork/employmentandemployeetypes/bulletins/uklabourmarket/january2019#actual-hours-worked and 'Trends in self-employment in the UK', 7 February 2018, https://www.ons.gov.uk/employmentandlabourmarket/peopleinwork/employmentandemployeetypes/articles/trendsinselfemploymentintheuk/2018-02-07

3. That's 37 multiplied by 46.4 weeks (52 weeks minus statutory holiday entitlement of 5.6 weeks) multiplied by 50.

4. '80% of workers ignorant of legal rights', *The Times*, 8 October 2019, https://www.thetimes.co.uk/article/workers-ignorant-employment-rights-605s387c8?utm_source=newsletter&utm_campaign=newsletter_121&utm_medium=email&utm_content=121_7411059&CMP=TNLEmail_118918_7411059_121

5. Fifty-two weeks, comprising twenty-six weeks' 'ordinary maternity leave' and up to twenty-six weeks' 'additional maternity leave'.

6. Any employee who earns on average at least £118 per week and has worked continuously for their employer for at least six months at the date of the fifteenth week before the expected week of childbirth.

7. Statutory Maternity Pay is paid at 90 per cent of your average weekly earnings (before tax) for the first six weeks, and then at either 90 per cent of your average weekly earnings or £148.68 – whichever is *lower* – for the remaining thirty-three weeks.

8. Yes, you do, and it is paid. We'll look a little more at this later.

9. No.

10. Your job must be kept open for you to resume when you return from maternity leave.

11. 'Employment tribunals are legalised extortion', This is Money, 6 January 2011, https://www.thisismoney.co.uk/money/article-1710536/Comment-Employment-tribunals-are-legalised-extortion.html. This is Money is owned by DMG Ltd, the owners of the *Daily Mail* and *Mail on Sunday*.

12. D. Martin, 'Jackpot tribunal payouts face axe: Plan to limit discrimination at work claims', *Daily Mail*, 11 May 2011, https://www.dailymail.co.uk/news/article-1385731/Jackpot-tribunal-payouts-face-axe-Plan-limit-discrimination-work-claims.html

13. L. McKinstry, 'An end to abuse of the employment tribunal system', *Daily Express*, 31 July 2014, https://www.express.co.uk/comment/columnists/leo-mckinstry/493899/Leo-McKinstry-on-the-employment-tribunal-system

14. R. Littlejohn, 'Unsuitable work for a woman', *Daily Mail*, 20 February 2014, https://www.dailymail.co.uk/debate/article-2564235/RICHARD-LITTLEJOHN-Help-My-ID-stolen-Call-Fraudbusters.html

15. A. West, 'First Farce: Royal Mail paid employees £70k compo after vile racist KKK note was pinned up at sorting office', the *Sun*, 15 February 2018, https://www.thesun.co.uk/news/5583559/royal-mail-employees-70k-after-racist-kkk-message/

16. 'Tesco worker SUES supermarket for £20k after colleague "FARTS in his face"', *Daily Star*, 19 October 2018, https://www.dailystar.co.uk/news/latest-news/737392/Tesco-supermarket-store-grocery-London-discrimination-muslim-employment-tribunal

17. M. Beckford, 'Pictured: Female PC who won £15,000 for sexual discrimination after failing a fitness test to become a dog handler – because she couldn't carry an Alsatian', *Daily Mail*, 14 January 2018, https://www.dailymail.co.uk/news/article-5266731/Policewoman-wins-dog-carrying-discrimination-case.html

18. David Davies MP, cited in *Daily Mail*, ibid.

19. R. Tyler, 'Employment tribunal system "broken" claim employers', *Telegraph*, 5 January 2011, https://www.telegraph.co.uk/finance/yourbusiness/8241409/Employment-tribunal-system-broken-claim-employers.html

20. D. Martin, 'Jackpot tribunal payouts face axe: Plan to limit discrimination at work claims', *Daily Mail*, 11 May 2011.

21. *R (on the application of UNISON)* v. *Lord Chancellor* [2017] UKSC 51, at [39].

22. Statistics cited in the Supreme Court judgment in *UNISON*, ibid, at [35–7].

23. *R (on the application of UNISON)* v. *Lord Chancellor* [2017] UKSC 51, at [98].

24. Industrial Relations Act 1971. Unfair dismissal should not be confused with **wrongful dismissal**, a claim where a person is dismissed without the notice to which they are contractually or statutorily entitled and is seeking their notice pay.

25. An 'employee' is distinguished in employment law from a

'worker'. An employee, put very loosely, is somebody who is under the ultimate control of an employer, where there are continuing mutual obligations to provide and perform work. A worker is a broader concept of someone personally contracted to perform work, but who may not be an employee – such as a company director or agency worker. Different rights apply depending on whether you are an employee or a worker.

26. This 'qualifying period' has changed repeatedly since 1971 – falling to as little as six months – and from 1999 up until 2012 was twelve months. Part of the coalition government's response to business criticisms of employment law was to double the qualifying period to two years, which, the government stated, would 'improve business confidence' and satisfy the 'general aim' of 'reducing the number of tribunal claims'. See Department for Business, Innovation and Skills, *Resolving Workplace Disputes: Government response to the consultation*, November 2011, https://assets.publishing.service.gov.uk/government/uploads/system/uploads/attachment_data/file/229952/11-1365-resolving-workplace-disputes-government-response.pdf

27. A quick word about **constructive unfair dismissal**. Where an employer commits a fundamental breach of the contract of employment, an employee can terminate the contract without notice and treat herself as 'constructively dismissed'. An example might be an employer unilaterally changing employment terms, such as cutting your pay in half. Often, the alleged breach will be of the implied duty of mutual trust and confidence that the courts have recognised exists in all employment contracts. This covers a broad range of serious misbehaviours, including bullying. If a tribunal finds that you have been constructively dismissed, it then proceeds to look at whether that dismissal was fair, as above.

28. Sex Discrimination Act 1975.

29. Race Relations Act 1976.

30. Unlike unfair dismissal, discrimination law applies to workers, not solely employees.

31. Direct discrimination is only permitted where there is a 'genuine occupational requirement' – such as where a male actor is required to play a male role.

32. Or, in the words of the legislation, 'a proportionate means of achieving a legitimate aim'.

33. Also, where A engages in unwanted conduct of a sexual nature

(sexual harassment), or where A treats B less favourably as a result of B rejecting or submitting to unwanted sexual conduct.

34. A. West, 'First Farce: Royal Mail paid employees £70k compo after vile racist KKK note was pinned up at sorting office', the *Sun*, 15 February 2018.

35. Or because you have been a witness in discrimination proceedings.

36. Employers also cannot treat a disabled employee unfavourably because of something arising as a consequence of disability. It is intended to cover, for instance, a situation where an employer dismisses someone who is disabled because of their disability-related absence, and the employer says they would have dismissed anyone who had been absent for so long.

37. 'Code of Practice on disciplinary and grievance procedures', ACAS, https://www.acas.org.uk/article/2174/ Discipline-and-grievance-Acas-Code-of-Practice

38. R. Littlejohn, 'Grandad, Grandad, You're fired! After a 61-year-old sales rep given the nickname "Gramps" wins compensation, RICHARD LITTLEJOHN says poor treatment of staff in their late 50s and early 60s is all about money', *Daily Mail*, 22 March 2016, https://www.dailymail.co.uk/debate/article-3503687/ Grandad-Grandad-fired-61-year-old-sales-rep-given-nickname-Gramps-wins-compensation-RICHARD-LITTLEJOHN-says-poor-treatment-staff-late-50s-early-60s-money.html

39. David Davies, Conservative MP for Monmouth, TheyWorkForYou, https://www.theyworkforyou.com/mp/11719/ david_davies/monmouth/divisions?policy=6703 (accessed 30 January 2019).

40. M. Beckford, 'Pictured: Female PC who won £15,000 for sexual discrimination after failing a fitness test to become a dog handler – because she couldn't carry an Alsatian', *Daily Mail*, 14 January 2018.

41. '"End B.A. Discrimination" Says Monmouth M.P.', 20 October 20016, https://www.david-davies.org.uk/news/ end-ba-discrimination-says-monmouth-mp

42. This is known as the 'basic award', and is calculated according to your length of service (capped at twenty years), age and weekly pay (capped at £489 per week). The maximum basic award is £14,670. This can be reduced, potentially to zero, if you have received a redundancy payment or other ex gratia payment from your employer.

43. This is known as the 'compensatory award', and is meant to compensate for the loss suffered as a result of the dismissal. This may include immediate loss of wages, loss of fringe benefits (such as company car or accommodation), loss of pension rights, expenses incurred looking for new work, and future loss of wages. The latter inevitably involves a degree of crystal-ball gazing, with the tribunal guessing how long it will take for the employee to find a new job (if they haven't already done so). Generally, future losses tend not to extend beyond twelve months.

44. D. Martin, 'Jackpot tribunal payouts face axe: Plan to limit discrimination at work claims', *Daily Mail*, 11 May 2011.

45. This is because, under EU law, financial remedies in the domestic law of member states *must* allow for full compensation for loss where there is a breach of EU rights. Discrimination and equal pay are examples of EU rights.

46. Currently the cap on the compensatory award is £80,541 or fifty-two weeks' gross pay, whichever is lower.

47. *Armitage, Marsden and HM Prison Service* v. *Johnson* [1997] IRLR 162.

48. There are four 'bands' for injury to feelings. The lower band (into which most awards fall) provides for awards between £800 and £8,400; the middle band, £8,400 to £25,200; the most serious cases in the upper band, £25,200 to £42,000; and exceptional cases, over £42,000.

49. Ministry of Justice, 'Employment Tribunal and EAT statistics 2009–10 (GB), 1 April 2009 to 31 March 2010', 3 September 2010, https://assets.publishing.service.gov.uk/government/uploads/system/uploads/attachment_data/file/218501/tribs-et-eat-annual-stats-april09-march10.pdf

50. Ministry of Justice, 'Tribunals and gender recognition certificate statistics quarterly: July to September 2018', 13 December 2018, https://www.gov.uk/government/statistics/tribunals-and-gender-recognition-certificate-statistics-quarterly-july-to-september-2018

51. R. Tyler, 'Employment tribunal system "broken" claim employers', *Telegraph*, 5 January 2011.

52. Brian Binley MP, Draft Employment Tribunals and the Employment Appeal Tribunal Fees Order 2013, First Delegated Legislation Committee Stage, Session 2013–14, 10 June 2013, Hansard, column 15–16, https://publications.parliament.uk/pa/cm201314/cmgeneral/deleg1/130610/130610s01.htm

53. Report of the Royal Commission on Trade Unions and Employers' Associations (1968), Cmnd 3623 (para 578).

54. Less complex unfair-dismissal claims, wage claims and breach-of-contract claims will now often be heard by an employment judge sitting alone.

55. R. Tyler, 'Employment tribunal system "broken" claim employers', *Telegraph*, 5 January 2011.

56. 'Employers concerned about return to the past on tribunals, says BCC', British Chambers of Commerce, 26 July 2017, https://www.britishchambers.org.uk/news/2017/07/employers-concerned-about-return-to-the-past-on-tribunals-says-bcc

57. Ministry of Justice, 'Tribunals and gender recognition certificate statistics quarterly: July to September 2018', Main Tables, ET3, Percentage of disposals by outcome and jurisdiction, 2007/8 to Q2 2018/19, https://www.gov.uk/government/statistics/tribunals-and-gender-recognition-certificate-statistics-quarterly-july-to-september-2018

58. P. Aldrick, '"Malicious" tribunal claims hit business', *Telegraph*, 8 March 2011, https://www.telegraph.co.uk/finance/jobs/8367670/Malicious-tribunal-claims-hit-business.html

59. M. Gibbons, 'Better Dispute Resolution: A review of employment dispute resolution in Great Britain', Department of Trade and Industry, March 2007, https://www.effectivedisputesolutions.co.uk/wp-content/uploads/2014/09/mgibbons-review.pdf

60. Ian Murray MP, Draft Employment Tribunals and the Employment Appeal Tribunal Fees Order 2013, First Delegated Legislation Committee Stage, Session 2013–14, 10 June 2013, Hansard, column 20, https://publications.parliament.uk/pa/cm201314/cmgeneral/deleg1/130610/130610s01.htm.

61. Baroness Whitaker, Added Tribunals (Employment Tribunals and Employment Appeal Tribunal) Order 2013, 8 July 2013, Hansard, volume 747, column 83, https://hansard.parliament.uk/Lords/2013-07-08/debates/13070845000225/AddedTribunals(EmploymentTribunalsAndEmploymentAppealTribunal)Order2013

62. Employment Tribunal Rule 37(1).

63. Employment Tribunal Rule 39(1).

64. Employment Tribunal Rule 76(1).

65. Ministry of Justice, 'Tribunals and gender recognition certificate statistics quarterly: July to September 2018', Main Tables, ET3,

Percentage of disposals by outcome and jurisdiction, 2007/8 to Q2 2018/19.

66. A. Beecroft, 'Report on Employment Law', 24 October 2011, https://assets.publishing.service.gov.uk/government/uploads/system/uploads/attachment_data/file/31583/12-825-report-on-employment-law-beecroft.pdf

67. See Ian Murray MP, Draft Employment Tribunals and the Employment Appeal Tribunal Fees Order 2013, First Delegated Legislation Committee Stage, Session 2013–14, 10 June 2013, Hansard, column 21.

68. A. Porter and R. Winnett, 'Firms get powers to sack the slackers', *Telegraph*, 9 January 2011, https://www.telegraph.co.uk/finance/economics/8249491/Firms-get-powers-to-sack-the-slackers.html

69. See Lord Monks, Added Tribunals (Employment Tribunals and Employment Appeal Tribunal) Order 2013, 8 July 2013, Hansard, volume 747, column 83, https://hansard.parliament.uk/Lords/2013-07-08/debates/13070845000225/AddedTribunals(EmploymentTribunalsAndEmploymentAppealTribunal)Order2013

70. See 'A truly remarkable democratic mandate', The Secret Barrister, 27 June 2016, https://thesecretbarrister.com/2016/06/27/a-truly-remarkable-democratic-mandate/

71. *R (on the application of UNISON) v. Lord Chancellor* [2017] UKSC 51, at [8].

72. Ibid, at [35–7].

73. See Ian Murray MP, Draft Employment Tribunals and the Employment Appeal Tribunal Fees Order 2013, First Delegated Legislation Committee Stage, Session 2013–14, 10 June 2013, Hansard, column 22.

74. 'Survey of Employment Tribunal Applications (SETA) 2008: findings', Department for Business, Innovation and Skills, 23 March 2010, https://www.gov.uk/government/publications/survey-of-employment-tribunal-applications-seta-2008-findings

75. Lord Monks, Added Tribunals (Employment Tribunals and Employment Appeal Tribunal) Order 2013, 8 July 2013, Hansard, volume 747, column 83.

76. Baroness Whitaker, Added Tribunals (Employment Tribunals and Employment Appeal Tribunal) Order 2013, 8 July 2013, Hansard, volume 747, column 84.

77. Added Tribunals (Employment Tribunals and Employment Appeal Tribunal) Order 2013 (SI 2013/1892).
78. R *(on the application of UNISON)* v. *Lord Chancellor* [2017] UKSC 51, at [39].
79. Ibid, at [40–2].
80. House of Commons Justice Committee, 'Courts and tribunal fees', 16 June 2016, at §71 https://publications.parliament.uk/pa/cm201617/cmselect/cmjust/167/16701.htm
81. Ibid.
82. R *(on the application of UNISON)* v. *Lord Chancellor* [2017] UKSC 51, at [43–4].
83. House of Commons Justice Committee, 'Courts and tribunal fees', 16 June 2016, at §69.
84. A. Grice, 'Vince Cable interview: Charging fees for employment tribunals was "a very bad move"', *Independent*, 29 April 2015, https://www.independent.co.uk/news/uk/politics/generalelection/vince-cable-interview-charging-fees-for-employment-tribunals-was-a-very-bad-move-10213703.html
85. The government expected a recovery rate of 'around a third'. The recovery rate for 2014/15 and 2015/16, after remissions, was 13 per cent. See *Unison* at [56].
86. *Unison*, at [58–9].
87. *Unison*, at [57].
88. The Council of Employment Judges, 'Submission on the Review of the Introduction of Employment Tribunal Fees', 24 July 2015, https://consult.justice.gov.uk/digital-communications/review-of-fees-in-employment-tribunals/supporting_documents/cejfeesreviewsubmission.pdf
89. *Unison*, at [55].
90. R *(on the application of UNISON)* v. *Lord Chancellor* [2017] UKSC 51 at https://www.supremecourt.uk/cases/uksc-2015-0233.html

## 5. Our Human Rights

1. 'Theresa May speech in full', 4 October 2011, http://www.politics.co.uk/comment-analysis/2011/10/04/theresa-may-speech-in-full
2. The names are disguised to protect the identity of the victims.

'Fiona' is referred to in the proceedings as 'DSD'. 'Manisha' is referred to as 'NBV'. The facts are taken from the High Court judgment in 2014: *DSD and another* v. *Commissioner of Police of the Metropolis* [2014] EWHC 436 (QB).

3. Ibid, at [308].

4. In such cases, claims may be made (as they were by Fiona and Manisha) against the offender himself, where he has means to pay, and/or to the Criminal Injuries Compensation Authority, but, prior to this judgment, claims could not be made against the police.

5. *Commissioner of Police of the Metropolis (Appellant)* v. *DSD and another (Respondents)* [2018] UKSC 11.

6. See I. Drury, 'Folly of human rights luvvies: As actors fight plans to axe Human Rights Act, how thousands of foreign convicts use it to stay in Britain', *Daily Mail*, 27 May 2015, https://www.dailymail.co.uk/news/article-3098327/amp/Folly-human-rights-luvvies-actors-fight-plans-axe-Human-Rights-Act-thousands-foreign-convicts-use-stay-Britain.html

7. J. Slack, 'Europe's war on British justice: UK loses three out of four human rights cases, damning report reveals', *Daily Mail*, 11 January 2012, https://www.dailymail.co.uk/news/article-2085420/Europes-war-British-justice-UK-loses-human-rights-cases-damning-report-reveals.html

8. 'No excuses, Dave, end this Yuman Rites farce: RICHARD LITTLEJOHN says case of three Libyan sex offenders seeking asylum must incite government to act on appalling Human Rights laws', *Daily Mail*, 2 October 2015, https://www.dailymail.co.uk/debate/article-3257056/No-excuses-Dave-end-YUMAN-RITES-farce-RICHARD-LITTLEJOHN-says-case-three-Libyan-sex-offenders-seeking-asylum-incite-government-act-appalling-Human-Rights-laws.html

9. 'May: Scrap the Human Rights Act', the *Sun*, 2 October 2011, https://www.thesun.co.uk/archives/news/813593/may-scrap-the-human-rights-act/

10. 'European Court of Human Rights is undermining democracy', Policy Exchange, https://policyexchange.org.uk/press-release/european-court-of-human-rights-is-undermining-democracy/

11. 'Human rights laws are protecting the wrong people', *Telegraph*, 24 April 2011, https://www.telegraph.co.uk/comment/telegraph-view/8470149/Human-rights-laws-are-protecting-the-wrong-people.html

12. A. Little, 'Human Rights Act has DEVALUED Magna Carta, blasts David Cameron', *Daily Express*, 15 June 2015, https://www.express.co.uk/news/politics/584454/David-Cameron-Prime-Minister-Magna-Carta-speech-human-rights-plan

13. 'No excuses Dave, end this Yuman Rites farce: RICHARD LITTLEJOHN says case of three Libyan sex offenders seeking asylum must incite government to act on appalling Human Rights laws', *Daily Mail*, 2 October 2015.

14. J. Slack, 'Unelected euro judges are bringing terror to the streets of Britain', *Daily Mail*, 18 January 2012, https://www.dailymail.co.uk/debate/article-2087831/Abu-Qatada-human-rights-Unelected-euro-judges-bringing-terror-streets-Britain.html

15. Chris Grayling MP, quoted in H. Phibbs, 'Grayling's message of toughness and tenderness', ConservativeHome, 30 September 2014, https://www.conservativehome.com/thetorydiary/2014/09/graylings-message-of-toughness-and-tenderness.html

16. L. Brown, 'Another Human Rights Fiasco!', *Daily Mail*, 15 December 2017.

17. D. Bamber, 'Prisoners win their claim that hardcore porn is a human right', *Telegraph*, 10 November 2002, https://www.telegraph.co.uk/news/uknews/1412742/Prisoners-win-their-claim-that-hardcore-porn-is-a-human-right.html

18. J. Doyle, 'Human rights laws are a charter for criminals, say 75% of Britons', *Daily Mail*, 16 April 2012, https://www.dailymail.co.uk/news/article-2130224/Human-rights-laws-charter-criminals-say-75-Britons.html

19. 'Theresa May speech in full', 4 October 2011.

20. M. Spurrier, 'After Worboys, the Met will have to take rape victims seriously', *Guardian*, 21 February 2018, https://www.theguardian.com/commentisfree/2018/feb/21/worboys-met-rape-victims-theresa-may

21. R. Mason, 'David Cameron eyes Human Rights Act repeal', *Guardian*, 8 August 2013, https://www.theguardian.com/law/2013/aug/08/david-cameron-human-rights-act

22. W. Woodward, 'Cameron promises UK bill of rights to replace Human Rights Act', *Guardian*, 26 June 2006, https://www.theguardian.com/politics/2006/jun/26/uk.humanrights

23. R. Merrick, 'Theresa May to consider axeing Human Rights Act after Brexit, minister reveals', *Independent*, 18 January 2019, https://www.independent.co.uk/news/uk/politics/

theresa-may-human-rights-act-repeal-brexit-echr-commons-parliament-conservatives-a8734886.html

24. 'Dominic Cummings's Blog', 24 March 2018, https://dominiccummings.com/2018/03/24/on-the-referendum-24c-the-whistleblowers-and-channel-4-observer-accusations/ (accessed 29 July 2019).

25. S. Hughes, 'EU can't kick out Abu Qatada', the *Sun*, 18 Janaury 2012, https://www.thesun.co.uk/archives/news/311309/eu-cant-kick-out-abu-qatada/

26. 'EU human rights court order Italy to pay Amanda Knox £15,600 in damages for violating her rights during Meredith Kercher murder investigation', @DailyMailUK, Twitter, 24 January 2019, https://twitter.com/DailyMailUK/status/1088397934494994434

27. Victoria Friedman, 'Orban: "EU court of human rights is a security threat to Europeans"', Breitbart, 31 March 2017, https://www.breitbart.com/europe/2017/03/31/orban-eu-court-human-rights-security-threat/

28. See reference to 'EU court' in J. Bell, 'Could ROBOT judges replace humans in dishing out justice in court?', *Daily Star*, 24 October 2016, https://www.dailystar.co.uk/news/latest-news/556341/robot-judges-court-justice-study

29. D. Bentley, 'Call for withdrawal from EU human rights court', *Independent*, 7 February 2011, https://www.independent.co.uk/news/world/europe/call-for-withdrawal-from-eu-human-rights-court-2206647.html

30. David Cameron stated in 2014 that, 'It's not just the European Union that needs sorting out – it's the European Court of Human Rights.' See O. Bowcott, 'Cameron's pledge to scrap Human Rights Act angers civil rights groups', *Guardian*, 1 October 2014, https://www.theguardian.com/politics/2014/oct/01/cameron-pledge-scrap-human-rights-act-civil-rights-groups

31. 'May: Scrap the Human Rights Act', the *Sun*, 2 October 2011.

32. M. Torrance, 'Maxwell Fyfe and the origins of the ECHR', *The Journal*, 19 September 2011, http://www.journalonline.co.uk/magazine/56-9/1010095.aspx#.XFmNgS10eis

33. 'The Prime Minister must defy the European Court', *Daily Express*, 11 February 2011, https://www.express.co.uk/comment/expresscomment/228451/The-Prime-Minister-must-defy-the-European-Court

34. Article 22 of the European Convention on Human Rights.

35. 'Human Rights in Europe: Explainer', RightsInfo, https://rightsinfo.org/infographics/human-rights-uncovered/

36. 'European Court of Human Rights: The ECHR in 50 questions', February 2014, https://www.echr.coe.int/Documents/50Questions_ENG.pdf

37. J. Slack, 'Europe's war on British justice: UK loses three out of four human rights cases, damning report reveals', *Daily Mail*, 11 January 2012, https://www.dailymail.co.uk/news/article-2085420/Europes-war-British-justice-UK-loses-human-rights-cases-damning-report-reveals.html

38. A. Hough and T. Whitehead, 'ECHR: Britain loses 3 in 4 cases at human rights court', *Telegraph*, 12 January 2012, https://www.telegraph.co.uk/news/worldnews/europe/9008904/ECHR-Britain-loses-3-in-4-cases-at-human-rights-court.html

39. C. Woodhouse, 'Euro judges go against UK in 3 out of 5 cases', the *Sun*, 24 August 2014, https://www.thesun.co.uk/archives/politics/1053158/euro-judges-go-against-uk-in-3-out-of-5-cases/

40. A. Wagner, 'No, The Sun, "Euro judges" do not "go against UK in 3 out of 5 cases". More like 1 in 100', UK Human Rights Blog, 27 August 2014, https://ukhumanrightsblog.com/2014/08/27/no-the-sun-euro-judges-do-not-go-against-uk-in-3-out-of-5-cases-more-like-1-in-100/

41. Human Rights Joint Committee, 'Seventh Report: Human Rights Judgments', 4 March 2015, at §2.2, https://publications.parliament.uk/pa/jt201415/jtselect/jtrights/130/13002.htm

42. J. Slack, 'Europe's war on British justice: UK loses three out of four human rights cases, damning report reveals', *Daily Mail*, 11 January 2012.

43. Human Rights Joint Committee, 'Seventh Report: Human Rights Judgments', 4 March 2015, at §2.6; see also Lady Hale, 'Celebrating 70 years of the Universal Declaration and 20 years of the Human Rights Act', British Institute of Human Rights Annual Lecture 2018, 7 November 2018, https://www.supremecourt.uk/docs/speech-181107.pdf

44. Home Office, 'Rights Brought Home: The Human Rights Bill (Cm 3782, 1997).

45. Ibid, at §1.14.

46. Ibid, section 6.

47. Ibid, section 8.

48. Ibid, section 3.

49. Ibid, section 2.

50. Ibid, section 4.

51. Often included in summaries of the 'main' rights are also articles 1 to 3 of protocol 1 to the convention, which prescribe the right to peaceful enjoyment of property, the right to education and the right to free elections.

52. Original *Daily Mail* front page available to see at C. Tobitt, 'Daily Mail runs front page IPSO ruling on inaccuracies in Iraq compensation claim report as staff told making similar errors again would "put careers at risk"', *Press Gazette*, 27 July 2018, https://www.pressgazette.co.uk/daily-mail-runs-front-page-ipso-adjudication-on-iraq-compensation-claims-as-staff-told-making-similar-error-again-would-put-careers-at-risk/

53. *Alseran & others* v. *Ministry of Defence* [2017] EWHC 3289 (QB).

54. D. Bamber, 'Prisoners win their claim that hardcore porn is a human right', *Telegraph*, 10 November 2002; see also 'How do you label a goat?', *Daily Mail*, 20 November 2006, which reported that 'The Human Rights Act 2000 [sic] allowed serial killer Dennis Nilsen to win a case to look at hardcore pornographic magazines in his cell.' https://www.dailymail.co.uk/news/article-417637/How-label-goat.html

55. See Department for Constitutional Affairs, 'Review of the Implementation of the Human Rights Act', July 2006, p. 30, https://webarchive.nationalarchives.gov.uk/+/http:/www.dca.gov.uk/peoples-rights/human-rights/pdf/full_review.pdf

56. A Judicial Communications Office statement, dated 4 October 2011, confirmed that 'the cat had nothing to do with the decision [not to deport]': P. Henley, 'Theresa May in deportation cat flap', BBC News, 4 October 2011, https://www.bbc.co.uk/news/uk-england-15174254

57. H. Phibbs, 'Grayling's message of toughness and tenderness', ConservativeHome, 30 September 2014.

58. *Vinter & others* v. *United Kingdom* (2013) Application 66069/09, 130/10 and 3896/10.

59. Lord Justice Laws, at [112].

60. Section 30 of the Crime (Sentences) Act 1997.

61. *R* v. *McLoughlin* [2014] EWCA Crim 188.

62. *Hutchinson* v. *United Kingdom* (2015) Application 57592/08.

63. T. Parsons, 'Why the Human Rights Act is just so wrong', *Sun on Sunday*, 14 December 2014, https://www.thesun.co.uk/archives/news/603603/why-the-human-rights-act-is-just-so-wrong/

64. HC Deb, 22 October 2013, Col 156.

65. T. May, 'It's MY job to deport foreigners who commit serious crime – and I'll fight any judge who stands in my way', *Mail on Sunday*, 17 February 2013, https://www.dailymail.co.uk/debate/article-2279828/Its-MY-job-deport-foreigners-commit-crime--Ill-fight-judge-stands-way-says-Home-Secretary.html

66. T. Parsons, 'Why the Human Rights Act is just so wrong', *Sun on Sunday*, 14 December 2014.

67. Home Office, 'Foreign criminals successfully appealing against deportation using Article 8 of the ECHR', 16 January 2014, Annex A, figures for April 12 to March 13, https://www.gov.uk/government/publications/foreign-criminals-successfully-appealing-against-deportation-using-article-8-of-echr

68. Section 32 of the UK Borders Act 2007.

69. Per Master of the Rolls in *MF (Nigeria)* v. *Secretary of State for the Home Department* [2013] EWCA Civ 1192.

70. T. Parsons, 'Why the Human Rights Act is just so wrong', *Sun on Sunday*, 14 December 2014.

71. J. Doyle and J. Narain, 'Asylum seeker who left girl, 12, to die after hit-and-run can stay in UK . . . thanks to the Human Rights Act David Cameron promised her father he'd scrap', *Daily Mail*, 17 December 2010, https://www.dailymail.co.uk/news/article-1339142/Asylum-seeker-Aso-Mohammed-Ibrahim-let-girl-12-die-stay-UK.html

72. T. McVeigh, 'Asylum decision on hit-and-run driver embarrasses PM', *Guardian*, 19 December 2010, https://www.theguardian.com/uk/2010/dec/19/asylum-ruling-fury-rights-cameron

73. 'Anger as asylum seeker death-crash driver stays in Britain', *Metro*, 17 December 2010, https://metro.co.uk/2010/12/17/anger-as-amy-houstons-dad-slams-decision-to-allow-driver-aso-mohammed-ibrahim-to-stay-614118/

74. *Secretary of State for the Home Department* v. *R* [2010] UKUT B1, at [70].

75. Ibid, at [74].

76. Ibid, at [56].

77. Ibid, at [70].

78. Lord Wilson, 'Our Human Rights: A Joint Effort?', The

Howard J. Trienens Lecture, 25 September 2018, https://www.
supremecourt.uk/docs/speech-180925.pdf

79. 'Patrick Stewart sketch: what has the ECHR ever done for us?'
written and directed by Dan Susman, https://www.youtube.com/
watch?v=ptfmAY6M6aA

80. See P. Weatherby QC, 'Truth and justice', *Counsel* magazine,
November 2016, https://www.counselmagazine.co.uk/articles/
truth-and-justice

81. O. Bowcott, 'MoD paid £750,000 on legal fees denying
responsibility for soldier deaths', *Guardian*, 12 September
2017, https://www.theguardian.com/politics/2017/sep/12/
mod-paid-750000-on-legal-fees-denying-responsibility-for-soldier-
deaths

82. *Smith & others* v. *Ministry of Defence* [2013] UKSC 41.

83. C. Coleman, 'Mother wins MoD apology over "Snatch" Land
Rover death', BBC News, 18 August 2017, https://www.bbc.
co.uk/news/uk-40958686

84. R. Mason, 'Mid Staffs: Labour Government ignored MP
requests for public inquiry into deaths', *Telegraph*, 17 February
2013, https://www.telegraph.co.uk/news/uknews/9875660/
Mid-Staffs-Labour-Government-ignored-MP-requests-for-public-
inquiry-into-deaths.html

85. L. Donnelly, 'Stafford Hospital: the scandal that shamed the
NHS', *Telegraph*, 6 January 2013, https://www.telegraph.co.uk/
news/health/heal-our-hospitals/9782562/Stafford-Hospital-the-
scandal-that-shamed-the-NHS.html

86. N. Duffy, 'Theresa May claims European Human Rights treaty
has "added nothing" . . . despite LGBT rights victories', Pink
News, 25 April 2016, https://www.pinknews.co.uk/2016/04/25/
theresa-may-claims-european-convention-on-human-rights-has-
added-nothing-despite-lgbt-rights-victories/

87. G. McKinnon, 'Theresa May saved my life – now she's the
only hope for the Human Rights Act', *Guardian*, 15 November
2016, https://www.theguardian.com/commentisfree/2016/nov/15/
theresa-may-saved-my-life-human-rights-act

88. *Sutherland* v. *United Kingdom* (1997) (25186/94).

89. L. Eleftheriou-Smith, 'Last week The Sun wanted to
abolish the Human Rights Act, this week they want to
use it to protect their journalists', *Independent*, 6 October
2014, https://www.independent.co.uk/news/uk/crime/

last-week-the-sun-wanted-to-abolish-the-human-rights-act-this-week-they-want-to-use-it-to-protect-9778190.html

90. 'A nation imperilled by the Human Rights Act', *Daily Mail*, 27 August 2015, https://www.dailymail.co.uk/debate/article-3181945/DAILY-MAIL-COMMENT-nation-imperilled-Human-Rights-Act.html

91. See *R (Associated Newspapers Ltd) v. Lord Justice Leveson* [2012] EWHC 57 (Admin); and *Associated Newspapers Ltd v. His Royal Highness the Prince of Wales* [2006] EWCA Civ 1776.

92. 'Eight reasons why the Human Rights Act makes the UK a better place', Amnesty, 8 October 2018, https://www.amnesty.org.uk/eight-reasons-why-human-rights-act-has-made-uk-better-place-british-bill-of-rights

93. British Institute of Human Rights, 'Getting with the Act: Our Human Rights Act', https://www.bihr.org.uk/hraebook

94. 'My HRA: Jenny Paton', Liberty, 22 February 2013, https://www.libertyhumanrights.org.uk/news/blog/my-hra-jenny-paton

95. R. Clegg, 'Council sued over polling station access', BBC News, 23 April 2015, https://www.bbc.co.uk/news/election-2015-32414123

96. *R (Bernard) v. London Borough of Enfield* [2002] EWHC 2282 (Admin).

97. I. Drury, 'Folly of human rights luvvies: As actors fight plans to axe Human Rights Act, how thousands of foreign convicts use it to stay in Britain', *Daily Mail*, 27 May 2015.

98. Human Rights Joint Committee, 'Seventh Report: Human Rights Judgments', 4 March 2015, at §2.4, https://publications.parliament.uk/pa/jt201415/jtselect/jtrights/130/13002.htm

99. *P (by his litigation friend the Official Solicitor) (Appellant) v. Cheshire West and Chester Council and another (Respondents); P and Q (by their litigation friend the Official Solicitor) (Appellants) v. Surrey County Council (Respondent)* [2014] UKSC 19; Judgment, 19 March 2014, https://www.supremecourt.uk/cases/docs/uksc-2012-0068-judgment.pdf

## 6. Our Access to Justice

1. 'An overdue end to the abuse of legal aid', *Daily Mail*, 16 November 2010, https://www.dailymail.co.uk/debate/

article-1329896/Kenneth-Clarke-An-overdue-end-abuse-legal-aid.html

2. 'We [. . .] still have by far the most expensive legal system of legal aid in the world', Lord Chancellor Ken Clarke MP, interviewed for International Bar Association, November 2011, https://www.ibanet.org/Article/NewDetail. aspx?ArticleUid=F4A4D433-36F9-4D3B-A3CA-ED94A30EF09A

3. D. Wooding, 'PRICE OF JUSTICE: Fat-cat lawyers raking in £3 million per trial for defending suspects in rape, terror, murder and fraud cases', the *Sun*, 1 January 2017, https://www.thesun. co.uk/news/2511999/fat-cat-lawyers-raking-in-3-million-per-trial-for-defending-suspects-in-rape-terror-murder-and-fraud-cases/

4. Interview with Ken Clarke MP, International Bar Association, November 2011.

5. L. McKinstry, 'Legal aid is now a racket that only benefits lawyers', *Daily Express*, 6 June 2013, https://www. express.co.uk/comment/columnists/leo-mckinstry/405287/ Legal-aid-is-now-a-racket-that-only-benefits-lawyers

6. N. Parker, 'AID FOR PAEDOS: Rochdale paedophile gang handed £1m in legal aid to fight deportation', the *Sun*, 10 February 2019, https://www.thesun.co.uk/news/8398308/ rochdale-child-sex-abuse-gang-legal-aid/

7. Name changed. See *R (Rights of Women)* v. *Lord Chancellor and Secretary of State for Justice* [2016] EWCA Civ 91, at [33] – see the case of 'M'.

8. See I. Pinter, 'Cut off from Justice: The impact of excluding separated migrant children from legal aid', The Children's Society, June 2015, https://www.childrenssociety.org.uk/sites/ default/files/LegalAid_Summary.pdf

9. Name changed.

10. W. Flack, 'How The Legal Aid Means Test Excludes People With No Accommodation From Receiving Free Advice and Assistance', William Flack Blog, 15 January 2019, http://wflack. com/how-the-legal-aid-means-test-excludes-people-with-no-accommodation-from-receiving-free-advice-and-assistance/

11. Name changed.

12. P. Butler, 'Tribunal restores benefit payments to acid attack victim', *Guardian*, 19 April 2019, https:// www.theguardian.com/society/2019/apr/19/ tribunal-restores-benefit-payments-to-acid-attack-victim?

13. Magna Carta, Section XXIX, 1297, http://www.legislation.gov.uk/aep/Edw1cc1929/25/9/section/XXIX

14. Per Lord Keith, *R* v. *R* [1991] UKHL 12.

15. The Poor Prisoners Defence Act 1903 provided some defendants of limited means with legal aid, where the court considered that they had a defence.

16. See Sir Henry Brooke, 'The History of Legal Aid 1945–2010', at Appendix 6 of the Bach Commission on Access to Justice, September 2017, https://www.fabians.org.uk/wp-content/uploads/2017/09/Bach-Commission-Appendix-6-F-1.pdf

17. This is an exceptionally basic explanation of the adversarial/inquisitorial traditions. For a deeper dive, see Chapters 8 and 9 of *The Secret Barrister: Stories of the Law and How It's Broken* (Picador, 2018).

18. See Sadiq Khan MP, Shadow Justice Secretary, quoted in, 'Legal Aid spending cuts to total £350m', *Guardian*, 15 November 2010, https://www.theguardian.com/law/2010/nov/15/legail-aid-clarke-spending-cuts

19. E.g. B. Witton, 'Suzy Lamplugh murder suspect "claims more than £60,000 legal aid while in jail"', *Mirror*, 2 December 2018, https://www.mirror.co.uk/news/uk-news/suzy-lamplugh-murder-suspect-claims-13679598 ; J. Corke, 'Cop killer Dale Cregan racks up almost £311,000 in legal aid funded by taxpayers', *Mirror*, 8 December 2018, https://www.mirror.co.uk/news/uk-news/cop-killer-dale-cregan-racks-13706928

20. G. McKelvie, 'Telford child sex monsters handed almost £2.5 MILLION in legal aid', *Mirror*, 28 April 2018, https://www.mirror.co.uk/news/uk-news/telford-child-sex-monsters-handed-12447244

21. N. Parker, 'AID FOR PAEDOS: Rochdale paedophile gang handed £1m in legal aid to fight deportation', the *Sun*, 10 February 2019.

22. S. Osborne, 'Fury as terrorist gets £250,000 legal aid handout to FIGHT deportation out of UK', *Daily Express*, 13 June 2017, https://www.express.co.uk/news/uk/816478/Convicted-terrorist-legal-aid-funds-deportation-battle

23. J. Slack, 'Clarke to slash legal aid bill for asylum seekers at Ministry of Justice seeks cuts', *Daily Mail*, 18 August 2010, https://www.dailymail.co.uk/news/article-1303718/Ken-Clarke-slash-legal-aid-asylum-seekers.html

24. C. Ikonen, 'Staggering cost of legal aid given to James Bulger killers REVEALED', *Daily Star*, 7 April 2018, https://www. dailystar.co.uk/news/latest-news/694392/james-bulger-jon-venables-legal-aid-robert-thompson-liverpool-news

25. Department of Health, 'Reference Costs 2015–16', December 2016, https://assets.publishing.service.gov.uk/government/uploads/system/uploads/attachment_data/file/577083/Reference_Costs_2015-16.pdf

26. A critical feature of our criminal justice system, for which there is insufficient space here, is that criminal barristers, contrary to popular belief, are not allowed to mislead a court by saying something they know to be untrue. So, if, for instance, a client admits to their barrister that they stole an apple, the barrister cannot stand up in court and suggest that their client did not. If, however, the evidence is overwhelming but the defendant insists that he is innocent and the fifty witnesses are mistaken, then the barrister will advise, robustly, but, if the client maintains that he is not guilty, the barrister's job is to fight fearlessly for their client.

27. 'How much money does legal aid save the country?', Full Fact, 8 January 2016, https://fullfact.org/law/how-much-money-does-legal-aid-save-country/

28. G. McKelvie, 'Telford child sex monsters handed almost £2.5 MILLION in legal aid', *Mirror*, 28 April 2018.

29. Jonathan Djanogly MP, Former Minister for Legal Aid and Courts, Address to Cambridge Union, 16 March 2015, http://www.jonathandjanogly.com/content/jonathan-djanogly-speaks-cambridge-union-debate

30. See interview with Ken Clarke MP, International Bar Association, November 2011.

31. D. Barrett, 'Britain has largest legal aid budget in Europe, says report', *Telegraph*, 9 October 2014, https://www.telegraph.co.uk/news/uknews/law-and-order/11149868/Britain-has-largest-legal-aid-budget-in-Europe-says-report.html

32. 'Justice for everyone need not cost the earth', *Telegraph*, 5 June 2013, https://www.telegraph.co.uk/comment/telegraph-view/10100926/Justice-for-everyone-need-not-cost-the-earth.html

33. C. Carter, 'Legal firms rake in millions from legal aid', *Telegraph*, 5 June 2013, https://www.telegraph.co.uk/news/uknews/law-and-order/10099863/Legal-firms-rake-in-millions-from-legal-aid.html

34. 'Legal aid spending cuts to total £350m', *Guardian*, 15

November 2010, https://www.theguardian.com/law/2010/nov/15/legail-aid-clarke-spending-cuts

35. J. Chapman, '£15m for just one firm on legal aid gravy train: Scale of taxpayers' bill revealed as Coalition vows to save £200m', *Daily Mail*, 5 June 2013, https://www.dailymail.co.uk/news/article-2336003/15m-just-firm-legal-aid-gravy-train-Scale-taxpayers-revealed-Coalition-vows-save-200m.html

36. 'Blair's asylum stance "chilling"', BBC News, 30 September 2003, http://news.bbc.co.uk/1/hi/uk_politics/3152982.stm

37. J. Slack, 'Legal aid payouts to fat cat lawyers will be slashed by a third, says Justice Secretary', *Daily Mail*, 10 April 2013, https://www.dailymail.co.uk/news/article-2306630/Legal-aid-payouts-fat-cat-lawyers-slashed-says-Justice-Secretary.html

38. Dominic Raab MP, Review of Legal Aid Reforms, Commons Chamber, 31 October 2017, Hansard, volume 630, column 688 [901517], https://hansard.parliament.uk/Commons/2017-10-31/debates/782C0020-9535-4E1A-BD38-7973DB3472AF/ReviewOfLegalAidReforms

39. S. Rogers, 'Public spending 2009/10 by UK government department', *Guardian*, 18 October 2010, https://www.theguardian.com/news/datablog/2010/oct/18/government-spending-department-2009-10

40. R. Bowles and A. Perry, 'International comparison of publicly funded legal services and justice systems', University of York, Ministry of Justice Research Series 14/09, October 2009, https://webarchive.nationalarchives.gov.uk/20100208125113/http:/www.justice.gov.uk/publications/docs/comparison-public-fund-legal-services-justice-systems.pdf

41. Ibid, p. iii.

42. Council of Europe, European Commission for the Efficiency of Justice, 'European judicial systems, Edition 2010 (data 2008)', 2010, Figure 2.23, https://www.uihj.com/en/ressources/21628/75/european_judicial_systems_-_2010.pdf

43. Council of Europe, European Commission for the Efficiency of Justice, 'European judicial systems, Edition 2016 (data 2014)', 2016, Figure 2.5, https://rm.coe.int/european-judicial-systems-efficiency-and-quality-of-justice-cepej-stud/1680786b58

44. I. Drury, 'We spend seven times more on legal aid than the French: £2bn Britain spends each year dwarfs every other country in Europe', *Daily Mail*, 9 October 2014, https://www.dailymail.

co.uk/news/article-2787276/We-spend-seven-times-legal-aid-French-2bn-Britain-spends-year-dwarfs-country-Europe.html

45. Council of Europe, European Commission for the Efficiency of Justice, 'European judicial systems, Edition 2014 (data 2012)', 2014, Figure 2.2. England and Wales allocated 1.8 per cent of its annual budget to the justice system; France allocated 1.9 per cent. http://www.just.ro/wp-content/uploads/2015/09/editia-2014-en.pdf

46. If you are wondering why I am flitting between the statistics for expenditure on the 'judicial system' (courts, legal aid and prosecution) for 2010 and expenditure on the justice system (judicial system, plus prisons, plus probation etc.) for 2016, and then back to the judicial system for 2018, it's because of the maddening inconsistency of the Council of Europe's methodology, which changes, apparently on a whim, each year.

47. Council of Europe, European Commission for the Efficiency of Justice, 'European judicial systems, Edition 2018 (data 2016)', 2018, https://rm.coe.int/rapport-avec-couv-18-09-2018-en/16808def9c

48. G. McKelvie, 'Telford child sex monsters handed almost £2.5 MILLION in legal aid', *Mirror*, 28 April 2018.

49. 'Becky Watts killers received £400,000 in legal aid', BBC News, 3 March 2016, https://www.bbc.co.uk/news/uk-england-bristol-35705555

50. 'Lee Rigby's killers received more than £200,000 in legal aid', *Guardian*, 29 July 2014, https://www.theguardian.com/uk-news/2014/jul/29/lee-rigby-killers-legal-aid

51. J. Chapman, '£15m for just one firm on legal aid gravy train: Scale of taxpayers' bill revealed as Coalition vows to save £200m', *Daily Mail*, 5 June 2013.

52. 'Legal aid: Government claims barristers earn £84,000 "misleading"', BBC News, 18 March 2014, https://www.bbc.co.uk/news/uk-26635572

53. R. Sabur, 'Terrorist who entered the country illegally handed £250,000 in legal aid', *Telegraph*, 13 June 2017, https://www.telegraph.co.uk/news/2017/06/13/terrorist-entered-country-illegally-handed-250000-legal-aid/

54. N. Parker, 'AID FOR PAEDOS: Rochdale paedophile gang handed £1m in legal aid to fight deportation', the *Sun*, 10 February 2019.

55. Civil Legal Aid (Remuneration) Regulations 2013, Part 2

(Hourly Rates, Controlled Work), and see C. J. McKinney, 'Legal aid lawyers aren't on £200 an hour', Full Fact, 6 July 2015, https://fullfact.org/law/legal-aid-lawyers-arent-200-hour/

56. Criminal Legal Aid (Remuneration) Regulations 2013, para 24.

57. 'Legal aid: Government claims barristers earn £84,000 "misleading"', BBC News, 18 March 2014.

58. P. Worrall, 'Should barristers keep their wigs on?', Channel 4 News Fact Check, 6 January 2014, https://www.channel4.com/news/factcheck/factcheck-violins-barristers

59. D. Wooding, 'PRICE OF JUSTICE: Fat-cat lawyers raking in £3million per trial for defending suspects in rape, terror, murder and fraud cases', the *Sun*, 1 January 2017.

60. J. Doyle, 'The multi-millionaire criminals claiming a fortune from legal aid', *Daily Mail*, 26 November 2012, https://www.dailymail.co.uk/news/article-2238716/The-multi-millionaire-criminals-claiming-fortune-legal-aid-Loophole-gives-50-rich-defendants-300-000-EACH.html

61. Otterburn Legal Consulting, 'Transforming Legal Aid: Next Steps. A Report for The Law Society of England and Wales and the Ministry of Justice', February 2014, pp. 5–8, https://consult.justice.gov.uk/digital-communications/transforming-legal-aid-next-steps/results/otterburn-legal-consulting-a-report-for-the-law-society-and-moj.pdf

62. Council of Europe, European Commission for the Efficiency of Justice, 'European judicial systems, Edition 2018 (data 2016)', 2018.

63. Ministry of Justice, 'Reform of Legal Aid in England and Wales: the Government Response', CM8072, June 2011, https://assets.publishing.service.gov.uk/government/uploads/system/uploads/attachment_data/file/228890/8072.pdf

64. O. Bowcott, 'Poorest priced out of justice by legal aid rules, says Law Society', *Guardian*, 20 March 2018, https://www.theguardian.com/uk-news/2018/mar/20/poorest-priced-out-of-justice-by-legal-aid-rules-says-law-society

65. P. Bredon, 'PLP Research Briefing Paper: The Civil Legal Advice Telephone Gateway', Public Law Project, May 2018, https://publiclawproject.org.uk/wp-content/uploads/2018/05/The-Civil-Legal-Advice-telephone-Gateway.pdf

66. 'Enforcing Human Rights', Joint Committee on Human Rights, 19 July 2018, https://publications.parliament.uk/pa/jt201719/jtselect/jtrights/669/66902.htm

67. Ibid, §39–44.

68. Ibid.

69. House of Commons Library, 'The future of legal aid', 31 October 2018, CDP-2018/0230, https://researchbriefings. parliament.uk/ResearchBriefing/Summary/CDP-2018-0230; see also, House of Commons Library, 'The spending of the Ministry of Justice', 1 October 2019, CDP-2019-0217, https://researchbriefings.parliament.uk/ResearchBriefing/Summary/CDP-2019-0217 – fullreport

70. Or 'non-molestation orders', as they are termed in the family courts.

71. *R (Rights of Women) v. Lord Chancellor and Secretary of State for Justice* [2016] EWCA Civ 91, at [45].

72. O. Bowcott, 'MoJ scraps legal aid restrictions for victims of domestic violence', *Guardian*, 4 December 2017, https://www.theguardian.com/society/2017/dec/04/moj-scraps-legal-aid-restrictions-for-victims-of-domestic-violence

73. *Re A (A minor)* [2017] EWHC 1195 (Fam) at [62]; *PS v. PB* [2018] EWHC 1987.

74. Ibid, [60].

75. 'Justice for all? Inside the legal aid crisis', *Financial Times*, 27 September 2018, https://www.ft.com/content/894b8174-c120-11e8-8d55-54197280d3f7

76. Dr J. Organ and Dr J. Sigafoos, 'The impact of LASPO on routes to justice', Equality and Human Rights Commission, September 2018, https://www.equalityhumanrights.com/sites/default/files/the-impact-of-laspo-on-routes-to-justice-september-2018.pdf

77. 'Justice for all? Inside the legal aid crisis', *Financial Times*, 27 September 2018.

78. E. Dugan, 'This Leaked Report Reveals The Stark Warnings From Judges About Defendants With No Lawyer', BuzzFeed News, 8 May 2018, https://www.buzzfeed.com/emilydugan/the-government-tried-to-conceal-this-testimony-from-judges

79. Only homelessness, possession cases and disrepair cases where there is a 'serious risk of harm to health and safety' remain within scope, subject of course to strict means tests, which mean, as we saw with Rita earlier, that even homeless people do not necessarily qualify.

80. Housing and Legal Aid Debate Pack, House of Commons, CPD-2018-0120, 15 May 2018.

81. Law Centres: Written question – 273435, https://www.parliament.uk/business/publications/written-questions-answers-statements/written-question/Commons/2019-07-04/273435/

82. Dr J. Organ and Dr J. Sigafoos, 'The impact of LASPO on routes to justice', Equality and Human Rights Commission, September 2018.

83. 'The Right to Justice: The final report of the Bach Commission', September 2017, at Appendix 5, p. 36. http://www.fabians.org.uk/wp-content/uploads/2017/09/Bach-Commission_Right-to-Justice-Report-WEB.pdf

84. A. Buncombe, 'Trump administration admits migrant children as young as 3 appearing in court alone for their own deportation proceedings', *Independent*, 28 June 2018, https://www.independent.co.uk/news/world/americas/child-immigrants-us-court-border-family-migrant-immigration-trump-latest-melania-a8422101.html

85. Bach Commission Report, Appendix 11.

86. C. Franchi, 'Windrush and Legal Aid: how free legal representation could have avoided a national scandal', Open Democracy, 3 May 2018, https://www.opendemocracy.net/uk/caterina-franchi/windrush-and-legal-aid-how-free-legal-representation-could-have-avoided-national

87. Ministry of Justice, 'Legal aid for unaccompanied and separated children', 1 August 2018, https://www.gov.uk/government/publications/legal-aid-for-unaccompanied-and-separated-children

88. Coram Children's Legal Centre estimated that there are several thousand children in local authority care likely to be affected. See 'Legal aid restored for migrant children in care', Family Law, 16 July 2018, https://www.familylaw.co.uk/news_and_comment/legal-aid-restored-for-migrant-children-in-care#.W2hoS4WcHcs

89. C. Grayling, 'The Judicial review system is not a promotional tool for countless Left-wing campaigners', *Daily Mail*, 6 September 2013, https://www.dailymail.co.uk/news/article-2413135/CHRIS-GRAYLING-Judicial-review-promotional-tool-Left-wing-campaigners.html

90. 'Enforcing Human Rights', Joint Committee on Human Rights, 19 July 2018.

91. J. Hyde, 'MoJ chief admits cuts rushed through without research', *Law Society Gazette*, 4 December 2014, https://www.

lawgazette.co.uk/law/moj-chief-admits-cuts-rushed-through-without-research/5045500.article

92. Interview with Ken Clarke MP, International Bar Association, November 2011.

93. J. Chapman, '£15m for just one firm on legal aid gravy train: Scale of taxpayers' bill revealed as Coalition vows to save £200m', *Daily Mail*, 5 June 2013.

94. L. McKinstry, 'Legal aid is now a racket that only benefits lawyers', *Daily Express*, 6 June 2013.

95. M. Fouzder, 'Fury over MoJ "betrayal" on legal aid at inquests', *Law Society Gazette*, 8 February 2019, https://www.lawgazette.co.uk/law/fury-over-moj-betrayal-on-legal-aid-at-inquests/5069214.article

96. Ministry of Justice, 'Post-Implementation Review of Part 1 of the Legal Aid, Sentencing and Punishment of Offenders Act 2012', February 2019, https://assets.publishing.service.gov.uk/government/uploads/system/uploads/attachment_data/file/777038/post-implementation-review-of-part-1-of-laspo.pdf

97. Legal-aid expenditure fell from £2.55 billion in 2010–11 to £1.62 billion in 2017–18. House of Commons Library, 'The future of legal aid', 31 October 2018, CPD-2018/0230.

98. J. Hyde, 'MoJ chief admits cuts were rushed through without research', *Law Society Gazette*, 4 December 2014.

## 7. Our Liberty

1. The views of a complainant will usually be taken into account when the state is considering whether to prosecute, but are not determinative.

2. R. Littlejohn, 'One-legged Albanian KILLER on benefits (even I couldn't make him up)', *Daily Mail*, 24 May 2016, https://www.dailymail.co.uk/debate/article-3605844/RICHARD-LITTLEJOHN-One-legged-Albanian-KILLER-benefits-couldn-t-make-up.html

3. It is still possible to bring a private prosecution, but this is rare, and the Crown Prosecution Service still retains a power to take over the case and proceed with it or dispose of it as it sees fit.

4. Ministry of Justice, 'Criminal Justice Statistics quarterly, England and Wales, October 2017 to September 2018', 21 February

2019, https://assets.publishing.service.gov.uk/government/
uploads/system/uploads/attachment_data/file/780612/criminal-
justice-statistics-quarterly-september-2018.pdf

5. This is a fairly broad simplification. For greater detail on the
operation of the magistrates' courts and how and when cases
are allocated to the Crown Court, see Chapter 2 of *The Secret
Barrister: Stories of the Law and How It's Broken* (Picador, 2018).

6. Barristers can and do appear in the magistrates' court,
and solicitors can obtain qualifications (known as 'Higher
Rights') that allow them to appear in the Crown Court as
'solicitor-advocates'.

7. In circumstances where the number of jurors drops from twelve
to ten – for instance, where a juror falls ill and is discharged – a
majority verdict can be agreed by nine of them.

8. *The Thin Blue Line* (1995–6), Broadcast by the British
Broadcasting Corporation (BBC), produced by Tiger Aspect
Productions. For full details, see https://www.imdb.com/title/
tt0112194/companycredits?ref_=tt_dt_co

9. See, 'Ten questions posed by Vicky Pryce jury', BBC News, 20
February 2013, https://www.bbc.co.uk/news/uk-21521460

10. Ibid.

11. J. Delingpole, 'Are some people just too stupid to serve
on a jury?', *Daily Express*, 22 February 2013, https://
www.express.co.uk/comment/expresscomment/379367/
Are-some-people-just-too-stupid-to-serve-on-a-jury

12. *Woolmington v. DPP* [1935] AC 462.

13. K. Rahman, 'Viewers are left outraged as Sir Cliff Richard tells
Loose Women he'd rather 10 guilty people go free than one
innocent person suffer after he was wrongly accused of historical
sexual offences', *Daily Mail*, 28 November 2018, https://www.
dailymail.co.uk/news/article-6436193/Viewers-outraged-Sir-Cliff-
Richards-comments-Loose-Women.html

14. See the comments of the London Victims' Commissioner to
the *Independent*: L. Dearden, 'Tens of thousands of rape cases
dropped because "police traumatising victims", report suggests',
*Independent*, 31 July 2019, https://www.independent.co.uk/news/
uk/crime/rape-prosecutions-dropping-uk-police-phones-trauma-
cps-a9028181.html

15. Per London Victims' Commissioner, reported in, S.
Gallagher, 'Just 3% Of Rape Allegations In London Result

In Conviction. This New Study Suggests Why', HuffPost UK, 31 July 2019, https://www.huffingtonpost.co.uk/entry/just-3-of-rape-allegations-in-london-result-in-conviction-this-study-suggests-why_uk_5d4151ebe4b01d8c9783aa07

16. S. Carrell, 'Scottish civil court rules that acquitted man did rape student', *Guardian*, 5 October 2018, https://www.theguardian.com/uk-news/2018/oct/05/scottish-civil-court-rules-that-acquitted-man-did-student

17. Court of Appeal (Criminal Division) 2016–17 Report (2018), https://www.judiciary.uk/wp-content/uploads/2018/08/coa-criminal-div-2016-17-2.pdf

18. S. Morris and A. Topping, 'Ched Evans: footballer found not guilty of rape in retrial', *Guardian*, 14 October 2016, https://www.theguardian.com/football/2016/oct/14/footballer-ched-evans-cleared-of-in-retrial

19. K. Gladdis, J. Narain and C. Brooke, 'Ched Evans' teammate suspended over Twitter comments about rape conviction', *Daily Mail*, 23 April 2012, https://www.dailymail.co.uk/news/article-2133792/Ched-Evans-rape-victim-named-abused-Twitter-girlfriend-stands-Wales-footballer.html

20. 'Ched Evans' rape victim had to change name and move five times, says father', *Guardian*, 28 December 2014, https://www.theguardian.com/football/2014/dec/28/ched-evans-rape-victim-change-name-move-house-father

21. See Twitter, https://twitter.com/search?f=tweets&vertical=default&q=ched%20evans%20liar&src=typd

22. A. Adu, 'COURT CONTROVERSY: Britain's top prosecutor sparks outrage by saying many men cleared of rape have NOT been falsely accused', the *Sun*, 10 October 2017, https://www.thesun.co.uk/news/4656366/men-cleared-rape-not-falsely-accused-alison-saunders/

23. T. Morgan, 'Magistrates raise "difficulty" of historic sex cases as Dr Fox blasts prosecutors after being cleared of assaults', *Telegraph*, 14 December 2015, https://www.telegraph.co.uk/news/uknews/crime/12048990/Dr-Fox-verdict-DJ-cleared-of-sex-assaults-on-radio-colleagues-and-teenage-girls.html

24. *Crown Prosecution Service* v. *Neil Fox* (2015), https://www.judiciary.uk/wp-content/uploads/2015/12/Neil-Fox-verdict.pdf

25. For the facts in this case and the proceedings, I am reliant on and grateful to the work of Matthew Scott, whose blog

provides not only a comprehensive analysis, but a rich source of links to the available primary sources. M. Scott, 'Everything we know suggests that the CPS was right to drop murder charge against John Broadhurst', Barrister Blogger, 24 December 2018, http://barristerblogger.com/2018/12/24/everything-we-know-suggests-that-the-cps-was-right-to-drop-murder-charge-against-john-broadhurst/

26. S. Wilkinson, '"Rough Sex" Doesn't Kill, Domestic Violence Does', *Grazia*, 18 December 2018, https://graziadaily.co.uk/life/real-life/domestic-violence-natalie-connolly-john-broadhurst-sentence-harriet-harman-attorney-general/

27. *R v. Brown* [1993] UKHL 19.

28. While deliberate infliction of injury as part of sexual activity is unlawful, the law makes for a distinction where there is consensual penetration of the vagina using an object, and foreseeable injury is unintentionally caused. This played a part in the Broadhurst case, as the evidence tended to suggest that this particular injury to Natalie was caused by consensual penetration. See Jim Meyer, 'John Broadhurst found not guilty of attacking Natalie Connolly', Tuckers Solicitors, 21 December 2018, https://www.tuckerssolicitors.com/john-broadhurst-found-not-guilty-of-attacking-natalie-connolly/

29. J. Merrick, 'Accepting "rough sex" as a man's defence for killing a woman makes a mockery of our justice system', *Independent*, 19 December 2018, https://www.independent.co.uk/voices/natalie-connolly-john-broadhurst-case-trial-murder-rough-sex-domestic-violence-manslaughter-a8690961.html

30. B. Ellen, 'Prosecutors thought no jury would accept Natalie Connolly was murdered. What does that say?', *Observer*, 23 December 2018, https://www.theguardian.com/commentisfree/2018/dec/23/prosecutors-thought-no-jury-would-accept-natalie-connoolly-was-murdered?CMP=share_btn_tw

31. 'No5 counsel secure jail term for young mother's killer', No5 Barristers Chambers, 18 December 2018, https://www.no5.com/media/news/no5-counsel-secure-jail-term-for-young-mother-s-killer/

32. Quoted in D. Barrett, 'Judges weaken rules on paedophiles', *Telegraph*, 20 August 2011, https://www.telegraph.co.uk/news/uknews/law-and-order/8713203/Judges-weaken-rules-on-paedophiles.html

33. For a full exploration of the competing theories as to the origins of the right to silence, see H. Quirk, *The Rise and Fall of the Right of Silence* (Routledge, 2016).

34. Cited in ibid, p. 44.

35. Criminal Justice and Public Order Act 1994.

36. H. Mills and T. Kirby, 'Ending the right to silence "is breach of human rights": "Hanging and flogging charter" condemned', *Independent*, 7 October 1993, https://www.independent.co.uk/news/uk/ending-the-right-to-silence-is-breach-of-human-rights-hanging-and-flogging-charter-condemned-heather-1509089.html

37. See *O'Donnell v. UK Application 16667/10* in J. Bennathan, 'Right to Silence and the ECHR', Doughty Street Criminal Appeals Bulletin, Issue 3, November 2015, http://doughty-street-chambers.newsweaver.com/Appeals/e2aj8l8hdog?a=1&p=698900&t=174031

38. See C. Baksi, 'Going "no comment": a delicate balancing act', *Law Society Gazette*, 24 May 2012, https://www.lawgazette.co.uk/analysis/going-no-comment-a-delicate-balancing-act/65781.article

39. 'My vision for Britain: by Tony Blair', *Observer*, 10 November 2002, https://www.theguardian.com/politics/2002/nov/10/queensspeech2002.tonyblair

40. J. Bindel, 'Why will I, a committed anti-rape campaigner, now advise victims to think twice before going to court? Because the Ched Evans judges have created a rapists' charter', *Daily Mail*, 16 October 2016, https://www.dailymail.co.uk/debate/article-3840261/JULIE-BINDEL-committed-anti-rape-campaigner-advise-victims-think-twice-going-court-Ched-Evans-judges-created-RAPISTS-CHARTER.html

41. C. Chaplain, 'Harriet Harman calls for ban on lawyers asking rape victims about sexual history after Ched Evans Trial', *Evening Standard*, 24 March 2017, https://www.standard.co.uk/news/politics/harriet-harman-calls-for-ban-on-lawyers-asking-rape-victims-about-sexual-history-after-ched-evans-a3498921.html

42. See J. Bindel, 'Juries have no place in rape trials. They simply can't be trusted', *Guardian*, 21 November 2018, https://www.theguardian.com/commentisfree/2018/nov/21/juries-rape-trials-myths-justice

43. L. Hoyano, 'The operation of YJCEA 1999 section 41 in the Courts of England & Wales: views from the barristers' row. An independent empirical study commissioned by the Criminal Bar

Association', Oxford University, 2018, https://www.criminalbar. com/wp-content/uploads/2018/11/REPORT-PROVIDED-FOR-CBA-WEBSITE-.pdf

44. House of Commons, Notices of Amendment, Prisons and Courts Bill, 23 March 2017, https://publications.parliament.uk/pa/bills/cbill/2016-2017/0145/amend/prisons_rm_pbc_0323.1-2.html

45. See J. Corke, 'One-eyed police killer gets £310k in legal aid', *Sunday Express*, 9 December 2018, https://www.express.co.uk/news/uk/1056481/dale-cregan-cop-killer-310-000-legal-aid-mental-health

46. The gross figure is adjusted slightly to reflect the number of people in the household. Means-testing is a highly complex exercise, the details of which are set out in the Legal Aid Agency's *Criminal Legal Aid Manual: Applying for legal aid in criminal cases in the magistrates' and Crown Court*, July 2019, https://assets.publishing.service.gov.uk/government/uploads/system/uploads/attachment_data/file/816112/criminal-legal-aid-manual_July_2019.pdf

47. 'Disposable' income, used when means testing eligibility for Crown Court, involves, as the name suggests, a more involved consideration than merely 'gross household income'. Certain allowances are allowed for living expenses. Again, the full details are set out in the *Criminal Legal Aid Manual*, ibid.

48. D. Brown, 'GP accused of paedophilia by "fantasist" loses fight for costs', *The Times*, 28 April 2018, https://www.thetimes.co.uk/article/gp-accused-of-paedophilia-by-fantasist-loses-fight-for-costs-96xj5ptkv

49. 'MP Nigel Evans: Trial made me realise impact of legal aid cuts', ITV News, 13 April 2014, http://www.itv.com/news/story/2014-04-13/nigel-evans-wants-cps-to-pay-130k-legal-bills/

50. A. Blake, 'Donald Trump's attack on Hillary Clinton for defending an accused child rapist, explained', *Washington Post*, 10 October 2016, https://www.washingtonpost.com/news/the-fix/wp/2016/10/09/why-donald-trump-just-attacked-hillary-clinton-for-defending-an-accused-child-rapist-explained/?utm_term=.5c97c98497ed

51. P. Bump, 'The GOP's chief strategist pitches the party's new "Willie Horton-style" ad', *Washington Post*, 3 October 2016, https://www.washingtonpost.com/news/the-fix/wp/2016/10/03/the-gops-chief-strategist-pitches-the-partys-new-willie-horton-style-ad/?utm_term=.d20eea41af6c

52. R. Booth, 'Tories step up attempts to link Sadiq Khan to extremists', *Guardian*, 20 April 2016, https://www.theguardian.com/politics/2016/apr/20/tory-claims-sadiq-khan-alleged-links-extremists

53. See, C. Friedersdorf, 'In Defense of Harvey Weinstein's Harvard Lawyer', the *Atlantic*, 3 March 2019, https://www.theatlantic.com/ideas/archive/2019/03/defense-harvey-weinsteins-lawyer-ronald-sullivan/583717/

54. K. Taylor, 'Harvard's First Black Faculty Deans Let Go Amid Uproar Over Harvey Weinstein Defense', *New York Times*, 11 May 2019, https://www.nytimes.com/2019/05/11/us/ronald-sullivan-harvard.html

55. S. Greenhill and N. Sears, '£25,000 to help catch smirking killer', *Daily Mail*, 2 January 2019, https://www.dailymail.co.uk/news/article-6549743/Jack-Shepherd-got-six-years-jail-killing-date-24-going-run.html

56. T. Wells, 'KILLER'S HANDOUT: Boat killer Jack Shepherd got £100k in legal aid funded by taxpayers – while he's still on the run', the *Sun*, 1 December 2018, https://www.thesun.co.uk/news/7877697/boat-killer-jack-shepherd-legal-aid/

57. S. Greenhill and N. Sears, 'The reality TV lawyer whose firm has received £93,000 aid for the case', *Daily Mail*, 2 January 2019, https://www.dailymail.co.uk/news/article-6549743/Jack-Shepherd-got-six-years-jail-killing-date-24-going-run.html

58. 'Response to the Daily Mail', Tuckers Solicitors, https://www.tuckerssolicitors.com/response-to-the-daily-mail/

59. C. Coleman, 'Speedboat killer: Jack Shepherd's lawyer receives Nazi death threat', BBC News, 28 January 2019, https://www.bbc.co.uk/news/uk-47029302

60. M. Porter, 'Dangerous drivers should not be allowed to choose trial by jury', *Guardian*, 8 April 2016, https://www.theguardian.com/commentisfree/2016/apr/08/drivers-who-kill-remove-right-to-trial-by-jury-death-cyclists-pedestrians-justice

61. Crown Prosecution Service Annual Report and Accounts 2016–17, Tables 3 and 7, https://www.gov.uk/government/uploads/system/uploads/attachment_data/file/628968/CPS_annual_report_2016_17.pdf

62. 'Cyclist fails in first UK private prosecution against motorist for dangerous driving', *Independent*, 10 March 2016, https://www.independent.co.uk/news/uk/crime/cyclist-fails-in-first-uk-private-

prosecution-against-motorist-for-dangerous-driving-a6922176.html

63. Office of National Statistics, 'Sexual offences in England and Wales: year ending March 2017', 8 February 2018, para 9, https://www. ons.gov.uk/peoplepopulationandcommunity/crimeandjustice/articles/ sexualoffencesinenglandandwales/yearendingmarch2017#reporting-of-sexual-assault-by-rape-or-penetration

64. See figures cited in, A. Topping and C. Barr, 'Revealed: less than a third of young men prosecuted for rape are convicted', *Guardian*, 23 September 2018, https://www.theguardian.com/ society/2018/sep/23/revealed-less-than-a-third-of-young-men-prosecuted-for-are-convicted

65. Ministry of Justice, 'Criminal court statistics quarterly, England and Wales, January to March 2018 (annual 2017)', 28 June 2018, Figure 14, https://assets.publishing.service. gov.uk/government/uploads/system/uploads/attachment_data/ file/720026/ccsq-bulletin-jan-mar-2018.pdf

66. Dr Dominic Willmott at the University of Huddersfield conducted simulated trials involving mock jurors, and found that many jurors took preconceived rape myths into the retiring room notwithstanding the judicial directions, with others displaying a troubling reluctance to convict young male defendants even where they found that, legally, the offence had been proved. See A. Topping and C. Barr, 'Revealed: less than a third of young men prosecuted for rape are convicted', *Guardian*, 23 September 2018. It should be noted, however, that a 2019 study by the UCL Jury Project, led by Professor Cheryl Thomas, based on questions asked of real-life jurors, reached the opposite conclusion: *Law in Action*, 'Rape Myths', BBC Radio 4, 27 June 2019, https://www.bbc.co.uk/programmes/m000671m

67. J. Bindel, 'Juries have no place in rape trials. They simply can't be trusted', *Guardian*, 21 November 2018.

68. Ministry of Justice, 'Criminal court statistics quarterly, England and Wales, January to March 2018 (annual 2017)', 28 June 2018.

69. Parklife.

70. In 2017, the Institute for Fiscal Studies calculated that, in the decade since 2010/11, the MoJ's budget was to be cut by around 40 per cent. Spending plans were in 2019 revised upwards so that that total MoJ budget in 2019/20 was around 25 per cent lower than in 2010/11. See House of Commons Library, 'The spending of the Ministry of Justice', 1 October 2019, CDP-2019-

0217, https://researchbriefings.parliament.uk/ResearchBriefing/Summary/CDP-2019-0217 – fullreport

## 8. Equality and Due Process

1. 'Harman warning on Goodwin pension', BBC News, 1 March 2009, http://news.bbc.co.uk/1/hi/uk_politics/7917361.stm
2. W. Martin, '"It sent a tremor down my back": Alistair Darling reveals how Britain came within hours of the "breakdown of law and order"', Business Insider, 28 May 2018, https://www.businessinsider.com/alistair-darling-uk-breakdown-of-law-and-order-financial-crisis-2018-5?r=US&IR=T
3. House of Commons Treasury Committee, Ninth Report, 'Banking Crisis: reforming corporate governance and pay in the City', 12 May 2009, paragraph 97, https://publications.parliament.uk/pa/cm200809/cmselect/cmtreasy/519/51902.htm
4. Although, had Goodwin been dismissed, rather than 'requested to leave', his pension entitlement would have been lower – a deferred pension of a meagre £416,000 per year. There was a significant dispute between Lord Myners, the minister who had overseen the negotiations, and RBS as to whether the latter had acted appropriately in requesting, rather than enforcing, Sir Fred's departure, with RBS insisting they had no choice. See Treasury Committee report, ibid.
5. See, A. Hirsch, 'What are the legal options?', Guardian, 27 February 2009, https://www.theguardian.com/business/2009/feb/27/goodwin-pension-legal-options
6. 'Harman warning on Goodwin pension', BBC News, 1 March 2009.
7. D. Summers, P. Wintour and J. Treanor, 'Angry Brown will recoup some of Goodwin's pension if law allows', Guardian, 27 February 2009, https://www.theguardian.com/politics/2009/feb/27/prescott-goodwin
8. J. Treanor and D. Hencke, 'HSBC boss to waive bonus as pension row escalates', Guardian, 2 March 2009, https://www.theguardian.com/business/2009/mar/02/hsbc-bonus-waived
9. A. Sparrow and H. Mulholland, 'Brown plays down Harman's threat to cut Fred Goodwin's pension', Guardian, 2 March

2009, https://www.theguardian.com/politics/2009/mar/02/brown-harman-goodwin-pension

10. 'Sir Fred Goodwin and Harriet Harman – pensions and bonuses row', 3 March 2009, http://www.boris-johnson.com/2009/03/03/bankers-pension-row-masks-real-issue/

11. T. Bingham, *The Rule of Law* (Penguin, 2011), p. 8.

12. For this historical summary, I have drawn on the research of Tom Bingham in Chapter 1 of *The Rule of Law*, ibid.

13. D. Macintyre, 'Major on crime: "Condemn more, understand less"', *Independent*, 21 February 1993, https://www.independent.co.uk/news/major-on-crime-condemn-more-understand-less-1474470.html

14. J. E. Cronin, *New Labour's Pasts: The Labour Party and Its Discontents* (Routledge, 2004), p. 360.

15. B. Franklin and J. Petley, 'Killing the Age of Innocence: Newspaper Reporting of the Death of James Bulger', in J. Pilcher and S. Wagg (eds.), *Thatcher's Children? Politics, Childhood and Society in the 1980s and 1990s* (Falmer Press, 1996).

16. *Secretary of State ex parte Venables and Thompson* v. *R* [1997] UKHL 25, per Lord Steyn.

17. *T and V* v. *United Kingdom* (1999) (24724/94).

18. Quoted in J. Petley, '"Kill a kid and get a house": Rationality versus Retribution in the Case of Robert Thompson and Jon Venables, 1992–2001', in S. Wagg and J. Pilcher (eds.), *Thatcher's Grandchildren? Politics and Childhood in the Twenty-First Century* (Palgrave Macmillan, 2014).

19. Ibid.

20. F. Mayhew, 'The Sun calls on police to "say sorry" for Operation Elveden after paper's last convicted journalist is cleared', *Press Gazette*, 28 October 2016, https://www.pressgazette.co.uk/the-sun-calls-on-police-to-say-sorry-for-operation-elveden-after-papers-last-convicted-journalist-is-cleared/

21. 'Operation Elveden a "misconceived witch-hunt" says Sun journalist's counsel', *Guardian*, 1 April 2015, https://www.theguardian.com/uk-news/2015/apr/01/operation-elveden-a-misconceived-witch-hunt-says-sun-journalists-counsel

22. 'THE SUN SAYS: Operation Elveden must go down as one of the most shameful and haphazard episodes in British legal history', the *Sun*, 28 October 2016, https://www.thesun.co.uk/news/2066478/operation-elveden-must-go-down-as-one-of-the-

most-shameful-and-%C2%ADhaphazard-episodes-in-british-legal-%C2%ADhistory/

23. 'The day press freedoms received a devastating blow', *Telegraph*, 23 October 2018, https://www.telegraph.co.uk/news/2018/10/23/day-press-freedoms-received-devastating-blow/

24. 'Sir Philip Green: From "king of the High Street" to "unacceptable face of capitalism"', BBC News, 25 October 2018, https://www.bbc.co.uk/news/business-36139828

25. 'Lord Hain defends naming Sir Philip Green over harassment claims', BBC News, 26 October 2018, https://www.bbc.co.uk/news/uk-45987084

26. @Andrew_Adonis, Twitter, 25 October 2018, https://twitter.com/Andrew_Adonis/status/1055484108137205761

27. @aak1880, Twitter, 25 October 2018, https://twitter.com/aak1880/status/1055463775044804609

28. M. Savage, 'Lord Hain named Philip Green "to promote justice and liberty"', *Observer*, 27 October 2018, https://www.theguardian.com/business/2018/oct/27/philip-green-to-lodge-complaint-against-peer-who-named-him

29. *ABC & others* v. *Telegraph Media Group Ltd* [2018] EWCA Civ 2329.

30. J. Waterson, 'Philip Green ends "gagging order" action against Telegraph', *Guardian*, 28 January 2019, https://www.theguardian.com/business/2019/jan/28/philip-green-ends-legal-action-against-telegraph

31. 'Lord Hain defends naming Sir Philip Green over harassment claims', BBC News, 26 October 2018.

32. A. Lloyd, 'Shamima Begum: Bring me home, says Bethnal Green girl who left to join Isis', *The Times*, 13 February 2019, https://www.thetimes.co.uk/article/shamima-begum-bring-me-home-says-bethnal-green-girl-who-fled-to-join-isis-hgvqw765d

33. L. Dearden, 'Shamima Begum: Manchester Arena bombing "justified" because of Syria airstrikes, Isis teenager says', *Independent*, 18 February 2019, https://www.independent.co.uk/news/world/middle-east/shamima-begum-isis-interview-manchester-bombing-terror-attack-syria-airstrikes-a8784741.html

34. @toryboypierce, Twitter, 23 February 2019, https://twitter.com/toryboypierce/status/1099243819189583872

35. N. Bartlett and D. Bloom, 'Shamima Begum: Tory MP demands law of TREASON is restored over Brit ISIS bride', *Mirror*,

18 February 2019, https://www.mirror.co.uk/news/politics/ shamima-begum-tory-mp-demands-14016673

36. T. Sculthorpe, '"Quite frankly, the British people don't like it and neither do I": Williamson slams Shamima Begum's bid for legal aid as he accuses the Jihadi bride of "turning her back on this country"', *Daily Mail*, 16 April 2019, https://www.dailymail. co.uk/news/article-6928637/Gavin-Williamson-slams-Shamima-Begums-bid-legal-aid.html

37. T. Newton Dunn, 'NO ENTRY: Pregnant jihadi bride Shamima Begum faces ban from Britain as "permanent exclusion is an option" – after she asks for NHS care for her baby', the *Sun*, 14 February 2019, https://www.thesun.co.uk/news/8431345/ jihadi-bride-exclusion-british-citizenship/

38. R. Littlejohn, 'She's not the same little girl who ran away – and that's what worries me', *Daily Mail*, 14 February 2019, https:// www.dailymail.co.uk/debate/article-6706765/RICHARD-LITTLEJOHN-Shes-not-little-girl-ran-away-thats-worries-me.html

39. L. Bannerman, F. Elliott, S. O'Neill, J. Simpson, 'Family of Isis bride Shamima Begum make plea for mercy', *The Times*, 15 February 2019, https://www.thetimes.co.uk/article/family-of-isis-bride-shamima-begum-make-plea-for-mercy-gdz5qwv0r

40. 'Shamima Begum: What is her legal status?', BBC News, 21 February 2019, https://www.bbc.co.uk/news/uk-47310206

41. In February 2020, the Special Immigration Appeals Commission refused Ms Begum's appeal against the Secretary of State's decision, finding that the decision to revoke her citizenship did not make her stateless (notwithstanding the publicly reported comments by Bangladeshi officials) – see *Shamima Begum* v. *Secretary of State for the Home Department* Appeal No. SC/163/2019 https:// www.judiciary.uk/wp-content/uploads/2020/02/begum-v-home-secretary-siac-judgment.pdf There are also separate judicial review proceedings before the High Court. At the time of writing, no decision had been given relating to the judicial review.

42. 'Shamima Begum will not be allowed here, Bangladesh says', 21 February 2019, https://www.bbc.co.uk/news/uk-47312207

43. Home Office, 'CONTEST: The United Kingdom's Strategy for Countering Terrorism', June 2018, https://assets. publishing.service.gov.uk/government/uploads/system/ uploads/attachment_data/file/716907/140618_CCS207_ CCS0218929798-1_CONTEST_3.0_WEB.pdf

44. For commentary see M. Honeycombe-Foster, 'Sajid Javid accused of Tory leadership pitch as he strips Isis teen Shamima Begum of UK citizenship', PoliticsHome, 20 February 2019, https://www. politicshome.com/news/uk/political-parties/conservative-party/ news/101980/sajid-javid-accused-tory-leadership-pitch

45. N. Clark, '"YOU BACK TERROR": Sajid Javid blasts moaning Shamima Begum's plea to come home and tells her "you and your death cult hate our country"', the *Sun*, 18 February 2019, https://www.thesun.co.uk/news/8453781/ sajid-javid-shamima-begum-isis-bride-death-cult/

46. Cited in R. Greenslade, 'Sajid Javid is pandering to rightwing press over Shamima Begum', 24 February 2019, https://www.theguardian.com/commentisfree/2019/feb/24/ sajid-javid-pander-rightwing-press-shamima-begum

47. Ibid.

48. @MichaelVaughan, Twitter, 17 February 2019, https://twitter. com/michaelvaughan/status/1097136760851759105?s=21

49. A. Pearson, 'Thank God, Sajid Javid grasped Shamima Begum is the one person uniting Britain – against her', *Telegraph*, 19 February 2019, https://www.telegraph.co.uk/women/life/ thank-god-sajid-javid-grasped-shamima-begum-one-person-uniting/

50. L. Clarke-Billings, 'Katie Hopkins slams "pandering Brits" as Shamima Begum STRIPPED of UK citizenship', *Mirror*, 20 February 2019, https://www.mirror.co.uk/news/uk-news/ shamima-begum-katie-hopkins-syria-14023635

## 9. Democracy

1. 'IAIN DUNCAN SMITH: Why it's crucial that the judges who could decide the fate of Brexit ARE scrutinised', *Daily Mail*, 7 December 2016, https://www.dailymail.co.uk/debate/ article-4007894/IAIN-DUNCAN-SMITH-s-crucial-judges-decide-fate-Brexit-scrutinised.html

2. 'PM statement on Brexit: 20 March 2019', https://www.gov.uk/ government/speeches/pm-statement-on-brexit-20-march-2019

3. Iain Duncan Smith, quoted in J. Tapsfield, T. Sculthorpe and M. Dathan, '"There is NO turning back!" David Davis warns Remoaner MPs they will face the full wrath of the public

if they use Supreme Court ruling to block Brexit', *Daily Mail*, 24 January 2017, https://www.dailymail.co.uk/news/article-4150822/Judges-ruling-PM-executive-powers-trigger-Brexit.html

4. Douglas Carswell MP, quoted in J. Slack, 'Enemies of the people: Fury over "out of touch" judges who have "declared war on democracy" by defying 17.4m Brexit voters and who could trigger constitutional crisis', *Daily Mail*, 3 November 2016, https://www.dailymail.co.uk/news/article-3903436/Enemies-people-Fury-touch-judges-defied-17-4m-Brexit-voters-trigger-constitutional-crisis.html

5. Iain Duncan Smith MP and Dominic Raab MP, quoted in ibid.

6. Iain Duncan Smith, quoted in P. Dominiczak, C. Hope and K. McCann, 'Judges vs the people: Government ministers resigned to losing appeal against High Court ruling', *Telegraph*, 3 November 2016, https://www.telegraph.co.uk/news/2016/11/03/the-plot-to-stop-brexit-the-judges-versus-the-people/

7. 'IAIN DUNCAN SMITH: Why it's crucial that the judges who could decide the fate of Brexit ARE scrutinised', *Daily Mail*, 7 December 2016.

8. See D. Boffey, D. Glaister and P. Maguire, 'Brexit high court decision means nothing has been ruled out', *Observer*, 6 November 2016, https://www.theguardian.com/politics/2016/nov/06/brexit-high-court-decision-nothing-ruled-out

9. J. Slack, 'Enemies of the people: Fury over "out of touch" judges who have "declared war on democracy" by defying 17.4m Brexit voters and who could trigger constitutional crisis', *Daily Mail*, 3 November 2016.

10. Cited in S. C. Nelson, 'MailOnline Attacks Brexit Judge For Being "Openly Gay"', HuffPost, 3 November 2016, https://www.huffingtonpost.co.uk/entry/mailonline-online-attacks-brexit-judge-for-being-openly-gay_uk_581b344ee4b0ab6e4c1ba5ff

11. P. Dominiczak, C. Hope and K. McCann, 'Judges vs the people: Government ministers resigned to losing appeal against High Court ruling', *Telegraph*, 3 November 2016.

12. F. Gibb, 'Next stop the Supreme Court as Brexiteers condemn judges', *The Times*, 4 November 2016, https://www.thetimes.co.uk/article/next-stop-the-supreme-court-as-brexiteers-condemn-judges-fr3mgs2kx

13. Quoted in J. Slack, 'Enemies of the people: Fury over "out

of touch" judges who have "declared war on democracy" by defying 17.4m Brexit voters and who could trigger constitutional crisis', *Daily Mail*, 3 November 2016.

14. 'After judges' Brexit block now your country really needs you: We MUST get out of the EU', *Daily Express*, 4 November 2016, https://www.express.co.uk/comment/expresscomment/728602/ Brexit-judges-block-leave-EU-referendum-High-Court

15. Quoted in P. Dominiczak, C. Hope and K. McCann, 'Judges vs the people: Government ministers resigned to losing appeal against High Court ruling', *Telegraph*, 3 November 2016.

16. 'Theresa May defends press attacks on High Court judges', *Financial Times*, 6 November 2016, https://www.ft.com/content/ c0cad18e-a441-11e6-8898-79a99e2a4de6

17. W. Worley, 'Liz Truss breaks silence on judiciary but fails to mention Brexit ruling backlash', *Independent*, 5 November 2016, https://www.independent.co.uk/news/uk/politics/liz-truss-brexit-ruling-high-court-judges-criticised-a7399586.html

18. 'Enemies of the people: Lord Chancellor Liz Truss says it would be dangerous to tell Daily Mail what to print', *Press Gazette*, 1 March 2017, https://www.pressgazette.co.uk/ enemies-of-the-people-lord-chancellor-liz-truss-says-it-would-be-dangerous-to-tell-daily-mail-want-to-print/

19. G. Adams, 'The judges and the people: Next week, 11 unaccountable individuals will consider a case that could thwart the will of the majority on Brexit. The Mail makes no apology for revealing their views – and many have links to Europe', *Daily Mail*, 3 December 2016. https://www.dailymail.co.uk/news/article-3995754/ The-judges-people-week-11-unaccountable-individuals-consider-case-help-thwart-majority-Brexit-Mail-makes-no-apology-revealing-views-links-Europe.html

20. C. Hope, 'Farage to lead 100,000-strong march on Supreme Court on day of historic Brexit court hearing', *Telegraph*, 7 November 2016, https://www.telegraph.co.uk/news/2016/11/06/nigel-farage-to-lead-100000-strong-march-on-supreme-court-on-day/

21. 'IAIN DUNCAN SMITH: Why it's crucial that the judges who could decide the fate of Brexit ARE scrutinised', *Daily Mail*, 7 December 2016.

22. J. Tapsfield, T. Sculthorpe and M. Dathan, '"There is NO turning back!" David Davis warns Remoaner MPs they will face the full

wrath of the public if they use Supreme Court ruling to block Brexit', *Daily Mail*, 24 January 2017.

23. Dominic Raab MP, quoted in, J. Slack, 'Enemies of the people: Fury over "out of touch" judges who have "declared war on democracy" by defying 17.4m Brexit voters and who could trigger constitutional crisis', *Daily Mail*, 3 November 2016.

24. *Daily Mail*, ibid, and 'After judges' Brexit block now your country really needs you: We MUST get out of the EU', *Daily Express*, 4 November 2016.

25. The European Union (Notification of Withdrawal) Act 2017 was introduced in Parliament on 26 January 2017 and was enacted without amendment on 16 March 2017.

26. J. Slack, 'Enemies of the people: Fury over "out of touch" judges who have "declared war on democracy" by defying 17.4m Brexit voters and who could trigger constitutional crisis', *Daily Mail*, 3 November 2016.

27. *R. (Miller & others)* v. *Secretary of State for Exiting the European Union* [2016] EWHC 2768 (Admin), at [5].

28. *Case of Proclamations* [1610] EWHC KB J22, available at https://www.bailii.org/ew/cases/EWHC/KB/1610/J22.html

29. Ibid.

30. [2016] EWHC 2768 (Admin) at [108].

31. The Liberal Democrats have argued that the Salisbury Convention does not apply to minority governments, see House of Lords Library, N. Newson, 'Salisbury Convention in a Hung Parliament', LLN-2017-0030, 20 June 2017, https://researchbriefings. parliament.uk/ResearchBriefing/Summary/LLN-2017-0030

32. V. Bogdanor (ed.), *Politics and the Constitution: Essays on British Government* (Dartmouth Publishing, Aldershot, 1996), p. 5.

33. The Parliament Acts of 1911 and 1949 mean that the House of Commons can (in most circumstances) override the House of Lords if there is a gridlock, although this is rare. The most recent instance of the Parliament Acts being invoked came in 2004 and the enactment of the Hunting Act 2004 banning the hunting of wild mammals with dogs.

34. Prior to the United Kingdom leaving the European Union, our courts were required to disapply an Act of Parliament if it was contrary to EU law, as confirmed in the case of *R (Factortame Ltd)* v. *Secretary of State for Transport* [1990] UKHL 7. In practice this was exceptionally rare, and the reason the courts

were required to do so is because Parliament, in section 2(4) of the European Communities Act 1972, legislated to make European Community law supreme in certain areas.

35. J. Tapsfield, T. Sculthorpe and M. Dathan, '"There is NO turning back!" David Davis warns Remoaner MPs they will face the full wrath of the public if they use Supreme Court ruling to block Brexit', *Daily Mail*, 24 January 2017.

36. C. de Montesquieu, *The Spirit of the Laws* (1748), Chapter 11.

37. See Lord Hodge, 'Upholding the rule of law: how we preserve judicial independence in the United Kingdom', Lincoln's Inn Denning Society, 7 November 2016, https://www.supremecourt.uk/docs/speech-161107.pdf

38. Section 17 of the Constitutional Reform Act 2005.

39. Section 3(1) of the Constitutional Reform Act 2005.

40. Section 7(2)(a), Constitutional Reform Act 2005.

41. Theresa May, 'It's MY job to deport foreigners who commit serious crime – and I'll fight any judge who stands in my way, says Home Secretary', *Daily Mail*, 17 February 2013, https://www.dailymail.co.uk/debate/article-2279828/Its-MY-job-deport-foreigners-commit-crime--Ill-fight-judge-stands-way-says-Home-Secretary.html

42. Theresa May MP, House of Commons, 22 October 2013, Hansard, column 162, https://hansard.parliament.uk/Commons/2013-10-22/debates/13102262000002/ImmigrationBill?highlight=Care%20COL:%20162

43. 'Blair's asylum stance "chilling"', BBC News, 30 September 2003, http://news.bbc.co.uk/1/hi/uk_politics/3152982.stm

44. N. Stadlen, 'Brief Encounter: David Blunkett', *Guardian*, 9 October 2006, https://www.theguardian.com/politics/2006/oct/09/davidblunkett

45. R. Verkaik, 'Judges are out of touch, says furious Blunkett', *Independent*, 15 May 2003, https://www.independent.co.uk/news/uk/crime/judges-are-out-of-touch-says-furious-blunkett-104765.html

46. N. Stadlen, 'Brief Encounter: David Blunkett', *Guardian*, 9 October 2006.

47. 'Is sentencing too tough?', BBC News, 1 July 2003, http://news.bbc.co.uk/1/hi/programmes/newsnight/3035512.stm

48. J. Rozenberg, 'Judges were right to snub Blunkett's dinner date', *Telegraph*, 19 October 2006, https://www.telegraph.co.uk/news/

uknews/1531796/Judges-were-right-to-snub-Blunketts-dinner-date.
html

49. N. Stadlen, 'Brief Encounter: David Blunkett', *Guardian*, 9
    October 2006.

50. House of Lords Constitution Select Committee, Sixth Report
    2006–7, at Chapter 2, https://publications.parliament.uk/pa/
    ld200607/ldselect/ldconst/151/15102.htm

51. *R (on the application of Miller)* v. *Prime Minister*; *Cherry &
    others* v. *Advocate General* [2019] UKSC 41.

52. 'Parliament suspension: Queen approves PM's plan', BBC News, 28
    August 2019, https://www.bbc.co.uk/news/uk-politics-49493632

53. M. Weaver, 'Suspending parliament not done to stifle
    Brexit debate, says Wallace', *Guardian*, 12 September
    2019, https://www.theguardian.com/politics/2019/sep/12/
    suspending-parliament-not-shut-down-brexit-debate-ben-wallace

54. See David Allen Green, 'The curious incident of the missing
    witness statement', *Financial Times*, 6 September 2019, https://
    www.ft.com/content/11983298-d08e-11e9-99a4-b5ded7a7fe3f

55. 'Kwasi Kwarteng criticised for "biased judges" comment',
    BBC News, 12 September 2019, https://www.bbc.co.uk/news/
    uk-politics-49670901

56. K. Schofield, 'Jacob Rees-Mogg brands Supreme Court ruling a
    "constitutional coup" as MPs prepare to grill Boris Johnson',
    PoliticsHome, 25 September 2019, https://www.politicshome.
    com/news/uk/political-parties/conservative-party/news/106811/
    jacob-rees-mogg-brands-supreme-court-ruling

57. M. Fouzder, 'Supreme Court appointments may need
    MPs' approval – Attorney General', *Law Society Gazette*,
    25 September 2019, https://www.lawgazette.co.uk/news/
    supreme-court-appointments-may-need-mps-approval-attorney-
    general/5101571.article

58. A. Woodcock, 'Boris Johnson appears to contradict his own
    claim that parliament suspension was "nothing to do with
    Brexit"', *Independent*, 24 September 2019, https://www.
    independent.co.uk/news/uk/politics/boris-johnson-brexit-news-
    latest-supreme-court-parliament-prorogue-a9118576.html

59. J. Longworth, 'The Supreme Court has sided with usurping
    Remainers over the people', *Telegraph*, 24 September
    2019, https://www.telegraph.co.uk/politics/2019/09/24/
    supreme-court-have-sided-usurping-remainers-people/amp/

60. A. Wickham, 'Cabinet Ministers Are Privately Threatening A Radical Overhaul Of The Courts After The Supreme Court Brexit Judgment', Buzzfeed News, 25 September 2019, https://www.buzzfeed.com/alexwickham/cabinet-ministers-supreme-court-brexit-decision

61. For an analysis as to how and why the decision was 'rooted in well-established constitutional principles', see Professor Mark Elliott, 'The Supreme Court's judgment in Cherry/Miller (No 2): A new approach to constitutional adjudication?', Public Law for Everyone, 24 September 2019, https://publiclawforeveryone.com/2019/09/24/the-supreme-courts-judgment-in-cherry-miller-no-2-a-new-approach-to-constitutional-adjudication/

62. 'IAIN DUNCAN SMITH: Why it's crucial that the judges who could decide the fate of Brexit ARE scrutinised', *Daily Mail*, 7 December 2016.

63. See Desmond Swayne MP, @ITVNewsPolitics, Twitter, 25 September 2019, https://twitter.com/ITVNewsPolitics/status/1176811495876943872?s=20

64. 'Death row trip for Tory MP who wants death penalty', BBC News, 16 July 2012, https://www.bbc.com/news/uk-politics-18858496

65. C. Greenwood, '"Criminals" aged just 3: Children responsible for hidden crimewave, including rape and vandalism . . . and there's nothing police can do', *Daily Mail*, 27 June 2011, https://www.dailymail.co.uk/news/article-2008403/Criminals-aged-just-3-Children-responsible-hidden-crimewave-including-rape-vandalism--theres-police-do.html?

66. '"Re-train soft judges" says Shipley MP Philip Davies', *Telegraph & Argus*, 26 February 2014, https://www.thetelegraphandargus.co.uk/news/11035877.re-train-soft-judges-says-shipley-mp-philip-davies/

67. S. Wright, 'MP Philip Davies to ask questions about justice system after day with city's top judge', *Telegraph & Argus*, 18 August 2014, https://www.thetelegraphandargus.co.uk/news/11415427.mp-philip-davies-to-ask-questions-about-justice-system-after-day-with-citys-top-judge/

68. G. Nicks, 'MPs: Judge dreadful should get the sack', *Daily Star*, 7 September 2012, https://www.dailystar.co.uk/news/latest-news/271032/MP-s-Judge-dreadful-should-get-the-sack

69. Joint Committee on Privacy and Injunctions, 'Privacy and

Injunctions', 12 March 2012, https://publications.parliament.uk/
pa/jt201012/jtselect/jtprivinj/273/27302.htm

70. A. Sparrow, 'John Hemming faces calls to resign for
    abusing parliamentary privilege', *Guardian*, 24 August
    2011, https://www.theguardian.com/politics/2011/aug/24/
    john-hemming-resign-abusing-privilege

71. J. Martinson, 'Theresa May and her man from
    another world', *Guardian*, 21 May 2017, https://
    www.theguardian.com/politics/2017/may/21/
    theresa-may-and-her-man-from-another-world

72. Q. Letts, 'Judges blew their hallowed status with the Supreme
    Court ruling and will now be fair game for public scrutiny',
    the *Sun*, 24 September 2019, https://www.thesun.co.uk/
    news/9998887/judges-supreme-court-public-scrutiny/amp/

73. See e.g. C. Woodhouse, 'Britain's weakest judges revealed
    following case reviews of lenient sentences', the *Sun*, 2 January
    2016, https://www.thesun.co.uk/archives/politics/934360/
    britains-weakest-judges-revealed-following-case-reviews-of-
    lenient-sentences/

74. House of Lords Constitution Select Committee, Sixth Report
    2006–7, at Chapter 2.

75. C. Hope, 'Farage to lead 100,000-strong march on Supreme
    Court on day of historic Brexit court hearing', *Telegraph*, 7
    November 2016.

76. V. Oliphant, '"THIS WILL BLOCK BREXIT" – Eurosceptic fury at
    High Court BETRAYAL on Article 50', *Daily Express*, 3 November
    2016, https://www.express.co.uk/news/uk/728349/High-Court-
    Article-50-Brexit-vote-parliament-Eurosceptics-UKIP-furious

77. W. Chalk and K. Virk, 'Leave.EU "now a far-right organisation",
    Labour MP says', BBC News, 4 April 2018, https://www.bbc.
    co.uk/news/newsbeat-43633204

78. R. Wearmouth, 'Leave.EU Condemned For "Perverse"
    And "Bigoted" Anti-Muslim Tweet', HuffPost, 3
    April 2018, https://www.huffingtonpost.co.uk/entry/
    leaveeutweet-suspended_uk_5ac386e2e4b04646b6465e25

79. @LeaveEUOfficial, Twitter, 23 December 2016, https://twitter.
    com/LeaveEUOfficial/status/812319361373343746

80. @LeaveEUOfficial, Twitter, 1 August 2018, https://twitter.com/
    LeaveEUOfficial/status/1024591138664181762

81. J. Halliday, 'How Tommy Robinson put Huddersfield

grooming trials at risk', *Guardian*, 19 October 2018, https://www.theguardian.com/uk-news/2018/oct/19/how-tommy-robinson-put-huddersfield-grooming-trials-at-risk

82. D. Smith, 'Trump diplomat lobbied UK over Tommy Robinson – report', 14 July 2018, https://www.theguardian.com/uk-news/2018/jul/14/us-raises-concerns-with-uk-about-safety-of-tommy-robinson-jailed-edl-founder

83. 'Suspect package delivered to the judge who jailed Tommy Robinson at Leeds Crown Court', *Yorkshire Evening Post*, 9 November 2018, https://www.yorkshireeveningpost.co.uk/news/suspect-package-addressed-to-judge-who-jailed-tommy-robinson-at-leeds-crown-court-1-9436693

84. @jk_rowling, Twitter, 3 November 2016, https://twitter.com/jk_rowling/status/794217086599962624?lang=en

85. F. Gibb, 'Sir Terence Etherton: "I'm not an activist, but I think it is my duty to be open"', *The Times*, 31 May 2018, https://www.thetimes.co.uk/edition/law/sir-terence-etherton-im-not-an-activist-but-i-think-it-is-my-duty-to-be-open-r5st3p88s

86. O. Bowcott, 'Lord chief justice attacks Liz Truss for failing to back article 50 judges', *Guardian*, 22 March 2017, https://www.theguardian.com/politics/2017/mar/22/lord-chief-justice-castigates-liz-truss-for-failing-to-defend-judges

87. C. Davies, 'Thousands spent on judges' security amid growing hostility', *Guardian*, 27 February 2017, https://www.theguardian.com/law/2017/feb/27/thousands-spent-on-judges-security-amid-growing-hostility

88. C. White, 'Man leaped out of dock to attack judge after being found guilty', *Metro*, 15 May 2017, https://metro.co.uk/2017/05/15/man-found-guilty-of-burglary-so-attacks-judge-in-the-courtroom-6638178/; C. Gorman, 'Woman judge assaulted in family court', *The Times*, 12 December 2015, https://www.thetimes.co.uk/article/woman-judge-assaulted-in-family-court-6c3pztpj5q8

89. 'Why US top court is so much more political than UK's', BBC News, 6 October 2018, https://www.bbc.co.uk/news/world-us-canada-45632035

90. 'US reverses travel ban over court ruling as Trump fumes', BBC News, 4 February 2017, https://www.bbc.com/news/world-us-canada-38868571

91. 'Chief Justice Roberts rebukes Trump's "Obama judge" gibe',

BBC News, 22 November 2018, https://www.bbc.co.uk/news/
world-us-canada-46294734

92. A. Boult, '"See you in court" – Trump's furious tweet
mocked on social media', *Telegraph*, 10 February
2017, https://www.telegraph.co.uk/news/2017/02/10/
see-court-trumps-furious-tweet-mocked-social-media/

93. 'Poland reinstates Supreme Court judges following EU ruling',
BBC News, 17 December 2018, https://www.bbc.com/news/
world-europe-46600425

94. C. Morris, 'Reality check: The numbers behind the crackdown in
Turkey', BBC News, 18 June 2018, https://www.bbc.com/news/
world-middle-east-44519112

95. J. Woods, 'A Hungarian judge to BBC: there
is a general climate of fear', Daily News
Hungary, 1 May 2018, https://dailynewshungary.
com/a-hungarian-judge-to-bbc-there-is-a-general-climate-of-fear/


## Epilogue

1.  M. Weaver and E. Durkin, 'BBC cameraman shoved and
abused at Trump rally in El Paso', *Guardian*, 13 February
2019, https://www.theguardian.com/media/2019/feb/12/
bbc-cameraman-shoved-and-abused-at-trump-rally-in-el-paso

2. E. Stewart, 'Trump calls media the "true Enemy of the People"
the same day a bomb is sent to CNN', Vox, 29 October 2018,
https://www.vox.com/policy-and-politics/2018/10/29/18037894/
donald-trump-twitter-media-enemy-pittsburgh

3. E.g. see F. Mayhew, 'Tommy Robinson supporters chant "scum"
at journalists as EDL founder calls media "enemy of the
people" in attack on free press outside court', *Press Gazette*, 23
October 2018, https://www.pressgazette.co.uk/tommy-robinson-
supporters-chant-scum-at-journalists-as-edl-founder-calls-media-
enemy-of-the-people-in-attack-on-free-press-outside-court/

4. A. Wagner, 'Joshua Rozenberg resigned Telegraph post after
editors sexed up human rights story', UK Human Rights Blog,
19 February 2015, https://ukhumanrightsblog.com/2015/02/19/
joshua-rozenberg-resigned-telegraph-post-after-editors-sexed-up-
human-rights-story/#more-25397

5. I. Hardman, 'Brexit has revealed MPs' flaws – and our own',

*Observer*, 13 January 2019, https://www.theguardian.com/commentisfree/2019/jan/13/brexit-mp-flaws-parliament-britain

6. Attorney General's Office and R. Buckland QC MP, 'Our vision for legal education', 31 October 2018, https://www.gov.uk/government/news/our-vision-for-legal-education

7. House of Lords, Select Committee on Citizenship and Civic Engagement, Report of Session 2017–19, HL Paper 118, 'The Ties that Bind: Citizenship and Civic Engagement in the 21st Century', 18 April 2018, Summary of conclusions and recommendations, paragraph 16, https://publications.parliament.uk/pa/ld201719/ldselect/ldcitizen/118/11813.htm#_idTextAnchor256

8. See the Bach Report, Chapter 6 and appendices, reproduced at https://sirhenrybrooke.me/2017/10/12/the-bach-report-19-public-legal-education/

9. Ibid.

10. M. Cross, 'New tech to "halve" transcript costs', *Law Society Gazette*, 1 April 2019, https://www.lawgazette.co.uk/news/new-tech-to-halve-transcript-costs/5069820.article

11. B. Thornton, 'The mysterious case of the vanishing court reporter', The Justice Gap, 7 April 2017, https://www.thejusticegap.com/mysterious-case-vanishing-court-reporter/

12. F. Mayhew, 'Cairncross Review: Key facts and findings you might have missed', *Press Gazette*, 22 February 2019, https://www.pressgazette.co.uk/cairncross-review-key-facts-and-findings-you-might-have-missed/

13. The average length of custodial sentence is 20.4 months and has steadily increased since September 2008 – see Ministry of Justice, 'Criminal Justice Statistics quarterly, England and Wales, October 2017 to September 2018', 21 February 2019, https://assets.publishing.service.gov.uk/government/uploads/system/uploads/attachment_data/file/780612/criminal-justice-statistics-quarterly-september-2018.pdf

14. A. Travis, 'England and Wales have highest imprisonment rate in western Europe', *Guardian*, 14 March 2017, https://www.theguardian.com/society/2017/mar/14/england-and-wales-has-highest-imprisonment-rate-in-western-europe

15. House of Commons Library, G. Sturge, 'UK Prison Population Statistics', CBP-04334, 23 July 2019, https://researchbriefings.parliament.uk/ResearchBriefing/Summary/SN04334

16. M. Robinson, 'Brazen prisoners FILM a cell raid on smuggled mobile phone and taunt the inmate led away by officers in riot gear at jail as they dub "Butlins with bars"', *Daily Mail*, 23 October 2017, http://www.dailymail.co.uk/news/article-5008749/Brazen-prisoners-FILM-cell-raid-officers-riot-gear.html

17. S. Walters, 'Criminals face new "spartan prisons": Justice Secretary plans tough regime with uniforms, no Sky TV and less pocket money', *Mail on Sunday*, 2 February 2013, https://www.dailymail.co.uk/news/article-2272572/Criminals-face-new-spartan-prisons-Justice-Secretary-s-tough-regime-uniforms-Sky-TV-pocket-money.html

18. M. Smith, 'Where is the most fertile ground for a new party?', YouGov, 1 August 2018, https://yougov.co.uk/topics/politics/articles-reports/2018/08/01/where-most-fertile-ground-new-party

# Index